35 MISSIONS to Hell and Back

A Mighty 8th Air Force, 390th Bomb Group (H) History

CHARLES J "CHUCK" RICHARDSON

Copyright © 2019 Charles J "Chuck" Richardson
All rights reserved
First Edition

PAGE PUBLISHING, INC.
Conneaut Lake, PA

First originally published by Page Publishing 2019

ISBN 978-1-64701-020-1 (pbk)
ISBN 978-1-64701-023-2 (hc)
ISBN 978-1-64701-022-5 (digital)

Printed in the United States of America

To all the very young men who flew bombers in World War II, willing to die for their country high in the sky over enemy territory, half a world away from home.

And to those at home who loved, supported, and waited for them, many in vain.

Contents

Foreword 9
Acknowledgments 11
Editor's Note 13

CHAPTER 1: INTRODUCTION 15
  The Yellow Cab Caper 17
  Pearl Harbor 19
  The Split-Fingered Fastball 22
  You Have A Letter 23

CHAPTER 2: CAMP CROFT, SOUTH CAROLINA 25
  The Mysterious Big Switch 28
  The Big Question 34
  Back To Basics 36

**CHAPTER 3: THE MAKING OF A SOLDIER
(FROM FORT JACKSON TO
MIAMI TO SOUTH DAKOTA)** 39
  Moon Over Miami 41
  The Miami Monster 44
  Dead Before We Finished Basic 45
  A Real Snafu (Situation Normal: All Fouled Up) 47
  The Badlands Of South Dakota And Radio School 49
  Mohammad Going To Move That Mountain 55
  Aerial Gunnery School 56
  Still No Shooting! 64

CHAPTER 4: THE CREW COMES TOGETHER 71
   Oh, No! Lost Records And…Finally 73

CHAPTER 5: DALHART, TEXAS (WHERE?) 76
   Butch 83
   The Night The Lights Went Out In Texas 87

CHAPTER 6: KEARNEY, NEBRASKA 90
   An Angel Named Nick 94

CHAPTER 7: TO THE WAR 96
   Awol? 98
   Goose Bay 100
   The Wizard 104
   I Remember Iceland 107

CHAPTER 8: THE MIGHTY EIGHTH 108
   A Nazi Trick 112
   Jolly Old England 113
   The Scotch Is Where? 114
   The Train, "Peep-Peep," Rolled South 117

CHAPTER 9: THE 390ᵀᴴ BOMB GROUP (HEAVY) 120
   Instruction And Indoctrination 124

CHAPTER 10: FRAMLINGHAM—HOME FOR A WHILE 130
   The Bitch Of Berlin And The Double-Cross System 132
   "And The Devil Take The Hindmost" 151
   They Killed Our Friends 153

CHAPTER 11: D-DAY 167
   An Uplifting Event 184
   London Town 185
   Piccadilly Circus 189
   Madame Tussaud's Waxworks 193
   A Chuck's Vignette 203

CHAPTER 12: ADVENTURES IN RUSSIA AND BEYOND 220
Boys Will Be Boys 225
A Russian Trap 245
I Flew In A P38 And Lived To Tell The Story: A Wild, Wild Ride 264

CHAPTER 13: MISSION TO MUNICH 282

CHAPTER 14: TIME-OUT FROM THE WAR 309
Those "Blawsted" Germans 309
Off To The Flak-Happy Farm 341
Flak Leave At Bournemouth, England 345
The Day The Earth Trembled 354
Stonehenge 355

CHAPTER 15: BACK TO THE WAR 358
The Zeitz Fireworks 363
The 390th Bomb Group 100Th Mission Party 370

CHAPTER 16: THE PREHISTORIC MONSTER 380
Love Lifted Mcgee 387

CHAPTER 17: AGAINST ALL ODDS 405
The Haystack Caper 406

CHAPTER 18: THE HOME STRETCH 409

CHAPTER 19: AT LAST, I FINALLY MEET THE QUEEN .. 412
The Good Old USA 415

CHAPTER 20: HOME AT LAST 416

Addendum, 2012 417

Foreword

This book is a personal history of the 8th Air Force, 390th Bomb Group and was penned in memory of the brave men who served with me on the Good-O-Yank crew and all the other men who have served their country with bravery and courage.

Acknowledgments

My sincere gratitude to Len Krentzler, aviation artist, for authorization to use his artwork on the cover of this book; to Mick Tipple from the Parham Airfield Museum in Framlingham, England, for his hours of research and information shared; to Edward Stoy for allowing the reprint of the letter from Herb Strate, cousin of Good-O-Yank crew pilot Ray Strate; to my cousin, Harry Booker, for providing the typewriter on which the original manuscript, an account of my personal journey leading up to and during World War II, was typed.

My thanks to Lieutenant Colonel William F. "Bill" Pennebaker, squadron commander of the 571st Squadron, 390th Bomb Group, USAAF, stationed at Framlingham, England. He distinguished himself as having never lost a plane on the many missions he flew as command pilot. Bill verified that the facts in this book are true and accurate.

To the 390th Bomb Group Museum in Tucson, Arizona, for their help in furnishing accurate information concerning the thirty-five missions I completed in the European Theater against the Germans. I encourage any readers to visit this wonderful museum.

Many thanks to my family—my wife, Eleta, my inspiration for writing this book; my son, Ron, a veteran of the Vietnam War; and my daughter, Carol. Their encouragement and support during the twenty-plus years of writing about the World War II years provided me the way to completion of this history.

I am especially indebted to Mrs. Emily Wilson for the endless hours of research, typing, and editing. With "bulldog" determination, she was able to find and interview relatives of every single member of the original Good-O-Yank crew, learning who they were, where they lived, places of burial, what they would like to share of their family memories. Well done, Emily.

Last, but not least, I thank the Boeing Aircraft Company and all those who helped build this remarkable airplane, the B17 bomber. Those of us who flew as crew on one of these planes could feel the loving care and knew we were blessed. Many times, we found hidden notes, written by those builders, in parts of our plane wishing, "Good Luck and God Bless."

Editor's Note

Twenty-plus years in the writing and, for an additional ten years, this gut-wrenching, heartwarming story has been silently biding its time, awaiting a channel for expression. A compelling story of young boys bound by faith, courage, blood, sweat, and tears and how that bonding created the brave young men they became.

Hopefully, all who read this account will feel the deep emotions of terror, disappointment, frustration, laughter, love, peace, and joy experienced by the author during his service as a radioman/gunner on a B17G during World War II.

Stationed in Framlingham, England, Mr. Richardson, 8th Air Force, 390th Bomb Group, 571st Squadron, was the recipient of numerous major awards, medals, and commendations including:

- The Distinguished Flying Cross
- The Air Medal, with four oak leaf clusters
- Two Presidential Citations
- The Russian Medal of Victory in the Great Patriotic War (on behalf of Russian Premier Boris Yeltsin)
- Certificate in Recognition of Contribution/Service in Liberating France and Participation in the Invasion of Normandy, signed by French Secretary of Defense John-Pierre Messeret
- French Liberty of Justice Medal
- French Legion of Honor Medal

CHARLES J "CHUCK" RICHARDSON

Born on June 7, 1923, Mr. Richardson is the author of six additional books of fiction, nonfiction, and poetry and is currently working on a seventh.

CHAPTER 1

Introduction

It was hot in August 1941. I lived right beside Derita High School with my parents, Mr. and Mrs. Frank Richardson; my brothers, Eddie and Preston. My sister, Jeanie, had just been married and moved downtown.

The war in Europe was heating up and going very badly for the French and English, but that was far away and I had my own problems.

I was still delivering papers (*Charlotte News*), but as I was not saving much money, I began to look for a better job. It so happened that my uncle, O. Hal Hamby, was sales manager for Southern Bearings and Parts Company. They were a very large wholesale distributor for home appliances such as Crosley radios, Norge refrigerators and washing machines, and phonograph records by Columbia and Okeh. But, more importantly for me, they distributed automotive parts from hundreds of companies. The automotive division needed a parts delivery man to deliver parts to service stations and garages all over the county. My Uncle Hal asked me if I would like to apply for the job. I said, "Boy! Oh boy! Would I?"

The next week, I dressed up and went down to 315 North College Street, scared but confident. Southern Bearings was located on the lot that is now the main building of the Charlotte Public

Library. It has an alley that is still in use that runs from North Tryon Street, between the library and Discovery Place, to College Street.

I was interviewed by several officers of the company, and I could tell they were very dubious about hiring me because of my age and size. I could see I had to do some selling if I was to get that job. I told them I had been working on a farm, which was long, hard work, had delivered newspapers for the *Charlotte News*, having never missed a day of work, and was certain I would make a reliable employee. They asked if I could drive a truck, and I said, "I can handle it." The truth was, I had never driven a truck and actually had done very little driving at all. The next question shocked me. "When can you start to work?" "Right away, but give me a few days to get someone to take my paper route."

It dawned on me that I did not have a driver's license, so I asked my Uncle Hal if he could help. He took me to the driver's license office which, at that time, was across the street from the county courthouse. We went straight in to the commander's office and were introduced. In fifteen minutes, I walked out with my license…no tests, no driving, no nothing. While there I was introduced to the sheriff, the chief of police, and the mayor. You see, my Uncle Hal, the commander of the highway patrol, the sheriff, the chief of police, and the mayor were very close friends and all members of the Scottish Rite. I made the remark right then, "I have got to get into the Scottish Rite, whatever it is, because it opens doors."

Things were really looking up. I had a job, and my first check was $13.46. Man! Oh, man! I am rich, driving around town, and the company is paying for the gas. Not only that, it just so happened that my girlfriend Eleta's home, at 317 West Seventh Street, was on my way to the post office where, twice daily, I picked up the company mail. I got to spend a few minutes with her every afternoon, usually to make plans for seeing her that night or for the next weekend.

THE YELLOW CAB CAPER

One afternoon I had loaded my pickup, a 1935 Chevy, with Prestone Antifreeze to be delivered to customers all over town. Antifreeze was in short supply, and everyone would take all they could get. I loaded at a side door in the alley and slowly eased into North College Street which, back then, was a two-way street. I couldn't see because the building next door obstructed my view of the oncoming traffic. I blew my horn, but too late. A Yellow Cab was passing going south, and, because of the heavy antifreeze, I could not stop in time. My front bumper caught the cab's right rear fender just behind his right rear wheel. It ripped his rear fender and knocked his rear bumper off. "Oh, no! There goes my plush job and, probably, everything else I own."

My boss came out of the building, shaking his head and looking things over. The cabdriver was jumping up and down and hollering like crazy. Everyone in our store was on the sidewalk staring, and I wished I could find a hole and jump into it. As soon as the police left, my boss said, "Charlie, if you don't get going you are not going to get back by closing time." So I took off, thinking that this was probably my last day!

My boss let me stew for about a week and then called me into his office. "Charlie, do you know how much it cost to fix that cab?" "No, sir," I said, "but I will be glad to pay it back." He laughed. "Charlie, do you know if you paid it back at your salary of $13.46 per week, it would take you just about four years?" I was shocked. He said, "No, you do not have to pay it back, we have insurance for that. But, I do want you to be real careful coming out of that alley. We have known for some time that sooner or later there was going to be an accident happen there."

After promising to be really careful, I left his office on cloud nine. Again, I think you can begin to see, as I did that day, I had an angel watching over me. I never had another accident while working there for the next thirty-one years. However, I was called back into the office in October. I remember because it was just before Eleta's birthday on October 11. She was sixteen, and I was wondering what gift I could get her. Anyway, my boss said, "Charlie, have a seat. You know, Charlie, you have gotten our payroll department in quite a quandary!" I said, "Sir, what is it that I have done?" He looked over his glasses, saying, "You have worked here since August, and you have not cashed a single one of your payroll checks! What in the world are you going to do with them?" I replied, "I have been putting them in my sock drawer at home. I live with my mom and dad and have not needed the money." "Well, Charlie, I am going to give you one week, and I want you to cash those checks. Is that understood?" "Yes, sir, it sure is, but I don't know what I am going to do with the money." As I was leaving his office he said, "Try putting it in a bank." On November 6, I opened a checking account at Wachovia Bank and Trust. That same week I bought Eleta a birthday gift, a gold locket. Ever since, I have found a million ways to use that money.

PEARL HARBOR

On the afternoon of December 7, 1941, my friend of many years Craig "Red" Black had picked me up to cruise through town in his older brother's 1939 Olds Rocket 88. We ended up, as usual, at the drive-in, the Minute Grill at Tryon and Morehead streets. I remember we had ordered a hamburger and a Coke and the waitress had just attached the order tray to the car door when a message came over the radio station, WBT. *"We interrupt this program to inform you that the Japanese have just bombed Pearl Harbor, Hawaii. All eight of our American battleships have been hit, including the* West Virginia, *the* Arizona, *and the* California, *along with three destroyers and three cruisers."*

WOW! As the news traveled around the many cars parked in the drive-in, it got deathly quiet. The music that was always playing over the loudspeakers went silent, and for minutes, nothing moved. Red and I sat looking at each other in disbelief. Soon the noise and horn blowing began, and many of the cars cranked up and drove away in confusion.

We decided to go home and be with our families and wait for more news. The radio had hinted that the Japanese may be about to invade California, and the American people, almost as one, were afraid and angry. **No one who lived through those terrible moments will ever forget it.**

At twelve noon on December 8, President Franklin Delano Roosevelt came on the radio with his famous speech. "Yesterday, December 7th, 1941, a date which will live in infamy, the United States of America was suddenly and deliberately attacked by naval and air forces of the Empire of Japan." And so, there it was. We were at war, and everyone was talking about it and running around wanting to do something, but didn't know what.

The German submarines were sinking ships off the coast of North Carolina, left and right. Finally, on December 11, Hitler declared war on the United States. The next day, after receiving a message from President Roosevelt, the Congress unanimously announced that a state of war existed between Japan, Germany, Italy, and the United States.

People everywhere were enlisting in the Army, Navy, and the Marine Corps. My brother, Eddie, signed up in the Navy and was promptly sent to the Great Lakes Naval Training Station in Michigan. I thought that was a dumb place for the location of the world's largest naval training station, a thousand miles from the ocean. But that was just one of the dumb things the armed services did.

Mom cried and cried when Eddie left, and I just did not have the heart to tell her that I wanted to sign up, too. I would wait for a while. I realized this war was causing a river of tears all over the country.

Christmas came, and I began to spend some of the money I had been saving. I remember I bought Mom a new Hot Point electric cookstove and she cried, again. I bought myself a portable radio and carried it just about everywhere I went. (Imagine that, I had one of the first boom boxes, thirty years before they became popular). I dated Eleta at least twice a week and had no transportation. It was at least six miles from her house to mine, and I walked it all the time. That's when the radio came in handy. I listened to the war news, baseball games, and enjoyed listening to music. This was the era of big bands such as Glenn Miller, Tommy Dorsey, Harry James, Jimmy Dorsey, and many others. It was usually midnight as I walked home, and I could pick up broadcasts from Charlotte, Atlanta, New Orleans, Chicago, and New York. I remember hearing an announcer say, "And now, high atop the hotel New Yorker in beautiful New York City, we bring you the music of Mr. Guy Lombardo," and before I knew it, I was home. I really loved that little ole radio. One of the joys of that long walk to Derita was stopping at a place called Shorty's Grill. It is gone now, but was located on North Graham Street about at the intersection of Graham and Thirtieth Street. Shorty was famous for hamburgers and hot dogs, but his specialty was a steak sandwich that would melt in your mouth. He was a great guy to talk to, giving advice to a lot of young boys who might have gotten into a lot of trouble. If he were still around, he could make a million dollars selling those steak sandwiches.

The spring of 1942 was a magical time. I was in love with Eleta, and we spent a lot of time together. There were so many wonderful movies, a lot of musicals, war stories, and comedies (Jerry Lewis and Dean Martin, Abbott and Costello), and we liked to window-shop uptown. Belk's, Ivey's, and Efird's department stores were especially pretty for Easter, Thanksgiving, Halloween, and Christmas. We could shop for hours and then stop for a Coke at Walgreen's or Liggett's, and usually, we would meet friends there.

THE SPLIT-FINGERED FASTBALL

Southern Bearings had a softball team, and I spent some wonderful times playing in the City League. We had a pitcher, named Pete Balosky, who was almost unhittable. This was due to a freak accident he had when he worked for Swift and Company, a meat-packing company on North Tryon Street. Pete ran the meat grinder that made those Little Sizzler sausages. One day he got his finger caught in the machine, and it chewed it off. He quit working for Swift and came to work with us selling appliances. Pete swears the day he lost his finger, they never shut the machine off and someone, somewhere, got his finger, nail and all. Anyway, with that finger missing, Pete developed the very first split-fingered fastball I ever heard of. Ask any baseball fan now, and they will tell you it is a very hard pitch to hit. We had a very good team and played in the finals that summer. We lost to a team called Film Row, whose players worked for several companies that distributed movies to local theaters.

The summer of 1942 was one of the best of my life. It was warm and slow and easy with weekend trips to the local swimming pools that were so crowded, you could hardly get in the water. There was Williamette, and just a few blocks away was Suttles, both on Wilkinson Boulevard, and there was also Sustars, near Matthews. We could go and spend the day, and at night there was dancing, mostly jitterbug. The summer nights were so clear, with no pollution, and you could see thousands of stars. Things seemed to move in slow motion, which was fine with Eleta and me. One of the greatest pleasures in this life is walking with someone you like on a warm summer night, with a cool breeze blowing.

YOU HAVE A LETTER

On a cold evening in January, 1943, I came home from work and Mom met me at the back door. I could tell from the look on her face that things were not just right. Looking more closely, I could see she had been crying. I was quickly afraid that something had happened to Eddie, and said, "Mom, what is it?" "You got a letter today," she said. "Well, that is nothing to cry about. Let me have it." She gave it to me, and though I had known it was inevitable, I just didn't think it would be this soon.

I am copying the contents of that letter with a hope and prayer that you will never receive one like it. We had been told we would receive a notice stating that we would be drafted into the armed forces and had been led to believe it would be a little more dramatic, like, "Greetings from the president of the United States, you have been chosen to serve your country." As you can see, it is just a cold, hard notice from the local draft board.

Although it is dated January 9, 1943, I actually received it on January 13, which you will see plays an important part in my life. It says, "The President of the United States to Charles J "Chuck" Richardson, order number 12707. Greetings! Having submitted yourself to a local Board composed of your neighbors for the purpose of determining your availability for training and service in the Armed Forces of the United States, you are hereby notified that you have been selected for training in the Army. You will therefore report to the local Board named at 119 ½ East Fifth Street, Charlotte, NC at 7:00 a.m. on the twentieth day of January 1943."

I don't know why, but in the envelope with my induction notice, they inserted a free pass to any of the five different movie theaters, the Carolina, Broadway, State, Imperial, or the Dilworth. I think it worthy of preserving this piece of history, so I am sharing this information as I never got a chance to use it. I spent many wonderful hours in these theaters, all gone now. They were all within three blocks of Independence Square, except the Dilworth, which was on South Boulevard near Park Avenue.

I had one week to prepare myself to leave my home and friends, and I got goose bumps just thinking that I may never come home again. Telling Mom and Pop, my sister Jean and brother Preston goodbye was tough, but telling Eleta was the worst. I wanted to go fight for my country, but now that it was time, I really hated it.

When that fateful day came, I kissed Mom goodbye at our back door and told her not to worry, that I would have this thing straightened out in no time. Pop drove me to East Fifth Street to the rear of the same building where I received my driver's license. Pop shook my hand, hugged me, and said, "Do what they tell you, keep out of trouble, and do not volunteer for nothing."

I was surprised to see several of my high school classmates. There was Jack Hefner, a very close friend, and George Brannon and Richard Penninger. There were 117 of us on two busses, and we were hauled away to Camp Croft in South Carolina. This was a short trip through Gastonia and across the South Carolina state line, near Spartanburg. We were met by a corporal, very businesslike, who lined us up and checked off our names. He had us stand at ease, and we were told that at *1300* hours we would go across the base to a series of buildings for physical examination. This was the first thing we noticed different about Army life; it was no longer 1:00 p.m. in the afternoon, it was *1300*. We would go to the mess hall (not the dining room), for chow (not lunch).

I told Jack Hefner and George Brannon, "We have not been here thirty minutes, and already they are changing the way we talk!" And we didn't walk across the base, we marched.

When we got to the examination area, we were sent into the first building for dental exams, and although the doctors were pretty rough, all in all, it went very nicely. As we chatted together in the mess hall, we all agreed that so far everything was okay. Even the food was not bad.

After eating, we marched back across the base. I commented to Jack, "Wonder why it is that wherever we go, it is across the base?" I had just learned my second rule, "Hurry up and wait," because we waited and waited and there were no benches or chairs on which to sit. We will have to make that a suggestion.

CHAPTER 2

Camp Croft, South Carolina

Being January, it was cold standing outside the physical examination building, and we were glad when a corporal came out with a clipboard and called out ten names to come into the warm exam building. It was a long one-story building with a wide hall down the center and small rooms on either side of the hall.

We were told to take off our clothes, down to our shorts, place them in a box, and fill out a paper identifying our clothes. Man! Oh, man! If we thought it was cold outside, it was twice as cold inside without our clothes.

We were given a small bottle to take to the latrine (a new word meaning bathroom), pee in the bottle, and take it back to the corporal at the typewriter. I will never forget the soldier that kept saying this over and over. That was his entire job, all day long, day after day for years, I guess. I laughed about it and hoped like heck that I would not get stuck with a job like that.

At the typewriter, the corporal typed our name on a sticky label and had us paste it on the side of our bottle. Some of the inductees were having a hard time, trying to pee on command in front of other people, but there was a sergeant roaming around yelling, "Come on! Keep it moving. We have a lot of people coming through here."

Next, we were directed to a room where there were tables and were told to take off our shorts. A lieutenant, I presumed was a doctor, started checking us from head to toe. Using a flashlight to look into any dark areas, I thought, *How embarrassing.* Some wanted to face the wall, but a sergeant told them to face each other. There were some snickers and moving around, and it was awkward because there were no pockets and no place to put your hands. First, the sergeant with the clipboard passed down the front of each line, examining our most personal parts, asking us to cough to see if there were any sign of hernia. Some of the guys coughed in his face, and he made it clear we were to turn our heads. This first exam for venereal disease was very uncomfortable and humiliating, but we were quick to learn *this would not be our last.* So much for what is known as the *short-arm inspection.* I have never seen so many naked men at one time in all my life. Now, I can look back and say, "Charlie boy, you ain't seen nothing yet."

They took blood samples by holding your thumb and mashing it down on what looked like a nail; the blood spurted out and was placed on a glass slide and given to a battery of technicians who determined your blood type. Later, they drew blood into a vial for other tests. I could not understand why they had to do the nail thing when they could have gotten it from the vial. Oh, well, things were moving too fast for discussion.

Did you ever have hepatitis, measles, mumps, smallpox, typhoid fever, diphtheria, yellow fever, whooping cough, scarlet fever, chicken pox, and a whole page of other stuff, some I never heard of? I could hear some guys saying, "I don't know. I'd have to ask my mom," and I could tell that wasn't the answer these guys wanted to hear. So I told them what I could remember having.

They checked our teeth, our eyes, our noses and ears, our throat, our lungs, our hearts, and all things south. I had never been examined by a doctor before, and this was a mountaintop experience for me. If there was anything they missed checking, I don't know what it would be.

By the time we were finished with the physical exam, it was late in the evening and we were told to put on our clothes and line up. As we came out the other end of the building, you guessed it, we marched for what seemed like miles, back across the base to a barracks. We were given a mattress and blankets, told to build a fire in a potbellied stove and report to the mess hall for chow at 1800 hours.

(See, I am already talking that Army talk.) Then they added, "The results of your tests and further orders will be posted on the bulletin board just outside your barracks at 0600 in the morning. Lights out at 2100 hours"(nine o'clock).

After we got the three potbellied stoves fired up, we sat around discussing the events of the day and agreed, everything considered, it had not been too bad. All the bad things we had been hearing about Army life were highly exaggerated.

The next morning at 0500 hours, a corporal came through our barracks blowing a whistle so loud, he could wake the dead. I don't understand to this day how it was possible to make that much noise with such a small instrument, and on top of that, he yelled at the top of his lungs, "All out, roll call at 0530."

After roll call, we marched across base to chow in an extremely clean mess hall, and we commented on how they kept it so spotless. They must pay someone a lot of money.

The corporal was waiting on us after breakfast (I mean chow), and we lined up and marched back across base to our barracks where the results of our physical exams were posted. All but four of our group had passed, and we were standing around wondering, what now? It was not long in coming. A sergeant appeared from nowhere and told us we were to report to base headquarters to be sworn in.

We marched for about forty-five minutes and arrived, huffing and puffing, directly in front of base headquarters. You could tell that something very important was about to happen. There was a MARCHING BAND, AND A COLOR GUARD, carrying the US flag, and a number of officers in full dress uniforms. After playing the national anthem, a lieutenant colonel said, "You will be sworn in as soldiers of the US ARMY." It was all very formal and proper with words like, "Do you solemnly swear to uphold the Constitution of the United States of America and to obey you superior officers?"

When we said, "I do," the colonel said, "I now declare you to be soldiers in the United States Army." The band played "God Bless America," and we all saluted the flag. AND JUST LIKE THAT, I WAS A PRIVATE!

THE MYSTERIOUS BIG SWITCH

FROM THAT MOMENT ON, EVERYTHING CHANGED, LIKE TURNING ON A LIGHT. It was amazing and it was frightening. A tough-looking sergeant appeared from nowhere and yelled, "ATTEN-HUT, FORM TWO LINES, STRAIGHTEN UP THERE. FROM NOW ON, NO MATTER WHERE YOU ARE OR WHAT YOU ARE DOING, IF YOU ENCOUNTER AN OFFICER, YOU WILL IMMEDIATELY COME TO ATTENTION AND SALUTE. UP UNTIL THIS MOMENT, YOUR HEART BELONGED TO YOUR MAMA, BUT NOW, YOUR TAIL BELONGS TO UNCLE SAM AND ME. IF YOU THINK YOU HAVE BEEN MARCHED UP UNTIL NOW, LET ME TELL YOU, YOU HAVEN'T SEEN NOTHING YET. NOW, RIGHT FACE, FORWARD, MARCH. HUT, HUT…" We never could figure what we had done to make that sergeant so mad at us.

We marched to the quartermaster building and, as we passed down a long hallway, there were soldiers handing out everything we would need as soldiers, including a set of dog tags. We were told to never take them off. From that moment on, I ceased to be Charles J "Chuck" Richardson. I am now 34602539.

They didn't ask you your size nor nothing; they just looked at my feet and gave me a pair of high-top brown shoes that felt like they weighed a ton. Socks, underwear, pants (summer and winter), shirts, jacket, dress uniform, fatigues, cap, helmet liner, blankets, shaving kit, mess kit, and toothbrush.

I had both arms full when I got to the end of the hallway. Then they gave us two barracks bags and told us to put all our gear in them. I laughed because there was no way it was going in there, but a growl from the sergeant changed my mind. He told us to guard it with our lives, and if we lost it, we would have to do without it until we got out of the Army, and, at this point, that chance was mighty slim.

We had to carry those bags all the way back to our barracks, and I was so exhausted, I just wanted to lie down and die. But in came the sergeant, with markers and stencils, and he wanted every piece of our stuff stenciled with our name and serial number.

He said, "You can forget your name, but you best never forget your serial number" (and to this day, sixty-one years later), I can recite it at a moment's notice, 34602539.

As soon as we finished marking everything, they brought us a stack of cardboard boxes. The sergeant said, "Take off all your clothes and jewelry, put it in the boxes, put your name on it, and in thirty minutes we are marching to the post office to mail these boxes."

I remember the only thing that fit was my fatigues, and that suited me just fine...except my shoes. They were too large, and I got blisters going to the post office. I got a sinking feeling, seeing my civilian clothes leaving on a conveyor belt, that I was losing a friend and part of my life that would never be the same again.

We didn't get a chance to think about it long. The sergeant had us doing HUP, TWO, THREE, FOUR, LEFT FACE, RIGHT FACE, ABOUT-FACE, HALT, AT EASE, ATTENTION, DOUBLE TIME, AND OBLIQUE MARCH. I COULDN'T EVEN SPELL IT, MUCH LESS DO IT! But not to do it and not to do it right soon came easy, for the punishment was ten push-ups and run to catch the formation.

CAMP CROFT, SOUTH CAROLINA, CO C, 26TH BATTALION 1943

By the time we got back to our barracks area, I was beginning to see a pattern for the Army life. I was assigned to B "Baker" Barracks, in C "Charlie" Company. My chow hall was in section 8, and my latrine was in section "X-Ray."

The latrine was another surprise. Jack and I went to take a bath, and there were no individual shower stalls, just one large room, with a bunch of showerheads sticking out of the wall. You would think that one would get used to it after a while, but I never did. Still worse, in the next room there were umpteen sinks or lavatories, side by side, down one wall. On the other side of the room, there were umpteen commodes, side by side, and the guys would just sit there and talk, like they were in a restaurant someplace. *Friends, when you go into the Army, let me warn you, leave your dignity at home. If you have large ears, crossed eyes, or freckles on your heinie, or six toes on one foot, the whole barracks will know about it the next day!*

As we were on our way back to our barracks, Jack said, "Chuck, I just heard one of the permanent party guys [soldiers that are stationed at this base permanently] say that we would be gone tomorrow." "Gone? Where?" Jack said, "I don't have the faintest." Gone tomorrow… Things are just moving too fast, and I can't keep up.

This time the rumor was true, and our orders read:

> **Headquarters, Main Recruiting and Induction Center, Camp Croft, South Carolina, Special Order 18, Jan 21, 1943**

HEADQUARTERS
MAIN RECRUITING AND INDUCTION STATION
CAMP CROFT, SOUTH CAROLINA

SPECIAL ORDERS)
:   -E-X-T-R-A-C-T-   January 21, 1943.
NUMBER   18)

3. Each of the following named men, white, privates, inducted into the AUS this date is released from active duty this date, is transferred to the ERC, and will proceed from this station, without delay to the place of his Local Board as indicated:

(a) L.B.#2, Mecklenburg County, Charlotte, N. C. -- 34-54

Puckett, Lewis L.	34602527	Rouse, John A.	34602528
Caldwell, William C.	34602529	Tate, Theron S.	34602530
Mullis, Ted J.	34602531	House, Horace D. Jr.	34602532
Barefoot, George B.	34602533	Lyles, William S.	34602534
Beachum, Ray B.	34602535	Earp, Troy R.	34602536
Allen, John R.	34602537	Klutz, Frank J.	34602538
Richardson, Charles J.	34602539	Godfrey, Luther J.	34602540
Kumpe, Joe K.	34602541	Francis, William J.	34602542
Mason, Howard L.	34602543	Lommonds, Craven R.	34602544
Matthews, Joe L.	34602545	Wood, Charles L.	34602546
Alexander, Lafayette M.	34602547	Raborn, Hoyte O.	34602548
West, Lauder M.	34602549	Stover, Elbert C.	34602550
Morris, Calvin O.	34602551	Thompson, Dale B.	34602552
Pope, William M.	34602553	Barley, Ernest C.	34602554
Zedaker, Homer B.	34602555	Williams, Parks O.	34602556
Pressley, Carl K.	34602557	Clontz, Harold E.	34602558
Mullis, Robert D.	34602559	Pennell, Lloyd R.	34602560
Morris, Charles S.	34602561	Davis, Harry C.	34602593
Pappas, Theodore G.	34602563	Moore, Thomas L.	34602564
Martin, George W. Jr.	34602565	McCarver, Milas D.	34602566
Threatt, George L.	34602567	Connell, Edward D.	34602568
Falkner, William E.	34602569	Moser, Lawson D.	34602570
Puckett, Arthur N.	34602571	Holleman, Jack R.	34602572
White, Francis J.	34602573	Fincher, Harold B.	34602574
Hefner, James R.	34602575	Putnam, Cyrus W.	34602576
McCall, Paul R.	34602577	Wentz, Charles S.	34602578
Rushen, James H.	34602579	McCall, Thomas D.	34602580
Warren, Emmett R.	34602581	Keesler, William R. Jr.	34602582
Diggs, Patrick D. R.	34602583	Huneycutt, Archie F.	34602584
McCorkle, Robert W.	34602585	Mullis, Stacy M.	34602586
Alexander, James F.	34602587	Howard, John A. Jr.	34602588
Craig, Jesse H.	34602589	Starnes, Paul B.	34602590
Lefler, Lenord L.	34602591	Mullis, Harvey W.	34602592

(66) Men. No meals authorized.
*Appointed acting corporal.

    Effective January 28, 1943, each of the above enlisted men of the ERC is called to active duty, and will proceed from the place of his Local Board as indicated to the Rec. Ctr., Ft. Jackson, S.C., reporting upon arrival thereat to the Commanding Officer for duty. It being impracticable for the government to furnish rations in kind, party meal tickets as indicated will be furnished separately for travel to the destination and return under provisions of AR-30-2215 for meals at the rate of not to exceed $0.75 per meal. The QM Corps will furnish necessary transportation and meal tickets. Travel directed is necessary in the military service and is chargeable to FD 31-F 431-02 A 0425-23. The above enlisted men were last rationed to include dinner, this date and will depart from this station on or about 1500 E. W. T.

OFFICIAL: *Leon E. Gardner*
LEON E. GARDNER
1st Lieut., C. E.,
Ass't. R & I Officer.

For the Commanding Officer:

LUTHER O. HINSON
Captain, Infantry,
R & I Officer

(66 Men)

> Each of the following named men, Privates, inducted into the US Army this date is transferred to the ERC, and will proceed from this Station without delay to the place of his Local Board, as indicated.
>
> Effective Jan 28, 1943, each of these men as called to duty, will proceed from this place of his Local Board, as indicated, to the Reception Center, Fort Jackson S.C., reporting upon arrival there to the Commanding Officer for duty. They will report at 1500 hours.

I am enclosing a copy of these orders, so you may see how the Army operates.

So, we were going home for seven days. Hallelujah!

As we were leaving Camp Croft, every marching formation we passed sang out, "You will be sorry."

We could have just brought our civilian clothes home, but the Army has its ways. I actually beat my old clothes home.

I called Eleta from the bus station, and she was really surprised. I told her to get dressed up as we were going out on the town. Jack and Ruth picked us up about six thirty, and away we went, searching for gas coupons so we could ride around.

Jack, Ruth, Eleta, and I went to the movies that night and, afterward, stopped at the Delmonico Grill on West Trade Street, which was right next door to the Hotel Charlotte. After a wonderful evening, it was time to say good night and go home. Eleta and I were doing some serious talking.

THE BIG QUESTION

Eleta said, "You are about to leave me again, and this time I don't know when I will see you again." I said, "Yes, I know, Butch, it's really tough and I am scared to death that when I do get home, you may have found someone else."

"What are we going to do?"

"There is only one thing we can do!"

"Will you marry me?"

"Yes, of course, I will. I love you, and I always will!"

"WOW!"

So our plans were made. Tomorrow evening, Jack and Ruth Hefner would drive us to York, South Carolina, as there was a no-waiting law in South Carolina.

We arrived at the justice of the peace's home, excited beyond belief, but not afraid. I will never forget his name, E. Gettys Nunn. Because of the war, he probably married more couples than anyone in North or South Carolina.

By 9:00 p.m., Eleta and I were married and on our way back to Charlotte, on "cloud 99." We were truly happy, and we were now together forever, no matter what happened.

What were we going to tell our parents? We agonized about that, not knowing how they would react. There was the expected crying and words like, "You are just children." That was true, but the war forced us to grow up in a hurry. Even after all our years together, we agree it was the right thing to do and if we had to do it all over again, we would. After everyone saw how happy we were together, they got used to it, and before long, everyone was pleased.

Those were the most wonderful days of my life, and I was convinced right then that Eleta and I would have a long and wonderful life together. Eleta was seventeen and I was nineteen. Now this does not mean in any way that we think others should marry early. If it had not been wartime, we probably would have waited until we were better off financially. It was very hard in those days, but LOVE conquers all. And, now, sixty-one years later, we can truthfully say it was the right thing to do.

We spent the rest of the week in the honeymoon suite at the Hotel Charlotte and made a promise that someday, after this mess is over, we would take a proper honeymoon in a far-off paradise. (The truth is it was almost forty years to the day before it happened). *But it did happen, and that is another chapter.*

Leaving Eleta this time was the absolute worst day of my life. My eyes were full of tears, my heart was bursting, and I was trying to act brave for her. The whole family was there to see me off again, knowing it would probably be a very long time before I got back. I was in a black funk for a week afterward.

BACK TO BASICS

The bus ride from Charlotte to Columbia, South Carolina, was torment; no one wanted to be on this trip. We had heard all kinds of rumors about what was at Fort Jackson, from permanent KP to MP training (military police), and we didn't want any part of those two choices. We were pretty apprehensive, but we told one another it couldn't be any worse than Camp Croft.

The sergeant that met us at Fort Jackson was mad at the world. We never found out why he was so mad, but he decided to take it out on us.

"All right, you guys, have you got lead in your tail? Get off this bus PDQ or I will have you on KP, guard duty, and running the perimeter night and day. Now pick up those barracks bags, line up for roll call, and sound off when your name is called." When that was done, he explained that he was to take us to quarters. **"Now, double time, and I don't want to see any stragglers."**

I could hardly lift those two barrack bags, and he wanted us to run with them? It was comical to see the wobbling, stumbling, and falling, but somehow, we made it. We couldn't believe our eyes; it was a tent. SURELY NOT? Oh, yes, and with a tent latrine down the way.

You could have heard the moan all the way to Charleston. The sergeant just grinned and said, "WELCOME TO THE ARMY AND FORT JACKSON."

He proceeded to tell us why we were here and if we were lucky, we could be shipped out in two weeks. TWO WEEKS? We could be dead in two weeks, sleeping in a tent, in the middle of winter, with no heat! Most certainly, it was a horrible dream.

After being assigned a tent, we were taken in a truck (that was an improvement) to get our mattress, blankets, and pillow. Soon, we were settled into our little home away from home. Camp Croft had not been so bad after all.

We got our potbellied stove going, and even though it had started to rain, we were dry and cozy. I had been a Boy Scout in my early years and had some camping experience, but some of the boys had a hard time coping. After chow, which we received at the mess tent, we cleaned our mess kits with water and sand from a nearby stream. We then returned to the mess tent, where they had fifty-five-gallon drums filled with boiling water. We dipped our mess kits to clean and sterilize them and learned you had to dip them a second time because the first time you dipped them, they got so hot, you would drop them on the ground like a hot potato.

Fort Jackson was a base for information, training, and testing. On our second day there, we were marched across the base (you didn't think that would change, did you?) to a series of large buildings where they began to lecture us about the ways of ARMY LIFE. We saw films on how to eat, march, make a bed, and dress. We were also shown the effects of the most gosh-awful diseases. YUCK.

We got into a routine of early morning chow, followed by two hours of calisthenics, then off to school.

After our Army life introduction, we began an aptitude stage to decide where each of us would best fit into the Army life. They tested us for days. Thank goodness, most of the questions were multiple choice. I had one chance in four of getting them right. It made me think, maybe, I should not try to pass the test. They might send me to some terrible place, but then again, if I didn't try my best, I might be sent to school for permanent KP. I decided to do my best.

On a truck, what is the fifth gear for?

What is the boiling point of water?

On a rifle, what is the firing pin used for?

Can you type?

Can you use a wheel barrow?

Have you any medical experience?

These are just a few of the questions that I remember. Boy, oh, boy, you could see where they were going to send you by the questions. Still, I tried to answer them truthfully.

After about a week of testing, they sent us to a large building which turned out to be like a large hall with tables and chairs in long rows. Each place had a set of earphones, and I asked Jack, "What is this all about?" "Beats me."

The instructor told us to have a seat and put on the earphones. He said, "This is an aptitude test for Morse code. I will tap the symbol for each letter in the alphabet, using dots and dashes, until you get used to the sounds. Then we will begin testing."

"For instance, A is dah-dit, B is dah-dit-dit-dit, C is dah-dit-dah-dit, and so on. When you first hear it, it sounds like a bunch of jumbled-up mess that no one could possibly understand. I listened, and after hearing the alphabet through one time, I began to hear a rhythm that helped me identify the letters. After an hour or so, the instructor asked us to write down on our paper the letters as he tapped them out.

Just when I was getting the hang of it, he threw in some odd sounds and laughed, explaining they were numerals, one through ten. Numbers were the easiest of all to identify because they ran in sequence. For instance, one is dit-dah-dah-dah-dah, two is dit-dit-dah-dah-dah, three is dit-dit-dit-dah-dah, and so on.

I really enjoyed this test. It was like playing a game, and it came very easy for me; not so for most of the other guys. The ones I had gotten to know said, "We thought there was something strange about you."

You could see it happening every day now. Some guys found some things easy for them, while others could not fathom it. So the Army puts you in a category that would determine what you would do while in the service.

CHAPTER 3

The Making Of A Soldier (From Fort Jackson To Miami To South Dakota)

Two weeks of testing, calisthenics, eating regularly, and sleeping regularly, along with the dang marching was already beginning to shape up a bunch of run-down civilians.

One afternoon at retreat, the base commander, a full colonel, told us we would be shipping out to permanent assignments or to schools for further training within the next few days. As the assignments were posted each day, we could see the original bunch being split up and sent to different bases all over the United States. Jack Hefner (with his plumbing knowledge) was shipped to Arizona (in the desert) to laundry school. They shipped George Brannon to aerial gunnery school in Texas.

George and I were the only two out of a class of five hundred to be sent to the Air Force. I had told them in an interview that I had always loved flying and, later in life, intended to get into the business. I don't know if that had anything to do with my going to the Air Force or not, but I was one happy camper. I never saw George again; he was killed in action in the Pacific. I never found out where Richard Penninger went because we shipped out before he was assigned. I heard it was to an armored division.

My orders came down the next morning and were hand delivered to me by a corporal, who said, "Get packed, turn in your bedding, and get gone. Transport will pick up at 1000 hours to take you to the train station in Columbia."

I was on cloud nine. First of all, I was getting out of that miserable tent; secondly, I was going to take my basic training in (where else) Miami Beach, Florida. Warm Miami! How lucky could a guy be! I will bet you can already guess what day it was…February 13, 1943.

Usually when the Army moved you, it was by the hundreds, but here I was, Private Richardson, riding first class, by myself, with a handful of meal vouchers, eating in the dining car like I was a general. I even got to spend one night on the train. I thought of Eleta and Mom and home and was sad, too, because with every clickety-clack of that train's wheels, I was getting farther and farther from home.

MOON OVER MIAMI

When I stepped off the train, I said, "Oh! No!" I was wearing winter clothes, and it was eighty degrees. Transportation was waiting, not only for me, but also others, officers and enlisted men. I felt very uncomfortable, having to salute every officer I met.

Pretty soon I learned to look the other way.

Boy, this is a beautiful place! The palm trees, everything green, and the ocean. I am really going to enjoy being here.

I don't know what I was expecting when we got to headquarters, certainly not the fact that headquarters was in the famous Fontainebleau Hotel, right on the beach. WOW! The year that Jack Hefner and I graduated from high school, we came to Miami and stood in this very same spot to watch movie stars coming and going, with huge spotlights following their every move and big-name bands playing inside. It was a very glamorous place.

As we went in, I could see that all the glamour had been removed and replaced with row upon row of desks, tables, and chairs. They were very efficient, and soon we were sent to a beautiful high-rise hotel right on the Indian River, which runs parallel to the ocean about two blocks away. Once inside, all the fancy interior had been removed, and the elevators had been stopped. I climbed nine flights of stairs to my room, shared with others, carrying two barracks bags full of equipment and clothes. We then went to the second floor, which was used as a storage room for quartermaster, to receive a folding cot and a blanket. We talked about needing a blanket in eighty-degree weather, but believe me, that first night I was colder than I had been in a tent in thirty-degree weather in Columbia.

We soon learned, from others that had been there a while, to put newspapers on our cots to keep the cold from getting to us from underneath. Being on the ninth floor was bad, but it could have been worse... There were guys on the sixteenth floor. We were instructed to get out our summer uniforms, to turn in our winter ODs (olive drabs), and hold on to our receipt if we ever wanted to get them back later.

The next morning, we were jarred awake at 5:00 a.m., told to dress in fatigues and report to the street in thirty minutes. We lined up, counted off, and marched north to Thirty-fourth Street to the mess hall. It was a very large building, covering an entire city block. There were soldiers wall to wall, and the chow line stretched for blocks. Thank goodness, it moved very fast. We had excellent food with all the oranges and grapefruit we wanted. There were even large bowls of tropical fruit, some I had never seen or heard of before.

It was here that I got my introduction to other guys from all over the country. Some I could hardly understand, and I was upset and embarrassed when they laughed at how I spoke. But it was all in fun, and soon we boys from the South were more than holding our own. When they laughed at our "You'alls," we laughed at their "Youse guys." We quickly made a lot of friends, some that lasted until we were back home from overseas.

I met a boy named Rex Stanley, from Dodge City, Kansas, and as you will see later, it seems that everywhere I was sent Rex was sent also. Rex was a nice-looking boy with jet-black hair, who could have easily been a movie star. He lived on a large ranch in Kansas and was a true cowboy. Being a cowboy caught my attention because I always loved cowboy and Indian movies. We spent a lot of time together, and he was the only person I ever met in the Army that I couldn't beat, at least once, playing ping-pong. He was so good, he gambled with a lot of guys and I never saw him lose. He was patient with me and we played for fun. We became close friends. His mother's name was Mary and so was mine. He had a brother named Edward and so did I. His home phone number was two longs and a short (on the old party line, hand-crank telephone), and my home phone number was two longs and a short. It was amazing how many similarities we had as we sat and talked way into the nights, sitting by the Indian River.

When they told us we were going to have calisthenics in the morning, I had no idea they meant the *entire* morning. Soon after roll call and chow, we marched over to Miami Beach, and there, on the white sand for as far as you could see, were platforms about six feet high, with a second lieutenant on top counting cadence for every kind of jump, squat, push-up, stoop, bend, and side-saddled spread you could imagine, with several squadrons of soldiers (to be), huffing, puffing, grunting, and groaning. To be sure, you did not goof off; they had a sergeant (mad at the world), roaming around just waiting to give you extra duty, like KP or guard duty, and added push-ups. Lunch came too slow for me and I found I could eat like a horse. Then came marching, we marched up and down the streets, which were closed to civilians.

After the first two weeks, we were divided into companies. Each company was made up from men from different areas of the country. I was put in a company of all North Carolinians, and there were groups from New York, Pennsylvania, Michigan, and New Jersey, to name a few. The purpose was to give camaraderie and to give incentive to achieve the best performance. We would march, count cadence, sing, and shout...*and it worked!* Every afternoon at 1600 hours (4:00 p.m.) we would parade to retreat and lowering of the flag. The commanding officers would review and grade us and give the winners recognition. The North Carolina boys were good and won several "best of the day" awards, but we could not beat Michigan, Illinois, or Pennsylvania. We finally agreed it was because they had more guys taking ROTC training in high school.

One morning our platoon sergeant said, "It is now time to separate the men from the boys." "Oh! No!"

THE MIAMI MONSTER

The Monster Obstacle Course

We had heard rumors about It, and some marching companies had even written about It in their marching cadence songs. When we were marching to the cadence beat, "One, two, three, four," our DI (drill instructor) would sing out, "Look sharp, boys, here comes Michigan," who would start to sing, "Fight, fight, for ole Michigan." We would counter by cranking up, "Hark, the sound of tar heel voices, ringing clear and true." They would end their song with "The Monster will get you if you don't watch out." By the time we got to It, we were already afraid of It.

Built, using the Marine base at Camp LeJeune as a model, the Marine course had been shown on movie theater screens on Pathe News. It was described as a killer course. With full pack, we were introduced to the first obstacle, an eight-foot dirt wall with a post on top. Attached to the post was a rope that swung across to the far side of a pool of water eight feet deep, more mud than water. Very few of us made it across without dropping into that mudhole. Now, with all the mud dripping off, you would weigh at least ten pounds more. And, the course got worse with ten-foot board walls, fields of barbed wire, ditches filled with water, running through tires and crawling through pipes, all with a bunch of loudmouthed sergeants yelling at you.

About the time you thought you had mastered it, off we went to the firing range. It's a wonder anyone survived. Bullets were flying everywhere. They ran us through an area covered with barbed wire, crawling on our bellies and firing over our heads, with live ammo.

DEAD BEFORE WE FINISHED BASIC

One afternoon after noon chow, we were marched up to Forty-eighth Avenue (about fifteen blocks), to a training area we had not been privileged to see or hear about. On the way, we passed another formation from Pennsylvania, and they were not their usual selves… no singing, no cadence, no cockiness. UH! OH! There is something wrong here. As they passed, it looked for the world like they were crying. Crying? Soldiers don't cry. We didn't get any catcalls, like usual, except one from a guy near the end of his formation who almost whispered, "You'll be sorry."

"Men, this is a **poison gas** training area. You will be instructed in the use of gas masks, using the real thing." "Is this guy kidding us, they wouldn't gas raw recruits, would they?" But yes, they did. "It is extremely important that you fit your gas mask to your face," said the instructor. The testing is done in a building with no furniture, no windows, and a door on each end. In we went; bang went the door, darker than black, hotter than blazes, sweating like crazy. All of a sudden, the sergeant instructor yells, "Gas," and drops a canister, spewing yellow smoke. Wherever we are wet from sweating, it began to sting like a hundred bumblebees, and, wouldn't you know, there were no doorknobs on the inside of those doors. The instructor finally got us calmed down by telling us he had only lost a few men this way, and we would only be there for ten minutes. Boy, when he opened those doors, he did not have to tell us to leave. We exploded out the nearest door, yanking off the mask and gasping for breath. The instructor explained that we had experienced a mustard gas attack, and had we not had on our masks, the mustard gas would have entered our bodies and burned our insides, causing death. We were told to wash off the areas that were burning and take a ten-minute break.

We were rejoicing that this part of our training was over, but *not so fast*! The sergeant said, "Gas mask on, in you go for another test," this time with a different gas. We were reluctant to go back in that building, but this time it was not bad. Carbon monoxide is odorless, tasteless, and you cannot see it, but they said if we had not had on masks, we would all be dead after it was over. Now, we were ready to go, but no, we still had one more test to endure.

This time when the instructor dropped the canister, it hissed and skittered all over the floor with a white smoke that looked more like steam. He did not have to tell us what it was, because, no matter how tight your face mask, your nose and eyes told you it was tear gas. It even burned my ears. My eyes were watering so badly, and I wanted to blow my nose, but could not get to it. For ten minutes, we were in pure misery. Even after we washed out our eyes and noses, we boo-hooed.

We somehow managed to make our way back to our company area and found a surprise; we got paid. I got eight dollars. The rest of the twenty-one dollars I had sent home to Eleta.

After doing this for four weeks, they declared us proficient and ready to be shipped out. Of all the things they put us through, to me the worst was getting ready for retreat. You see, after the calisthenics and sweating and lying on the sand, onto that nasty obstacle course and firing range, and marching all over Miami Beach, we were brought back to quarters in the hotel at 15:30 hours. We were told to clean up, dress, and be back in formation for retreat in thirty minutes.

Everyone would run up the stairs, turn on the shower (no hot water), and get soapy. At the same time, thousands of soldiers just like us, up and down the beach, were doing the same thing. The result was chaos... The water pressure dropped to zero. We would dry ourselves with a towel, and unable to get the soap off, we began to itch like poison ivy, and marching in the sun, it got worse. I learned to take a shower in the dark, after lights out. Ahhh, it felt so good to get that dried soap rinsed off.

A REAL SNAFU (SITUATION NORMAL: ALL FOULED UP)

It was late February, and we were on the move again. Once on the train, the officer in charge revealed we were being sent to the US Air Force Technical Training School for radio operators and mechanics at Scott Field, Illinois. I was one of only a few that knew anything about Scott Field. It is one of the best places in the United States to be stationed. It is well established and a base for not only radio operator school, but also for engine mechanics, pilots, bombardiers, and navigators. I was pleased that we were going there.

I met Jimmy Basinger and Duke Moser on the train, both from Charlotte. I had not known them before, although I felt I knew Jimmy because of his father. His father, Jim Basinger, was manager of Belk Brothers Department Store on College Street in Charlotte, and I saw him almost every week. He was a very outgoing person, and everyone loved him and bought most of their clothes and household goods from him. He never met a stranger, and Jimmy is just like him. We became close friends, along with Dale Moser.

Sometime during the night, our train arrived at Scott Field, and the car we were in was separated from the rest of the train and left on a side track. I woke up cold and hungry, and soon there were a bunch of cold and hungry, grumbling soldiers. Several hours passed before a second lieutenant came and informed us that there had been a SNAFU. There was no room for us at Scott Field; we were to be reassigned. Meanwhile, we were trucked over to the mess hall. Now, remember, this was still late February, there was snow on the ground, and we were in our summer khakis with no coats. We had not yet been issued our winter clothes.

After spending most of the day in a building they called a dayroom, playing cards, ping-pong, and writing letters, they came to get us and put us back on the same train car. They told us we would be leaving shortly for radio school in Sioux Falls, South Dakota. "*South Dakota*," we shouted. "That's got to be the end of the world." I had heard that it sometimes got colder there than Alaska and even the North Pole. Good grief, how can this be? How can the US Army be so screwed up? Then came the banging and jerking as we were coupled to an engine and then to other cars to form a train headed west. It was a sad night as we rolled across the Great Plains. As we rode across the open country from Chicago to Sioux Falls, I was struck by the mile after mile of farmland with no trees. I asked Jimmy Basinger, "Where have all the trees gone?" He laughingly said, "They are out there. They are just under all that snow." It was white from here to eternity. The longer we rode on that clickety-clack railroad, the grimier we got, because they only had coal-burning locomotives and the black soot crept through the cracks. We all looked like coal miners.

Several of our group, being tired of playing cards and shooting dice, started getting off the train when we came to a small town. They would race into the station, looking for anything they could find to eat and for cigarettes. The trick was to find it, pay for it, and get back on the train before it departed. To my knowledge, we only lost two guys, but there were fifty close calls, running and diving on the last car platform.

THE BADLANDS OF SOUTH DAKOTA AND RADIO SCHOOL

Picture this: 160 raw recruit privates, fresh from basic training on the beach at Miami, Florida, where the temperature averaged over 80 degrees, arriving in Sioux Falls, South Dakota, at 3:00 a.m., in the dead of winter, with summer khakis on. The train car was parked on a side track, and the heat left when the engine left. At four o'clock, a second lieutenant arrived and had us line up outside, called the roll, and apologized because the Army had not told them we were coming…a mix-up at Scott Field. The temperature was now minus 18 degrees. That meant we came from Miami with an 80-degree average to minus 18 in one week. We spent the night in the base dayroom, but first, we had to build fires in three potbellied stoves.

The lieutenant said, "Welcome to Sioux Falls. You will get used to this weather after about 30 days."

When daylight came, there was snow everywhere. After breakfast, we were introduced to walking in snow, packed down, snowed on, and packed down some more. We were issued blankets, winter clothes, and rubber overshoes, which were very inconvenient, but we soon learned them to be a blessing.

One thing stuck in my mind when we arrived here. As you came in the front gate, off to the right, was this huge coal pile. It looked like a mountain. We learned that everything on this base was heated using coal, and we noticed right away that this mountain of coal was smoking, much like a volcano. We were told it had been smoldering ever since it was placed there.

The next thing we noticed was the technical school buildings. There were rows of buildings placed side by side that stretched for about a mile. They were connected near the center of each building by a very long hallway. After settling in, we started school by marching on the outside (where many of the days were below zero) to the farthest building. There was absolutely no reason at all why we could not have walked through that long hallway, which was heated, except that was the way it was and we may as well get used to it. There were twenty-two buildings, and we spent one week in each building. The good news was, we didn't have as far to go in the cold each morning.

The first week, we took one hour of Morse code and five hours of radio mechanics and theory. As we progressed, we got more code and less mechanics. For twenty-two weeks, we moved one building at a time until the twenty-second week, the last building, we were very near the headquarters building, the PX, the mess hall, and our barracks.

During the coldest weeks, we marched around the base for our physical exercises. They had a rule while marching there would be no talking and you could not put your hands in your pockets. These were strictly enforced. One evening, after school, we were marching back and forth, up and down the streets near our barracks, and someone was detected talking. Our second lieutenant stopped the formation and, after berating the formation, determined to find the culprit, threatening KP, guard duty, and all kinds of punishment if we did not point out the talker. We all knew who it was, but no one told. The officer said, "Very well, you will all receive the punishment. You will assemble Sunday morning at 7:00 a.m., in front of the headquarters building in full pack, for a twenty-mile forced march. Any questions?" No one said a word. "Dismissed." Sunday morning was freezing cold and drizzling rain, but we went and we suffered. I got blisters on my blisters; I ached all over. When we got back, we skipped chow and a shower and went straight to bed. We didn't do much talking in the ranks for a while, but we were pleased that we didn't rat on one of our friends.

I found some letters that I had written to my mom from Sioux Falls, and on April 18, 1943, I wrote that I had passed a test on receiving Morse code at ten words per minute on Monday of that week, twelve words per minute on Tuesday, and fourteen on Thursday. Once you got the hang of it, you could really pick up your speed. Many of the instructors were civilians, hired by the Air Force to teach, and they were really nice to us and made it easier to learn. They would use catchy phrases to help us remember a certain letter like Q. "Q" is sent as dah-dah-dit-dah. By repeating it over and over again and saying into our earphones, dah-dah-dit-dah, *pay day to day*, we got the rhythm and we remembered.

After listening to Morse code for hours every day, dit-dah-dit, dit-dah-dit, dit-dah-dit, dah-dit-dah-dit, some students would jump up from their desk, rip the earphones off, screaming. I remember one in particular, wild-eyed, standing on his desk, shouting, "I'm a transmitter dawdee-daw!" On the wall in the rear of each classroom hung a restraining jacket, or several of them. The instructor would call base security, and they would come and take the "code happy" student away. Fortunately, the affliction was only temporary, and they would usually be back in class the next day.

About halfway through our twenty-two weeks, we finished the course on radio receivers and were told we would take an exam, which we must pass or go back to building number 1 and start over. That alone was enough to scare you to death, but the method of testing would make you want to go running to the chaplain, or want to go AWOL and home to Mama.

The test room was set up in one of the buildings, and each student was called in separately. When you went in, there was a long table behind which were five or six of the school's instructors. In the center of the table was a large box, filled with radio receiver parts, wire, condensers, resistors, tubes, dials, and a soldering gun with solder.

"Private Richardson," the head instructor said, "build us a radio receiver that works." The blood seemed to flow from my head to my feet, but after a few minutes, I began to assemble the parts I needed, and thinking about starting the course over, I worked rapidly and finished quickly.

One of the instructors picked it up, looked it over, and said, "We won't know until we plug it in, will we?" He plugged it in; nothing happened and my heart sank. Then he turned a dial, and a radio station in Milwaukee came in loud and clear. All the instructors grinned, congratulated me, and said, "Send in the next student." WOW! I was one happy dude.

The next day was Saturday, and all who had passed were given a pass to go into Sioux Falls. Rex Stanley and I went into town, and we found the people there to be warm and kind. They seemed to have an unusual understanding and compassion for a bunch of homesick boys a long way from home.

There was not a lot to do, but we ate hamburgers, did some shopping, and went to a movie. Wherever we went, we found the folks of Sioux Falls the same, down-home and easy to talk with. Thank the Lord, for it helped preserve our sanity. If you ever get to Sioux Falls, tell them "Thanks" for me.

There were other things I remember about Sioux Falls. One was the wonderful ice cream. Never, before or since, have I tasted ice cream that good. We would buy it by the half-gallon carton, eat what we wanted, and set the rest outside the window of our barracks for later use. The weather during the winter months never got warm enough to melt it.

It snowed two feet on Easter Sunday, and a visiting general was due at the airfield to inspect the base. All the students were sent to the airfield, which was named after the base commander, Colonel Cole. We were marched up and down the runways to smash down the new snow so the general's plane could land. When the general's plane landed, we stood in formation at attention while the general and his entourage rode by in jeeps to inspect us. The only thing we could think of that the visit was for was the wonderful Easter ham dinner we had.

We had made friends with a very nice boy from the Bronx in New York City, whose name was Herby Goldstein. He was very much Jewish, and Jimmy Basinger, my friend from Charlotte, and I liked to listen to him talk, and he liked to listen to us with our Southern drawl. I asked Herby, "Why is it that Jews are always well-off?" Almost every jewelry store in my hometown was owned by Jews. He laughed and said, "If you were familiar with the Jewish section in the Bronx, you would know that most Jewish people are not wealthy, but on the other hand, you would know that many have done well because they work longer and harder and concentrate their attention and work together. We are taught from the time we are babies not only about our religion, but also, how to be prosperous and how to make money." He was not a jeweler but could look at a diamond and tell if it were real and how much it was worth, and the same with watches. He taught us how to divide a ten-dollar bill with a razor blade, then divide a one-dollar bill, glue them back together, and end up with two ten-dollar bills. Of course, it would be ten dollars on one side and one dollar on the other. He said it was used a lot in New York City.

Herby liked to tell jokes, mostly about his own people, the Jews. He told the story of the two Jewish brothers, partners in the clothing business for over forty years. Abbe and Harry had worked long and hard and were very successful. Neither had ever taken a vacation or any time off. One day, Abbe said to Harry, "I am going to take some time off and visit the land of our fathers, and I would like you to do me a big favor. As you know, I have a pet cat that I am very, very fond of, and I need someone who I can depend on to take care of it while I am gone." "Sure, sure, say no more," said Harry. "I am your brother, and you can positively depend on me." So Abbe went to Jerusalem. After a very pleasant week, he received a telegram from Harry. "Dear Abbe, your cat is dead. Harry."

Abbe was devastated. He cut short his trip and hurried home. Very upset with his brother Harry, and upon arriving home, he proceeded to read Harry the riot act. "What happened?"

"Well," said Harry, "you know I live upstairs over our store, and your cat just fell out of the kitchen window and was killed on the sidewalk below." "Oiy-yi-yi!" exclaimed Abbe. "You almost gave me a heart attack. When you have to tell someone something bad has happened, you should break it to them gently. For instance, if it had been your cat, I would have wired you, 'Dear Harry, please do not worry but your cat is missing. I am sure we will find him as he has crawled out on the roof, Love, Abbe.' Then several days later, I would have wired you again. 'Dear Harry, we found your cat, but I am sorry to tell you your cat has passed away.' Don't you see how much easier that would be?" "Yes, I see what you mean."

Years later Abbe decided to go back and finish his trip to the land of his fathers, Isaac, Jacob, and Abraham.

Two weeks into his trip, he received a telegram from Harry. "Dear Abbe, our dear mama crawled out of the kitchen window and on to the roof, but don't worry, I am sure we will find her. Love, Harry."

We learned to love Herby. He was different; he came from a different culture, but he was a great guy.

As May and June rolled around and the weather went from cold to cool to hot (they don't have much springtime there; it just jumps right into summer), they started giving two hours of calisthenics every afternoon after school. We marched about two miles to a parade ground; this was really nice after being inside for so long. Our physical training director, a second lieutenant (former football coach at Stanford University), really gave us a workout.

One afternoon, we had not been working out very long when a terrible-looking black cloud appeared in the distance and seemed to be heading right for us. The lieutenant was supposed to march us back to our barracks, but he waited too late and the storm broke right on top of us. There was thunder and lightning, rain, hail, and wind, like a tornado. The lieutenant yelled, "Dismissed," and hightailed it to the officer's quarters about two blocks away. It was an awful storm, and we ran helter-skelter as fast as we could. Well, sir, being from the south, I had seen thunderstorms of different magnitude and intensity, but this one was new to me. It grew dark as pitch, and the lightning danced and crackled around our heads, and the rain began to sting like beesting. It hurt; it was hail. I had always been trained to seek shelter or a ditch, but there was none. I looked at my arms, and there was blood running down. I thought, *I am not going to make it*. Closer examination revealed the blood was actually mud. Well, this lil ole country boy had seen lots of storms, but I had never been in a mud storm before. We were running along the street leading back to our barracks when I noticed a car with its lights on stopped and a window rolled down. Someone was shouting, but we paid them no mind. With mud dripping off us, we had no time for conversation. We found out later that one of our guys did stop and the driver was base commander, Colonel Cole. He wanted to know why we were in such disarray. We later learned the second lieutenant was demoted to private, but I didn't blame him; he probably had never seen a mud storm either. We were told it is not uncommon to see these storms in the plains states where the wind creates dust storms with rain and, many times, tornados.

MOHAMMAD GOING TO MOVE THAT MOUNTAIN

One clear day in May, Colonel Cole decided that he was going to stop that mountain of coal from burning and smoldering. He had truckload after truckload moved about one hundred yards across the street. Each truckload was thoroughly doused with water. It quit smoking, and everyone was saying what a smart guy he was. But, just a few days before we shipped out in July, we noticed blue smoke drifting out the top of the mountain.

Radio school was grinding down, and my code speed was getting faster and faster. Our final test on Morse code was really tough. We were tested individually for code speed, transmitting, and receiving, and were tested on a key pad and also on light transmission and reception. We were tested on ground to ground, ground to tower, tower to tower, ground to air, tower to air, air to air, and back.

Our final exam on radio mechanics and theory was a doozy, two and a half hours of written and two and a half hours of hands-on mechanics. We had to completely dismantle radio receivers and transmitters and a radio compass, and put them back together so they would function. It was simple this time as it was not in the dark.

Graduation day was busy, but the best part was we were promoted to PFC (private first class), which meant a little more money. I was pleased that I had done well in radio school and was ready to move on.

AERIAL GUNNERY SCHOOL

On July 9, 1943, I received my orders to report to aerial gunnery school at Wendover, Utah. I asked around, but no one had ever heard of it. I finally asked our mess sergeant whose hometown was Salt Lake City. He whistled and said, "Man, you are going to the end of the universe. It is 120 miles from Salt Lake City, straight out over the salt flats." I felt like crying! But I had already learned not to believe everything soldiers tell you.

Possibly you may be realizing, as I did, that I was being moved from a very warm base, to a very cold base, to a very warm base, alternately.

As we passed through Salt Lake City on the train, I told Rex Stanley, "This is a beautiful place, and after the war, I would like to come back here for a visit." I had heard of the Mormon Tabernacle all my life, and I got a glimpse of it as we passed.

As we neared Garfield, Utah, which is at the very south end of the Great Salt Lake, I could already see that this was going to be a very hot place. The Western Pacific railway cuts across the Great Salt Lake Desert toward a pass in the mountains of Nevada. Wendover, a town of 278 souls, is very near the border of Nevada and is built at the base of the mountains.

The Air Force has built an airfield in the edge of the desert and calls it Wendover Field, and on the side of an 8,000-foot mountain, they have built a gunnery school to train both enlisted men and officers in the art of shooting machine guns from bombers.

So now, those of us that came from radio school in Sioux Falls, South Dakota, knew that we were going to be radio operators / gunners on bombers. We saw the possibility of flying combat in either B25, B26 twin-engine medium bombers, or B17 or B24 four-engine bombers. On the day of our arrival in Wendover, we hit the ground running. We could not figure out why everyone was in such a hurry because everywhere we went, we had to wait.

Naturally, the first thing was a physical inspection. "Take off your clothes and line up in two rows, facing each other." In came a doctor and a sergeant with a clipboard. They were not interested in what I thought would be the important things, like eyes, ears, nose and throat, lungs, or heart. All they wanted to check was our bottom half to see if we had contracted any of the dreaded venereal diseases.

Their being satisfied, off we went up the mountain to our living quarters. Of course, we were marching, but they did send our barracks bags along in a truck. About halfway up the mountain, it began to get cold. That's where we came to a series of tar paper-covered buildings. One was headquarters, one was quartermaster (where we picked up our bedding), one was the mess hall, and three were barracks for permanent party. There were a PX (post exchange), post office, and a large building used as a garage to repair trucks, about ten school buildings and four or five buildings used for guns and ammunitions.

"Hey," someone said, "where are our barracks?" "Over there beyond the latrine and laundry," said the sergeant. I said, "Oh, no! Surely we are not going to live in those tents." But that is exactly where they put us…not really tents, just the top half. The bottom was boarded up about waist high. "Six men to a tent, and I want it cleaned every day," said the sergeant. "Yes, sir." So we made our cots and built a fire in the potbellied stove, in the middle of the tent, that never went out the whole time we were there.

There we were in the middle of the desert, in the middle of the summer, with a fire going all out. The explanation was that we were halfway up the mountain. The first week, after getting all our records brought up-to-date, we were given our school schedules. I was designated tent captain, and I could see it was going to present some problems. The good news was that I could pick who I wanted, and that turned into a blessing because I got five really good guys. We had no lights in our tent, so we had to get it cleaned up before sundown. Fortunately, there was a dayroom with lights where we could go to read, listen to music on the radio, or write letters.

In addition to being the tent leader, I was put in Squadron A and made leader of Section 13. (There is that number again. I was pleased, as I have explained before; the number 13 was turning into my lucky number. I forgot to mention that I arrived in Wendover on the thirteenth of August.) One of my tent buddies was PFC Dale

Vandiver from New York, and he was very intelligent. Later on, he became invaluable because he kept a wonderful book of notes, which we all shared. He played chess with his father by mail and wrote him almost every day. They were still playing the day we shipped out.

One of the first things they did was march us off to the pressure chamber. If we could not make it here, there was no need to go any further. There were 9 of 252 that left the next day, one with a busted eardrum.

They jumped us right into gunnery school, but we were anxious to start shooting. We were told that we had to learn everything about guns, ammunition, and theory before we ever touched a weapon; otherwise, everyone on the base would be dead.

DAY ONE

Staff Sergeant A. J. Stuart stood in front of us in our first class, introduced himself, and said, "Long after you have left here and forgotten my name, you will remember that you were introduced to this machine gun. It is the US Air Force Browning 50-caliber M2, fixed and flexible automatic rapid-fire machine gun."

As he spoke, he reminded me of a preacher paying great respect to someone of great honor:

> Love it like you would your Mother,
> Respect it like you would your Father,
> Live with it like you would your Sister,
> Wrestle with it like you would your Brother,
> Care for it like you would your own Body,
> Study it like you would your Bible,
> Fear it like a Snake,
> Wash and clean it like you would your Child,
> Use it to defend yourself, your comrades, and your Country.
> Properly used it will save your Life,
> Treat it well as it is your Friend.

He wasn't a preacher, he was a prophet. He said:

> It weighs 64 pounds.
> Its bullet weighs 1.71 ounces.
> Its cartridge weighs 4.20 ounces.
> Its 100-round belt weighs 30 and 1/4 pounds.
> Its barrel is 36 inches.
> Its overall length is 56 and 1/8 inches.
> Its muzzle velocity is from 2,660 to 2,900 feet per second.
> Its chamber pressure is 50,000 pounds per square inch.

Its rate of fire is from 750 to 850 rounds per minute.
Its maximum range is 7500 yards or 4 and 1/2 miles.
Its bullet diameter is 0.510.

These were his opening remarks, and each day, as he unfolded the anatomy of this gun, I was amazed at how complicated it was. We learned to break down the gun into its many groups and parts and to list its nomenclature:

Back plate group: 17 parts
Bolt and driving spring rod assembly group: 21 parts
Oil buffer group: 28 parts
Barrel group: 8 parts
Receiver and barrel jacket group: 50 parts
Cover and belt feed group: 27 parts
And on and on.

We would work on a group until we understood each part and what its function was and how it related to the other groups and parts. We did it over and over until we memorized it, keeping in mind our final exam, which he told us would consist of disassembling a completely assembled gun, laying each group part in order, and doing it in a pitch-dark room. We would be timed, and an instructor would evaluate. (I had been there before at radio school).

We learned what could go wrong (malfunction) and how to fix it. We had to recite from memory, "*The sequence of fire and the cycle of operation*," which is eleven pages long.

We had a class in ballistics, which is the science of motion, force, and impacts of projectiles. One day the instructor asked, "How many different directions can a missile go at one time?" I got into a discussion with the instructor. He had taught that it could go in many directions, such as upward, spinning, tumbling, etc. I, however, disagreed saying that it could only move in one direction at any one given moment. I was told in no uncertain terms that I was not teaching the class and that I was not at liberty to discuss it in class again. He must have been right, but I still think he was wrong.

While we were spending much of our schooltime learning about guns and ammunition, we were also taking classes on other things about which we would need to know when we got into combat... things like parachutes. There were four types—seat, chest, triangle, and back. Seat packs were used by pilots. Chest packs were used by all other crew members. Triangle chutes were used to drop supplies, and backpacks were used by fighter pilots. Chutes were divided into five parts: (1) a canopy with 24 panels, (2) shroud lines, which were tested at 7,200 pounds, (3) harnesses, tested at 3,000 pounds, (4) the pack, and (5) the rip cord.

Chutes were checked every 10 days and repacked every 60 days. We were put into a chute harness, lifted 250 feet to a tower, and released. Boy! That will get your heart pumping. It looked like fun and games, but I am here to tell you, the ground meets you like a sledgehammer. We had guys with broken legs, ankles, arms, and a bunch of sore heinies.

In each chute, there is packed a Form 58, telling when and who packed the chute. The story was relayed to us that when you bailed out in combat and the chute failed to open, you could look in the chute pack, pull out the Form 58 so you would know who made the mistake in packing, and look him up later.

We had classes on oxygen masks. Used were the A9 Air Force high-pressure system and the A8B, along with the A10, demand-type regulator. This enabled us to use oxygen when we inhaled, rather than a continuous flow.

We were put into a pressure chamber, simulated flying at 30,000 feet where the temperature dropped to minus 60 below zero. When we reached 18,000 feet, we were told to put on our masks, and we could feel ourselves getting light-headed and dizzy.

Classes were given on identifying aircraft, both friendly and enemy. We watched films every day until we could identify a plane in a fraction of a second. We had to know their fuselage lengths and wingspans, which helped to tell how far away they were. We learned their maneuvers, how they were likely to attack, and what their armament was.

One of the fun classes was on turrets. At the time we were in school, there were four turrets we could expect to see in combat. Later on, a chin turret was used on B17s. The Martin upper turrets, used on B24 and B26 bombers and on PBM flying boats, were electrically operated, and you could sit in them. By using two control levers, you could whiz around in all directions using the two levers to raise and lower the two 50-caliber machine guns that were mounted in them.

The Sperry upper turret was similar, but was electrohydraulically operated and could be operated either sitting or standing. It carried 800 rounds of ammunition and was used on B17s.

The Sperry lower ball turret was retractable. It was used on B17s and B24s. Also electrohydraulically operated, it carried 675 rounds for two 50-caliber guns. You had to be very small (very brave or a little crazy) to get into it, but once inside, knees jammed up under your chin, you could spin around like crazy. It took a special kind of guy to get down in this turret, flying at 25,000 feet, all alone, with nothing between you and the ground. (Not to mention, someone shooting at you). This was definitely not for me, but wouldn't you know, I had to do it.

Then there was the consolidated tail turret, used on B24s only. It carried 425 rounds for the left gun and 400 for the right.

We had to become proficient in operating these turrets and knowing how to disassemble and reassemble them. **But, we still had not fired a shot**. I thought we would never get around to shooting.

We had classes over and over on fire drills and bail-out procedures and how to put on and remove our flying equipment...oxygen mask, chute harness, Mae West life preserver, electrically heated flying suits, heavy sheepskin flying suits, and boots.

We were made familiar with emergency kits, which were attached to our chute harnesses. They included *a mosquito net, a knife or machete, two boxes of D rations, 20 rounds of ammunition, a compass (in England, we were given 3 compasses of various sizes, one small enough to be inserted into the rectum), fishing line and hooks, a waterproof container of matches, a bottle of iodine to purify water, a bottle of quinine, for disease prevention.* In England, we were given a fake French passport with our picture on it, 10,000 French francs, and a book showing French and German phrases with the English translation. Some kits included a 45-caliber handgun, usually just in the officer kits.

We spent hours of instructions on how to use a life vest (Mae West). There were two types and were activated by CO_2 in a small metal bottle. The vest was always worn under the chute harness.

Life rafts was a course taken very seriously, and hour after hour was spent practicing what very likely could save our lives. Two types were used on B17s and B24s…the five-man and the seven-man. There were two on each plane, located in the fuselage near the wings, and a lever released them with spring tension. Their contents included *a complete set of fishing equipment, including a harpoon, 10 cans of water, a first aid kit, an emergency radio (with hand crank), 2 collapsible oars, rubber patching, bullet-hole plugs, a hand pump, a flare gun, three cans of luminous paint, a camouflage cloth, pliers, scissors, a flashlight, twelve Type K rations, and a sail mast.* We had mock-ups of the fuselage of B17s and B24s, and we practiced, daily, deploying the rafts, inflating them, and climbing aboard. We could do it in our sleep.

STILL NO SHOOTING!

They took solid weeks to teach us about the different gunsights we would be using, and how to tell the speed and distance of an enemy plane just by looking through these gunsights. Used only on the turret guns, some of the sights were very high-tech and complicated.

We were taught formation flying tactics and shown how, by placing planes in a certain formation, it could give maximum firepower against enemy attacks. We were schooled in briefings and debriefings, and why it was important to remember what we saw to help in later missions.

One morning, they told us, "All right, you guys have been itching to do some shooting, so today is your chance." A roar went up and everyone was gung ho.

Instead of taking us to the firing range, we were marched into a long building and could see targets set up at the far end. As we were about to learn, you don't fire any weapon without going through all the safety precautions and learning how to dismantle, clean, and reassemble the weapon.

"Gentlemen, the weapon we will be using today is the Army A12 air rifle, better known as the BB gun," said the sergeant.

What? Oh! No! We couldn't believe our ears. The Air Force was going to teach us how to shoot BBs! After about a week, we could very well understand why it was taught. With still targets, we were shown when shooting at farther distances, we had to compensate the elevation by raising the sights. With moving targets, we had to fire ahead as well as compensate the elevation. It was, as the instructor said, "like looking at firing larger guns in miniature." The BBs were painted, and we could follow their flight path to the target. We were disappointed but agreed it was a very good course.

We were moved from BBs to 22-caliber rifles the second week. First, in the indoor range, where we had to dismantle, clean, and reassemble our weapon. The instructor pointed out that the 22-caliber had a higher muzzle velocity and we needed less elevation in order to hit our target. Safety precautions were more important because the chance of injury was greater. On the outdoor range, using the mountain as backdrop, we went from still to moving targets, and this is where they began to separate the men from the boys. Almost everyone could score well on the fixed targets, and I thought, *Man, this is fun*. I was knocking the middle out of those targets. "So far, so good!"

Then came the moving target shaped like an airplane. They mounted it on a steel frame and fastened it atop a jeep, which ran along a track behind a concrete bunker about a hundred yards long. As the jeep ran from one end of that range to the other, we each got ten shots going each way. Twenty-five men in my squadron, not ONE HIT. We said, "You are giving us blanks." Our instructor laughed, picked up a rifle, and got twenty hits. Amazing! He said, "You must get fifteen hits out of twenty to pass this course." He proceeded to show us how, by learning how to squeeze off our shots instead of jerking, to lead our targets and to judge our elevation. After a week of instruction, we all made it.

Next came the 45-caliber handgun. This weapon turned out to be one of the hardest for me to shoot. I couldn't hit the side of a barn with it; I couldn't hit the barn if I were standing inside the barn. It's a good thing it was not required.

We moved to the Army carbine. A 30-caliber semiautomatic rifle. It was lightweight, had a short barrel, was fun to shoot, but, it had a short range. We began to get used to rapid fire, and we were all over the place. Just when we thought we were making progress, they shot us a curve.

Like most things, we were beginning to see this shooting is not as easy as it looks. Like most things, it comes natural to some, while others had to struggle. If I struggled with some weapons, I came into my own the next week.

It was the 16-gauge automatic shotgun, and we went to the skeet range. Trapshooting, as it is called, has the shooter fire from different angles. In our case, it was eight stations, shooting at clay pigeons (clay discs) that are thrown or hurled by a spring-loaded machine, or trap, to simulate birds in flight. This was my thing, and I really enjoyed it. The only thing was my shoulder went from red to green to purple after about two days. It was fun and a wonderful way to learn how to lead a moving target. I really hated to move on to bigger and heavier weapons.

Meanwhile, I was finally getting around to writing more letters home and, best of all, receiving some mail. Eleta had taken a waitress job at the very upscale Mecklenburg Hotel and was doing well. Pop and Mom told of their vegetable garden and how hard it was to get hardly anything. Everything was rationed and being sent to the armed services. It really hurt to see how the Army wasted things, especially food. As I wrote letters home one night, I heard a loud moaning sound. Someone shouted, "Air raid warning!" I was cumbfounded. Surely the Japs could not be attacking us here in this forsaken place. We ran out of the dayroom and found it was a fire alarm, and not just a drill, but the real thing. The fire started in the post office, and it burned completely. Next to go was the PX. Those two buildings were very important to us, and our morale took a shot. Two permanent party barracks burned, as well as two school buildings. Thanks to the students pitching in, we formed a bucket brigade and wet down the buildings near the fire, thus saving the mess hall. They had a fire department, with one truck, but it ran out of water in ten minutes and left the firemen standing there with the hose dripping. The base commander phoned Salt Lake City, but the fire was out when they arrived. I felt sorry for them, driving 128 miles, across the desert, only to find they were not needed. It was a spectacular fire because all the mattresses and linens were stored in the back of the post office.

There was real excitement for a while and a lot of fun to see all those "ninety-day wonders" (second lieutenants) running around in circles.

It was back to school the next morning and time to learn how to fire the 50-caliber machine gun. At first, we were allowed only one round and fired from a platform where the gun was rigidly mounted on a steel frame. For a week, we only shot one shell at a time at a fixed target...first, at fifty yards, then seventy-five yards, then one hundred, two hundred, three hundred, four hundred, five hundred, and so on, up to five thousand yards. It was very difficult at first, and we thought we would never be able to hit anything, but slowly, our instructors taught us how to use the gun. We were then given an ammo belt with twenty rounds, and it is a good thing there was a mountain behind our firing range, for bullets were flying in many directions.

To make us familiar with the recoil, an instructor would stand behind us, reaching around us, clasping his hands over ours, and fire off twenty rounds. Man! Oh, man! That gun just about pulled my arms off, even with him holding. The instructor said, "You can see you are not going to hit much, firing continuously. The *secret* is in firing short bursts." And, eureka, after firing many hours, we could tear up a target at three hundred yards, with short bursts. Then came the dratted jeep with the moving target, and it was like starting all over again. Practice makes perfect, and that is certainly true when it comes to shooting a 50-caliber machine gun. One week later we were actually getting a few hits. Tracer bullets were then added to our ammo belts and that helped considerably.

One afternoon, when we got back to our squadron area, there was a lot of talk with rumors flying around that concerned a number of permanent party officers and enlisted men. It seems they had sneaked off the base and driven a couple of Army vehicles over the mountain into Nevada, where there was legal gambling. Gambling was strictly forbidden for all servicemen.

It turned out the rumors were true, and the base commander had given the men who had been caught two choices, a court-martial or extra duty. They chose extra duty without knowing what it was.

Their punishment was to construct a huge sign, with letters twenty feet tall, transport it to the seven-thousand-foot level on our mountain, erect it permanently, and paint it white. The SIGN spelled out the message, **"KILL OR BE KILLED."** I am sure you have seen the sign on the side of a mountain in California that spells out **"HOLLYWOOD."** Well, this was very similar. Every day we watched as those men loaded several Army trucks and backed in reverse up the side of the mountain, as the incline was too steep to go forward. Even so, they still had to carry the last one thousand feet by hand. It was a lesson to those men and a reminder to all who followed. ***DO NOT GET CAUGHT GAMBLING.***

Sometime later, we received a three-day pass and went by bus to Reno, Nevada. It was a terrible temptation not to play those one-arm bandits, but some did and had to paint that big old sign, **"KILL OR BE KILLED,"** which, by the way, is still in place on the side of the mountain near Wendover, Utah.

The last two weeks of gunnery school were spent learning to shoot from an airplane. We thought we had seen it all, but this added a new dimension. Where before we were firing from a fixed position, we would now be firing from a moving position, at a moving target. We flew in a B17, and our target was a long cylinder-shaped canvas target, towed by a C47 transport plane. The towline was very long for reasons I am sure you will understand.

Each person firing was given ammunition that had been painted a different color, and when the mission was over, your score could be calculated. After a while, this got to be real fun, and I got proficient enough to graduate. Yes, indeed, the tow plane did get a lot of holes.

Our last day of firing from the B17 was not shooting at a towed target, but flying very low over the desert firing range called "on the deck," shooting at targets of opportunity and choice. Our favorite choice was jackrabbits or coyotes. They were extremely hard to hit, but it was fun to see them jump and run.

Graduation was a time for celebration for two reasons. First, it meant we would be leaving this "end of nowhere" place, and secondly, I was promoted to sergeant. **HOT DOG!**

We rejoiced for a few days and teased the new guys coming in with, "You'll be sorry." It was short-lived, however, because with nothing to do, the commanding officer said, "Until you ship out, you will help with KP and LD" (kitchen police and latrine duty). After three days of that, we were happy to hear we were shipping out, but were concerned about to where. We received our orders the next day and found we were being split up and sent all over the place... some to Kansas, some to Arizona, and a lot to Texas. I was one of five being sent to Salt Lake City, Utah. It was just 128 miles away, but I was pleased because I had liked the looks of this beautiful city when we came through on our way to Wendover.

We said our goodbyes to our friends, promised to keep in touch, but, except for a few, never did. It was a sad time because we had come to know them very well and would like to have enjoyed having them as friends for the rest of our lives. The only close friend that went with me was Rex Stanley, the boy from Kansas, and I was glad.

As I look back on Wendover, I am thankful for the hard work that all those instructors tried their best to get us to learn. Their dedication meant that many hundreds of lives were saved because they insisted that we do it right. Knowing what I do now, long after the battles are over, there is one lesson they could not teach us, and that was with all the training they gave us, they could not simulate twenty ME 109s coming at you head-on, and twenty coming at your rear, darting and diving from all directions. They didn't fly straight and level like a C47 pulling a tow target, so we had to start from scratch to find a way to shoot a bee in a haystack.

When we arrived by bus from Wendover, we were driven to the US Air Force base, not far from downtown Salt Lake City. This is a well-established base and has brick barracks, steam heat, and inside latrine. After Wendover, what a blessing!

We began to ask, "What do we do now?" After we settled in and the inevitable physical inspection, we were assembled in a large meeting room, and the CO welcomed us to the US Air Force Western Division Staging Center. He said, "Here, you will meet your future crew members, get to know them, before being shipped out to one of the many training centers for flight training together. Here, you will meet your pilots, navigators, bombardiers, and all the other gunners. Once assigned, pilots will interview each crew member and determine if you are right for his crew. So look sharp and get selected to fly with a really good pilot. One more thing, as of tomorrow afternoon at 1500 hours, you will each be on a thirteen-day furlough, so get going, make your arrangements, and be back on time." YIPEEEEE! You could have heard us all the way to Chicago.

That evening I telegraphed Butch to wire me some money 'cause her ole man was coming home. The next morning, I had the cash, and transport trucks took us to the train station in Salt Lake City. Being soldiers, we had no trouble getting *on* the train. The only trouble was there were no seats available. We sat in the aisles on our barracks bags, but who cares, we were headed home. We slept on our barracks bags for three days.

The whole family met me at the train station, and my feet didn't touch the ground for a week. It was November and cold as a well digger's toenails, but Butch and I didn't mind a bit. We went for long walks, even took a picnic lunch to the park, and talked about raising a family when I came home for good.

A little over a week went by, and I sensed the festive mood began to change. At first, I could not figure out why, but then Butch said, "It is almost time for you to go back and you will be going overseas to fight and who knows what will happen to you." She began to cry, and from that time on, I tried to reassure her and Mom that somehow, I didn't know how, I would be coming home.

After a wonderful furlough, it was time to go. It hit me like a ton of bricks, and I was really in the dumps. I thought, *Man, this is awful. It is like dying.*

Halfway to Cincinnati, I discovered I had left my wallet at home. It was dinnertime, and a lady in the seat next to me noticed that I did not go to the dining car. She questioned me and when she found that I had no money, she gave me twenty dollars. That was plenty to get me back to Salt Lake City, and I wrote down her name and address so I could repay it. What a wonderful thing for her to do, and to this day, I would gladly send her one hundred dollars if I had not misplaced her name. All I know is, she was from Cincinnati and that city will always be special to me because of her.

I arrived in Salt Lake City in a snowstorm, and the city was like a fairyland. Snow covered everything, and I thought, *Well, old boy, you just might have a white Christmas.*

For the next couple of weeks, I watched as crew after crew was put together and shipped out. My old buddy, Rex Stanley, was long gone. Each day, I checked the bulletin board to see if I had been assigned.

CHAPTER 4

The Crew Comes Together

All I saw were notices, for those not yet assigned, to report to the duty officer for work detail. I worked on KP every day for two weeks. I remember opening cans of beans and putting them in a huge pot, four feet deep, and I opened over five hundred cans of peaches. The inspector general made an inspection one day and told the officer in charge of mess that he was wasting and throwing away too much food. As a result, signs were hung as you entered the mess hall, "Take all you want, but eat all you take." The mess sergeant was only allowed one gallon of scraps per day, and there was an officer at the mess hall exit checking each tray to be sure everything was eaten. If not, your name went on the duty roster. What he didn't know was how much was being flushed down the john.

Going into the third week, as I had been assigned to scouring floors and walls with a GI brush, I slipped off and went by squadron headquarters to see if I could find out why I wasn't being assigned to a crew. They were sympathetic and promised to check it out.

The duty sergeant called me on the loudspeaker to report to the orderly room. Good news and bad news…they could not locate my records but would continue to search. He took me off KP and put me on a cleanup crew at Camp Hamilton. Boy! I was happy to get out of that mess hall.

I should have known better. There's some kind of law in the military, "If things can get worse, they will." Camp Hamilton was an old Army base way up in the Wasatch Mountains, a base used to train Army and Air Force under winter conditions. There was permanent snow, even in the midst of summer, and the wind blew unmercifully and continuously. I knew I was in trouble the moment I got out of the truck that brought me there.

It seems they were demolishing some old barracks and our job was to take nails out of the old boards, save the lumber, and stack it in large piles. Rumor had it that the camp commander was having the lumber sent over to a nearby mountain to build himself a summer home.

Let me tell you, I nearly froze to death on that mountain. We were not allowed to put our hands in our pockets and I got caught and had to sew my pockets up. This was the second time for me; the first was in Sioux Falls, South Dakota. (Don't laugh; you try taking a lil ole Southern boy to South Dakota or to a snow-covered mountain in Utah and tell him he can't put his hands in his pockets. *He will bite you!*)

OH, NO! LOST RECORDS AND...FINALLY

Each evening we were brought back to our base in Salt Lake City to thaw out. The third day, I went by the orderly room to plead my case. The sergeant in charge listened, but I could see I was getting nowhere. I was desperate, and knowing full well I was committing a no-no by going over the sergeant's head, I asked to see the officer in charge. The good Lord was on my side, and the officer of the day was a Lieutenant Abrams from Clover, South Carolina. After listening to my sad story he said, "Wait right here." I waited patiently, but I could hear Lieutenant Abrams. He had that sergeant doing a few tricks to locate my records, and in a few minutes, in came the lieutenant with my records in his hands. HALLELUJAH! They located my records that had slid down behind the filing cabinet, along with several others. Before I shipped out, Lieutenant Abrams told me that a couple of the guys whose records were also lost had left the base and gone home.

Not only did Lieutenant Abrams get them cracking on assigning me to a crew, he gave me a three-day pass into Salt Lake City. I truly enjoyed visiting that beautiful city whose streets run directly north and south, and exactly east and west. They were laid out by Brigham Young and the leaders of the Mormon Church in 1847.

The magnificent granite Mormon Temple has a huge organ and a world-famous choir. The temple was built entirely without nails and can be seen for miles in all directions. What a joy it was to be able to worship there! Also in Temple Square is Seagull Monument. Early pioneers erected it to honor the gulls that came all the way from the Pacific Ocean to devour crickets that were destroying their crops.

For three days after I got back to base, I sat around doing nothing but reading and writing letters. I shall never forget Lieutenant Abrams... Bless him.

One evening after eating, I was sitting on my bunk writing to Eleta when someone yelled, "Ten-hut." I jumped up and stood at attention as three officers came walking through. One was a rather large man, heavyset. One was small, even smaller than I (I only weighed 125 pounds), and the other guy was in between, and it struck me that he was a very handsome man. The big guy said, "At ease, men," and everyone relaxed. He said, "I am looking for Sergeant Richardson, anyone seen him?" I said, "That's me, sir, Sergeant Charles J "Chuck" Richardson." He said, "My name is Lieutenant Ray Strate, and these other officers are Lieutenant George Curnes and Lieutenant Neal Payden." I was almost trembling and thought to myself, *What have I done now?* The only thing I could think of was not being on work detail for the last few days, and I was already running through my mind something I could say to them.

Lieutenant Strate said, "Sergeant, I just wanted to ask you a few questions." I replied, "Sure, won't you have a seat." We sat on my bunk and my footlocker. "Tell me what you can about the radio equipment on a B17." I didn't know what to say or where to begin. Lieutenant Payden noticed I was nervous and said, "Why don't you begin with the command set?" Once I got started I couldn't stop. Finally, after describing all the equipment and their uses, I slowed down and Lieutenant Curnes said, "Where did you go to school?" I told them and added that I was recently married and settled down. They apparently liked that as they smiled at one another.

Lieutenant Strate questioned me about armament and life-saving equipment and asked if I got along with other soldiers well.

Finally, he looked at Lieutenant Curnes and Lieutenant Payden and nodded. Then turning to me with a big grin on his face, said, "We are putting together a crew for combat, and we would like you to be our radioman." I jumped up and said, "Yes, sir, I would really like that, sir." "Do you mind if we call you Chuck?" "No, sir, I wouldn't mind that at all." "Well, Chuck, we will be in touch with you tomorrow after we talk to the rest of the crew." "Yes, sir," I said, "I'll be waiting."

"By the way," Lieutenant Strate said, "I'll be your pilot, Lieutenant Curnes will be your copilot, and Lieutenant Payden will be your navigator." "Sounds great to me, sir! Good night." I called out, "Attention," and as they were leaving, Lieutenant Strate said, "As you were, men." WOW! Was I excited! Finally, a real crew! All the other guys crowded around my bunk and congratulated me. They said, "It looks like you are getting some really great officers." "Yeah," I said.

A young boy of Italian descent from the Bronx in New York, named Antonelli Minotti (we called him Antsy), chimed in and said, "Yeah, sure, it will only take you a couple of months to get them trained." We all laughed, but I went to bed that night feeling really good.

Salt Lake City had been good; I loved the city, but all the extra duty, cleaning mess halls and latrines had me thinking it was time for me to move on. Before the week was out, I got my orders.

Description:	English: Dalhart Army Airfield—Texas—1943
Date	1943
Source	United States Army Air Force photograph
Author	United States Army Air Force
Permission	USGOV-PD

CHAPTER 5

Dalhart, Texas (Where?)

My orders read, "Transportation by rail to U.S. Army Air Force Heavy Bomber Training Command, Dalhart Air Force Base, Dalhart, Texas." Dalhart, I never heard of it. How do they come up with all these weird places? One thing's for sure, it was south and warmer. Everything seems to be following the same pattern…from hot to cold, back and forth. I asked the guys in the barracks if anyone had ever heard of it, and one kid from Texas said, "Yeah, I have heard of it. It's way up in the panhandle." I said, "Tex [we called everyone from Texas Tex], how far is it from where you live?" He replied, "If I am not mistaken it's over 700 miles." I could hardly believe it, even though I knew Texas was a big state. "I'm from Brownsville," he said, "and that is way down at the bottom of Texas." He knew very little about it except that it was in the Great Plains and the wind blew hard there. Man, alive! He was a prophet for sure. And, we found it was closer from Salt Lake City to Dalhart, than from Dalhart to Brownsville by about 250 miles.

About forty men were on the trains, and we rode through the mighty Rocky Mountains. They made my North Carolina Smoky Mountains look like anthills. There was snow everywhere, and I told one of the guys that I would like to come back someday and see the countryside. He told me it was cold and snowy like that almost year-round. Boy, this lil ole country boy from the South was getting an education.

It turned out Dalhart was a very small town of around 4,500 people, and as I looked out over the landscape, it was tabletop flat for as far as I could see. You will not believe it, but I did not see one tree, not one. It looked to be a perfect place for an airfield. I found out later that there were some trees, but very few and very small.

There were planes flying around the day we arrived, and I was delighted to find they were B17 Flying Fortresses. I had nothing against other bombers, but B17s were world-famous.

We went directly to our physical inspection, which we were finally getting used to, and then to our barracks. Our barracks were large Nissen huts that resembled a big metal pipe with the bottom sawed off.

It was colder than blazes when the sun went down, and the wind blew at a steady gale force. This was a "three wool Army blanket" kind of place, one on top and two underneath. (And I thought I was going where it was warm!) It turned out to be a base where they told you to be someplace at a certain time and otherwise they left you alone.

To give you an idea of Dalhart's location, it is in the Texas panhandle about eighty miles northwest of Amarillo, Texas, near the Oklahoma and New Mexico borders. The town of Dalhart was located nine miles from our base.

Almost every day now, Lieutenant Strate would come by my barracks to introduce a new crew member. He was taking his time examining each member's records. He told us if his life was going to be on the line, he was going to be certain that he got the very best crew members to be found.

The next man he brought by was Steve Przepiorka, whose home was near Detroit, Michigan. He had been trained in mechanics on General Motors cars at the factory. He would be our plane's engineer and top turret gunner. I was really impressed with Steve's knowledge of almost every part of a B17. The truth is he probably knew more about a B17 than any other person on the crew and would truly prove himself in the months to come.

Next came Sam McGee (quickly nicknamed Magee or Maggie), whose home was in Connecticut. He was to be our armorer and ball turret gunner (the ball turret hung beneath the B17). Magee knew everything there is to know about guns, ammunitions, and bombs. Believe me, it took a very special kind of person to mess with stuff that blows up, and to get down in that ball turret hanging out the bottom of a plane looking down from thirty thousand feet with nothing holding you but four bolts. And that was without anyone shooting at you. We often told him you had to be a genius, almighty brave and fearless, or just plain crazy to do what he did. I think it was all three. WOW! What a guy!

Next came our left waist gunner, Harvey Burr, from Conneaut, Ohio, handsome, soft-spoken, and a really nice guy. We became friends at once, because we had many common interests. We were to have many long talks together. He also proved to be an expert gunner.

From San Antonio, Texas, came our tail gunner, Rogelio Sanchez (nicknamed, right off the bat, Sandy). He was a strong, good-looking boy who taught me some Spanish that I remember to this day—a kind and gentle boy who grew up in combat and became a rock-solid crewman. *Them* Germans didn't mess with Sandy when he was in the tail.

My memory tells me that Jeff Fuller, our right waist gunner, came on later after another guy didn't make the grade. Jeff was from Oklahoma and was a joy to be around. He made us forget our problems and cares. In combat, he was never afraid of anything or, if he was, never showed it. We were lucky to get him as later he was promoted to togglier. (Our bombardier was bumped up to lead the squadron.)

Lieutenant Vic Estes was the last to come, and he was our bombardier. I can verify that he was exceptional because, as I went with him on bomb trainers that were set up in a large hangar, Vic would climb about twenty-five feet up a ladder into a box on a high platform (which was a simulator or mock-up of the bombardier's position on a B17), simulate dropping bombs, and his score was recorded on a paper target on a second platform (my position) near the floor of the hangar. This tower contraption was on wheels, and Vic could guide it. After a drop, I would call out his score, and he would start another run. We practiced for hours. He was so good, they took him away from us later on in our missions and made him a lead bombardier.

We had a few days to settle in to our new quarters, time to write home, and visit the PX, and time to learn how to dress for that cold wind that never quit. All the enlisted men on our crew moved into one barracks and all the officers into another, so we could get acquainted before we started training together.

There were days of orientation where gunners went to class, radiomen, engineers, and armorers to different classes. Once we had been instructed in what we were going to do, we got down to business.

GOOD-O-YANK CREW
BACK ROW, LEFT TO RIGHT: TECHNICAL SERGEANT STEVE PRESTON (PRZEPIORKA) STAFF SERGEANT HARVEY BURR, TECHNICAL SERGEANT CHARLES J "CHUCK" RICHARDSON, STAFF SERGEANT SAM MCGEE, STAFF SERGEANT JEFF FULLER, STAFF SERGEANT ROGELIO SANCHEZ

FRONT ROW, LEFT TO RIGHT: FIRST LIEUTENANT RAYMOND STRATE, SECOND LIEUTENANT GEORGE CURNES, SECOND LIEUTENANT NEAL PAYDEN, SECOND LIEUTENANT VICTOR ESTES

For days, pilots would fly with pilots who had already been in combat, fine-tuning their skills. The same was true for navigators, bombardiers, and all the other positions on the plane before we flew together as a crew.

These times sometimes seemed needless to us after all the training we had been through, but we would later come to appreciate their importance—things like formation flying, with wingtips practically touching, close contact with other members of our crew by intercom ("Are the flaps down?" "Is the ball turret positioned for landing?" "Are the wheels down?" "Are there other planes nearby? How many? Which direction?" "Reply by location with twelve o'clock straight ahead, six o'clock directly behind, two o'clock high or low.") We soon learned we were our pilot's eyes and ears.

At the end of the second week in Dalhart, we were called together and told that if we were married, we could apply to have our wives come live with us on base. There were a number of small house trailers available to airmen who were in final stages of training for overseas service. I applied immediately, even before asking Eleta if she could come. Harvey Burr also applied. That night I wrote Eleta and I was truly happy, not even stopping to consider the hardships we might encounter.

The next day we began flying as a crew, and one of the first things we did was gunnery target practice. As in gunnery school in Wendover, a B17 with a long, long rope pulled a cone-shaped cloth target, and we went over into the New Mexico badlands for target practice—first, a single B17 with all guns firing and later, whole formations. As before, each gunner had different colors painted on their bullets' nose. The formation flying gave us practice as it would be in combat. This also taught us to be careful not to hit any of our own planes. The noise from all those 50-caliber machine guns and the vibration was almost unbearable. After we learned that each crew would take turns pulling the target, we were more careful where we were shooting. In spite of all the instructions and training, we still had a number of hits on the tow plane. If your crew hit the tow plane or missed the target, you were put through extra hours of classroom and flying target practice.

Our crew received excellent results with Jeff, Harvey, Sandy, Steve, and Magee all getting multiple hits. I was happy when we finished this part of our training because we received several holes in our plane while we were pulling the target. A man could get killed before ever getting to combat.

One evening, after returning from gunnery practice, I was told to report to the orderly room. Walking over, I worried about what it could be. I was thrilled to learn that my application to have Eleta come to Dalhart had been approved. I wired Eleta that night to come on down, not realizing that I was asking my beautiful seventeen-year-old bride to get on a train and ride halfway across the United States alone. She wrote back that she was making arrangements and would come as soon as possible. Oh, happy day!

Harvey had also gotten permission, and his wife-to-be, Lou Nell, would be coming soon. We were really excited and were already making plans to have dinner together. It meant that Harvey and I would be moving out of our barracks and into one of the mobile homes, but we thought the rest of the crew could get along without us for a little while.

To tell you the truth, I was kind of glad we were getting away from that barracks for a while. There were a number of other crews sharing this same barracks with us, and about four bunks down, across the aisle, was this great big Indian from Oklahoma named William Manittaou, who was a genuine Pawnee chief. He was the most easygoing, likeable guy you would ever want to meet. That is, until he had a few drinks. Then he was a wild man and mean as a snake. One evening he came in the barracks hooting and yelling and mad at the world. Someone said something like, "PIPE DOWN, CHIEF. WE ARE TRYING TO SLEEP!" That set him off, and he turned over every bunk in the barracks and chased everyone out of the building. About an hour later someone found him fast asleep on the floor in the latrine. The next day he didn't remember a thing about it. I had always heard that Indians could not drink alcohol, and now I know it for sure.

The next few days were spent flying all over Texas, sharpening our skills on many things, such as opening and closing bomb bay doors, emergency drills (including getting into our parachutes and going to our exit doors), oxygen mask drills, Mayday, and SOS drills. These things seemed minor, but in a real emergency, they had to be second nature and properly executed.

We flew all around north Texas, into New Mexico, Colorado, and Oklahoma. I wanted to see the scenery, but was kept busy with my radios, practicing for any sort of emergency. We had to get a radio compass fix every fifteen minutes and keep a log of our location. A radio compass fix is a fairly complicated procedure. For instance, I would call the control tower in Dalhart, and when they answered, I could note the direction our radio compass was pointing from 0 to 360 degrees. Then call Roswell, New Mexico, and Denver control tower. Using a map, I then could chart where these three lines crossed. This was called navigation by triangulation or location by radio fix. I could also call a control tower and ask for a fix, and they would plot our location by calling two other control towers and relaying our exact location back to us. If we needed directions on how to proceed to a certain location, the control tower would radio us a heading of so many degrees. It worked like a charm, as I will explain later.

We had begun flying at night, and that really gets spooky. One evening we flew until after midnight, and we were really spent when Ray called me on the intercom, "Chuck, you are to report to the officer of the day as soon as possible." I thought, *What have I gotten into this time?*

The officer of the day drove up just as we shut down the engines. He was driving a 1939 Plymouth painted a drab olive green; the Army must have had ten thousand of them. He said, "Sergeant Richardson, your wife is in Dalhart at the train station, and I have already cleared you for a three-day pass." I turned to Lieutenant Strate and said, "Lieutenant Strate, may I go?" "You damn well better go, or I'll go in your place," he said. Then I thought, *The busses to Dalhart have quit running and there are no taxis. How am I going to get there?* The OD said, "Jump in, Sergeant, I'll take you." That officer's name was Lieutenant Christian McDermott from Wilmington, North Carolina. He drove me to my barracks for my dress uniform and shaving gear, then drove me to town in style, dropping me off at the train station. I said, "Lieutenant, I don't know how to thank you." He replied, "Chuck, if you are ever down in Wilmington after the war is over, look me up. Good luck." I said, "I will and thanks for everything." I did look him up, but he never came home.

BUTCH

My heart was pounding as I rushed up the platform, opened the door to the waiting room, and stopped dead in my tracks. The room was dark as pitch and cold as ice. "What the... Where is Eleta?" Then I noticed a sliver of light shining through the ticket window. I stumbled over some chairs and knocked on the window. An older man came to the window wearing a black cap like railroad conductors wear. He had a large rubber band around each arm, just above the elbows. Talking a mile a minute I said, "I am supposed to meet my wife. She came on a train earlier today. Do you know where she has gone?" The railroad man knew I was excited and said, "Slow down, Sergeant, she is here. You see there are no more trains this afternoon, so we turn off the lights and let the fire die down in the waiting room. Your wife is back here in the baggage room. Just go through that door behind you, and I'll take you to her." I went through the door, and there she was, my gorgeous Butch, dressed to kill in a black suit with black high heels. She had a long black coat with a fur collar and the cutest little black hat I ever saw. She was sitting on a wooden crate that must have held several hundred baby chicks, just chirping away. There was a big smile on her face, and she was swinging her feet back and forth. She was BEAUTIFUL.

I don't know how long we were there embracing and rejoicing. We were together again, and for the moment that was all that mattered. The Army, the Air Force, the war were a million miles away.

The ticket master stepped back and gave us some space and time. He had a huge grin on his face and was visibly pleased with our joy, seeming to take some satisfaction that he had played a small part in our reunion. We vowed we would never forget his name, but we did. We thanked him and asked where the nearest hotel was. He laughed and said, "There is only one hotel, and it is just two blocks away."

Eleta and I walked the two blocks expecting to find a really nice hotel. We laughed when we saw it. It looked for the world like one of the hotels you have seen a hundred times in old Western movies. It even had a hitching post outside. As we went in we both chimed,

"OH! NO!" Inside was a large lobby with a long desk on one end and a lot of stuffed chairs and couches scattered about. *There was a soldier in every one.*

The desk clerk greeted us with, "Sorry, we don't have any rooms." "Man, you have got to be kidding me. My wife has come 1,500 miles. Can't you do something for us?" The clerk shook his head slowly and said he was terribly sorry but could not help.

A soldier standing nearby overhead our conversation and said, "Sergeant, you can have my room." We could not believe it! And you think the good Lord was not watching over us? I have long forgotten the soldier's name, but I do remember he was from Illinois. Bless him.

We graciously accepted and climbed the two flights of stairs to our room. The lock on our door was the kind they used many years ago. When you took the key out of the lock, you could see through the key hole. We locked the door and left the key in the lock.

The room was clean but had very little furniture, a chair, a table, and a large cabinet used to hang clothes. No closets, no lamps, the light hanging from a cord in the center of the room. NO BATHROOM? The only bathroom was down the hall and served everyone on the floor. Oh, well, we didn't expect the Ritz, and it was warm and cozy. The one thing that Texas has is heat. They have natural gas seeping out of the ground. There were no drapes on the window, so we hung our bedspread over it. We were so glad to be together again; we talked on and on about our life together after the war. It was almost noon when we woke to a bright sunshine. We ate steak and eggs at a nearby café (Texans ate steak three times a day), and I liked it.

We caught the bus to the air base, and the sergeant in charge of our squadron had already made the arrangements for Eleta and me to have a mobile home parked near the base entrance. There was row upon row of these small mobile homes with a bedroom and kitchen combination and a bath. It was great until we could find something better. We had been there about a week when a sergeant I had known in radio school told me he was shipping out for overseas. He asked if my wife and I would like to live in town in a very nice home with an older couple. We grabbed it and met the most wonderful old couple.

The Mahons were in their late sixties and rented rooms and board to soldiers and their wives. Five or six rooms had been converted to bedrooms. Mrs. Mahon took an immediate liking to Eleta (I knew she would), and they became very good friends. So much so, she asked Eleta to stay and live with them until the war was over. Each week, Mr. Mahon handed my week's rent back to me, saying, "You need it worse than we do." I will forever be grateful not only that we lived there for nothing, but also for their love.

Our room had a very small bath, and I remember, one morning before leaving for the base, I was shaving. The longer I stood there looking in the mirror, the weaker I got. I didn't feel bad, but my knees started to buckle, and as I sank to the floor, Eleta came to see about me. She called to Mr. Mahon, who came in and helped me to bed. He said, "You had a close call. The trouble is you were inhaling natural gas." Each room in the house had a natural gas fixture mounted in the wall. It looked like a water fountain that you see in many public buildings. It had a pilot light, and when I closed the bathroom door, it blew the pilot light out. In this part of Texas, natural gas was so plentiful and very inexpensive. We had never seen anything like it. This was the first of many times that Butch has saved my life.

Something else we had never seen was a Texas panhandle snowstorm. The snow was falling, but it was coming at you sideways. The wind would almost take you off your feet, and snow would pile up against one side of a building like you could just walk right up on the roof. They called it a blizzard; I called it something you wouldn't say in church.

Our training was getting into high gear now, and we were taking longer trips, checking our navigation, and lining up on simulated bomb runs. Lieutenant Neal Payden continued to amaze me with the accuracy of his navigation. He was so consistently accurate, he made it look easy. I knew better. I could double-check him with my radio equipment as long as I had radio contacts with several ground stations, and he was always, always on the money. This was even more important when we started flying at night. You could not see a thing from the cockpit except the lighted instrument panel. No one knew where we were except Neal and possibly Ray.

One cloudy afternoon, we started out on a routine night navigation mission. The farther we flew out over the Grand Canyon, the worse the weather got. We headed north toward Denver, Colorado, and ran into thunder and lightning. Let me tell you, it was a frightening situation with thunder booming and lightning crackling and running along your wings like a thousand blue and white snakes, flashing and hissing. The plane was bumping and jerking in every direction. It was raining so hard, you could barely see your running lights on your wingtips. But the worst part is you are flying between mountain peaks of the highest mountains in the United States. If you think thunder is loud on the ground, wait until you are flying right through it.

Ray came on the intercom and said, "Hold on to your hats, boys, and tie everything down. We are in for a rough ride." Then he added, "Chuck, would you come up to the flight deck?" I said to myself, "What is this all about?" I very gingerly made my way up to the cockpit, through the bomb bay, across the narrow eight-inch catwalk while the plane was bucking like a Brahma bull doing its best to throw me down into the bomb bay. I knew those aluminum doors would not stop me falling twenty thousand feet into Denver.

When I got to the flight deck and looked out at what Ray was seeing, I really got scared. All we could see were a thousand lighted dials and gauges, blinking and flashing. I looked at Ray, and sweat was running off his head as if you had poured a bucket of water on him, and it was cold up there. He and George Curnes were struggling with the steering wheels. I said, "Yes, sir?" He said, "I am lost, and there are mountains all around us. Get me a heading for Dalhart." My eyes were as big as teacups, and I said, "Yes, sir," and flew back to my radio command set and keyed in a message. Almost before I was finished, Dalhart came back, "Heading 262 degrees." I went back to the flight deck and reported to Ray. He remarked, "Thanks, Chuck, that's what I thought." I figured the reason he didn't do all this on the intercom was because he didn't want the rest of the crew to get upset, but I was having a hissy. Ray told me later that was the exact heading that Neal had given him, but he just wanted to make sure. We landed in a blinding rainstorm, and I said to myself, "We have got the best pilot and navigator in the whole Air Force."

THE NIGHT THE LIGHTS WENT OUT IN TEXAS

We had been busy practice bombing on the bombing range about fifty miles northwest of Dalhart, and our bombardier, Lieutenant Vic Estes, had been tearing up the target. Flying at twenty to thirty thousand feet, he was dropping his one-hundred-pound practice bombs within a one-hundred-foot circle. Practice bombs were one hundred pounds of sand and white powder with a small explosive charge so we could see when they hit the ground. Everyone, including Vic, was amazed that he could be so accurate and consistent, but I knew how good he was because I had been practicing with him on the simulator.

We were getting pretty cocky, being one of the top crews in training. Then came night bombing. We were thinking, this will be easy because the bombing range, about forty miles northwest of Dalhart, was well lit and there was not a cloud in the sky. Ray took us into the IP (initial point), which was the start of the bomb run. Ray called out, "Bomb bay door open, check it, Chuck." I opened the door from the radio compartment to the bomb bay and called back, "Bomb bay doors open." I closed the radio room door because the cold air was flooding in. "It's all yours, Vic," said Ray, and Vic took over flying the plane, using the bombsight. "Bombs away," yelled Vic as he turned the plane back over to Ray. Ray said, "Check the bomb bay, Chuck." I opened the door and looked down at the ground, lit up like a Christmas tree. I reported, "All bombs away."

Sandy Sanchez (tail gunner) reported in, "Man, we plastered that target. All the lights are out." A few minutes later, Dalhart Control Tower recalled all planes to the base as soon as possible. Ray came on the intercom and said, "Boys, we have a problem. Someone has bombed the little town of Perico, Texas, knocking out their power and water systems." We didn't believe it was us. There were a lot of other planes bombing tonight. We were never told who turned off the lights in Perico, Texas, but it took a lot of apologizing and money to fix it. There were NO injuries!

Waist gunner, Harvey Burr, upon seeing how well Eleta and I were adapting, wrote Lou Nell, his wife-to-be back in Conneaut, Ohio to come on down. They were married in Dalhart Airfield Chapel on March 4, 1944 and the four of us became close friends. Lou Nell was very outgoing and a joy to be around. Harvey was tall and thin, and Lou Nell was very small. They were a beautiful couple.

Crewmen on other crews were constantly changing. They just could not seem to get fitted to one another. Our crew just seemed to fit from the start and, as a result, jelled into a smooth-running machine that was to play an important part in our success later.

We knew our time was getting short in Dalhart, and there was an air of urgency for us to finish our training. We needed only to look at the newspapers to realize why. There were reports of large numbers of bombers being shot down by the Germans. In one week, they reported 64 lost on one mission, 50 the next day, and two days later 119 lost. Two hundred and thirty-three planes in one week. The 8th Air Force in England suspended bombing in order to get replacement planes and airmen. So, from that point on, it was hurry, hurry, hurry! Training was cut short. Thank goodness, we were well along before this crisis, but then, we began to look at the facts. Two hundred and thirty-three planes lost meant 2,330 men lost. Crews were flying 25 missions before being rotated home. The odds of finishing 25 missions were getting worse; the average crew mission time was 14.5 missions. The 8th Air Force minimum mission, now 25, was rumored very soon to become 30. There seemed no way we could expect to finish our tour. I kept all this from Butch and Mom, but talked about it to the rest of the crew. Jeff said, "YOU didn't expect to get through this war in one piece, did you?" We all laughed and said, "You can stay here if you want, but the rest of us are going home."

As we neared the end of our training, we were called together, and our training officers told us that they had given us all the tools and training they could and from now on it was up to us and good luck.

I remember as we got ready to leave Dalhart, we had a few days to get our things together. Officers and enlisted men were not supposed to fraternize, but our crew was feeling more and more like family. We were told to be ready to leave at any time. As we said our goodbyes to the other crews, I found it very hard, and I never cease to marvel that boys from every part of the United States were so much alike. Some had different accents, but inside, most were just wonderful American boys.

When word came down that we were shipping out to Kearney, Nebraska, I asked the usual dumb question, "Where the heck is that?" Eleta decided to stay as close as she could for as long as she could; we made arrangements for her and Lou Nell to follow us on a civilian train. It was really tough for Eleta and me to tell the Mahons goodbye. They were like a second mom and dad. They told us if we ever wanted to come live with them, we would be welcome. We found the people of Texas to be great, with hearts as big as their state. It was, indeed, a pleasant memory.

CHAPTER 6

Kearney, Nebraska

After packing up, and another emotional parting with Eleta, we left Dalhart on a troop train heading northwest through New Mexico to Pueblo, Colorado, and all I could hear was the clickety-clack of the train's wheels and the voices of soldiers playing their never-ending card game, poker, and dice game, craps. "I'll raise you," "Shoot, you're faded." They began the first week I was in the Army, never quit, night and day, and were still going on when I was discharged. Ask any soldier or ex-soldier, they will tell you these games are eternal.

One of the best or luckiest gamblers I ever saw was my friend Rex Elmo Stanley from Dodge City, Kansas. I once saw him throw dice seven times in a row and win on every throw. If you want to verify what I say, call him up. He is in the book in Dodge City. I dare you!

Another great gambler was the big Indian kid from Oklahoma, Chief William Manittaou. His specialty was poker. He had a straight face showing no emotion, a perfect poker player. By the end of the third day on the train, he had cleaned out everyone in our car that wanted to play and had any money left. I said, "Chief, teach me how to play poker." He said, "I know you don't have any money so we will play for pennies." He would deal and talk, and after he won each pot, he would lay down his cards and show me what he had done.

Many times, he didn't have the cards to win but won anyway. He could bluff the best of them. We played for pennies, matches, and for nothing, but he always won. I know somewhere out there today, in the great Pawnee country, there is an Indian chief millionaire.

As we rode through Pueblo, Denver, and Cheyenne, some of the soldiers on the train were playing that old high-risk game of getting off the train every time it stopped. At small towns and large cities, they would charge off the train to buy whatever they could find—cigars, cigarettes, candy, or sandwiches. One of the biggest sought-after things was bubble gum. We received three large meals on the train, but that wasn't enough. When the train started to move there would be a mad scramble to run and jump on the last car. Most made it, but there were those who didn't. They usually caught the next train, but were demoted in rank to private. That really hurt since most were sergeants; but, the entire time I was in the Army, they never learned.

I will never cease to be amazed by the grandeur of the mighty Rocky Mountains. When we left the flat plains of the Texas panhandle, we started a gradual climb toward Pueblo, and by the time we got to Denver we were in the clouds. When we had an hour layover to pick up supplies, I stepped off the train. We were already a mile high, and I looked up at those mountains and it appeared as though you could climb right to heaven. We were already higher than Mount Mitchell in North Carolina, the highest mountain in eastern North America, and the mountains, high, rocky, treeless, snowcapped, forbidding, towered above me. Harvey Burr, who had never been out of his home state of Ohio, and I stood there with our mouths open. The rest of the guys just laughed.

At Cheyenne, we made a ninety-degree turn to the east and began dropping out of the big sky country, altitude six thousand feet, along the Platte River valley into southwest Nebraska. We followed the Platte River along a route that many early American settlers took along the Oregon Trail. There were many Indian wars fought along this trail, and it reminded me of when I was about twelve years old. I loved to go to the movies and see my favorite cowboys, Johnny Mack Brown, Ken Maynard, Buck Jones, Bob Steele, and Hopalong

Cassidy fight those Redskins. There were Apache, Sioux, Comanche, and Shoshone all along this very ground we were riding on.

We got to Kearney about midnight, and I didn't get to see very much. We did learn it was not a big city, population about ten thousand, but it had a tremendous air base just five miles east of town. Busses picked us up at the train station, and the trip to the base took only about fifteen minutes. The base was not well lighted, but we could see silver B17s parked all along the runway apron.

It was cold as blazes as we picked up our bedding and headed to our Quonset hut barracks. There were three potbellied stoves (just like everywhere else), and by now we had learned how to get them going in short order. Someone pulled out a pack of playing cards, shuffled them, and spread them facedown on a bed. Everyone drew a card, and the three that drew the three lowest cards were designated firemen to keep the fire going the rest of the night. I was glad it was not me; I was tired from that long ride on the train. Did I mention there are no beds on a troop train, just bench seats, and they don't sleep very well.

They let us sleep until 0600 (thanks a lot). We had breakfast and were told to report at 1400 hours for physical exam and orientation. We were then free to explore the base, the PX, and the flight line. Excitement abounded to see row upon row of brand-new, shiny B17s, the first we had ever seen with chin turrets. There was no lettering or paint. We were really tickled with the thought that we would soon have our very own plane.

Harvey, Maggie, Sandy, and I stopped by the PX to pick up candy bars and other junk for the next leg of our journey. We had not yet been told when or to where we would be going, but rumor had it we would leave in four to five days.

It was time to relax, write letters, or call home.

We had just settled into our barracks when a runner from squadron headquarters came in shouting, "Sergeant Charles J "Chuck" Richardson." If I live to be a hundred, I'll never get used to the chill that went up my spine when I was called out like that, even if you are expecting it. "Here I am." "Report to Lieutenant Lyerly at squadron headquarters PDQ." I remembered Lieutenant Lyerly's name because it scared me and also because Lyerly was the name of my favorite high school teacher. (He gave me As.)

"Lieutenant Lyerly, my name is Charles J "Chuck" Richardson. You sent for me?" "At ease, Sergeant. I wanted to tell you your wife is in Kearney at the Fort Kearney Hotel." "Thank you, sir. Am I going to be able to see her?" "Take it easy, Sergeant. Yes, you will be given an overnight pass with the condition you call this office before 0800 hours to see if your crew has received orders to ship out. If your orders have not come down, your pass will automatically renew for twenty-four hours. Is that clear, Sergeant?" "Yes, sir, thank you, sir." And I was off to see my lovely wife.

Kearney was a lot like Dalhart. There was only one movie in town and a couple of cafés, so after the first night, Eleta and I would catch the bus to the base where there were always first-run movies, good food, and a wonderful enlisted man's club.

The Army knew that time was getting short for us before leaving for overseas, and they brought in a lot of USO celebrities to entertain us. We truly enjoyed them, but the entertainment we enjoyed most was the talent of all the enlisted men. There were soldiers who came from Broadway in New York and from Hollywood. Some would play the piano, and we would all gather around and sing. One soldier was a short Mexican who was a stand-in for Mickey Rooney in all his movies. Whenever a movie called for Mickey to perform a hard stunt, they would use Peanut Alvarez. We became good friends, and he always wore a watch engraved on the back, "Best of luck, your friend, Mickey Rooney."

He taught me to sing in Spanish, and one song he taught me was "Yours," which I remember after all these years. "Cuando se quiere de veras." I made a recording on a recording machine furnished by Pepsi Cola for soldiers to record and send messages home before going overseas. Eleta brought it home, and I still have it except it is cracked too much to play.

AN ANGEL NAMED NICK

One of the strangest stories about my time during World War II was how I was selected to fly with my pilot, Lieutenant Ray Strate. When he decided to be a pilot, a cousin, Herb Strate, said, "I am going with you." And so off to war they went, together. All their training was done together; both were assigned to heavy bombers, and wherever one went the other followed. It so happened that in their training in Dalhart, they were both assigned crews that became friends. It is almost unbelievable that they would stay together, but it was just to be. The radio operator on Lieutenant Herb Strate's crew, Sergeant Nick Mamula, and I had been in radio school together. Though we were not close since our months of training in Dalhart, our two crews felt a sort of kinship. Since all radio operators had something in common, the other positions on the plane were friends as well. The last night we were in Kearney, I was told I couldn't get an overnight pass because our crew was on alert to leave the next day. My friend, Nick Mamula, was not on alert and he had a pass. He heard me say I was not going to be with my wife this last night in the USA, and he said, "Hey, Chuck, take my pass." And I did. I still have that pass dated April 9, 1944. I thought I would never get to thank Nick, but you guessed it, Lieutenant Herb Strate followed us to England and, against all odds, was assigned to our same bomb group.

Those last few days together with Eleta were wonderful and very different. We finally realized that this was it. The end of the road together for a long time, perhaps forever. There were many tears and promises to wait as long as it took until we were back together again.

I waited until just before 0800 hours to call my squadron HQ and a sergeant read me the orders. "All Air Force B17 crews, report to your squadron at once." We were leaving and we were leaving the United States. It was time to say goodbye. How do you tell someone you love so very much, newly married, goodbye? She had gone with me as far as she could go. She cried and I cried as we held each other for the last time for a long, long time. Goodbye, Butch, I love you.

When I arrived at the base there was a buzz of excitement in the air, with everyone making last-minute calls home and packing up to leave. I finished packing and got into a long line to call Mom. Mom answered on the first ring, and I said, "Mom, this is your number-two son calling from Kearney, Nebraska. Yeah, Mom, Nebraska. I am not quite sure I know where it is either, somewhere in the middle of the Great Plains. It's in what I call Indian country, Mom. No, there are no wild Indians here now. Mom, I called to tell you and Dad that I am shipping out today for overseas. I don't know where we are going yet, but I am pretty sure it is Europe. I will write to you as soon as I can. Don't cry, Mom. I'm going to be okay. I have felt it from the very first. Tell Dad and Pres I love them and to hang in there." She was gone before I could say, "Goodbye, I love you, Mom," but somehow, I was sure she knew that.

There was some unusual excitement on the flight line as we were trucked to our planes. It had been reported that there was a terrible shortage of Scotch whiskey in England, and word had trickled down that if you enjoyed it, you best take some with you. Well, our pilot, Ray Strate, loved the stuff, and to be sure he could continue to enjoy it, he and some of the other officers (but not all) had two wooden cases delivered to our plane. One case was stashed in each wing in a compartment just outside the landing gear wheel wells. What a precious cargo…and ours was not the only plane that got loaded up.

For several days prior to shipping out, there was a lot of money that went into a "pot." It seemed the wager was "which soldier would be the last to be with a female before leaving," and many were witnessed and documented. There was a lot of bragging and laughing, and the issue was settled when we were taxiing and ready for takeoff. Near the end of the runway, the belly hatch opened, and out jumped this female, slowly walking off the field, hair blowing in the prop wash. I don't know his name, but he was a kid from Brooklyn, New York.

CHAPTER 7

To The War

When we got into the air, Ray Strate was all business, calling for position checks and informing us that the next leg before leaving the United States was Manchester, New Hampshire, for a short overnight layover to refuel.

I could not see anyone in the waist section of our plane from my radio compartment, but I knew Maggie well enough to know that the sawdust in his brain was burning and the gears in his brain were grinding and out of control. He would be saying to Harvey and the rest of the boys in the back, "That is right next door to where I live. I am going home before I go overseas."

It so happened that is exactly what he was thinking, and he began making plans and asked each one of the enlisted men on the crew to go home with him. It would only take a few hours, and we would be back long before our early morning takeoff time. The only one who took him up on it was Steve Przepiorka (engineer). I chose not to go, although I would have really enjoyed meeting his family and some of the great home cooking he was always talking about. But my mind told me that this was not the right time to break the rules.

As we flew from Kearney, Nebraska, toward New Hampshire, it became apparent to me that we would be flying over or near the hometown of some of our crew members. First was Ray Strate's (pilot) hometown of Minneapolis, Minnesota. The closest we came was Des Moines, Iowa, which is only 246 miles to the north. I was truly surprised that he did not take that detour. Next, came Moline, Illinois, hometown of Neal Payden (navigator). He didn't say anything, but we must have flown directly over his house. He could have waved to his beautiful girlfriend, Anna. I would have if I had only known.

Next came Detroit, Michigan, more accurately Hamtramck (a town within the city of Detroit), hometown of Steve Przepiorka (Preston) (engineer). We actually flew over Toledo, Ohio, which is just 62 miles from Detroit. We could have flung a rock that far. Flying from Toledo across the southern edge of Lake Erie, we flew over Conneaut, Ohio, hometown of Harvey Burr (waist gunner). We could have yelled down to Lou Nell had we known. When we passed Cleveland, Ohio, we were just 250 miles from Charleston, West Virginia, which was the hometown of our copilot, George Curnes.

We landed at Grenier Field in Manchester, New Hampshire, which is just a few miles from Maggie's (Sam McGee, armorer) home in Oakville, Connecticut.

That accounts for everyone in the crew except Vic Estes (bombardier), our right waist gunner, our tail gunner Sandy Sanchez, and me. Vic lived in Houston, Texas, and Sandy lived in San Antonio, which are both very near where we started. Jeff Fuller's home was in Enid, Oklahoma, just across the border from Dalhart. So those are all our crew members whose hometowns were lined up in a narrow corridor from Texas to New Hampshire, except for me. My hometown is Charlotte, North Carolina, and nowhere near any of the others. Did this somehow mysteriously mean I did not belong on this crew? I didn't dwell on it very long, because I knew we were a team that worked well together and our pilot was happy with us.

AWOL?

Then something happened that threatened to change all that. As I mentioned before, Maggie was determined to sneak off and go home. No one would miss him and he would be back the next morning, long before we were scheduled to leave. Maggie persuaded Steve to go with him, and we were no sooner on the ground at Grenier Field in Manchester, New Hampshire, when Maggie and Steve disappeared.

The enlisted men on our crew purposely avoided any contact with any of our officers for fear they might ask, "Where are Steve and McGee?" We were bound as comrades and by friendships to lie for them. Thankfully, it did not come up, but after a nice rest and a wonderful breakfast, which included pancakes with real honest-to-goodness maple syrup, we boarded our plane to leave. All the enlisted men gathered in a little knot and were saying, "Oh, no! Maggie and Steve are not back yet." "Man, oh man, this is awful!" "They could be shot for desertion for going AWOL when their unit was shipping out for overseas."

We turned our props through, a procedure we did before cranking the engines to prime the cylinders to circulate oil. Still, Ray had not been overly concerned about the two missing men. When we were all in our positions on the plane, and Ray asked for an intercom check, the manure hit the fan! "Where the hell are Przepiorka and McGee?" No one said a word. "Sergeant Richardson, come to the flight deck." (I supposed it was me because I was the highest ranking noncom and my position was closest to the cockpit). "YES, SIR?" "Chuck, have you seen McGee and Przepiorka?" "No, sir." "Chuck, this is serious, don't you lie to me. Do you know where they are? We are ready for takeoff, and the control tower has told us to move out. Now, WHERE THE HELL ARE THEY?" "Sir, they—" BAM, BAM, BAM. Someone was knocking on the side of the plane. Harvey and Jeff opened the waist hatch, and in POPPED the two wayward crewmen, panting and out of breath.

Harvey advised Ray the two were on board and the engines roared out to the runway. As soon as we were in the air and on our way, Ray called Maggie and Steve to the flight deck. Ray looked at me and said, "Saved by the bell. Why didn't you tell me? Never mind, I know why. Return to your position." WHEW! That was close.

I did not hear what Ray told them, but his voice was raised to the point of shouting and his ears were lit up like red lanterns. They both said later that they had never been chewed out like that before. Both were demoted from rank of sergeant to buck private, effective at once. The crew was very quiet throughout our long flight from Grenier Air Force Base in Manchester, New Hampshire, to our next refueling stop, Goose Bay, Labrador.

GOOSE BAY

"Goose Bay where?" Goose Bay is a very large military air base, covering 120 square miles in southeastern Labrador. It is located at the head of Lake Melville, a saltwater inlet 200 miles from the Atlantic Ocean. It was built in 1942, during World War II, primarily for US Air Force planes flying from the United States to England. There was and still is another large airfield in Canada named Gander. Both are still used today by commercial airlines as a refueling stop for planes flying between the United States and points in Europe.

During World War II, Goose Bay had a population of 1,500 people living near the town of Happy Valley on the Hamilton River, about four miles away.

It was clear that the very close comradery our crew had attained was being strained by the incident in New Hampshire and the subsequent punishment. We were flying over the most awesome scenery one could imagine. Ever since we left the United States near Presque Isle, Maine, the ground was covered with snow. We flew northeastward across the Canadian province of New Brunswick and across the Gulf of Saint Lawrence, over a place called Havre Saint Pierre in the province of Quebec to Happy Valley, Newfoundland.

Over the intercom came a deep bass voice, obviously disguised. "How does it feel to be a private again, Private McGee?" You could hear all the laughter all over the plane. Maggie came right back, "I don't know yet. I'll have to wait 'til payday. Why don't you ask Private Przepiorka?" More laughter. "I will get you for that later, Fuller," said Maggie. The ice was broken and even Ray felt better. He said, "I'm glad you two have put it behind us. If you work hard with no more violations, we will see about restoring you to corporal." More laughter.

The miles flew by, and it was a long trip of one thousand miles, but the best darn navigator in the Air Force did it again. Dead on the head we flew into Goose Bay Airfield.

We were talking about all those little Christmas trees in the snow, but when we landed, we looked out and the snow was so high, we could not see over the side of it. We discovered, to our amazement, that all those little trees were not small at all but large trees with just the tops sticking out. We learned that there were planes parked under that snow, and in an effort to find them, bulldozers and snowplows had damaged some planes. The snowplows worked around the clock to keep the main runways open. We also discovered why we had not seen any buildings on the base... They were completely covered with snow.

Man! Oh, man! There is not this much snow at the North Pole. And I thought it was cold in Sioux Falls, South Dakota. This lil ole Southern country boy was going from bad to worse. Goose Bay, Labrador Air Force Base, was leased to the United States by Canada during World War II and is located near the fifty-fourth parallel and dead on the sixtieth longitude, just fifteen degrees from the Arctic Circle. Surely this will be the coldest place I will ever be stationed.

This place is unbelievable. There are people living here that rarely go outside. The snow is so deep, the buildings are completely covered, and all you see when out on top of the snow are vent tubes and smokestacks. There are tunnels in the snow that go from one building to another. We laughed when they told us that if they have significant snowfall, they just add more smokestack. There was a very nice gym, and it was the only two-story building on which the upper windows were not covered with snow. We played basketball and volleyball and had calisthenics here every morning.

One day, a local hired worker asked if anyone would like to go fishing. We just laughed, but we went along to watch. The Hamilton River was not far away. An Army half-track took us to where some native Eskimos were fishing. They had figured a way to make a hole in the ice by first chopping a hole, then keeping it from freezing over by placing large, heated rocks in the hole. Most of the fishermen put up small tents to keep out the wind and cold. We saw them catch a number of good-sized fish, but it was just too cold for us to stay out there.

While I am talking about fish, I feel I must tell you my great fish story. Not far from where we were in Goose Bay is another famous bay, named Fundy Bay, where the highest tides on earth occur. The waters of the Atlantic Ocean rush into Fundy Bay, and at high tide the water is fifty feet deep.

My story takes place further up the bay where, believe it or not, the local fishermen go fishing in a two-horse wagon. When the tide is out it flows seven hundred miles to the ocean, and the fishermen set their nets on tall poles, about fifteen feet high. When the tide rolls in on a wall of water fifty feet high, fish by the thousands are caught in their nets, and the men wait again for low tide. They then take their empty wagons out into the bay and actually ride along the nets, standing in their wagons, releasing the caught fish and filling their wagons. Wow, what a great way to catch fish!

The weather over the North Atlantic had been terrible for the past two weeks, and all flights had been grounded. After a few days, we were very bored. There was a wonderful library and movies every day, but you can stand just so much. Most of us got caught up on our letters home, and I was homesick for Eleta and those 50- and 60-degree days back in North Carolina, where the snowfall was 2 to 3 inches per year. Occasionally, we got a 6-inch snow, and we considered it a blizzard. All the schools and businesses closed, and the grocery stores sold out of milk and bread. Compare that with lows of 30 to 40 degrees below zero and average snowfall of more than 150 inches in Goose Bay. This was April? Springtime? Just think what it was like in winter.

We always thought our last station was the worst, and it could not get worse, only better. If you are ever in the service, remember, I told you so. You can believe it when you are shipping out, and the guys along the streets on base are waving goodbye and yelling, "YOU'LL BE SORRY."

We had been told to be ready to ship out at a minute's notice, but you are never quite ready, especially at 0500 hours when a sergeant wakes you, yelling, "All right, all B17 crews, up and at 'em. Chow at 0530, briefing at 0600, hup two…"

So, we are moving again. Man, I was cold! My feet never got warm in Labrador. We scurried down the tunnels in the snow passageways from barrack to latrine, to mess hall to briefing room, and never got a glimpse of what it was like outside.

Briefing told us we were to fly singly from Goose Bay across Baffin Bay to near the southernmost coast of Greenland, close to a small village named Julianehab, on a course to Iceland. Boy, oh, boy, and I said it could not possibly get worse. There is nothing worse, unless it be the North Pole, and that would not surprise me.

Neal, with his stack of charts, began to plot a course, and we were amazed that this leg of our trip would be 1,542 miles. When we came out of our caves in the snow, it was a beautiful sunshine morning, and we went to work getting our plane ready to fly. All went well, and we bade Goose Bay goodbye. They had capped our fuel tanks just before takeoff, and we were carrying extra fuel tanks in the bomb bay. We were going to need it, and if we missed that little island of ICELAND, WE WOULD BE IN A HEAP OF TROUBLE.

We flew and flew, and the farther we flew, the worse the weather got. We had been warned of the treacherous storms of the North Atlantic, and we heard stories of earlier flights of B17s being lost. Some crashed in Greenland (one landed in a frozen lake and was not recovered until 1998), others landed near weather stations, and some were never heard from. There was almost no hope if you ran out of gas and landed in the Atlantic.

I can remember being concerned, but not afraid. We had confidence in our plane and in our crew. The flight went on for hours, and the clouds got higher and higher, until we were flying blind. At one point, Neal asked Ray to drop down under the clouds so he could get a sighting on the whitecaps in the ocean. We were almost in the water before we got under the clouds. The ocean was very rough, but Neal got his sighting, and we went back up into the thick clouds, which was okay by me. I didn't like the looks of that cold Atlantic, and I thought of the *Titanic*, which was under the waves not far from where we were.

I listened to my radios and tried picking up Iceland, but all I got was static. I could still receive Goose Bay and Gander and the station in Greenland. I could get a radio fix, showing exactly where we were, but what good would that do when over one thousand miles of water? After a while, I got sleepy, but was hoping like crazy that Ray and Neal didn't.

THE WIZARD

This writing would not be complete if I did not tell you about the Wizard. A man that knew where we were ALL the time. Navigating comes easier for some, but most people can get lost, utterly confused, and disoriented just driving around a large city. Send them to a big city or a foreign city, and the situation is compounded, or put that person in an airplane with the wind blowing hard, at night, add clouds and zero visibility and the results could be horrific.

I watched Lieutenant Neal Payden snap on a small light over his navigator's table and begin to do his magic. With a slide rule, a compass (showing true magnetic north), a chronometer (giving correct time), a sextant (showing direction and inclination of stars) to give him latitude and longitude, and using a protractor and a bearing circle, he would put a dot on his navigation chart and draw a line from his last dot (or fix) he had made, and that was exactly where we were.

Today, there are electronic devices that calibrate all the variables and show you these things instantly, but tonight (1944), these electronic marvels had never been thought of.

After hours and hours of flying in the clouds, Neal came on the intercom and said those words that I will never forget. "Okay, Ray, you can start your descent. If this isn't Iceland, I don't know where we are." WOW! That woke us all up, and Ray started his gradual descent.

We dropped well below one thousand feet (I was holding my breath), and when we broke out of those clouds, there was Iceland dead ahead. Not only was it Iceland, but dead on line for Keflavik, a very small town on the southernmost tip of Iceland about thirty miles from Reykjavik, the capital of Iceland. Back on our plane, there was yelling and clapping for the Wizard.

Keflavik had a huge air base, used mostly to refuel planes, both civilian and military. There were hundreds of planes parked along the long runways and on the airport tarmac. We wondered why there were so many and learned the next morning that there was a huge storm coming, with hurricane-force winds. We would surely be there for several days and possibly a week. Thank goodness, our own personal Wizard had gotten us safely here before the big storm. Not only had he gotten us here, but also, he did it in spades. My confidence in our pilot and our navigator really soared. No doubt about it, we were going to be a first-rate crew.

The next morning, shortly after breakfast, Ray got the crew together and said, "Boys, we have got some work to do. The storm that is coming is powerful enough to lift our plane right off the tarmac, even though it is tied down securely. The high winds could do serious damage to our wings, so we are going to get hundreds of sandbags and pile them on top of the wings until this monster storm passes."

We got busy filling sandbags and hauling them out to our plane, hoisting them up on the wings. We were give out when we finished, and it was a funny-looking sight. I wondered if Boeing ever dreamed of seeing a B17 with its wings all drooped down like that. The wind got stronger and stronger, and for two days no one was allowed to get out in the storm. The wind blew, and the rain came down in sheets. I thought for certain the island of Iceland would be blown away. We played cards, wrote letters, and slept.

When the storm had passed we took down all the sandbags, which was a whole lot easier than putting them up. Ray told us, after the sun came out, that he had another little job for us before we left. After this "little" job, he would see if he could get passes into Reykjavik, a city of about sixty thousand people (Iceland's capital city).

"What is it that we have to do?" we kept asking. Ray replied, "The Air Force has decided that we do not need the deicers on our wings and we are to remove them." We all agreed that didn't sound too bad, so we said, "Let's get at it."

Deicers consisted of a hollow, thick rubber sleeve mounted on the leading edge of each wing and held in place by thousands of sheet metal screws. The thousands turned into millions, or so it seemed. The screws had been installed with machine screwdrivers and were extremely tight. All we had were standard handheld screwdrivers. I had blisters after about a dozen screws and said to myself, "Oh, oh, this is going to be a nightmare." Ray hollered up to us, "And save the screws, you have to put them back in the empty holes." "Oh, nooooo," we screamed. Ray just smiled and rode off in a jeep. We learned later, he visited Reykjavik. We had been warned to be very careful when going into town. The women of Iceland are beautiful, with blonde hair, blue eyes, and fair skin. About 95 percent were of Scandinavian origin, and their men were extremely jealous. We heard some pretty wild tales about Americans who became involved with local girls… They disappeared never to be heard from again. I don't think anyone else on our crew ever went into town. My hands had blisters on top of blisters, red, raw, and oozing. To this day, I still don't like to use a screwdriver.

Iceland turned out to be a strange land. It originated from volcanos far below the ocean and is full of active volcanos now. It has steaming hot springs and geysers, side by side, with huge ice fields and glaciers. From the air, it appears black and white, black lava from the volcanos and sparkling white ice and snow.

We were actually closer to the Arctic Circle here than at Goose Bay, but because of the Gulf Stream which runs nearby, the climate is moderate. The average summer temperature is around fifty degrees, and the winter temperature along the south coast rarely goes below freezing. Icelanders have a unique way of heating their homes. They pipe hot water from their many hot springs directly into radiators in their homes and businesses.

Because Iceland is so far north, summer days are almost twenty-four hours long. In December, the sun only shines about four hours a day; that would take some getting used to. The people were friendly and liked Americans. They work very hard and long hours. We saw a field near our base, nearly a city-block square, where the local people were drying codfish in the sun, after salting them down. Reading is their favorite pastime (I can understand why because there is nothing else to do), and we soon were ready to get the heck out of Dodge.

One good thing happened in Iceland…I was reacquainted with my friend from radio school, Rex Stanley. He was still gambling and still winning. Little did we know that we were destined to meet again, but that is part of a future story.

I am not sure, but I think our pilot, Ray, and some of his buddies opened up the stash of Scotch whiskey hidden in our plane's wing compartments as he didn't seem to mind Iceland at all. It could be, however, that he felt at home because of his Scandinavian ancestry.

One bright, beautiful morning, we climbed aboard our great silver bird and bade Iceland farewell. It was then I noticed so many of their homes and buildings had bright red roofs in contrast to a very barren land.

I REMEMBER ICELAND

I remember Iceland as a very warm people in a cold, cold land,
Bright red rooftops built on black volcanic sand.

Soon, Iceland was a faint memory as the humming of our four big radial engines took us steadily on the next leg of our flight to England. Ray told us, just after takeoff, that our next stop would be Glasgow, Scotland. Being part Scot, I had always wanted to go to the land of my ancestors, and Glasgow was a good place to start.

After checking all my radios, I remembered to activate my IFF (identification friend or foe). We were entering the war zone, and IFF sends out a radio signal, identifying a plane as friendly, so your own personnel will not fire on you.

I made the necessary entries in my logbook, opened the door to the waist compartment, and there were Maggie, Harvey, Jeff, and Sandy spread out on the floor, fast asleep. It was 627 miles from Iceland to Glasgow, and I should have dozed off, too, but I was excited and wide awake with anticipation. Scotland, WOW! I never dreamed I would be going there.

CHAPTER 8

The Mighty Eighth

As our engines droned on, my mind began to wander as I thought about Scotland, England, and about the Mighty Eighth Air Force. I had done some reading about this outfit, and I was dreaming of being a part of it. Way back in 1907, just a few years after the Wright Brothers made their historic flight at Kitty Hawk, North Carolina (not too far from home), someone in the US Army, with a tremendous vision of the future, created an aeronautical division in what was then called the Signal Corps. The only thing they had wrong was the belief that flying machines and airplanes would never be used for anything but observation and reconnaissance.

In 1920, a young nineteen-year-old flyer named Carl Spaatz, following in the footsteps of another famous aviator, Glen Curtis, decided to make aviation his life's career. The aeronautical service at that time was changed to the Army Air Service by General John Pershing. Its main purpose was still for observation, but soon, these observation planes on both sides began trying to destroy each other. They began with pistols and rifles, and soon, there were machine guns mounted on the planes. This brought on strafing of the enemy on the ground and was soon followed by bombs dropped by hand.

The Air Force continued to change and soon became more important in the fighting. General Spaatz enlisted the aid of other great Air Force flyers, Ira Baker, Jimmy Doolittle, and Billy Mitchell. They attempted to sway the US Congress for more support, convinced that the Air Force was the way of the future, but old Army and Navy people opposed them.

In 1921, Billy Mitchell convinced Congress to watch a test of Air Force power as Navy planes destroyed a German U-boat near the mouth of the Chesapeake Bay. To further his cause, Mitchell used eight Army biplanes, flying at eight thousand feet and ninety miles per hour, to bomb a captured German battleship. The battleship, a cruiser, and a destroyer were sunk within thirty minutes. But you know, the US Congress was still not convinced and so devised a new test. In 1923, both Army and Navy big Brass watched the bombing of two old US battleships, the USS *Virginia* and the USS *New Jersey*, near Cape Hatteras, North Carolina. Eight planes, carrying two bombs six hundred pounds each, sank the battleships. Still, it was not to be until President Calvin Coolidge authorized funds for the new Army Air Corps.

In the 1930s, Spaatz worried about sending our bombers into enemy territory where they might easily be shot down by enemy ground fire. They thought it would be completely impossible to build a fighter to escort the bombers.

Another man, Carl L. Norden, in 1932, invented the Norden bombsight and made it possible for bombers flying above twenty thousand feet to hit targets with pinpoint accuracy. Now the first glimpses of large numbers of planes which could bomb any place in the world was becoming a reality. Then, a very serious question arose. How are you going to protect the bombers? In 1934, Boeing built the first B17. President Franklin Roosevelt brought pressure to bear and in 1939 production began.

Those first B17s had little firepower, only five 30-caliber machine guns, and were manufactured with no tail guns, no belly guns, and no armor. Changes came quickly, and soon, there were thirteen 50-caliber guns with power turrets top and bottom. A tail gunner's position was added, and still later came a chin turret to protect from head-on attacks.

Army chief of staff, George Marshall, authorized General Spaatz and General Ira Eaker to activate the Eighth Air Force in January 1942. It had been a long, hard fight from a handful of men to get what they were convinced could make the difference in winning future wars.

It is an interesting story and worth telling when in February 1942, General Eaker went to England as head of the Eighth Air Force. Arriving in England on May 11, 1942, were 39 officers and 384 enlisted men who followed. They had come to fight a war, but were completely inexperienced. They were cocky and ready to get on with it. The British looked down their noses at them, and rightly so, as they had been fighting alone for 3 years.

General Eaker was quick to see these differences and, after setting up headquarters at High Wycliffe, made a short speech to his English counterparts. It was a very, very short speech, in fact, just twenty-two words. He said, "We won't do much talking until we've done more fighting. We hope that when we leave, you'll be glad we came." And he sat down. He made a lot of friends that day.

The early months of the Eighth Air force were really disappointing. Not only were the crews in a strange country, the bases were hastily built, and almost all lacked running water and had outdoor toilets. The weather was awful and usually cold and rainy. Even our training flights were hazardous. Many men and planes were lost during training missions, sometimes getting lost in the clouds. The pilots would fly up and down the whole of England looking for a break in the clouds. Many times, it was after dark, and except for an ingenious plan devised by the English, many more would have been lost. The operators of the thousands of very large searchlights used to spot German bombers, learning that the planes, both American and English, were helplessly lost in the almost impenetrable clouds, would point the way with their light beam to the nearest landing field. As a plane would fly over a light, it would switch on and point the way. Soon, it would snap off, and another light pointing further ahead would snap on, until at the airfield, several lights would cross above the end of the runway, directing the pilot in on a safe approach. That is one group we never got a chance to thank, but they saved many lives.

The Eighth Air Force's early combat missions were just barely into France. It was getting late into the year of 1942, and the records for high-altitude precision bombing had been very disappointing. So ineffective that Sir Winston Churchill, on November 2, 1942, wrote to his air chief marshal, Sir Charles Portel, "The number of American Air Force personnel is about 5500 and so far the results have been pitifully small. Far from dropping bombs on Germany, they have not gone beyond Lille, France; whereas, English night-bombing Lancasters, are bombing Berlin, Cologne, and deep into Germany." He added, "For many months ahead, large numbers of Americans will be here playing very little part in the War."

Through December, the United States could only send seventy-five bombers on a mission. It took us awhile to get it together. On December 12, eighty-two B17s and B24s bombed an airfield just outside Paris…still a long way from the thousands General Spaatz had predicted and promised. But look out, Sir Winston, here we come…

A NAZI TRICK

"CHUCK." The intercom jolted me back to reality. "Yes, sir." "Come up to the flight deck." I had been daydreaming, and now I was fumbling and stumbling, getting my earphones, unplugging my heated suit and oxygen unplugged. What the heck have I done now? What is he calling me up there for when he could have just talked to me on the intercom?

When I got to the flight deck, Ray said, "Have you been monitoring our homing signal from Scotland?" "Yes, sir. I don't keep it on all the time, but I check it every thirty minutes for my log." "I don't want to concern the rest of the crew, but that signal is changing every little bit. Get us a position fix and bring it back up here." I rushed back to the radio compartment and, within minutes, took it back to Ray. Ray called Neal up to where we were. After doing some checking, Ray said, "Those blasted Germans are overriding our homing signal with a high-powered transmitter somewhere in the north of Germany, Norway, or Denmark, or maybe they have a submarine broadcasting." The signal changed our course by a few degrees so that if we followed the signal, we would fly right over the top of Scotland and end up in Germany, the North Sea, or Denmark. As a result, Ray took over flying from the automatic pilot and flew the rest of the way manually.

JOLLY OLD ENGLAND

With Neal's directions, we flew straight into Prestwick Airfield, which is about forty miles south of Glasgow. We crossed the northern tip of Ireland, and it was like a jewel. Shining in the water, it was a color of green I had never seen before. I had read of it in books, but it was breathtaking. Vic Estes (bombardier), up in the nose, said, "Wow, man, would you look at that!" And we did. Everyone was wide awake now as we flew across the Firth of Clyde, the bay leading into Prestwick.

As we shut the engines down and got ready to leave the plane, we were weary and exhausted, but very relieved. We were met on the hardstand by vehicles that seemed to be made for the express purpose of ferrying airmen from their planes. They reminded us to be sure to take everything out as they could not be responsible for anything left behind. We thought that a little strange, but we gathered up our A2 bags, stuffed everything we could find in, and were met and greeted by the brightest and bubbliest redheaded Scottish lass. She would be our guide and see that we were housed and fed. It was the first WAF (Women's Air Force) we had ever seen.

We were fed a hot meal and taken to a warm and comfortable building and were pleased we didn't have to fire the stove and keep it going all night.

CHARLES J "CHUCK" RICHARDSON

THE SCOTCH IS WHERE?

After breakfast, things began to happen very quickly. We were informed that our plane had been flown away to be modified for combat and that it was not our plane at all. At that news, Ray Strate went ballistic. Not only were we losing a wonderful new plane, but also it had two cases of the best Scotch whiskey money could buy, hidden in the wings.

What a paradox! Whiskey so lovingly distilled just a few miles from where we landed in Scotland, bottled, packed carefully with straw in a wooden box, shipped to America, making its way to Kearney, Nebraska (halfway around the world), there to be bought at a premium price. Having been assured you would not be able to buy it in England, secretly stashed in the wings of our big bird, flown through many hazards back to Scotland, only to have it flown away to God knows where, only to have some maintenance crews find a treasure worth its weight in gold.

Ray was mortified. He loved his Scotch and now it was gone. The good news was that Scotch was plentiful here. It had been a horrible scheme, and not only that, the Scotch was half the price. We all laughed for days, but not in front of Lieutenant Ray Strate. To him it was no laughing matter.

Arriving in Scotland gave us another shock. When the sun went down, it was darker than the Black Hole of Calcutta. The British blackout was complete. You could not see a speck of light anywhere. If we planned to go out after dark, we were told to memorize our movements so we could find our way back. Falling over obstacles, we felt our way to the latrine. Most of their buildings had two doors with a little space between them so you could close the first before opening the second. There were a lot of our crew members who smoked, and they were called down often for lighting up outside. The commanding officer put the fear of the almighty into them when the British wardens called it to his attention. If caught a second time, no smoking for thirty days, with a promise of no smoking EVER if caught again. Americans learn very quickly. We were told to be ready to leave early the next morning, but three o'clock seemed ridiculous. Grumbling, off we went in an English lorry to the train station in Prestwick. While waiting to board the train to Glasgow, we got our first glimpse of an English train. We were all talking and laughing at the small steam locomotive and a number of small passenger cars. The cars were half the size of their American counterparts, and instead of entering from a door to a platform on either end as we were accustomed, each compartment had a door that you entered from the station platform. To us it seemed rinky-dink, almost like a toy train. Instead of brakes operated by steam hydraulics, the English system consisted of two mushroom-shaped pads on either end of their cars, which served as a bumper. When the engine slowed, the rods on the first car, being compressed, applied the brakes and the first car activated the second, so the entire train could be slowed or stopped by slowing down the engine. How very clever of the Brits. The whole train system, while very new and odd to us, worked very well. The conductor blew a little whistle much like a bobby's (policeman's), and the engineer gave a toot-toot. Again, the sound was not like that we were accustomed to, more like peep-peep, but with a very smooth movement, we were off.

Each compartment had two bench seats facing each other, which was fine for our card-playing poker friends, but a little awkward looking straight into someone's face for hours. The windows were held in place by a leather strap. To close the window, you simply lifted it by the strap and fastened it near the ceiling. It worked and got the job done. It was the first of many things the English did that was new to us, but worked just fine. Americans were not the only ones that knew how to make things. After all, the first steam engine was invented by James Watts, right here in Glasgow in 1767, and the first train ran in England in 1814. This was long before the first US steam locomotive (The Friend of Charleston) began in Charleston, South Carolina, just two hundred miles from my home in North Carolina.

Another great country, living proof that they could produce things better than we Americans, was the mighty German war machine, superior to the Americans in almost every way. What we had was an ability to change and improve as we found the need, and we had begun to learn.

As we pulled out of Glasgow headed for London, I watched out the window and the sun shined beautifully on the heather and the green grass and I thought:

> Scotland, how fair,
> Spring was in the air.
> How could there be war here,
> In a land, so bright and clear.
> But the military were everywhere,
> On the land, sea, and in the air.
> A million jeeps a-jaunting,
> A zillion sheep a-yawning.
> There were sounds of bombs and siren,
> And peaceful meadows so serene.
> A Scottish lass with bright-red hair,
> In this land called Scotland, oh so fair.

THE TRAIN, "PEEP-PEEP," ROLLED SOUTH

"I'll have the porridge, please!" "Are you nuts?" shouted Maggie and Steve. "They have real pancakes with real butter." I said, "I have always wanted real live porridge." "What the heck is it?" said Burr. Jeff chimed in, "Everyone knows what porridge is. It's a bird some people call the quail." He laughed and Harvey said, "No, Jeff, you are thinking of partridge." They all looked at it like it was poison. Maggie said, "It looks like oatmeal," and I retorted, "You are exactly right."

In the United States many people eat oatmeal, but most eat it with sugar or fruit. My mom served it two ways, hot or cold. To make oatmeal or porridge, you just mix oatmeal with hot water or milk and stir it up. I always liked it with fresh butter melted over it. The only difference here is they mix it with heavy cream. YUUUM, eat it up! They ate their pancakes while I ate my real porridge, from a real porringer (a thick bowl), and I loved it.

As we passed through the mountains that separate Scotland from England, our first stop was Dumfries, and you guessed it, there were guys jumping off the train to buy things, anything to eat or smoke, or chew, or read. They only had American money and didn't know a sixpence from a bob, or a quid, or a pound. They just held up their dollars, and the merchants would make the change.

Some swapped cigarettes for things like fish and chips, which were to become the one thing I really liked to eat in wartime England. So many of their foods had fillers which made them have very little taste. We were told things like sausages were fortified with sawdust. I'm not sure that was true, but, what I can say is that is exactly what it tasted like. Welcome to England in wartime. These poor souls had already endured it for four years. There was just not enough food to go 'round, and food was just one of the items that was in short supply and nearly impossible to get. We received an early education on the hardships of war.

Our really first shock of wartime was received when we got to Manchester. It is in the heart of the manufacturing region of

England, and the German Air Force bombed it regularly, second only to London or, possibly, Birmingham. There was destruction everywhere, and it gave us cause to stop and think about the seriousness of why we were here.

In Manchester, we saw the canal that runs the 35 1/2 miles to Liverpool. It is 120 feet wide and 30 feet deep. The English people built it so oceangoing ships could sail inland; it is certainly strange to see such large ships right downtown. I am beginning to have more and more respect for these hardworking people.

The scenery turned ugly with the evidence of heavy bombing and the black sooty industrial areas. However, you could see where a building had been destroyed and the rubble was being quickly removed, as though a colony of ants would come out at night and clean the streets and railways. It must have been disturbing to the Germans when their reconnaissance planes came to survey the damage and there was very little rubble.

We headed south toward London, still not having been told where we were going. As we neared London, the destruction we had seen was nothing compared to London.

They were in an awful hurry to move us along as we came into London at the Euston Railway Station, where I remember a huge arch and a long covered station building. Euston is one of fifteen train stations that encircle London. No trains run through London. You must transfer by cab, truck, or subway to another station if passing through, and that is what we did. We went directly to Liverpool Station, boarded another train going northeast, with little or no sightseeing. We could tell we had arrived at war as there were soldiers and sailors of every description, from every country, going in every direction. Huge antiaircraft batteries caught my attention. They were as long as a football field and were somehow connected to one another so when one moved, they all moved. I thought to myself, I surely would hate to be a German plane that these guns locked on to. Wherever the Germans bombed in London, leveling whole city blocks, the London people cleared away the rubble. The empty spot would become batteries of antiaircraft guns. We rode into London, and there were literally miles of destroyed buildings. I wasn't sure how the rest of the crew felt, but I was ready to get the heck out of London.

At Liverpool Station, we boarded quickly and I remember it being a large station, built in the shape of a tunnel and covered with glass panels, giving it the look of a huge flower house (without the flowers). The conductor blew his little whistle, "Tweeeeeet," the engineer blew his whistle, "Peep-peep," and we were heading northeast toward the English Channel. Finally, someone said, "Ipswich in ten minutes," and that is when we knew where we were going. We passed through Ipswich and on to our new home at Framlingham. From there we were trucked three miles along a narrow one-lane road to a huge air base.

So now we knew, we had been assigned to the 390th Bomb Group (Heavy), which had four squadrons, the 568th, 569th, 570th, and 571st. Ours was to be the 571st, all B17s, thank goodness.

Framlingham was designated Station number 153 by the British Air Ministry because it was nearest the town of some size. The base was actually located in the English parishes of Parham and Glenham, while Framlingham was located three miles northwest. We were ninety miles northeast of London, twenty-eight miles north of Ipswich, twenty-five miles east of Bury Saint Edmunds, which I thought was a very unusual name. I inquired, and a local, who didn't think it unusual at all, informed me in the direct manner that is so English, "It is exactly what it says it is," he said. He explained its name was given from and founded by the last king of East Anglia. Saint Edmunds was a medieval patron saint of England who was hacked to death by swords when the Danes landed on the coast of England in the year 869. He was canonized and a shrine was built, thus the name is exactly what it says…a place where they buried Saint Edmunds. This was one of my many lessons about England.

Framlingham is only 11 miles from the English Channel and the North Sea, and has a wonderfully preserved medieval castle with a moat, which has become a popular tourist attraction. To the north of Framlingham lies Norwich, about 30 miles away. It has a world-famous landmark, Norwich Cathedral, whose spire is 315 feet high, built in the year of our Lord 1096. It is easily spotted by bombers returning from missions over Germany.

CHAPTER 9

The 390th Bomb Group (Heavy)

The 390th Bomb Group had its origin at Blythe Army Air Base in southern California, a B17 combat training base of the 34th Bomb Group. It was activated by headquarters, 2nd Air Force at Fort George Wright, in Spokane, Washington, on January 26, 1943. On April 1, 1943, 124 officers and enlisted men from Blythe were ordered to the School of Applied Tactics in Orlando, Florida, for one month of training, then on to Geiger Field in Spokane, Washington.

Major Thomas S. Jeffrey was assigned as deputy group commander, and Lieutenant Colonel Edward M. Wittan was made the first commanding officer of the 390th. Wittan and Jeffrey were a good match and had known each other since training together at a B18 bomber school in Langley, Virginia, in 1939. They added many fine officers, among them Major Bill Pennebaker. Within a few months, they gathered their equipment, planes, and men and set out to train for about six weeks at four different locations in Montana. They finished their combat training with a flight across the United States to Bermuda and back. After a thirty-day furlough, they flew to Prestwick, Scotland, and then on to Framlingham, arriving on July 15, 1943. The ground crews and equipment arrived on July 27. Colonel Edgar M. Wittan was group CO from January 26, 1943, until May 15, 1944. Colonel Frederick W. Ott was CO from May

15, 1944, until September 6, 1944. Colonel Joseph A Moller was CO from September 6, 1944, until May 21, 1945, and Lieutenant Colonel George W. Von Arb was CO from May 23, 1945, until June 26, 1945.

The 390th was assigned to the 13th Combat Wing, along with the 95th and 100th Bomb Groups. These three groups flew together for the entire war, and the 13th Wing was part of the 3rd Air Division which, along with the 1st and 2nd Air Divisions, made up the 8th Air Force.

Just 5 days after flying its first mission, the 390th was part of one of the most famous bombing missions in Air Force history. On August 12, 1943, they bombed Regensburg, Germany, where Messerschmitt Me109s were being made in record numbers. They were turning out 48 percent of all German fighters. The Germans defended it with all they had. One of the most feared targets in Europe, it was one of the fiercest air battles in history.

The day our crew arrived, the average life of a heavy bomber was 145 days, including the time it spent on the ground. With this in mind, we entered the security gate, but couldn't help noticing there was no high fence around the base. Could it be that people could just come and go as they pleased? That was just about the way it turned out. There was just a single strand of barbed wire, but mostly just a hedgerow.

We were driven directly to the 571st Squadron headquarters' Nissen hut and were surprised that it was so small. We were welcomed by Major Bill Pennebaker and assigned to our quarters. The enlisted men were assigned to a hut very near the headquarters building. As we put our bags away, the duty sergeant explained what we would be doing for the next few days. We were walked to the latrine, just two huts away, and then on to the mess hall. I remember the chow was not good and we were grumbling to ourselves. Harvey Burr said, "Oh, we will get used to it," and Jeff Fuller said, "I have been wanting to lose a little anyway."

We were much too excited to worry about food right now. We could see B17s everywhere, some coming in for a landing, shooting red flares. We learned quickly that these were the ones with wounded aboard. We were hypnotized as, one after another, the big, beautiful B17s landed. I thought to myself, *This is serious.*

One of the first things we noticed was that all the planes had a big black J painted on a white square, high on the tail. It was also painted on the wings and was used to identify different bomb groups when assembling for formation flying. The two other groups that were closely related to the 390th were the 95th with a square B and the 100th with a square D. The square D played a very important part in the fact that I survived the war, as you will see. Surviving was made possible by several other factors as well. First, and most likely one of the most important, was by direct intervention by General Dwight David Eisenhower, who overruled everyone under his command, stating the 8th Air Force would be used, beginning in May 1944, as tactical support for the long-awaited European invasion of ground troops. He practically had to courts-marshal generals and others, both American and British, who felt it was in the Allies' best interests that we continue to bomb far into Germany. Long-range bombing was beginning to take its toll on the German war effort, particularly in the fuel and aircraft industries.

It meant that the deep penetrations would be sharply reduced and delayed. This is where the Eighth Air Force had suffered its worst losses, both from fighters and antiaircraft fire. We would be bombing railroads, bridges, communication and aircraft centers, and troop concentrations closer to the coast to disrupt the German Army from reacting to the invasion. (This was happening just as our crew was starting its mission. Without a doubt, God was working His purposes out.)

Another very important part of my survival was the P51 Mustang fighter plane. Just now coming in ever-increasing numbers, fitted with wing tanks, they could escort the heavy bombers all the way to the targets and back.

I am convinced it was God's plan; otherwise, how could all these dramatic factors come into place just as our crew arrived in England. I am in no way saying that things would be easier. It was the fact that the odds of survival got better for me and the playing field became a little smoother.

One other factor was now in place. Most of the B17Fs still able to fly were being upgraded with chin turrets that attached just below the nose of the plane. All new plane replacements were the newest B17Gs with chin turrets installed in the United States, like the one we flew over. After the Germans learned (the hard way) that all our planes were equipped with chin turrets, the number of fighter attacks from twelve o'clock level (or dead ahead), dropped dramatically. They would now try to find a more vulnerable, unprotected area of our plane to attack.

INSTRUCTION AND INDOCTRINATION

The first few days on our new base and home were used to get us accustomed to our surroundings and to get into the flow of activity. All the new crews, and there were many, made us wonder, "Are the crews we are replacing finishing their tour of thirty-five missions, or are we losing more in combat?" It made me quiver and shiver.

We had hours of indoctrination sessions, and one of the guys with whom I went to radio school had just finished his 22nd mission. He called me aside after chow one evening, and after reminiscing about nearly freezing to death in Sioux Falls, South Dakota, he became very serious and leaned in close to me. In almost a whisper he said, "Listen, Chuck, I want to tell you something very important. It could mean the difference in whether you go home again." I can tell you, he got my full attention. He said, "The next few days, you will be listening to guys who have already completed their tours and have learned some hard lessons. They have been very good at what they had to do and have been lucky. Most of the new guys going into these sessions look at it as just another classroom talk, but you listen, and you listen hard, and tell your crew that what they hear in the next few days will be worth all the gold and diamonds in the world, your life."

I felt as though my dad were talking to me, saying, "Pay attention, Son." I thanked Sergeant William Schmidt and shook his hand. I went back to our crew hut with a lot on my mind. I did not know that in just a few days, on June 5, Sergeant Schmidt's plane would be hit by ground fire, a direct hit, causing it to collide with another plane. I never heard from Sergeant Schmidt again. I attempted to find him after the war, but could not. I told the guys on my crew what he had told me, and I could see it was getting through to all of us.

In the squadron briefing room the next day, our instructor was a tech sergeant who had finished his tour and wanted to tell us a few things, some of which we already knew, but did not understand. I was reminded of the story of the little boy who came home from school and told his mother that his teacher had taken him to the principal because she could not get him to behave in class. The mother was irate and called Johnnie's father, who blew a fuse and headed for the school on a dead run, determined to stomp the daylights out of the principal who dared to paddle his son. On arriving at the school, he charged right past everyone and was met by the principal, who was 6 feet, 4 inches tall, and weighed 225 pounds. There was a lot of noise and then all was quiet. As the boy's father left the school with a black eye, he went directly home and told Johnnie, "From now on, you do exactly what that teacher says. You see, Son, at first they just didn't 'splain it right."

The sergeant told us about being shot down on a mission to Brunswick, Germany, on January 11. His plane was attacked by about fifty Me109s right after they dropped their bombs. He said, "Things were happening so fast, it was like a whirlwind." The fighters knocked their plane out of formation, and as the pilot fought for control with two engines out, a wounded bombardier and navigator, they headed down into low clouds and home. All intercom was knocked out, so the pilot sent the copilot to check on the rest of the crew. Meanwhile, the fighters were making pass after pass to finish them off. The ball turret was gone from a direct hit; all others were okay.

Our sergeant instructor was a radio operator, and the point he wanted to make was "*when you hear the bailout bell ring, run like hell and get out.*" He pointed out that when the bell rang on his plane, he started looking around to see what was going on or to help others and it almost cost him his life. The pilot could see and knew what was happening and waited until the very last minute to tell the crew to jump. He had already instructed the copilot and engineer to put chutes on the bombardier and navigator and to shove them out. He rang the bell and jumped himself. Our instructor sergeant was the last to leave the plane. "Know where your chute is, be able to grab it, snap it on, and be gone when the BELL rings." Man, he had our attention, for sure!

A pilot was our next instructor, and he told us to know the basics of the jobs of the other members of the crew so we could fill in if an emergency arose. He told of a plane in which the pilot was badly injured, the copilot was killed in a raid over Leipzig, Germany, and the navigator and engineer flew the plane back to England. All members of the crew bailed out and were safe. The navigator and engineer elected to try to land in an effort to save the badly injured pilot. The Fortress named Ten Horsepower made four passes at landing, directed by radio from another B17, but crashed. Both men received the Medal of Honor, posthumously.

Know your position well and teach others enough that they can be called on, if needed.

Lieutenant R. Kennedy told us something that should have been part of the training for all aircrews. It was his misfortune to have to bail out over Holland, after being shot up pretty badly over the Rhur Valley in Germany. The plane burned slowly for a while, and the pilot fought to keep it flying. As they dropped out of formation, a Focke-Wulf 190 bore in for the kill. The pilot, realizing that he could not make it back to England, gave the order to bail out. All ten crew members got out and landed safely in Holland. Seven were captured, but Lieutenant Kennedy and two others evaded capture and, with the help of the Underground, made their way through Spain back to England.

What Lieutenant Kennedy wanted to tell us was this, "When you bail out at high altitude without oxygen and pull the rip cord too soon, more than likely you will pass out and odds are you will never regain consciousness." We were already aware of this, but what we didn't know, even after free-falling to get under ten thousand feet where we could breathe, was that almost every time, the jerk of the chute opening would snap your flying boots and heated inner socks off, leaving you barefoot in freezing temperatures. Frostbite, with the loss of toes and feet, was common. He told us to talk to our ground crews and use tape to secure our boots. Wonderful advice for those shot down, with the prospect of walking out of enemy territory.

A very wise second lieutenant told us about English customs and how to keep from getting into trouble when we were on infrequent leaves. To many English people, a favorite description of American soldiers, and particularly airmen, was that they were overpaid, oversexed, and over here. Americans that had preceded us, and again, airmen, had made the average Englishman wary of our fun-loving exploits. Our squadron CO told us, in no uncertain terms, we were to obey the British laws and customs or bear the wrath of the English police, the US MPs, or much worse, his own brand of punishment. Whatever that was, I did not want any part of it.

We were told we would get a ration each month which, of course, we would have to pay for. We were issued a small three-by-five card which was titled "U. S. Army Exchange Service Ration Card, ETO USA." The card listed the following things: beer, juice, tobacco, candy, cookies, matches, peanuts (four ounces), toilet paper, toilet soap, razor blades, toothpaste, soap, shaving cream, writing tablet, envelopes, and handkerchiefs. This ration card was signed by J. Foster, first lieutenant AC, who stated that if lost would not be replaced. I call this to attention, as there are a couple of items listed on the card that I wish to tell you about later.

On a more serious note, one of the guys that had been shot down and made his way back wanted us to take a few moments to write down the names and addresses of our crew members and also note their family members. Some of our crews did not make it, and he wanted someone who had been close to write the families and stay in touch with them.

One day, we were sent over to base headquarters to receive fake papers in case we were shot down over enemy territory. We were dressed in old clothes; some of us wore caps like the farmers in Europe wear. I still have pictures of some of the crew that were taken for our identification papers. These papers must have been very good, because a number of them were checked by the Germans, who were not suspicious of them.

A bombardier, who was shot down over Belgium, used his escape kit (which I described in a previous chapter) to evade capture, moving right through Paris and all of France and Spain, using the language interchange which had phrases in ten different languages translated from English to Spanish, Portuguese, French, Italian, Russian, Polish, German, Jewish, Chinese, and Japanese. With the help of the Underground, and by pointing to phrases like, "I am an American airman. How can I get to Spain?" he was told to pretend he was deaf and dumb and to follow different contact people. He told us the kit with the candy, cigarettes, D rations, along with the small compasses, and ten thousand French francs and the language interchange, really worked well and kept him from being captured.

Some of our instructors gave us tips that were not approved, such as scrounging up an extra parachute because, in combat, at least one was shot up and made useless, and to scrounge extra flak suits. Even our pilots were against this as it added much weight to the plane, which was already loaded to its limits.

We were told of one pilot who kept complaining to his ground crew that his plane was flying sluggish and tail-heavy and he could not trim it out. The crew chief solved the problem and reported to the pilot, "No wonder you could not fly it. Your tail gunner has surrounded his position with twelve flak vests, at twenty pounds each." Needless to say, the pilot checked each position and found there were even more throughout the plane.

The flak vests were made by Wilkinson Sword Company (the same company that makes razor blades) and were made of twenty-gauge magnesium steel. The steel plates were one and three-fourths inches wide and overlapped three-eighths of an inch. The plates were sewn into a heavy canvas vest. It would stop a 30-caliber bullet and saved countless lives. The vests were worn over the parachute harness and could be removed quickly by pulling a release cord…just one more thing you had to think about if you had to bail out.

In addition to the flak vest, we were issued a steel helmet, which we rarely wore until we heard the first burst of flak. I eventually modified my helmet as I had to wear earphones and couldn't get a helmet over them. I cut a hole in my helmet large enough for my earphones and had a flap welded to each side. It looked funny, but it worked. If you really want the truth, in combat, I ended up sitting on my helmet as that was the direction from whence the fire was coming.

We were given our new APO overseas address and told to get busy and write our loved ones so we could start getting some letters and cookies for everyone to enjoy.

The last thing I remember of our indoctrination was a review of our last will and testament, which we had recorded in Dalhart, Texas. It lent a tone of the seriousness and danger we were just beginning. It told all concerned that here was a soldier going into battle, and odds were he would not be going home.

It was Friday, May 19, 1944, and we were told that our missions as crew number 71, 571st Squadron, 390th Bomb Group, 3rd Air Division of the 8th Air Force would officially begin on Monday, May 22. We were ready, as far as we knew, and eager to get on with it and go home. We kept the crew number 71 until June 14, when it was changed permanently to number 86.

On Saturday, Harvey, Maggie, Steve, and I went to squadron headquarters to register for bicycles, which would be assigned to us for transportation around the base. We decided to check out Framlingham Air Force Base number 153. We first checked out the latrine and mess hall, then the infirmary and the officers' quarters, plus the enlisted men's club. Then, we rode out to the flight line and the control tower. There were B17s everywhere. Many were new and shiny, with just the identification numbers and, of course, the big square J painted on the tail. We could see farmers working in the fields adjoining the base. We rode by the village of Parham, which came right up to the edge of the base. We saw a very nice church and decided to ask permission to attend it the next day. I can't remember the sermon, but I sure remember how cold those seats were. The church was not heated, and the seats were made of granite. It reminded me of how comfortable and warm our churches at home are. Comfortable or not, many of us attended that church as often as we could. I recall the bell tower had three large bells, one which was inscribed "Made in 1350." The church was very near our barracks and a short walk. Harvey and I made the acquaintance of a very nice lady who was already doing laundry for a number of 390th personnel. She agreed to do ours and also some of the others on our crew. I don't remember precisely what she charged, but I do remember it was very reasonable. I've often thought of trying to contact our laundry lady to thank her.

CHAPTER 10

Framlingham—Home For A While

We were beginning to settle into our Nissen hut home, just two doors down from our latrine that served several other huts. There was hot water for a good bath in a communal area. Even so, we really appreciated it because many bases still slept in tents and had no hot or running water.

Squadron headquarters was nearby, and the mess hall was a short walk. We shared our hut with another crew and soon learned that it was painful to become close friends, as the turnover was rapid with some crews finishing their tours and others being shot down.

There was the "eternal potbellied stove" that kept going continually, and we had a radio that kept us up-to-date on news of the war in other areas.

Just after we arrived, one of the most disturbing things that happened to us was pointed out by the other crew in our hut. The second night after our arrival, right after evening chow and the crews were writing letters home, we were introduced to the voice on the radio, known as Lord Haw-Haw. Broadcast from Germany on a powerful transmitter, Lord Haw-Haw, in perfect English, would broadcast propaganda. On this second night of our arrival, he welcomed the crew of Lieutenant Raymond Strate to the US Air Force Base number 153 at Framlingham, in East Anglia. He said, "We welcome you and tonight we will send you a calling card. Listen for us."

And, sure enough, a German plane did come over and drop a couple of bombs, but nowhere near us.

We wondered, "How in the heck do they do that?" How did they know that when we hardly knew it ourselves? Many times, they called the names of the crew members, and we began to realize that we had a formidable foe.

A few nights later we tuned in to another propagandist, called Axis Sally. We loved to listen to her, with her low sexy voice, playing all the popular music from home. Her favorite trick was to call out a crew member's name, rank, and serial number, and say something like, "Sergeant Bill Smith, radio operator on Lieutenant Robert Best's crew, did you know your wife, Peggy, is out tonight with another man? Dancing and having a big time?"

THE BITCH OF BERLIN AND THE DOUBLE-CROSS SYSTEM

Not until after the war did we find out how they got the information about us. I think my readers will be interested in the story about Axis Sally, also known as the Bitch of Berlin.

Her real name was Midge Gillars, a girl from Ohio, who became a model in Paris. She met and married a German, Max Otto Koischwitz, and moved to Berlin. There she became a disc jockey. She had a wonderfully pleasant and sexy voice and, of course, spoke perfect American. Every evening she would play records of the latest American songs and taunt the listening GIs, saying, "Your wives and girlfriends at home are cheating on you." She welcomed many new American arrivals, giving name, rank, and serial number, plus their outfit and their location.

How did she do it? Because of what was known as the Double-Cross System.

The British made many outstanding contributions to the war effort. They were brilliant in technology and science. They gave us the proximity fuse, which allowed our artillery to shoot at a target and explode the target the second it touched. Whereas, the Germans, at least in the early days of the war, used a timed fuse that exploded by time. There were many times when German shells passed completely through our plane, leaving a perfectly round hole, and continued on to explode high above us. Had they been using a proximity fuse, I, for one, would not be here to write this account.

The British also gave us radar and sonar, two very important inventions for waging war. They also collaborated in the development of the atomic bomb. They had intelligence operations, second to none, and one of their most important discoveries was called Ultra. This was the top secret code word for the system of breaking the elite German Enigma encoding machines.

From 1941 on, we knew everything they were doing. It identified all the spies working in England. They were rounded up and "convinced" to work for the Allies, sending only information they were told to. The Germans never caught on because they thought the code could absolutely not be broken. They believed they were just too smart. The information about American troops in England was actually fed to Axis Sally and the German High Command by British Intelligence. It had to be the truth for the Double-Cross System to work.

After the war, Midge Gillars was tried and convicted of treason. She served approximately twelve years in the US federal prison. In 1961, she was released and taught music in Columbus, Ohio. She died in 1988 at the age of eighty-seven.

I can still hear her now, in her low sultry voice, singing, "Lillie Marlene," a sad and haunting tune, "Lily of the Lamplight, by the Garden Gate…" She was effective, and many American boys, after hearing her late in the evening, went to sleep with tears in their eyes.

Monday, May 22, 1944, 0500 Hours

I awakened with a jerk when the sergeant in charge of quarters banged open the door to our Nissen hut. It sounded like a bomb going off. "Okay, Lieutenant Ray Strate, crew number 71, up and at 'em. Chow at 0530, briefing at 0600. Get moving."

It was damp and dark and cold, and I was already wide awake. This was finally it, and I found my teeth chattering and my knees a little weak. We dressed in a hurry and half ran to the mess hall, where we were happy and surprised to find the mess crew, sleepy eyed, already had pancakes. We walked right into the mess kitchen and stood by the big iron stove, where we told the cooks how we wanted our fresh eggs cooked. This was the privilege for flying crews only. It reminded one of a prisoner about to be executed and getting to choose whatever he wanted before he died.

After eating, we went to the briefing hut and were told that Lieutenant Ray Strate's crew number 71 was to stand down, but not go back to quarters. After the other crews went back to their quarters, we were told the mission had been scrubbed. Due to bad weather over Europe, our crew was to fly a training mission. What a letdown!

When we arrived at our hardstand, the bombs had been unloaded, and instead, the ground crew was very gingerly lifting four tin tubs into the waist hatch. We asked what was going on and were told our pilot would explain.

Ray explained that we were flying a practice formation over "The Wash." The Wash is a large desolate area, like a huge swamp, over the north coast of England where planes, both English and American, went to practice bombing and weapons firing.

The four tin tubs were full of water and, at altitude, would turn to ice. The ice was to be used in the officer's mess and officer's club since the English had no ice-making machines and they drank their alcoholic drinks hot.

We also served as a weather ship, but the main reason for our flight was ice. All was not lost. Ray gave us a good ride, climbing to almost a stall then nosing over, as gravity disappeared. We were weightless and floating all over the airplane. Wow! That was fun!

Tuesday, May 23, 1944, 0500 Hours

Bang went that door again. From a dead sleep, I was startled and asked, "What is going on?" "Okay, Ray Strate, crew number 71, up and at 'em. Chow at 0530, briefing at 0600, hop to."

"Hey, Sarge, where we going?" "You'll find out, and you will be sorry." Uh-oh, I wished Jeff had not asked… Just gave me a little longer to worry about it.

We went through the same routine as yesterday. We didn't go, and when the crews came back, we talked with some of them. It was a rough mission, to Metz and Saarbrucken. We lost two B17s and one B24, with eighty-three planes damaged, twenty-two men killed, and ten missing. They also told of watching a B17 and a B24 collide during assembly. "Hey, wait a minute, this is serious!"

As we soon discovered, getting into formation before leaving England could be every bit as dangerous as flying over Germany. With literally thousands of planes taking off from different fields all over England, and eight out of ten times through cloud cover, we held our breath until we broke through on top of the clouds.

In the meanwhile, we felt that the powers that be were playing games with us, but we soon realized we needed this extra training. We flew in formation with other new crews like ours, and what we thought was flying close together was nothing compared to what we would see in combat.

Up and down England we flew. We had an opportunity to see all the preparations going on for what surely could not be far off, the Invasion of Europe.

Wednesday, May 24, 1944

We were not alerted this morning. We slept until about 0800 and just got to the mess hall before it closed. Harvey, Steve, Maggie, Sandy, Jeff, and I rode our bicycles out to the flight line. I had awakened around 0700 to the roar of our group taking off on a mission, and we wanted to see where they had gone and when to expect them back.

Our crew chief said, "You guys have got to be the luckiest crew on this base." We asked why, and he replied, "The group is leading the 3rd Division to Big B [Berlin]. Last Friday we bombed Berlin and lost 28 planes while you were making ice for the officer's club. Then, on Monday, we bombed Kiel and lost 5, and today we sent 516 planes back to Berlin. Just count your blessings." Wow, can you believe it? We were scheduled to fly, and by the grace of God, we didn't. Thank you, Lord.

When the planes came back in the afternoon, we found that 33 planes did not come back, nine from the 100th Bomb Group alone. Flying through some bad weather, the 100th got separated from the rest of the division and were pounced upon by 200 enemy planes. We felt it was a downright miracle that we did not fly today, as the 100th always flew on our wing.

Thursday, May 25, 1944, 0500 Hours

"All right, up and at 'em, Lieutenant Ray Strate, crew number 71. Chow in thirty minutes, briefing at 0600. Don't be late." Bang went the door, and he was off to the next hut. We could hear a lot of moaning and groaning going on.

This time it was for real, our first mission. Where would we be going? Would I choke up and be afraid to fight? Would this be my last day to live?

I hardly remember eating, wondering, worrying, "Are we going back to Berlin?" As we took our places in the new briefing room (the old one burned to the ground on May 15, just a few days before our arrival), there was a lot of talking going on and suddenly, "Atten-hut!" and everyone stood; there was deathly quiet. The squadron commanders, the group commander, the weather officer and the group briefing officers came quickly down the center aisle, and someone said, "Be seated, gentlemen."

You could almost hear the hearts pounding as we sat down and waited for the briefing officer to pull back the black curtain that covered a large map of Europe, revealing the mission route and target. I, for one, was expecting to see the long black ribbon stretching way across into deep Germany.

When the curtain was finally drawn, it was as if we all caught our breaths. The moment was electrifying and the adrenaline was really flowing. Much to my surprise, our division was to bomb gun emplacement batteries in Normandy, on the coast of France at Fecamp and Saint Valery, which are located just across the Channel from Brighton, England. There were 38 planes in our flight, and our 390th Bomb Group was assigned to bomb the guns at Saint Valery.

The main force, with 247 B17s and 103 B24s, was to hit rail marshaling yards in Brussels, Belgium, while the 1st Division would be bombing airfields at Nancy and Liege and rail yards at 4 other locations along the French coast.

It was a clear day; however, our 390th Bomb Group had been chosen to take part in an experiment, dropping our bombs when the lead plane in our flight dropped theirs. If results are good, it would be adopted for use in future missions. It was to be called saturation bombing and was to be used when the target is obscured. (The lead plane is a PFF or Pathfinder plane equipped with radar.) It was apparent that this was in preparation for the forthcoming invasion. All the bombing this day was a softening-up mission and was really a milk run, or easy mission.

When the main force headed into Belgium, the Germans shifted their air defenses to meet them. As a result, we did not see any enemy aircraft, but we did get a lot of flak. Since it was our first mission, we thought the flak to be heavy and terrible. Little did we know, as one of the older crews said after the mission, "Man, you ain't seen nothing yet."

There were 4 planes lost and 145 damaged, but results were listed as good.

Heading home we were in great spirits, laughing and kidding one another. Maggie said, "Did you see all those Germans running away when they saw us coming?" "Yeah, ole Hitler is running scared since we got here," said Jeff (Fuller right waist gunner). "Okay, pipe down, you guys," Ray broke in, "something tells me we have been very, very lucky today."

We, of course, did not know it at the time, but the fact is, on the exact day we flew our first mission, General Eisenhower had overruled a lot of other generals and even Winston Churchill himself, stating that he was to be in charge of **ALL** Allied forces, including land, air, and sea. For the near future at least, everything would be focused on preparation for the Invasion of Europe. Both British and American Air Forces pitched a flying fit, especially since we were just now making our best advances of the war.

"Nevertheless, you will do it my way or get yourself another man for this job," said Dwight David Eisenhower. The midnight oil burned, and there was a lot of gnashing of teeth, but in the end, Eisenhower prevailed.

We were back at Framlingham early, and our ground crews came running out to meet us and were delighted that we all returned, with no holes to patch.

I wrote to Eleta and Mom that night, telling of our successful first mission and saying it looked like we had now turned the tide of the war. This, of course, was merely wishful thinking because each of us knew that very soon now, we would be sorely tested.

Friday, May 26, 1944

Our squadron did not fly. However, the 390th Group went back to Saint Valery to knock out more of those coastal guns.

It was an eerie kind of morning. Our squadron was not alerted, and the usual noise of engines being run up and planes taking off made us think something was wrong. However, it was just one of those days when our entire group did not fly, and I, for one, was glad. I needed a day to let my heart slow from flying our first mission.

Breakfast on a nonflying day was really bad. We almost always had an orange, and if we could get by with looking down at that large square pan of powdered eggs as green as grass, we might get nerve enough for one spoonful. Most of us went for pancakes or French toast, with syrup so watery it would not stay on our metal trays. Someone said the formula is one teaspoon of sugar to a gallon of water. We did get fresh milk most of the time, which we could use with corn flakes.

Some of us took this quiet time to take our laundry down to our laundry lady in Parham. She was always glad to see boys from the base and treated us like one of her own children.

As we walked back to our hut, Harvey asked, "Hey, Chuck, can you speak French?" I didn't know if he was kidding, and I cautiously said, "Oui, monsieur." He was dead serious and said, "You know, it might just come in handy if we happen to be shot down." So, that very evening, we began to learn a little more French. I was lucky to have had two years of French in high school, and had I been able to foresee the future, would have paid more attention in class. (Years later, at a high school reunion, my old French teacher was there and I told her about this. She said, "Yes, Charles, I kept trying to tell you." And I thanked her again for what I *did* learn.) By late afternoon we saw the red alert flag go up at squadron headquarters, telling us to start worrying as we would be flying in the morning.

Saturday, May 27, 1944

I was wide awake when the duty sergeant called our name and number. "Let's go, girls," he said in a high, squeaky voice. "It's your time to rise and shine. Hey, looka here, some of you guys are already dressed. I'll have to tell the ole man how eager you are." He just made it through the door when someone threw a shoe at him.

This being our second mission, we were not quite as uptight and on edge, but we knew we had some rough days coming. Breakfast was very good, and we gathered at the briefing hut, chatting with other crews. But everyone had the same thing on their minds. *Where are we going today?*

We did not have to wait long as no sooner had we sat down when the briefing sergeant yelled, "Tens-hut." Everyone jumped up as a group of officers made their way from the door at the back of the room, up the center aisle, to the platform at the front. The procession was led by the group briefing officer and followed by the 390th Bomb Group commander, Colonel Frederick W. Ott, our 571st squadron commander, Colonel George Von Arb, and the commanding officers of the 568th, 569th, and 570th Bomb Squadrons. There were also officers from weather and intelligence.

Colonel Ott said, "Be seated, gentlemen," and the adrenaline began to stimulate my heart 'til I could feel each beat in my temples. There was something in my throat that wouldn't go down, my mouth was dry as cotton, and there was a ringing in my ears.

"Men, today is a maximum effort." (Whatever was in my throat now hit the bottom of my stomach.) "Everything that can fly, will fly." (It's Big B, for sure, and the sweat rolled down my back.) "We are sending 1,126 B17s and B24s to strike Hitler a mighty blow." He pulled the cord that opened the black curtain and there were oohs and aahs and "Oh, nos" all over the room.

"As you can see this is not just a single strike, but many. All the targets are important as we prepare the way for the Invasion, which will come soon. There will be 150 planes hitting a large communication center in Ludwigshaven. This is a deep penetration and is certain to draw a lot of enemy fighters.

"There will be 125 planes hitting the rail marshaling yards at Mannheim, next door to Ludwigshafen, and there will be a host of flak guns here, in addition to fighters. There will be 18 planes hitting the airfield at Lachen/Speyerdorf. They may get off the ground, but we want to fix it so they can't go home.

"In addition, there will be 25 planes hitting other rail facilities near Mannheim. Ninety-eight planes will be bombing the rail yards at Karlsruhe, which is located on the Rhine River, just inside Germany on the border of France. This is an important crossroad for land transportation, both auto and rail. There is also a huge plant for making munitions. *Whatever you do, don't miss this target.*

"There will be 369 planes bombing rail shipping and marshaling yards at Saarbrucken, Neunkirchen, and Konz, all of which are near Karlsruhe and well protected by both flak and fighters.

"But, the 390th, which is us, will be concerned with the rail yards at Strasbourg, a transport hub 300 miles east of Paris, right on the German border. The target lies right in the midst of a hotbed of fighters and flak." [It has been called the crossroads of Europe, kind of like our modern Atlanta... If you are flying, you must go through Atlanta.]

"General Dwight Eisenhower has declared that we must render these targets useless, so when the Invasion comes, the Germans will not easily be able to shift ground forces and supplies from one area to another."

The intelligence officer outlined the areas where we could expect fighters and flak, and reminded the bombardiers that the target is a huge rail yard just west of the old city of Strasbourg. Located in the center of town, it would look like a bull's-eye because it is surrounded by the Ill River, which divides and then comes back together. In addition, there is the Cathedral of Notre Dame with a spire 466 feet high, which was begun in the year 1176 and completed 300 years later, in 1439. It can be seen for miles in all directions, and we were told to avoid hitting the Cathedral.

The weather officer's speech was short and sweet. "Thin cloud cover near the target. Otherwise, clear all the way."

Colonel Ott added, "Men, you will have 102 B17s, with 170 P38s, 238 P47s, and 302 P51s flying cover for you." That brought a loud "all right." "But, don't forget, the enemy is getting his back against the wall, and he is extremely dangerous and capable." Using our motto, he said, "Good hunting and Sur le Nez [translation is "On the Nose"]. Atten-hut! As you were." And he was gone.

BOEING B17G FLYING FORTRESS WITH NORTH AMERICAN P51 MUSTANG.

REPUBLIC P47 THUNDERBOLT (OUR "LITTLE FRIENDS")

We picked up our equipment (flying suits, parachutes, flak vests, Mae Wests, etc.) and headed to the flight line. The mood of the crew was quite good; we were excited, but not glum. We are going deep into enemy territory, and this time, our lives were truly on the line.

Ray called us together just before we boarded the GOOD-O-YANK, a name he gave our plane. He picked the name from an expression that everyone in England seemed to be using, meaning everything is A-OK.

He said, "Men, this mission is going to be a test for us. I am going to need each one of you doing your best and then some. They are going to be doing their damnedest to shoot us down and kill us. Keep your eyes open and don't let up for a moment. Help me and I will bring this big bird home safely."

We all pulled the propellers through to lubricate the engines before cranking them. The crew chief stood by with a giant fire extinguisher, while another ground crewman hooked up the auxiliary cranking unit to the number 1 engine (the engine farthest to the pilot's left). It ground, coughed, bucked, and roared like a huge wild lion awakened from sleep. As the running got smoother, the ground crew moved to the next engine, until all four were running smoothly. Since this would be a long trip of over one thousand miles, our fuel tanks were topped off.

We were now on strict radio silence because the Germans were listening. They needed to get every little clue about where we were going and when. To them, this was a deadly serious war, and they were confident and determined to exterminate this hive of bees that were coming to destroy their fatherland.

I listened as I checked out my radio equipment to be sure everything was working right. I looked up over my radio command set, where I had taped Butch's picture and marked a big hash mark, denoting that I had completed one mission, and now only thirty-four more to go.

I heard the snap of a Very pistol from the control tower and, looking out my radio room window, could see the flare arching high into the morning sky. Almost simultaneously, the roar of engines all over the base told us we were on our way. One of the sounds I can vividly remember, after over sixty years, is the sound of brakes being applied on all those B17s that were lining up for takeoff. We would roll a little ways and then *screeeech*, the brakes would wail.

Nose to tail, like a string of circus elephants, we lumbered out to the runway for takeoff. The roar was deafening as all the planes that were to fly today were cranked and rolling.

Finally, at 0930 hours came the flare from the tower and the first plane moved off down the runway. Imperceptibly at first, then gaining momentum as it neared the end of the runway, it ever so slightly lifted off. With no runway left, it cleared a one-wire barbed wire fence used principally to keep farm animals off the runway. We could see the landing gear rise up into the plane then, every thirty seconds, another plane would roar away. Each pilot would race his outboard engines, then stop, over and over until all were airborne.

Flying an elongated box-shaped pattern, ever climbing, we assembled our group right on time, then began looking for the other two groups who always flew together, the Ninety-fifth and the One-hundredth. Today, we were flying the low squadron in the high group and we were spaced so it looked like a huge stairway, all the way to heaven.

At ten thousand feet, Ray (Strate), our pilot, called on the intercom, "Okay, boys, you can test your weapons." The first few times you hear this sound it will definitely "scare your mule." But you soon get used to it, knowing that it's for your own protection. The gun mounts were fitted directly to the frame of the airplane, and when all thirteen guns were firing, the vibration would rattle your cage. The smoke from the guns drifted back through the plane and smelled exactly like the smoke you smell after a large fireworks.

"Chuck," came a voice on the intercom. It was Neal (Payden), our navigator, "You can put on your oxygen mask now. We don't want to lose you before the fun starts." Then Jeff (Fuller), our right waist gunner, chimed in, "Let him go a little longer. He gets to acting so silly about eighteen thousand feet without oxygen." The reason for reminding me was that my earphones were plugged into my radio as this is an important time for coded messages from England, which could cancel our mission. I could not listen to radios and intercoms at the same time. (I fixed this after a few missions.) "Thanks, Neal and Jeff, don't forget your oxygen line runs through the radio compartment."

With the ever-increasing altitude, the colder it got. We all looked like men from Mars, with heavy "long john" underwear, flight coveralls, heated suits, heavy lamb's wool flying suits, Mae Wests (life preserver), flak vests, lamb's wool leather boots, parachute harnesses, sheepskin caps, helmet liners and helmets, oxygen masks, eye goggles, earphones with wires coming out of our ears and mikes worn around our necks, and oxygen tubes coming from our mouths. We were a bunch of funny-looking, weird-walking spacemen. I think it was Jeff who said, "If we can't shoot them, we will surely scare them to death."

If you think that is bad, just contemplate for a second what you would have to do to go to the bathroom. Don't even dare think it. If you were to go in your flying gear, you would be electrocuted. *I tried not to think about it!*

We were now at seventeen thousand feet, and we can see the French coast coming up. Ray kept us posted on the altitude and told us to shape up and be ready for anything from this point on. In the combat zone when on the intercom, we used our position when we talked, such as copilot to ball turret, so we would instantly know where the crew member was.

"Bombardier to crew, flak at twelve o'clock high." Looking out my window and forward over the left wing, I could see small puffs of black smoke, but not close enough to hear it yet. The coastal gunners were telling us, "We see you, come and get it." Each plane in our squadron pulled in closer and closer, for the fighters were sure to be coming.

As we crossed the French coast near Calais, just south of Dunkirk, I got my first taste of coming under enemy fire, and I did not like it one bit. *Thump. Thump. Thump. Karumpt.* It got closer and louder. My mouth was dry, my teeth were chattering uncontrollably, and my legs were weak as water.

"Fighters at three o'clock high," called out Jeff. "They look like Spitfires." "Pilot to crew, hold your fire 'til they get a little closer. We don't want to shoot any of our 'little friends.'" "Right waist to crew, they just waggled their wings so we could get a good look. They are definitely Spitfires." "Thanks, Jeff," said Ray. "It looks like we have just gotten out of range for the flak batteries along the coast, but be alert and sing out if you see anything."

I looked back toward the French coast, and the sky was black where we had just been. I was sure glad that was behind us.

We were moving deep into France now, and we could see hundreds of planes in other formations. Some were drawing flak that seemed to be bursting above them. We neared Metz and swung south to skirt the heavy flak batteries there. There was also a very active fighter base stationed here, but so far, so good.

Steve, in the top turret, was the first to see them, and he called out, "Top turret to crew, bandits at twelve o'clock high, about twenty of them. Get ready, here they come." Then we heard, "Bandits at six o'clock high, Me109s, coming fast." Our plane was shuddering as several of our crew begin firing. Maggie, in our ball turret, reported the group in back of us was staying just out of range, to draw our attention, while the main force came streaking in from the front. Vic Estes, our bombardier, and Neal Payden, navigator, were firing away; then Steve in the top turret opened up. There were a series of loud bangs all around us as the first wave of Me109s came slashing through our formation. The best way I can describe how those twenty-millimeter cannons on all the German fighters sounded was like that of a cherry bomb exploding under a tin washtub.

I looked up through the window above my head as one of the German pilots came through. He was rolling over on his back and peeling off, straight down. It was so quick, I could not swing my gun around fast enough to get a shot. There was a noise; the closest description I could think of was similar to when I used to trim shrubbery and a wasp would come out right by my ear, *r-r-rr-rppp*, and he was gone. This was much louder.

Vic (bombardier) called out, "Hold your fire, boys, the cavalry has arrived." And then I saw them, those wonderful, beautiful P47s crisscrossing above us, in groups of four. Oh, how we loved them. The Me109s hightailed it when the P47s arrived. It was not that they were afraid; it was because they could not afford to lose any more fighters.

We were coming up on the target at Strasbourg, and we could clearly see the Ill River and the rail yards. Just as our briefing officer had said, the river divided at one end of the old town and then came back together further on, making an almost circular route around that huge cathedral. I silently prayed that all the civilians had taken cover and that we did not hit the cathedral.

"Pilot to bombardier [Vic Estes], it is all yours, Vic." We made an almost perfect bomb run, although the flak became very heavy during those few minutes on the bomb run from the IP (initial point) where the bomb run began until "bombs away." The bomb bay doors opened with a thud, the flak gunners got their best shots at us because of the drag slowing us down; additionally, we had to be straight and level for the Norden bombsight to do its job. They sure took advantage of it as the GOOD-O-YANK was bounced all over the place, with shells exploding all around us. Then I heard a new sound, like someone throwing a handful of gravel on a tin roof. I realized it was shrapnel hitting our plane and passing right through, leaving holes. Some were small (pea size), others as large as two fists held together.

Vic yelled, "Bombs away! Bombardier to pilot, back to you." Immediately, we began to dive and turn to the left, and Ray said, "Pilot to radio, check the bomb bay, Chuck." I was already opening the door to the bomb bay. "Bomb bay clear," and the doors to the bomb bay began to close. I could see straight down to the ground five miles below. There were flak bursts everywhere.

As we made a wide turn toward England, I heard Vic say, "Woweee, right on the money. Ain't no trains going through there for a while." "Pilot to bombardier. Good job, Vic. Pilot to crew, be alert! The fighters usually come back just after the bomb run, and it looks like our 'little friends' had to head home after they dropped their wing tanks."

I didn't see it, but Sandy (tail gunner) said he saw one of our group go down in flames. The Germans like to single out one group and one squadron and one plane and pick them off one at a time. Any stragglers were certain to be pounced on.

We were well on our way, but we still had to cross France from one side to the other. It seemed the further we went, the more intense the flak became. Plus, their fighters had time to land, refuel, and get more ammo. We were told later that some German pilots would make up to four landings and return to the fort formations. What we needed were more fighter escorts that would somehow have the ability to fly with us all the way to the target and back. It seemed like an impossible wish at the time.

Finally, we flew over the English Channel, and British Spitfires escorted us 'til we made landfall near Norwich (not far from our base at Framlingham). Our formation was ragged and shot up. As we neared the control tower, several planes shot off red flares, signifying they had wounded aboard. They were given immediate priority to land. The rest of the group went into a normal landing pattern, and it was a beautiful sight to see each plane peel off to touch down on that friendly soil.

By the time I shut down my radios, finished my entry in my logbook, and broke down my 50-caliber machine gun, we were turning into our parking space. Ray raced the number 4 engine and turned the plane around, ready for the next mission. He shut the engines down, and I could hear whooping and hollering. *We made it!*

I wrote in my diary:

> **Saturday, May 27, 1944**
> Mission #2, Strasbourg, France
> Target: Train Marshaling Yards
> Purpose: To disrupt transportation during Invasion
> Results: Good to excellent Losses: 7 B17's MIA, 89 planes damaged, 70 men killed or missing, 8th Air Force lost 25 planes and 250 men, not counting fighters
> Opposition: Moderate to heavy flak; fighters, light but intense

At debriefing, it was good news to learn that of the 710 escort fighters, they claimed 36 enemy destroyed, while losing only 7.

Our crew was dead tired and, without eating, went straight to our hut and to bed.

"AND THE DEVIL TAKE THE HINDMOST"

The British Air Force had tried on many occasions to use their large bombers against the highly fortified German Luftwaffe in daylight raids, but had failed miserably. As a result, this type of attack was discontinued; it simply would not work. American powers that be were convinced it would and set out to prove it. It just made sense that planes like the B17s and B24s, bristling with thirteen 50-caliber machine guns, could ward off any enemy fighters. To arrange hundreds of these planes in flying formations, stacked in a V, was a formidable task.

Eighth Air Force leaders worked feverishly trying different formations to arrange the planes so, when attacked, the maximum number of guns could fire at the attacking German fighters without hitting our own planes.

In late 1943, there was considerable improvement, but no matter how they changed it, the last plane in the low squadron was usually the first to be shot down. Thereby, it was designated as the coffin corner and tail-end Charlie. This position was almost always flown by the newest and least experienced crews.

New crew pilots quickly realized that, if at all possible, being assigned to the coffin corner was to be avoided. But, some of the older crew pilots learned it did have one advantage. When attacked, they could take evasive action that other positions did not allow because they were boxed in with other planes all around them.

Pilot Ray Strate, through early experiences, summed up the tragic danger of flying in the coffin corner, quoting an early sixteenth-century English proverb, although I suspect he did not know its origin.

After flying one of our first missions and realizing the ever-present danger, four Me109 German fighters got on our tail and repeatedly attacked the last plane in the entire Eighth Air Force formation. We swung wildly to the left, climbed quickly to our right, and dropped suddenly below the formation. Those Germans must have thought, *That B17 pilot is nuts*, but it saved us to fly again.

Ray realized there was no one to help us. Our fighter cover had left us to return to their bases in England, and all the planes in our formation were well ahead of us. We were all alone and on our own. Ray said to us on our intercom, "They run all away and cry, 'the Devil take the hindmost.'"

Many times, later, we saw the last planes in our formation shot up badly, causing them to lose power and fall behind. Easy prey for the German fighters, Ray would always tell us, "And the devil take the hindmost."

Sunday, May 28, 1944

Again, I am convinced that God was looking after me and our crew. Our 390th Group was sent, along with 1,341 planes, to bomb oil depots and storage tanks at Konigsberg and Magdeburg, deep into the center of Germany, not far from Berlin. It was a terribly costly mission as we lost 32 bombers and 9 fighters. Our 571st Squadron did not fly, and I surely was glad.

THEY KILLED OUR FRIENDS

His cousin Lieutenant Herb Strate, together with whom he had joined the Air Force and finished pilot's training, was shot down and killed on this mission.

Our two crews were very close, and although we did not know it at the time, some of the crew escaped, but rather than tell their story, let me copy from an account of this tragic story as told by Ed Stoy. Tech Sergeant Edward Stoy was the engineer and top turret gunner.

> *My story starts on the morning of May 28th, 1944. We were flying out of Framlingham, England and were awakened at six am on Sunday. We had breakfast and could have anything we wanted. Everyone seemed in a good mood except the left waist gunner. He was just 18 years old and was very nervous about this mission. We had a bad mission the day before with anti-aircraft fire over our target, which was Strasbourg, France. One of the shells exploded under our plane and the plane was thrown straight up so hard it buckled my legs. I think this effected the waist gunner and I knew that he would not make 35 missions. He was a hero on this mission as you will see later. Before I forget, the name of our plane was Decatur Deb.*
>
> *We went to the briefing of the weather and our target and then we picked up our parachutes and went out to our plane. Everything checked out O.K. and we were ready for takeoff. Assembled with the lead Group at twenty thousand feet over the English Channel, our position in the Group was the lower left corner of the lead Group, which was called "the Coffin Corner". This position was the preferred section for the German pilots to hit, which we did not know at the time. While we were crossing the English*

Channel, the pilot informed me that the generator on Engine Two was not working. I checked everything but could not locate the reason for the malfunction. Everything else seemed to be working O.K. I suggested we turn back but the pilot and the co-pilot decided to go on. We had taken off at 1022 am and would reach the target at 2 PM. Our plane was equipped with eleven 50 caliber machine guns and two 30 cal. guns. We also carried 38 100-pound bombs. We were escorted by P51 and P47 fighter planes. The escort planes left our Group just before we reached our target due to the length of the mission and their fuel capacity. We crossed the English Channel into France. It was a beautiful view and my position in the top turret gave me a beautiful view of all the B17's above and behind us, leaving contrails behind them. Something I will never forget—All the way to our target, which was the oil depot at Magdeburg, Germany, we encountered anti-aircraft fire which kept our waist gunners very busy throwing chaff out the window to confuse the German gunners about our position and our altitude. The black puffs were pretty to look at but were very deadly. As we approached our target, the bombardier opened the bomb bay doors. The 38 bombs were hung on 4 racks on each side of the catwalk, 19 on each side. It is now seven minutes after two and we are starting our bomb run. This is a period when all planes cannot alter their course for any reason until the bombs are released over the target. There was no anti-aircraft fire and everything seemed to be O.K. but, at this moment, someone called over the intercom, "Enemy planes at twelve o'clock". In the distance, I could see a lot of small spots straight ahead. Within a few seconds, the German fighters were all over us, up and down, right and left, just like in the movies, but for real. At this time, our plane was met with 20mm cannon fire, which shot off part of the vertical stabilizer and set the front of the plane on fire. I dropped down from the turret as the plane tried to recover for a few seconds, but then went into a dive. I had trouble getting loose from my equipment but finally got my chute on. The pilot and co-pilot were both down in the passageway to the escape door and the front of the plane. Smoke was coming out around them which left me with nowhere to go to get out except the bomb bay. With the plane in a dive, I had trouble pushing the bulk up and open. I had put on my chest-pack parachute and, with the plane in a spiral dive, I knew there was not enough room between the bombs and the bulkhead for me to jump, so I crouched low and took a dive headfirst between the bombs and the bulkhead. It did not work. The bottom of my jacket caught on the arming prop on the lower bomb and left me hanging upside down on the bomb, with no way to get loose. I was thinking of my wife and my mother and how they would feel when they learned of my death. Everything was very quiet. I have to tell you that the only way the bombs could be released was either by the bombardier or by a lever next to the catwalk in the bomb bay. I was the only one in there and everything was very quiet when, all of a sudden, all the bombs were released with me on the bottom bomb, upside down. I was thrown headfirst into the corner of the fuselage and the bulkhead, the bombs hitting me in the head, the left side of my back as they tore out the bomb bay door and the side of the fuselage next to me. The plane was on its side and I found myself on the side of the plane. God was looking out for me. I checked my chute for damage and it was alright. I did not want to dive out over

> *the jagged edges of the fuselage, so I turned around and rolled out backwards. As soon as I left the plane, I straightened out and, looking up, I could see the plane just above me. It was burning completely from one end to the other. It was so close I thought it was falling on me. I pulled up my knees and rolled into a ball to fall faster and get away from it.*

There is much more to this remarkable account, but that is still another story. Let me hasten to tell you that Tech Sergeant Ed Stoy parachuted safely, but with cuts and bruises and a banged-up knee. He was captured and spent the rest of the war in a German concentration camp until General Patton's troops liberated him. As of July 2004,[1] he was alive and well. I talked with him on the phone, and he graciously furnished me with this account. The radio operator on this crew, Tech Sergeant Nick Mamula, played a part at another time in these accounts.

As you can see, it was terrible news. Our crew members were good friends. I knew Nick Mamula very well as we had some classes together in radio school.

Losing a crew that we ate with, slept, played, and fought with was tough, and I know it was really bad for Ray, but he was a very strong man and we could not see that it affected his performance. It may be that he let down with his fellow officers, but somehow I doubt it.

---

[1] Ed Stoy passed away in August 2005.

Monday, May 29, 1944

This was another bloody and costly mission, and our 571st Squadron did not fly. There were 993 bombers dispatched to bomb an oil refinery at Politz. I felt for all those crews. It was a terribly long mission with part of the force bombing an airfield and an aircraft factory at Leipzig. Leipzig was a place deep into Germany, well past Berlin, a place we all dreaded to go because we always sustained heavy losses. This one was no exception. We lost 34 bombers and 10 fighters, but the Germans paid a heavy price, also. Our bombers shot down 62, damaged 37, and our fighters shot down 39. Bombing results were fair to good.

We watched as our 390th Group returned. They were badly beaten up, and we saw plane after plane unload wounded. We were deeply depressed to find one of the crews that did not come back were close friends of ours. I lamented, "Man, alive. I hate what this war business is doing to these fine young boys, fresh out of high school." I felt like fighting, but I felt more like crying.

The red alert flag was flying when we got back to our area. "Can it be that we are going back deep into Germany after two days of planes dropping like flies?" I wrote Butch a short letter and took it by the officers' quarters, and even Lieutenant Neal Payden was solemn. I said, "Lieutenant Payden, do you really think they can fix enough planes to fly tomorrow?" He said, "Yeah, I am afraid so, Chuck, but you know what, let's just be thankful we were not on those last two missions." "Yes, sir. You are right about that. See you in the morning."

I just was not ready for the fact that we would flying missions so close together. I thought we would maybe fly once a week and kind of ease into this war, but it looked as if they were hell-bent to kill us all as soon as possible. Four new crews arrived just as we were going to bed, and as usual, someone called out, "You'll be sorry."

Tuesday, May 30, 1944

It turned out to be a beautiful spring morning in England. We had a leisurely breakfast, even though we knew we were flying. Things were just moving slowly, like we were walking in molasses. Even when we got into briefing, no one was pushy or hyped. Everything went smoothly, and the operations officer pulled back the dreaded black curtain, revealing our target for today. There were no whistles or moans, just let's get on with it.

Our target for today was the rail marshaling yards at Troyes, France. Despite our heavy losses recently, the 8th Air Force put 938 planes in the air, not counting 672 fighters.

General Eisenhower was making sure German troops and equipment are not able to move very easily when the Invasion comes. We, of course, had no idea when it would come, but you could feel it in the air. It would certainly be soon.

Troyes is 95 miles east of Paris on the Seine River in the heart of the Champagne country. They want the world to know they are the capital of Champagne. They even went so far as to form the historic center city in the shape of a huge Champagne bottle cork, with the large bulb-like top formed by a big bend in the river Seine, a handsome landmark which was hard to miss from the air.

We were told, near the end of our briefing, that we would have an escort of 186 P38s, 184 P47s and, for the first time, 302 P51s that would be with us all the way to the target, going and coming. There was a loud cheer you could have heard for miles, and I was one of them.

Now that put a smile on our faces and a spring in our steps. 'Twas a real morale booster and just when we needed it. Thank you, Lord.

This was our third mission, and already we were getting into a routine that made it easier each time we fly. There were actually hundreds of things that needed to be done or checked before we were airborne. In my radio room, I had a checklist of 32 items to check off. McGee was our onboard armorer, and whereas every crew member was able to assemble, fire, and disassemble the 50-caliber machine guns, Sam had been schooled in all the armor on a B17, including the upper turret, just above the pilot's compartment, the chin turret, just under the nose, and the ball turret, in the floor just behind the radio compartment. He was familiar with all the ammunition we used and how to belt it. He had hands-on knowledge of all the types of bombs we carried, including how to arm and disarm them. He could look at a weapon that had malfunctioned and tell you exactly what was wrong with it and how to fix it. In addition, he was an expert at making homemade bombs, which I will tell you about one day when we are not flying.

Each man and each position on the plane had his series of checks and duties before we rolled down the runway for takeoff. The pilot and copilot had a checklist that would make you dizzy. Today went smoothly, and as our 390th Group formed up at 9,000 feet, along with the 95th and 100th Bomb Groups to form the 3rd Bomb Division, I looked over and saw the 1st and 2nd Bomb Divisions getting themselves into formation. I really felt for them, going back again deep into central Germany to bomb aircraft plants at Oschersleben, Dessau, Oldenburg, Munster, and Halberstadt. There were 268 B17s in the 1st Division and 369 B24s in the 2nd Division. They lost 12 bombers and had 152 damaged, while we in the 3rd Division with 250 B17s had no losses and 48 damaged. We saw no enemy aircraft. The rail yards at Troyes were plainly visible under clear skies, and we had excellent bombing results. All the fighter escorts were beautiful, but we were especially thrilled as P51s went all the way to the target with us.

The flak was moderate and accurate, but once we cleared the target area, we had clear sailing for home. Flying back to England was uneventful, and as we parked on our hardstand, I reached up and gave Eleta's picture a kiss. Boy, was she beautiful! I made another hash mark on my radio room wall. This was number 3, only 32 more to go.

I wrote in my diary:

> **Tuesday, May 30th, 1944**
> Mission #3: Troyes, France
> Target: Rail Marshaling Yards and Repair Shops
> Purpose: To disrupt rail transport prior to Invasion
> Dropped: 800 tons of 500 lb. general purpose bombs
> Results: Good to excellent
> Losses: All 8th Air Force, 12 bombers, 9 fighters
> 209 damages, 123 men MIA
> 58 enemy aircraft destroyed

After debriefing, we slowly made our way back to our squadron area only to find a BLUE FLAG, alerting us for a possible mission tomorrow. We grumbled, went to chow, wrote some letters, and, without much conversation, hit the sack.

Wednesday, May 31, 1944

At 5:30 a.m., bang went the door.

"All right, all right, you sleeping beauties. Lieutenant Ray Strate, crew number 71, up and at 'em. Are you going to sleep all day? You have a war to fight."

"Oh, no. Will someone shoot that guy? We just got to sleep."

"Chow in thirty minutes, briefing at 0630."

"Somebody, shut that recording off."

Steve said, as we walked to the mess hall, "Look at it this way, men, the quicker we fly them [missions], the quicker we go home." "You are right," said Jeff. "Let's go kick Hitler's tail."

The black curtain was pulled back, and there were whistles and moans. Our target for today was Osnabruck, Germany, and again, they were the rail marshaling yards. Our 3rd Division was to hit 4 targets, all rail yards, with 188 B17s; 54 planes were to hit Schwerte, 52 planes Oeske, and 50 planes to hit Hamm, all in the heavily defended Ruhr Valley.

The 1st Division was bombing mostly rail yards, but also some airfields in the Netherlands and Belgium.

I preferred those types of targets for several reasons. First, we would be bombing areas where few civilians would be killed. Secondly, these targets usually did not have heavy concentrations of flak guns, and thirdly, they were relatively short. Osnabruck is about 120 miles from the English Channel and almost directly on line with our base at Framlingham.

The bad news is that it was cold and rainy, and the clouds were right on the ground. Sandy (our tail gunner) said, "There is a good chance we will not go today. I can't even see the control tower." Harvey (waist gunner) said, "I hope you are right, Sandy. I just don't like to fly up through this mess, with a thousand planes going every which way. I am sure we have good pilots, but the odds are that a large percentage are not going to know where they are going." I said, "Yeah, I hold my breath 'til we break out on top of all the clouds." Steve remarked, "Yeah, and just think, we have to come back down through this stuff."

When the flares went up for us to start taxiing for takeoff, I could barely make it out as it made a long arch through the fog.

The weather people assured us we would break through on top just above 8,000 feet and we would have clear skies over the overcast to the target. We later learned that one flight kept climbing past 26,000 feet and still did not get on top. They were forced to take a secondary target. We went straight across the English Channel and across the Netherlands into Germany. And, although there were 682 fighters assigned to go with us, I, personally, did not see one. Nor did I see any enemy fighters. We had a lot of flak, but it was very inaccurate. We had "bombs away" right on schedule and skedaddled for home. Out of 1,029 that flew today, it amazed me that the whole 8th Air Force only lost one plane, which must have been some sort of record.

Today was the first (and I think the last) time that the 8th AF used a new type of bombing, called AZON, which was a radio-controlled bomb used specifically to bomb special targets, such as dams and bridges. It was highly successful.

As our wheels touched down at Framlingham, I thought to myself that we must have the best pilots and navigators in the world. How is it possible to fly and navigate in pea soup? As we left our plane, I could see Lieutenant Strate was soaking wet. I said, "Thank you, sir." He looked at me very seriously and, with a sigh, said, "It wasn't easy, Chuck." He was truly exhausted.

Wednesday, May 31st, 1944
Mission #4, Osnabruck, Germany
Target: Rail Marshaling Yards
Dropped: 1720 tons of bombs
Results: Fair
Losses: One bomber and 3 fighters
Opposition: Moderate to heavy flak; 4 enemy fighters destroyed

I could see a pattern to our bombing missions over the past week, and I am sure, the Germans did also. We were hitting rail yards and airfields in the Netherlands, Belgium, and northern France, down the coast of France to about Calais. Surely the Germans were thinking this was an attempt to soften up their ability to move troops and equipment around in the northern section of Europe, anticipating the inevitable invasions. They had no way of knowing *where* it would actually come.

As we rode back to the squadron area, we stopped at headquarters, where we were met by an American Red Cross vehicle. It was a van with windows on the side which folded down into a countertop. It was piled high with doughnuts and coffee. The Red Cross girls told us to help ourselves, and we gorged ourselves. The girls were allowed to fraternize with the officers, but not the enlisted men.

After a few minutes, we were told to line up. A table was set up, and a corporal called out our name, rank, and serial number. As we walked down the line, we received immunization shots in both arms and were paid our monthly pay. I had agreed to keep eight dollars a month and send the rest home to Eleta. What did I need money for? We also received a monthly ration of fruit drinks, candy, tobacco, toothpaste, etc.

By the time they were done with us, I was really dragging. All those doughnuts and coffee on an empty stomach, plus the shots, I was ready to throw up, so I went straight to bed. I missed chow but heard it was mutton, again, and I was happy to have missed. When mutton was being served, you could smell it long before you got to the mess hall. It was yuuuuuck! On those days, they served half as many meals. Another bad meal was horse meat. They told us it was beef, but it was really red and long and stringy. It was so tough, the more you chewed it, the bigger it got.

Jeff came in later and said, "No flag tonight." I could have kissed him. Naw, I wouldn't go that far. Butch didn't get a letter today.

Thursday, June 1, 1944

The orange juice cans were empty and sitting around everywhere. I noticed Maggie (Sam McGee) volunteering to pick them up and get rid of them. Man, what a nice guy.

The fireworks began when someone went to the latrine and came back and lay down on his bunk. The first thing I noticed was a line of fire coming in the door on the floor. It turned to the left and ran up the wall in a large arch, then back down, under a bunk, and across the room to the other wall, back down under another bunk, then BLAM. I was halfway out the door when all the snickering began. It went off under Harvey Burr's bunk and raised him about a foot. It sounded like someone slamming a door at the end of a long hallway. Man, oh, man, that was as scary as German flak.

Before our tour was over, everyone on our crew got one of these "awakenings." These "bombs," for lack of another name, were made from empty juice cans. When we drank them, we punched a hole in each side of the top to relieve the air pressure. Black powder, taken from 50-caliber machine gun bullets, was poured into a can through one of the holes, and a cigarette was stuck into the opening. The amount of the charge could be regulated by how much powder was put in the can; half full would have taken down the hut. The cigarette was then saturated with lighter fluid and the fire trail was then squeezed to wherever the path was determined to go.

Once the "victim" was in his bunk, someone outside the hut lit the liquid fuse, and you could watch it run and dance before it got to the can. Usually, you had about thirty-nine seconds to make your move, or since you did not know whose bunk it was under, just curl up in a ball and wait to see if it was your turn to be "airlifted."

Of course, it was dangerous. Sure, we were nuts. But so was everything else we did. I heard these explosions many times, but I never heard of anyone being hurt. *Payback can be hell, and it can come when you least expect it.*

Friday, June 2, 1944

The British have a favorite expression for getting you up in the morning, like, "I will knock you up at eight o'clock." The Americans liked the expression and adopted it. When the red alert flag went up, someone stopped by the squadron HQ to ask, "What time will you knock us up?" The answer came back, "We will knock you up at 0530." Everyone would laugh and start preparing to face death or whatever was to come our way. You can take it from one who has been there; the toughest of the tough pray. They like to do it in privacy, usually in bed, at lights out. They were not ashamed. To the contrary, most just thought it very personal to talk to God, one on one. It was not uncommon for one crewman to ask another to remember him in their prayers.

Catholics have a way of witnessing that many of them don't even realize. I happened to like it, even though I am Protestant. They cross themselves. It tells everyone "I believe."

All went smoothly today, and when the briefing officer pulled back the curtain, there were shouts of "all right" from every corner of the room. The 8th Air Force was being sent to a number of places, but our targets were the airfields and rail yards of Paris, France. It was such a short mission that everyone was happy…so short that headquarters decided to fly two missions.

The first was 926 planes bombing weapon sites at Pas de Calais with a total of 2,506 tons of bombs. The second, 319 planes to bomb Paris, Conches, Beaumont, sur-Oise, Bretigny, Criel, and Villeneuve, dropping 841 tons of bombs. There were 341 fighters escorting the first mission and 397 on the second. Clouds hindered bombing, but results were good. These missions were what we called milk runs, but none were easy. Our 390th lost one plane, and they were friends.

We were back in time for lunch and a game of softball.

I wrote in my diary today:

Friday, June 2nd, 1944
Our Crew Mission #5
8th Air Force Mission #385
Target: Rail yards and air fields near Paris, France
Dropped: 3000 tons of bombs
Results: Good
Losses: 7 bombers, no fighters
Note: Records indicate that fighter bombers destroyed a bridge at Ostend, France, leading the Nazi's to believe the coming invasion would be near Calais. We were told this is the beginning of Operation "Cover", to deceive the Germans into thinking the Invasion would be at Calais.

Saturday, June 3, 1944

Our 390th Group was flying, but not our 571st Squadron. Five hundred sixty-eight bombers pounded Pas de Calais with 1,580 tons of bombs. There were 429 fighters flying cover for them. The weather was so bad, all bombing was done by radar. There were no losses and no enemy sightings.

CHAPTER 11

D-Day

The 8th Air Force did it again, and you guessed it, Pas de Calais. Two missions, the first, with 257 bombers, dropped 567 tons of bombs, and again, they were bombing through the clouds. The second mission flew 314 planes and dropped 804 tons of bombs, all on Calais. The Germans must have thought we were invading today. Our 390th Bomb Group and 448 other bombers hit rail bridges and airfields, bridges at Massey, Palaiseau, Versailles, Matelots, Villeneuve Saint Georges, and Melun, and airfields at Romorantin, Prunieres, Alvord, and Bretigny. Our bombs fell on Bourges, in the center of France, and all around Paris. There were no bombers lost due to enemy action, but one 390th plane crashed near Easthorpe, England, from undetermined causes.

After our mission today, we were told to report, in our dress uniforms, to base headquarters at 1600 hours. Having no idea what was happening, we were called to attention in strict formation. The base commander and the four squadron commanders presented us and other crews with Air Medals. It was all very formal. Later, we asked Lieutenant Strate what we had done to earn the medals, and he said, "You completed five missions over enemy territory. You can feel proud and, I might say, lucky." "Yes, sir!"

Sunday, June 4, 1944
Mission #6, Bourges, France
Target: Bridges and airfields
Munitions: 1079 tons of 500-pound general purpose bombs
Losses: 0 Planes
Escort: 412 fighters, who lost one plane

Monday, June 5, 1944

When the black curtain was drawn, it was almost like, "I told you so." The main strike was Cherbourg, but we also had strikes at Pas de Calais and coastal defenses at Le Havre, Caen, and Boulogne.

The weather was still bad, but the Germans were so concentrated that it didn't matter where we dropped our bombs; we would still do major damage. We dropped 1,896 tons of bombs with good results. The lowest private could look at our bombing and know where it was going to happen.

Monday, June 5, 1944
Mission: Cherbourg, France
Target: Coastal defenses
Munitions: 1896 tons of 500-pound general purpose bombs
Results: Good
Losses: 6 bombers, 0 fighters

It was in the air; you could feel it. D-Day was about to happen. Everyone was expecting it. It was all anyone wanted to talk about.

Tuesday, June 6, 1944, D-DAY

At 0200 hours, June 6, 1944, they woke us and we knew this was something special, and at our briefing, we knew this had to be IT. The big day. D-DAY. And when the curtain was pulled back showing our mission for today, everyone exploded with shouts and cheers from all over the room. Now, we were finally getting down to business. When we were told there would be 3,500 escort fighters, we hollered for 10 minutes.

The B26 medium bombers were to go first, flying at 500 feet and carrying 12 250-pound bombs each. The B17s and B24s were to go in next at 20,000 feet (10,000 feet below our normal bombing altitude). Each Fortress carried 16 500-pound bombs, 4 more than normal, made possible because we would not need much fuel just to fly to Normandy and back.

The Allies were to put up 3,467 heavy bombers and 1,645 medium bombers, plus 5,409 fighters and fighter bombers in the air on D-DAY. Not one was lost to enemy fighters, but flak claimed 113 planes.

D-DAY (Code name OVERLORD, The Invasion of Europe) had been postponed many times, sometimes because of bad weather in the English Channel. The bad weather could have made this invasion a complete disaster. Most people are not aware of how rough the English Channel can be. It can change from calm to raging, hurricane-type weather in a matter of hours.

D-DAY was delayed by the spring thaw on the Russian front, because the Russians were to start a huge offensive timed with the invasion. It was delayed by a little known, highly secret exercise, named Exercise Tiger, which was to be a training exercise for tens of thousands of American troops at a place called Slapton Sands, a secluded beach very similar to the beaches of Normandy. This was to be a very realistic landing of men and equipment in LSTs, using live ammunition.

General Dwight Eisenhower, the supreme commander, watched from the deck of a battleship in April 1944, as a force of 300 ships and 30,000 men began an assault on the beach, just 6 weeks before

D-DAY, when Exercise Tiger went completely wrong. The planes covering this invasion rehearsal did not show up, the landing craft were late, and the amphibious tanks going toward shore fired in the wrong place, hitting soldiers who were wading ashore. Tanks that were to float didn't.

From out of nowhere, nine very fast German torpedo boats came racing up and sank several LSTs loaded with hundreds and hundreds of American soldiers. In the confusion, General Eisenhower had no way of knowing if the German torpedo boats had picked up survivors, some of whom had top secret information about the real D-DAY invasion, including the correct dates.

Still another delay came because two high-ranking American officers revealed invasion plans at a party, revealing areas of invasion, number of ships and troops, and dates. A general and a navy captain were demoted and returned to the United States.

The most disturbing incident concerned crossword puzzles published in the London *Daily Telegraph*. In successive days, words appeared in the puzzles that were highly secret words concerning the invasion. On May 2, the word *Utah* appeared, and two weeks later, the word *Omaha*. Both were top secret words for the beaches where the American troops were to land in Normandy. A schoolteacher, who wrote the puzzles, was secretly followed. Then came the word *Mulberry*, the invasion secret code for the artificial harbors being built in England to be towed to Normandy. Next, came the word *Neptune*, which really shook up the intelligence units, as this was the secret word for all amphibious actions. The teacher was arrested, but finally cleared when intelligence found it was an almost impossible coincidence.

One of our biggest secret code words, BIGOT, was an unimaginable gathering of information about the invasion landing area, information from high-altitude photo reconnaissance, from single unarmed planes, flying at less than thirty feet, from spies inside France, and from frogmen, mapping where the German defenses were.

Composite maps were made showing where almost every German gun or underwater mine was located. If this information had gotten into German hands, it would have been catastrophic for our landing forces.

A number of conditions went into the selection of the D-DAY date. The main reason concerned the moon and the tides. The Navy wanted to cross the Channel in daylight to avoid confusion with all the ships and boats and to see where they were shooting their big naval guns.

The Air Force wanted daylight so they could best see where to drop their bombs and to avoid the confusion of getting into formation in the dark.

The Army ultimately got their way, crossing at night to ensure the greatest surprise, up to the very last minute, landing just at daybreak in order to have a full day.

The Allies needed at least a half moon to get enough light for the Navy to operate and drop paratroopers behind German lines.

The landing needed a rising tide so the landing craft could run right up on the beach, then float free after unloading as the tide rose.

A rising tide with the right moon occurred twice during June, the fifth, sixth, and the seventh, and on June 19 and 20. Eisenhower picked June 5 for D-DAY and the French coast, from Cotentin and Calvados of lower Normandy, would be the place.

German Field Marshal Rommel had prepared the beaches well to meet the Allies' attack, stating that the only chance the Germans had for defending Europe was to stop the Allies in their tracks at the beaches. He used many devices, including floating and anchored mines, metal hedgehogs, and Belgian gates and cement obstacles, with miles of barbed wire. Since he had no idea where the invasion would come, he fortified the coast from Norway to Spain, and he guessed incorrectly many times on *when* the invasion would come.

On June 1, he declared that there were no good times until after the 20th of June and on June 2, he wrote his wife, Lucie, "There is no sign the invasion is imminent."

Hitler's guess was even worse, when, on April 6, he was quoted as saying, "I can't help feeling that the whole thing [Invasion] is a shameless charade."

Rommel took leave, having bought his wife a birthday gift in Paris, and went home to celebrate her birthday.

It is ironic and surprising as I write about all these preparations for the invasion along the south coast of England, from Land's End to the mouth of the Thames, that sixty years later, my son Ron is vacationing along these same beaches from where the invasion began.

General Eisenhower must have surely been going bonkers with all the distractions, but finally, it was decided to go on May 1, 1944. Eisenhower, however, changed it to the first suitable day after June 1, citing as his reason for delaying to get another month's production of LSTs and other landing craft.

Then this was it! What the whole world had been waiting for.

I was really surprised to find there was no alternate plan for the invasion, no plan B or C. It was all or nothing at all, sink or swim, live or die. One shot only. It had to work.

The United States and England had spent billions to build an armada of ships and aircraft, but WOW! How were they going to use them? There was no question or argument on how to use them on D-DAY. Everyone agreed that just before H hour and throughout D-DAY, every Allied aircraft that could fly would be used to attack the Normandy coast.

Beyond this, there were great disputes between the air and ground forces. General Spaatz of the US Air Force and Sir Arthur Harris, chief marshal of the Royal Air Force Bomber Command, thought they could best win the war by bombing deep inside Germany, crippling Germany's factories and transportation. General Eisenhower and the Allied Expedition Force staff thought the Air Force should support the ground forces along the front lines.

The fight grew worse with Ike demanding complete control of all bomber and fighter operations, US and English. Churchill said, "NO," so Ike told Churchill, "Give me command or I simply will have to go home!"

The War Cabinet gave Eisenhower "supervision" of the Air Forces; General "Hap" Arnold changed it to "command." The British refused this, leaving Eisenhower furious, and on March 22, 1944, he wrote in his diary, "If a satisfactory answer is not reached, I am going to take drastic action. I will request relief from this command."

The English capitulated!

WOW! Can you imagine, just days away from the greatest battle in the history of human warfare, worse even—hours—and the top general's ultimatum: "We are going to do it my way, or I'll take my marbles and go home." Thousands, no millions, of soldiers ready to go into battle and the generals were squabbling.

I thought, and I am sure all those in my bomb group thought, that headquarters had it together and knew, for certain, what they were doing. Had we known what was going on, our morale would have hit bottom. Thank God, we didn't know.

When we were flying over England, leaving and returning from missions over France and Germany, it was a wonder to behold the preparations all over England and Scotland. Troops and equipment were everywhere. It was like a zillion ants literally covering the earth.

Perhaps the words of Steven Ambrose in his book *D-DAY* paint a better picture when he wrote, "Starting the first week of May, 1944, the soldiers and sailors of the Allied Expeditionary forces began descending on southern England. They came by sea in a never ending stream, in transports and LST's. The ships came out of the Firth of Clyde, and Belfast, down the Irish Sea, past the Isle of Man, from Liverpool and Swanson and Bristol. They got into formation, twenty ships, forty ships, hundreds of ships to sail out into the Atlantic Ocean and around past Land's End, to turn left at their designated ports, Plymouth, Torquay, Bournemouth, Southampton, and many others."

They came by land, sea, by train, bus and truck, or on foot, men and equipment from Northern Ireland, Scotland, the Midlands, and Wales. They formed up by the hundreds in companies and battalions, by thousands in regiments to march down narrow English roads, headed south. When they arrived in their marshaling areas, they formed up by divisions, by corps, and by armies in the hundreds of thousands, altogether almost two million men and half a million vehicles. It took 5,400 men to provide necessary services for them, including 4,500 cooks.

It was the greatest mass movement of armed forces in the history of American and British armed forces. It culminated with a concentration of men and weapons such as the world had never seen and perhaps would never see again.

And I saw it unfolding, out the windows of our B17. It was so huge, so overpowering, it made me think of a great hymn we used to sing when I was very young, "Onward Christian soldiers, marching off to war." I was glad that God had placed me on the right side.

From 5,000 feet, the roads and highways looked like water running through small rivers and creeks, emptying into larger rivers and lakes. What a monumental task, to feed and clothe and get all those men and machines in the right place and at the right time. As we flew above this, I could not help thanking God that I was where I was and not down there getting ready to invade Hitler's stronghold.

D-DAY was the greatest show ever staged. As dawn broke on D-DAY, one could observe one of the most important and impressive sights of any wartime action. Wave after wave of light, medium and heavy bombers could be seen sweeping down the invasion beaches to drop their bombs. It was the longest air armada ever gathered. Totally, there were more than 14,000 planes used. Many bomb groups flew two or three missions; our 390th flew two.

The foot soldiers envied, and some resented, the airmen. Complaining that the flyboys hung around their bases, did nothing at night, went into town to be with the English girls, had warm beds, plenty of food, and much rank. Yet, many others said, "You flyboys can have it. I want my feet on solid ground where I can run if I have to." What many of the foot soldiers did not see or know was that the airmen suffered differently. In bad weather, they spent quiet but stressful lives. Once every three months, they were given passes to London or other places. You can believe me, you didn't want to be in London, where every day it was like an early childhood story of Chicken Little, "The sky is falling."

On the way to their targets, they were cramped, cold, tense, and fearful. When in enemy territory, they were shot at constantly by the world's best guns (88s) and gunners, with maybe the exception of the gunners around London. When they entered action, they entered hell, with flak explosions so thick, you could not see where you were going or where you had been. With enemy fighters coming at you from every angle, it was an hour or more of pure terror.

In the twelve months preceding D-DAY, the Air Force lost twelve thousand men and more than two thousand planes.

The plan for the Air Force was that on D-DAY minus 2, half of all our bombers would bomb Pas de Calais, making the Germans think this was to be the invasion point. The next day, half the crews rested. The RAF would bomb, at midnight, the coastal batteries of Normandy and a German stronghold at Caen. At dawn, with 1,200 B17s and B24s, the 8th Air Force would bomb the invasion beaches for a half hour, while the medium B26, P51, and P47 light bombers bombed Utah Beach. If the sky was clear, the bombing would cease 5 minutes before our troops went ashore. If cloudy, it would be 10 minutes.

When we got to our planes early that D-DAY morning, we were very excited about finally getting the big show on the road. When we looked at our plane, we went deadly silent. The ground crew armorers were just finishing hanging two monster bombs underneath each wing. No one, except Maggie, had ever seen these used before. Lieutenant Strate went straight under the wings to examine and touch them. What he was thinking was, *How in the world are we going to get all this weight off the ground and airborne?* His concern soon carried over to our crew, and our mood turned sour. We were told again that the additional weight would be compensated, in part, by a much lighter fuel load. Our plane, now named Good-O-Yank, seemed to be squatting and straining under the weight of those extra bombs. And to my prayers that morning, I added, "Lord, please let us get off the ground safely."

As Ray and George taxied the big bird, Ray told George, "Give us as much running room as you possibly can. We are going to need every inch of it." Our plane seemed to creak and groan more than usual as we made our turn onto the long runway. With full throttle and release of brakes, we didn't seem to move, but just sat there bouncing up and down a few times, then slowly rolled off. The engines were screaming when Ray called out, "Okay, boys, hold your hats, here we go."

Once we were rolling, our plane seemed to say, "Don't worry, boys, I can handle it." I looked out my window as faster and faster we went, and I could see the end of the runway coming up fast. We went past the point where we were usually airborne, and Ray had not even attempted to get us up. At the last possible moment, I felt us lift, but then drop back onto the runway and with a mighty heave, we bounced off. With the engines still roaring, George pulled up the landing gear, giving us less wind resistance, and ever so slowly, we began to climb. I finally got my breath and looked back in the waist compartment at Jeff and Harvey who were grinning and giving me the two thumbs-up sign. Whew, I was wet with sweat, and we had not even gotten into formation yet. Later, I talked with Lieutenant Neal Payden about what that takeoff was like, and he said, "If you think it looked bad from where you were sitting, you should have been up there in the nose when we got to the end of the runway and were still on the ground. I just wanted to climb right out the top." The Good-O-Yank was groaning and straining in an unusual way, almost as if saying, "I'm giving you everything I have." She was a brand-new B17G with all the latest modifications, easily identified by the new chin turret operated by Lieutenant Vic Estes, our bombardier. Due to weight constraints, modifications had also taken place in the radio compartment, including removal of the 50-caliber machine guns and the additional ammo boxes stored in the floor. In the space over the old command set, where I had Eleta's picture and the hash marks denoting my finished missions, there was an improved command set. I already had |||||-||, not counting today. Things were accelerating, and my head was spinning.

As we poked our head through the thick overcast, there were literally planes in every inch of space, all over England. I thought how awful it would be to die in a blinding collision while trying to form up to go fight, but many did. Once above the overcast at twelve thousand feet, we quickly found the other members of our group. Each group had a distinctive flare color or combination of colors, fired at intervals, so we could locate one another. With all those planes and all those Very pistol flares (invented by Lieutenant Edward W. Very) arching through the sky, it was the granddaddy of all fireworks and seemed to be saying, "Look out, Herr Hitler, today we are going to celebrate."

At ten minutes before dawn, we came sweeping down the Normandy beach, just minutes before the landing of tens of thousands of Allied soldiers, between Le Havre and Cherbourg. It was a completely overcast sky, and I could only pray that our bombs would hit our targets and not any of our own men. It occurred to me that, hopefully, all the clocks and watches were correct and synchronized. Here was the greatest production in history, and everything depended on split-second accuracy, the shelling by the big ships offshore, the maneuvering of the landing craft, the dropping of the bombs, the troops going ashore, all timed to the minute. In spite of how hard we worked at getting it right, in at least one case, we got it wrong. We dropped some bombs too soon, and five hundred American boys died. "Killed by friendly fire," the report read.

A lot of planning went into preparations for D-DAY. In 1941, the British started planning how in the world to get all the men and equipment across the English Channel to invade France, especially against the Germans, who had concrete fortifications all along the entire coast.

They came up with the LST (Landing Ship Tank) and the LCT (Landing Craft Tank). The LST was very large, 322 feet long with a flat bottom, and very hard to control at sea. It was capable of landing tanks, trucks, and soldiers. When it beached, two large doors to each side and a large ramp or gangplank were deployed, and dozens of tanks and trucks could drive ashore.

The LCT was smaller, about 110 feet, and could carry 8 to 10 tanks or trucks. When the United States came into the war, they took over the building of the LSTs and the LCTs and made considerable improvements. These became the workhorses of the Allies. The men who used them insisted that LST stood for "Long Slow Targets," for they would be easy targets for the German gunners. They were just not right for landing platoons of fighting men. What was needed was a much smaller, faster boat that could reach the beach, discharge, and return to its mother ship for more soldiers.

Many manufacturers in the United States competed for the right to build such a boat, and the US Navy came up with the LCI (Landing Craft Infantry). One man, Palmer Putnam, had an idea. He took a standard US truck (the hardworking deuce and a half) and made it amphibian. It would do five miles per hour in the water and fifty miles per hour once on land, fully loaded with soldiers and equipment. It worked, and was called the DUKWID, but was soon shortened to the DUCK."

Production was slow, too slow, when a small boat builder in New Orleans entered the competition. He was a hot-tempered and loudmouthed Irishman, who drank a bottle of whiskey a day and built his boats of wood instead of metal.

At first, the powers that be wanted nothing to do with him, but he proved to have the best and, once he got the contract, proved to be a genius at mass production. He assembled three thousand workers and built thousands of Eureka boats, LCVPs.

A square bow was used that was actually a ramp, thirty-six feet long and ten feet wide. It could carry a platoon of thirty-six men or a jeep and a dozen men. Called the Higgins Boat, there were over twenty thousand built. General Eisenhower once said, "He is the man who won the war for us." Without his boat, the whole strategy of the war would have been different.

Another invention that helped win the war was the Douglas DC3 transport plane. Utilized in every branch of the Armed Forces, the Army called it the Dakota. It had no armor but was extremely versatile. Slow moving at 230 miles per hour, it was the most dependable, rugged, and best designed airplane ever built. Many are still flying all over the world today (60 years later). The DC3 carried the 82nd Airborne and the 101st Airborne behind the German lines and pulled countless gliders across the English Channel.

Of all the paratroopers who jumped on D-DAY, only one group landed in the right location and, because of bad weather, it was almost a disaster. Each paratrooper was given a clicker similar to the one children play with. Because they jumped in darkness, they used it to communicate with other jumpers. One click was answered by two clicks.

In spite of the utter confusion of the paratroopers being scattered all over the place and the inability to link up with their own units, all was not lost. They came together in twos and fours and tens and twelves to do enough damage behind the German lines to justify the effort. The complete confusion of the Allied paratroopers was bad, but you can imagine how baffling it was to the Germans. What the enemy was doing made no sense to the Germans, so they concluded it was just an exercise, a rehearsal for the real thing.

Meanwhile, we had dropped our bombload on the beachhead, very near the town of Caen. As we released our bombs something unusual happened. Good-O-Yank jumped straight up. It was like being on one of those scary rides at the fair back home. Ray came on the intercom and said, "WOWEEE, ride 'em, cowboy." Vic called out, "Bombs away," and when I could get my breath, I answered, "Bomb bay all clear," and away we went to Framlingham. When the two one-thousand-pound bombs hanging under each wing, plus our regular load of twelve five-hundred-pound general purpose bombs, were suddenly released the weight sent us heaven bound. For a few moments, I thought I was going through the floor of the plane, and the next few, I was up on my tippy-toes, barely touching the floor. Whoa! What a surprise.

As we passed over the Normandy beaches and the English Channel, I looked down, and at first light, I could see through an opening in the clouds. What I saw was indescribable, for as far as the eye could see, there were ships so close together it looked as if you could walk from one to the other. At this moment, for the very first time, I knew it was all over for the Germans. It was almost over for us, also, getting back down through the overcast and, literally, dodging others doing the same.

Our radios, tuned to our homing channel, brought us right over the coast of England. We peeled off one by one, and I sure was glad to hear our wheels go *vurr-rrrp*. We taxied to our hardstand and were met by the entire ground crew, waving and shouting. Something else we saw were our ground crew armorers bringing load after load of bombs out to our hardstand and our petrol trucks standing by ready to fill our tanks. We went straight to debriefing and were told to go to the bathroom, to chow, and be back at briefing in one hour.

We were going again.

The official records do not show it, as our crew only got credit for one mission on this day, possibly because it was such a short mission. We assembled more quickly than usual and headed back to the invasion beaches, this time to be certain we didn't drop on our own troops. We bombed the city of Caen, just fifteen miles inland from the beach. The Germans were firmly entrenched here, and our bombing played havoc with their efforts to get reinforcements and material to their defenses along the lower Normandy coast.

I was saddened to later hear that we were responsible for damaging or destroying many old buildings, some built in the year 1060 by William the Conqueror. During the next two weeks, the Battle of Caen completely devastated the city and a fire raged for eleven days. Most of the destruction has long since been repaired and rebuilt, and I am told there is now a wonderful World War II memorial there.

We, thankfully, saw no enemy fighters and lost only one bomber to enemy action.

I wrote in my diary:

> **D-DAY, June 6, 1944**
> Mission: The beach heads for Allied invasion of France and Caen, France
> Target: Coastal defenses and reinforcement positions
> Munitions: 4852 tons multi-purpose bombs
> Results: Good to excellent
> Losses: 4 bombers and 25 fighters
> Note: It is worth noting that this day, June 6th, 1944, began one of the most important battles in the history of mankind and I had been a part of it. We witnessed it firsthand, from a grandstand seat. The scope and horror of it all will go with

me to my grave, but the *Glory* of it all will live as long as we can read and write about the ongoing history of the planet Earth.

As noted by Roger Freeman in one of his books about World War II, the most detailed eyewitness reports of the Normandy landing received by the Allied commander on D-DAY came from none other than the head of the 8th Air Force. Two P38 Lightnings took off from Bovington, England, that morning, piloted by Lieutenant General James Doolittle and Major General Earle Partridge, the commander and deputy commander of the 8th Air Force. It is unlikely that any other fighter plane formation ever carried this much rank. The two generals flew back toward England to try to locate a hole in the clouds so they could go back at low level. General Doolittle found a hole, but General Partridge did not, and radio contact between the two was lost. Doolittle flew back to the beaches at 1,500 feet and observed the invasion for an hour and a half before returning to Bovington. Thankfully, the twin fuselage of the P38 was easily recognized by the gunners on the ships and Doolittle wasn't shot down.

The event of June 6, 1944, marked in history the date of the cross-channel invasion of occupied Europe…D-DAY. It was also the occasion of another monumental event. On the morning of the assault, an estimated 17,000 aircraft were in the air over southern England, and I was somewhere in the midst of it all.

Wednesday, June 7, 1944, was my twenty-first birthday; however, I did not get the day off! I made a *huge* mistake in telling my fellow crew members it was my birthday. They didn't say much, just wished me a Birthy Hapday and seemed to forget it.

"All right, all right, rise and shine. Wipe the sleep out of those eyes. Shake those cobwebs loose. Do you think the Krauts are sleeping? They are over there right now scheming how they are going to knock the 390th out of the sky. Lieutenant Ray Strate crew number 86, let's go."

"Hey, Sarge, wait a minute! What's going on here, our crew is 71?" "Not anymore it isn't, changes have been made. Lieutenant Vic

Estes has been promoted to lead bombardier, and from now on you will have a togglier. Lieutenant Strate will explain at the briefing."

Sometimes our sergeant, charge of quarters, waxed poetic and philosophical. Some days he was all business. Today, he stopped just before leaving our hut and said, "Good luck, boys."

Steve said, "What was that all about? Does he know where we are going or something?" We wondered.

We were expecting the worst when they pulled back the black curtain, and to our surprise, the target was Nantes. Nantes was an important transportation and communications center, about twenty miles from the Atlantic Ocean, south of the Brittany peninsula on the Loire River, with several important bridges. If these bridges were taken out it would surely disrupt the German troop movements. It was also just twenty-five miles from Saint Nazaire, the huge German submarine base, and of course, that meant it would be well protected with both fighters and flak. It was here we were introduced to a new German tactic. The Germans mounted a number of their feared 88-millimeter antiaircraft guns on flat bottom barges and roared down the river, firing at us. This gave them twice as long to be in range. Being masters in the art of war, they are devilishly wicked and cunning, always coming up with some new and highly effective ways to kill us.

The 8th Air Force had two missions today, the 397th and the 398th. The first, with 473 planes, struck 8 targets in northwest France, dropping 1,159 tons of bombs on tactical targets in direct support of the invasion troops.

The second mission was to towns along the Loire River. We were a part of the second strike, which bombed 11 targets with 1,172 tons of bombs using 572 heavy bombers hitting bridges, airfields, train rail yards, main roads, and river transportation.

At briefing, which was late, Ray told us about the crew change. Lieutenant Vic Estes was indeed moved to lead bombardier, and Staff Sergeant Jeff Fuller, our right waist gunner, was chosen to be our togglier. His job was to watch the lead plane in our squadron, and when they dropped their bombs, there were two smoke bombs indicating when to flip the toggle switch, releasing our bombs. This was all part of a new way of bombing called carpet bombing. It was no longer necessary for each plane to line up on a target. It proved to be simple and effective and made it easier to keep our planes in better formation.

I did not see the ground from the time we left England until we got back. We dropped our bomb by Pathfinder radar.

When our formations were returning to our bases, the Germans followed us in the cloud cover, and we lost several planes right over our bases. Those sneaky Germans; you just could never let up.

AN UPLIFTING EVENT

After chow, we received our first mail and I was one-more happy camper. I was sitting on my bunk, with a silly, homesick look on my face, deep into reading a wonderful love letter from my beautiful wife, Eleta, when I looked up and saw it. It was snaking in the door, down between two bunks, up the wall almost to the top of the Nissen hut. Then it curled back down the wall, under two more bunks, and headed straight for me. I had no sooner realized it was a barracks bunk bed bomb, with its fuse of liquid lighter fluid, when I hit the floor, stumbling, half crawling, and scratching off. Then, **BLAM**! The entire building shook and reverberated. Everyone spilled outside, and by now, half the squadron was out looking at the sky and asking, "What the h—was that?" Then I heard someone say in a cool, clear voice, "As you were, men. It's just Chuck's birthday celebration." I think it was either Jeff or Maggie. Everyone laughed and disappeared. I inspected my bunk, and I thought, *Good gosh, that thing could have killed me!*

I could hear giggling long after lights out. That's okay, boys. We have a saying back in North Carolina that goes like this, "What goes around, comes around. I don't get mad, I just get even." From that point on, no one told their birthday.

Thursday, June 8, 1944

We were not flying, but it looked as if everyone else was. One thousand one hundred seventy-eight bombers and 1,353 fighters were in the early morning sky, headed toward rail targets and airfields in France. They dropped 1,876 tons of bombs on 28 different targets. We lost 3 bombers and 22 fighters.

LONDON TOWN

At breakfast, we met Lieutenant Ray Strate, our pilot, who told us we could have a three-day pass to visit London or Cambridge, or some other points of interest. Maggie said, "When does it start?" "Right now, but you best be back here by Saturday night midnight, or I'll have your *~%#^ on a stick. Is that understood?" "Yes, sir, you can count on us, sir." Whooopeee. "Where we gonna go?" London, everyone agreed.

Within thirty minutes, we were dressed and riding in the back of a GI truck, headed for Framlingham and the train station.

On the train to London, we were discussing where to go and what to see. There were so many interesting sights that hardly anyone could agree on which way to go. We arrived into Liverpool Station after lunch and caught a cab for downtown.

There were so many bombed and burned-out areas everywhere, and as we paid the cabbie, he offered some very good advice. "I advise you Yanks to get about early. Get your sightseeing and whatever done before dark. You'll not be able to find your way around, and Jerry will be sure to find you if out after dark." We found this to be excellent advice.

We checked into an older hotel near Charing Cross and took off to see the Tower of London. I was really surprised by the fact that early England was so bloody. We spent hours seeing and hearing about British royalty, from William the Conqueror in the eleventh century, to Henry the VIII in the sixteenth century. All of them had lived right here in this palace and fortress.

We saw the remarkable Crown Jewels and collections of arms and armor. There is one tower called the Bloody Tower, where even small children, princes, were murdered. I didn't like the Tower of London, too depressing.

From there we went to Saint Paul's Cathedral, a true miracle of architecture, built by Sir Christopher Wren, completed in the year 1710. A guide took us to the whispering gallery, located several hundred feet above the floor in the great dome. The acoustics are so good, you can hear someone whisper on the floor or 107 feet across the come. So remarkable was the sound, a paper clip dropped from that high balcony could be heard loud and clear when it struck the floor.

There were several scaffoldings in the church where repairs were being made. One large scaffold surrounded a hole through the roof and right through the floor. We could not see how far it went, but the guide said a German bomb made a direct hit but did not explode.

Just imagine how the men felt whose job it was to go down into those holes and defuse those bombs that had not exploded. Some were true duds, but others were on timers or slow fuses that would explode hours or even days later, killing those brave souls working to defuse them. They were true heroes.

Aircraft spotter on the roof of a building in London. Saint Paul's Cathedral is in the background. 306-NT-901B-3. National Archives Identifier: 541899.

"Standing up gloriously out of the flames and smoke of surrounding buildings, St. Paul's Cathedral is pictured during the great fire raid of Sunday December 29th." 1940. 306-NT-3173V. National Archives Identifier: 541922.

We looked around for a place to buy a Coke or, as the members of our crew from north of the Mason Dixon Line would say, a soda. There were no places to be found. In the USA, you could get a refreshing drink at any corner drugstore. In England, a drugstore is called a chemist. Another surprising thing we learned was that four o'clock every day is teatime, and the *world comes to a halt at teatime*. Usually, you were served a cookie, but don't dare call it that in England; it's a biscuit or crumpet. We ended up visiting a pub, which I thought was a bar. Au contraire, mon ami. In England, a pub is an institution where friends and neighbors gather for fun, relaxation, food, conversation, and, of course, drinks. You can play cards or checkers, chess, or throw dart, or just plain bull.

Most often the Englishman would order a pint of bitters (an English beer). I gave mine away, as it was not even cold. They laughed at us for wanting something cold; they didn't even have ice. We did find something we liked a lot, and it was so good, I have never forgotten it. On a stand on the street we ordered fish and chips. The man handed us a generous helping of fried or baked white fish and a handful of piping hot potatoes, in chunks like a quartered potato. All this was rolled in a couple pages of newspaper. We sat on a bench and devoured our feast. Man, was that good! I am not sure if we were just hungry or whether this was just good, basic food that we had not seen for a while. The whole time in London we ate at the hotel dining room or some other really nice restaurants, but things were so bad in England, no one really had much to eat. For instance, the sausage we ate for breakfast was half sawdust. Sawdust was used as a filler in many foods, but the fish and chips were for real. If you ever get to London, be sure to try the fish and chips.

PICCADILLY CIRCUS

We decided we had best get started back to our hotel for the night, and we stopped at Piccadilly Circus on the way. Piccadilly Circus is not really a circus, but a large roundabout at the intersection of several streets. To our delight we found an American USO where they were playing American pop music and dancing to a live band. They had cold drinks and doughnuts and this was "the" gathering place for American GIs in London. We could sit and drink or write letters, and everything was furnished free.

After a really enjoyable time, we walked down two flights of stairs to the street and were almost to the corner when we noticed the busses, trucks (lorries), and taxis stopped and pulled over to the side of the street. We asked, "What is it?" and someone said, "Listen." We listened and heard an odd-sounding engine *putt, putt, putt*. Someone yelled, "There it is!" It was a German V1 buzz bomb coming right down the street about three or four hundred feet high. Now, everyone was diving for cover. It was barreling down Shaftesbury Avenue. I was hypnotized, and then, as the motor stopped, it nosed over and hit the ground about two blocks away. The noise was horrifying, and the ground shook like an earthquake. The concussion came rushing down the street like a windstorm, and smoke and debris were everywhere. Wow! What an explosion. How do the English people stand it, day after day, never knowing where one of these devilish things will land?

BUZZ BOMB. Life in London during the war. View of a V1 rocket in flight, circa 1944. 306-NT-3157V. National Archives Identifier: 541919.

It was time for us to get back to the hotel, and we were wondering if we should not just get back on the train and get the heck out of Dodge. The sirens were blaring constantly.

After a dinner of roast beef and potatoes and a delicious plum pudding, we sat in the hotel lobby and wrote letters home.

Soon after dark, the air raid sirens wailed, an awful sound like a moaning cry, warning of death. The air raid warden allowed us to stand on the sidewalk and watch as hundreds of powerful searchlights snapped on. The lights crisscrossed the sky, illuminating hundreds of huge balloons tethered with steel cables, floating over the city. We could hear the antiaircraft batteries swing into action and realized we were standing in the middle of war.

We were fortunate; for tonight, the Germans were bombing the southeast section of London along the Thames. We could see the huge fires lighting up the sky, and we felt for the weary and exhausted firefighters.

We went to our rooms, were told to stay there and, if the bombing got any closer, we would be directed to an air raid shelter in the subway tunnels, called tubes. After what seemed like hours of explosions, things settled down, and we drifted off into a fitful and uneasy sleep.

We just had to do it. We left word at the desk that we would like to be knocked up at 8:00 a.m. We were disappointed when our phone rang at 8:00 a.m., as we were expecting a rap at the door.

Another custom the English have that is most interesting is when you retire at night in the hotel, you leave your shoes just outside your door and some mysterious shoe fairy picks them up during the night, cleans and shines them, and redeposits them at your door the next morning.

We all laughed about this, and Jeff said, "If you did that in America, the next day you would be buying new shoes, for the shoe fairy would have pawned them."

Friday, June 9, 1944

We had a really good breakfast of orange juice, toast with many kinds of jelly, sweet buns, a large bowl of fruit, and coffee. We could have ordered sausage (ersatz), but we already knew about the sawdust.

We couldn't all agree on what we would like to do today, so Jeff, Steve, and Maggie went to a couple of museums, while Harvey, Sandy, and I went to see the Changing of the Guard at Buckingham Palace. I wanted to see Westminster Abbey, and even though it was reinforced on every side with scaffolding, we spent several pleasant hours there. I felt it was a very reverent place, much like the Catholics feel about the Basilica in Rome. Many of England's greatest people are buried in Westminster Abbey including Chaucer, Milton, Shakespeare, and all English royalty including Queen Elizabeth I, Mary Queen of Scots, and Henry V.

We really stepped up our sightseeing, visiting Trafalgar Square, which is the center of London. All distances in England are measured from this point, with a statue of Admiral Horatio Nelson high on a column, honoring one of England's greatest, victorious at the Battle of Trafalgar. Nearby is Saint Martin's in the Fields Church, with a towering spire similar to the steeples on many of our American early churches.

From there to 10 Downing Street, home of the prime ministers of England. Unfortunately, the Prime Minister was not receiving guests today, the War, you know, 'er what.

The Houses of Parliament's grounds have statues of everyone you can think of, including our own Abe Lincoln. You can't miss the huge towers at the corners. First is Victoria Tower, 336 feet tall and the jewel tower; the second, Saint Stephen's tower or Clock Tower, which we know as Big Ben. We found that the clock in the top of the tower is not really Big Ben, as we had always thought. Big Ben, named after Sir Benjamin Hall, is a 13-ton bell deep within the tower, from where the sound emanates, when struck on the hour.

MADAME TUSSAUD'S WAXWORKS

We chuckled about the way the British, and particularly Londoners, gave directions. It's almost like they all got together and rehearsed it. We approached a bobby (London policeman) asking for directions to Madame Tussaud's famous Waxworks Museum. His answer was classic, "Oh, I say, old boy, you are hee-uh at the Royal Opera House, aren't you? Oxford Street will lead you to Regent Street. With a right turn, you will soon find yourselves at Baker Street, and just around the corner, you will find Madame Tussaud's. I say, you cawn't miss it. Good day to you." (I have often wondered if that bobby could have possibly been Bobbie Webb's father. Bobbie Webb sang in the Hickory Grove Presbyterian Church choir with me.)

Before arriving at Madame Tussaud's, we stumbled upon one of the most famous addresses in London, 221-B Baker Street. Oh, sure you have heard of it. Remember, the home of Sherlock Holmes? It is now a museum.

Madame Tussaud's Wax Museum is the third most popular tourist attraction in London. Her real name was Maria Grosholtz. She was born in 1711, and her father was killed two months before she was born. Madame Tussaud learned her trade from a doctor whose hobby was modeling wax. Becoming friends with King Louis XVI's sister, she lived in the Royal Court of France, in Versailles. She moved to London in 1802. By taking hundreds of precise measurements and using human hair, her wax figures became lifelike.

There was a long line, or queue (in England, you do not line up, you queue up). Woe be unto you if you break into a queue ahead of someone, for you will be bumbasted by everyone with a tongue lashing such as you have never heard before. The queue in England is sacred, so we waited patiently.

Once inside, we went through endless rooms of wax figures of famous people. The hair and eyes were colored perfectly. The figures were cast in their exact size, and their clothes were made by tailors according to the period or year in which they lived. They were so lifelike, you could stand as close as one foot and not know if they were dead or alive. Likenesses of such people as George Washington, Abraham Lincoln, Benjamin Franklin, and Thomas Jefferson were on display, as well as Queen Victoria, Mary Queen of Scots, Joan of Arc, and the British royal family, in all their finery.

We were directed down long hallways and to a dark stairway leading down, down to Madame Tussaud's infamous Chamber of Horrors. Much like an ancient dungeon, where there was little light, emphasis was that this was a terrible place. The hair on the back of my neck told me they had achieved their goal.

There were displays of every known method of torture, from the gallows to the rack and the guillotine, to knives, axes, spears, and guns.

She made likenesses of infamous people and others in gory detail, such as Marie Antoinette under the guillotine, with her bloody head in a basket. Also beheaded, there is King Louis XVI, and Jack the Ripper, a famous London killer, is lurking in a dark alley.

It was just about at this point that the earth shook, and with air raid sirens wailing, all the lights went out. After the initial shock of being several stories down in a dungeon with the worst killers the world has ever known just inches away, I caught my breath and said, "Harvey…is that you?" Harvey said, "Yeah, Chuck, I'm here, let's get the heck out of this place." I replied, "Yeah, but how the heck are we going to find our way out?" The thought occurred to us that the building might cave in, trapping us forever in this devilish place. For what seemed an eternity, we stood along with some other sailors, some of whom tried to be brave, and moaned, "Whooooeeeeee."

Finally, a young girl with a flashlight (torch to the English) came down the stairs and said, "All right, everyone, this way out." We, of course, knew we were in no danger, but nevertheless, we were happy to get out of there.

We made our way to Piccadilly Circus and, along with hundreds of other American GIs, sat and talked about how the war was going. Right on schedule, here came the buzz bombs. As we made our way back to the hotel, we watched a Spitfire diving after one. Buzz bombs were faster than any plane we had in level flight, but Spitfires could catch them coming out of a dive and shoot them down. We could hear them exploding all over London.

The weather was bad over southern England on this Friday night, and we heard only single planes dropping bombs here and there, and we were thankful.

Saturday, June 10, 1944

We had walked for two days, so we decided to ride the double-decker busses for a change. We rode way out to the west side to Kensington Gardens, Kensington Palace, and Hyde Park, where anyone at all can climb up on a box, tell the world and all who will listen what you think about any subject. There were several museums nearby, but it just took too long to take them all in.

We had to check out at noon, so we took the subway (tube) right to our hotel. After lunch, we took a cab to Liverpool Station and headed back to Framlingham and the war. It had been a restful break, and we were in no hurry to get back in action.

We were on the base by about 2000 hours (eight o'clock), and the sergeant at squadron headquarters where we signed in said, "Sergeant Richardson, you are to report to Lieutenant Strate as soon as possible." On the way over to the officer's quarters, I wondered why in the world my pilot wanted to see me.

He didn't waste any words. "Chuck, are you all back from your three-day pass?" I said, "Yes, sir, we are all back." "Did you enjoy yourselves?" "Yes, sir, we had a great time." "That's good. Pass along that we are flying tomorrow, and, Chuck?" "Yes, sir?" "Good night and thanks."

Whew, is that all he wanted? I thought as I walked back to our hut. But, as I looked at the sky and down toward London, the sky was lit like daytime. I thought, *Oh, no, they are getting it again tonight. How long are they going to be able to stand it? A couple of nights and we were a nervous wreck. Which is worse, flying over Germany, with a thousand guns shooting at you, or being in London, with their constant air raids?*

We talked with some friends on other crews to find out what had been going on while we were gone. We learned that a crew in the hut next to us were MIA. They had been part of heavy attacks on airfields and rail yards. One thousand one hundred seventy-eight planes dropped 1,876 tons of bombs, with losses of 3 bombers and 22 fighters.

On June 8, fighter losses were mainly because of dive bombing and strafing at ground level.

On Friday, June 9, 1944, bad weather prevented any missions, but on Saturday, June 10th, 883 bombers and 1,491 fighters hit tactical targets in France in support of ground forces. We lost 3 bombers and 8 fighters. Luckily, no one from our 390th Group was downed. There were a number of good bombing results from 1,825 tons of bombs dropped.

Sunday, June 11, 1944

Our crew was moving like molasses. We were getting ready to fly, but our hearts were not in it. Those few days off took a toll on us, but at the briefing we felt better when the black curtain revealed a very short mission to the Brittany coast. Actually, there were 20 different targets, all in support of our invasion forces. Airfields and rail targets from Paris to coastal defenses along the northern coast of Brittany were to be hit. The 390th target was Dinard, a beautiful coastal resort town, situated where the Rance River meets the ocean.

The Germans had fortified this area with 20-foot thick concrete bunkers, and it was our job to destroy as much as we could. We plastered the targets but were later told that our bombs bounced off those concrete bunkers like marbles. What was it going to take to get at these darn Germans? It wasn't much of a mission, but flak claimed one of the crews from our squadron. You can get killed on the easy missions, and you are just as dead.

There was no rejoicing at the 390th tonight. I wrote Butch a short letter and hit the sack.

> **June 11, 1944**
> Mission #10
> Target: Dinard, France, Tactical support for invasion forces.
> Deployed: 1055 heavy bombers and 914 fighters.
> Munitions: 210 tons of 500-pound general purpose bombs.
> Results: Poor to questionable.
> Losses: 3 bombers and 8 fighters with 31 men MIA.

Monday, June 12, 1944

Good-O-Yank did not fly, and we were so glad. Our morale was hitting rock bottom. The 8th Air Force flew missions to airfields and bridges in northern France. It was a clear day with 1,442 bombers and 988 fighters dropping 3,103 tons of bombs. With visual bombing, the results were very good; however, for the first time since D-DAY, enemy fighters and heavy flak accounted for 8 bomber losses and 16 fighters. I was glad we had the day off.

Tuesday, June 13, 1944

Because of extremely bad weather, only 260 bombers flew, dropping bombs by radar along the invasion corridor. Six hundred fifteen fighters flew bombing and strafing missions along the northwest French coast. We lost 2 bombers and 4 fighters with 627 tons of bombs dropped by both bombers and fighters. The Germans lost 6 planes.

Wednesday, June 14, 1944

The weather finally cleared, and the 8th AF took good advantage of it. There were 1,525 bombers and 908 fighters filling the skies.

Our 390th Group flew, but our 571st Squadron did not. I'm extremely thankful we didn't because the 8th Air force lost 14 bombers and 7 fighters on raids near the coast, from the Netherlands to Brittany, in France. Bombing was very effective, primarily due to good weather. All our noncom crew members rode our bikes out to the flight line to watch for our 390th planes' return. There were hundreds of ground crew people, and when all 27 of our group's planes appeared overhead, we let out a yell you could hear in London, 90 miles away.

In our three days of not flying, we all got a chance to catch up on our letter writing, and at mail call, I got seven letters from Butch. She also sent me a new diary to keep the records of my missions. On each page, in the top left-hand corner was written in very small letters, "I miss you and I love you." Harvey saw me reading and said, "What's the matter, Chuck. Bad news?" There were tears in my eyes as I replied, "No, not at all, just happy and homesick." He said, "Yeah, I know what you mean." His wife, Lou Nell, had sent him a bracelet, and he was lonely for her, also.

Thursday, June 15, 1944

We were flying today, and since we were awakened early, I suspected a long flight into Germany, but when they pulled back that ominous black curtain, the ribbon showing our target for today was just across the Channel at an airfield at Mons, Belgium.

The 8th Air Force was to hit 30 different targets, one of which was heavily defended Merseberg, Germany. Sure was glad we were not going there. Mostly in France, just ahead of the Allied troops, 1,361 bombers dropped 3,259 tons of bombs. There were 742 fighters escorting us, some of which carried and dropped 34 tons of bombs. The escorts kept the German fighters away, but they made up for it in flak. We caught a burst and had to feather engine number 1. Ray had everyone call in a damage report as he fought to regain control of the airplane. We slowly dropped out of formation, and Ray decided to head for home and drop our bombs in the Channel.

Ray called me on the intercom and said, "Chuck, get me a heading for home." With everything that had been going on, he had lost track of our location. I tapped a message on our emergency channel, screwed down the sending key, and was absolutely amazed at how fast the British triangulated our position. They came right back with our heading of 280 degrees, which I quickly relayed to Ray. "Thanks, Chuck, we are on our way. Pilot to crew. We are on our own, so keep your eyes open."

No sooner had he said it 'til Sandy said, "Bandits at seven o'clock high." "Pilot to crew, hold your fire 'til they are in range, then let them have it. We are going to have to fight our way home."

I snapped on my chute and got ready for battle. Mons was a town of about forty-five thousand on the river Lys, about twenty miles from the French border and seventy-five miles from the English Channel. Mons is located very near the place where Napoleon was defeated in the Battle of Waterloo and near the place of a great battle yet to come, the Battle of the Bulge.

Sandy came on the intercom again, "Tail gunner to crew, hold on, they are not Me109s, they are P51s." Just out of range, they gave us a "wing up" so we could see they were friendly. Someone shouted,

"Praise the Lord. They have come to escort us home." Wow! What a feeling of relief.

"Pilot to crew, okay, boys, this is our lucky day. We don't want to take our bombs home, and we don't want to drop them on these poor Belgians, so we are going to drop in the Channel." I heard the bomb bay doors open, and our togglier, Jeff Fuller, called out, "Bombs away." We all watched as they went into the water without a splash and, within seconds, spewed forth huge geysers.

We didn't bomb our target, but we got credit for a mission. We were the first plane for the 390th to land at Framlingham.

> Target: Airfields, Bridges, Oil Refineries
> Munition: 3293 tons of bombs
> Results: Good to excellent
> Losses: 2 bombers and 4 fighters.

When our engines stopped, we all piled out to wait for transportation to our debriefing. Ray came over to me and said, "Thanks, Chuck, 280 degrees was right on the money." I assured him I was just doing my job. He made no other comment, but I took it as a great compliment.

Friday, June 16, 1944

I don't see how anything could fly today. It was rainy, foggy, damp, and miserable. I was now convinced that the 8th Air Force can fly in anything…any kind of weather, including cyclones, typhoons, and hurricanes. Our 3rd division did not fly, but the 1st and 2nd did. I am not sure if it was because we had more sense or because we were scared and yellow. The two other divisions put up 370 bombers and 620 fighters.

The bombers dropped 893 tons of bombs on airfields and V-weapon sites in northwest France, while the fighters bombed and strafed communications and troops in and around Arras (about 70 miles southeast of Calais). In a new trick, P38s dropped their wing tanks as incendiaries on rail traffic.

I would bet the Germans felt as I did, "Those crazy Americans will fly in any kind of weather."

Total bombs dropped were 1,195 tons. Losses were one bomber and 3 fighters.

Saturday, June 17, 1944

Framlingham was socked in, but again, the 8th Air Force flew, hitting airfields in 12 different locations and a railroad bridge at Noyen. There were 332 bombers and 528 fighters.

A second mission with all B24s of the 3rd Division hit airfields at 6 locations in northern France. Five hundred twenty-eight bombers and 405 fighters were involved with the loss of one bomber and 4 fighters.

A CHUCK'S VIGNETTE

This is a good time in my story to tell you of some of the little everyday routine events that were part of our lives just as much as flying the death-defying missions. For lack of a better title, I will call it "A Chuck's Vignette."

Flying day after day, with someone shooting at you from the ground and every angle in the air, on oxygen, plus the danger we encountered flying in really bad weather and all the other ways you could be killed, tend to make you sweat. Particularly, these things make you sweat when you are using a heated flying suit, and after a while, you become aware of the odor. Each of us was issued a coverall flying suit which had pockets all over (I never figured out what all the pockets were for). Since we had only one of these suits, we used it every time we flew, and since we couldn't fly without it, we didn't have time to send it to the nice laundry ladies down in Parham.

An industrious ground crew sergeant found a way to clean them (for a price). The cleaning was thorough and left our suits like new. The best part was the cleaning only took a couple of hours. He would collect our suits on a morning we were not flying and bring them back after lunch, spotless. We were thankful, but curious about how he did it and dropped by the hangar area where he worked to see how it was done. To our surprise, it was a very simple procedure. He had acquired a fifty-five-gallon steel drum, cut the top out, and filled it with 100-octane aircraft fuel (courtesy of the US Air Force). The sergeant would drop a suit into the fuel and, with a rod with a crook on one end to retrieve it, hold it up a little to drain, then hang it on a clothesline to dry. The cleaning didn't take very long, and if the wind were blowing, the gasoline dissipated quickly. All this for a pound note (approximately five dollars). It was worth every penny.

Over in another area, you could take your leather A2 bomber jacket and get a sergeant, who had set up shop, to paint the name of your crew aircraft, such as ours (the GOOD-O-YANK), a picture of a bomb for every mission, and a swastika for every enemy fighter your crew had shot down. This guy was so busy, I didn't see how he had time for anything else. At five pounds a jacket, he was making more than our group commander. Figure it out, ten men on a crew and hundreds of crews at twenty-five bucks a throw. I had mine done.

Still another staff sergeant was a painting whiz and was kept busy painting the plane names and pictures on the plane noses. Ray never told us how much he paid the guy, but one morning just after our tenth mission, there she was, the GOOD-O-YANK, with ten bombs painted just under the pilot's side window. My gosh! She was beautiful!

The next guy will be nameless for fear of retaliation. On those cold, dreary, rainy days when we were not flying, we seldom got out of the sack to go to breakfast, and for some, getting up to go to the latrine was a real chore. One of our group (I dare not tell because 390th vets have been rumored to return from the grave for payback) decided he would put his Yankee ingenuity to use. He devised a tube with a funnel, which he kept by his bunk. One end of the tube ran through a hole in the side of our Nissen hut and the other to the outside. Simply, when he had to go, he would reach out, pick up the funnel with the tube attached, relieve himself, and promptly go back to sleep. But boys will be boys; someone found a cork to plug the tube outside the hut, and next time it was used, the fluid flowed back into the bed. I don't know which was louder, our friend's protests or the laughter from all who witnessed it.

This tube and funnel, by the way, were not his personal creation. Located in the bomb bay, it is the same tube and funnel used on our bombers while in flight. DO NOT, under any circumstances, announce you are going to use it, as the plane will gyrate in every direction while you are holding on with one hand.

Sunday, June 18, 1944

The red alert flag on Saturday night warned us we would be flying Sunday morning. The duty sergeant woke us very early, and we knew, from experience, that an early briefing meant we were going to be flying for a long time, and that meant Germany.

Just when the Germans thought they had figured out we would be hitting targets in front of our invasion troops, our high command would change things just to keep them guessing.

There were a lot of moans, groans, and whistles when the mission board was uncovered, and I was one of them. The mission was to be a maximum effort into the very heart of Germany, to the Hamburg, Bremen, Hanover area. There were 28 different targets for the B17s and B24s. Hanover was the deepest penetration and the one which the 390th drew. Hanover is a large city about 35 miles southeast of Bremen. This area, from Hanover to Hamburg, is often referred to as Fairy Tale Road and has some of the most spectacular scenery in all of Europe. It is a major transportation center, having shipping, rail, and automotive facilities. Also, located on a canal that runs east and west across Germany, called the Mitterland Kanal, it made an easy target for our bombardiers. We were after their oil storage tanks, which were enormous and, you guessed it, very well protected with both flak and fighters. We knew we were in for it when we had to pass through Germany's most heavily defended areas, just to get to our target. This was the first major mission into Germany since D-DAY, and I was foolishly hoping the Germans would not see us coming.

The weather was quite good when we were forming up, but we could see some clouds forming up over toward the Netherlands. We headed out over the North Sea, and Ray said, "Okay, boys, check your weapons, something tells me we are going to need them." Climbing higher and higher, we could see the Frisian Islands, a long string of islands stretching all the way from the Netherlands to the mouth of the Elbe River, just before Denmark.

This long string of islands, running along the north coast of Germany, reminded me of the Outer Banks along my own North

Carolina coast. However, I am convinced the only reason these Frisian Islands were there was to support five hundred miles of German anti-aircraft guns. There must have been a gun on every square foot of these islands. If you even looked as if you were going to cross them, the guns would open up on you. We stayed well off to the west and still got an occasional flak burst.

Almost to Denmark, we made a ninety-degree turn and headed into Germany, between Bremen and Hamburg. As soon as we crossed the coastline, the sky turned black from shells exploding. Jeff Fuller (togglier) said, "Woooeeeee, would you look at that." I didn't want to look, but I did. We were heading right into the blackest part of that man-made cloud. Then the sound came. Kaboom! **KABOOM!** Our entire plane shook and bucked like riding bareback on a Brahma bull. A B17 is a remarkable airplane. The concussion alone was enough to tear an ordinary plane to pieces, much less the zillion pieces of shrapnel that were flying in every direction. Once we got past Bremen and Hamburg, the flak settled down and we could see pillars of black smoke near Hamburg, where bombers ahead of us had already dropped their bombs.

I had noticed that we were carrying two different kinds of bombs, and I asked Maggie what those funny-looking bombs hanging in the bomb bay were. He said, "They are British-made incendiaries." I said, "Oh, no, they look bad just looking at them." Maggie replied, "Don't worry, Chuck, if we get hit, we will go off like the biggest Roman candle you have ever seen. They will be picking up our pieces all over Germany." I said, "That is what I am afraid of."

Ray came on the intercom and said, "Knock it off, boys, we are coming up on the IP, and I need your full attention." "Yes, sir," said Maggie, "I can see our target is going to be covered with clouds." "Yep, you're right, we will have to drop by radar." The heavy flak began again as we neared Hanover, and soon Jeff said, "Bomb bay doors open." As we waited for the lead Pathfinder plane to drop his smoke bombs, signaling Jeff and all the other planes in our group to drop, I noticed I was trembling and could not stop. I was busy throwing out handfuls of chaff (strips of aluminum foil) to throw off the German radar. We could soon tell the difference in the flak as it began to explode far below us.

The bomb run was just a few minutes long, but it seemed forever before Jeff yelled, "Bombs away. Check the bomb bay, Chuck." I opened the door to the bomb bay and, horrified, I reported, "Sorry, we have got one hanging." One of the bombs was hanging nose down; the clip on the rear had failed to release. "See if you can get it loose, Chuck, and be quick. We can't stay in formation with our bomb bay doors open." "Bandits, ten o'clock level," Steve yelled. "Oh, good Lord," I said. "What a time to be dropping out of formation. With our bomb bay doors open, we are a sitting duck."

I looked down through the bomb bay and could see nothing but clouds for thousands of feet. I reached out to get a walk-around oxygen bottle, mounted to the right of the door to the bomb bay when, KABLAM! BAM, BAM, BAM, KABLUM. ALL OUR GUNS WERE FIRING, and a violent jolt sent me flying against the side of the plane. The oxygen bottle was knocked out of my hand and rolling around on the floor. Half crawling, I chased it into a corner, plugged in, and stepped on to the 8-inch catwalk that ran from the bomb bay to the cockpit. Looking down from 26,500 feet, I realized, in case I fell, I did not have a parachute. There was no way, while the plane was bouncing wildly and vibrating like a riveting machine, I could wear a chest chute, hold on to an oxygen bottle, walk on an 8-inch walkway, hold on to the bomb racks, and dislodge this bomb. I left my chute on the floor of the radio room and stepped out on the walkway. I tried pushing the bomb from the side, but this was a 500-pound bomb, swinging like a pendulum, and I only weighed 140 pounds. That wasn't going to work, so I tried kicking it loose. The fins on the rear of the bomb caught my right-foot heated boot, ripping it off my foot. I watched it drop out of sight as it pulled me to my knees. Holding on for dear life with my one free hand, I pulled myself up, and then it dawned on me that this thing was armed. There is a small propeller on the nose of the bomb that is locked in a safe position by a wire that runs through the arming device, much like a cotter key. When the bomb is released from the bomb rack, the wire remains attached to the bomb rack, and as the bomb falls, the arming wire is pulled free from the bomb. It only takes a slight jolt for it to explode. To be sure the bomb has fallen a safe distance from the plane before exploding, the small propeller on the nose of the bomb must turn 500 revolutions. The wire to this malfunctioning rebel bomb had pulled free, and the propeller was spinning like crazy. I, of course, had disconnected my earphones and had no idea what was going on in the rest of the plane. I felt a tap on my shoulder and turned to find Maggie, our onboard armorer, motioning me back to the radio compartment. I quickly plugged back into my oxygen supply and the intercom when Ray said, "Chuck, let Maggie have a crack at it, he's the pro and, Chuck, we can't let the ball turret be INOP with our guns pointing straight down. Those Me109s know when no one is in there. Get down there and fill in 'til Maggie gets this bomb out of here." "Okay, Chief, just one more thing… That bomb is armed." I could hear moans from everyone on board.

I hopped down into the ball turret, and man, if that isn't the scariest place in the world, I don't know what is. Harvey Burr closed the hatch door and tapped it, indicating that it was fastened. It was then that I got claustrophobia of the worst kind. Imagine yourself balled up in a space hardly big enough for you to get into, with your knees jammed up under your chin, looking straight down 26,000 feet with nothing under you but a glass window, no chute, no room, knowing you can't get out by yourself. Holy cow! This is for the birds. By the time I plugged in my oxygen and my intercom, Ray had raised his voice a couple of octaves, "Chuck, are you in position? Ball turret, come in. Damn it, Chuck, can you hear me?" Yes, Ray, I can hear you loud and clear, and if I can find the darn mike switch, I am going to tell you if you can do it any faster, be my guest. But I didn't. I finally found it and said, "Yes, sir, ball turret, A-OK." I grabbed the control handles that guided the turret and swung around toward the rear of the plane, realizing that German fighter pilots looked for planes with their bomb bays open and their ball turret's guns pointing downward, meaning there was probably no one in it. I made a 360-degree turn to be sure there were no bandits around and could see all the planes in our formation, as well as the hundreds of planes in the other divisions. I have never seen a sight like this, airplanes as far as the eye could see. I no longer felt attached to the plane; in fact, I didn't feel attached to anything. It was as if I were all alone.

I turned the turret facing the bomb bay and the front of the plane just in time to see a Me109 flash by, the flashes from his wings winking. It was like a streak of lightning. I wheeled the turret around in time to see the Me109 pilot stand it on its nose and dive for the ground. I didn't even get a shot off. Jeff, in the nose, called, "Hold your fire, boys, here come a couple of P51s going after the Me109." Man, I would not have been in that Me109s position for nothin'. I didn't see it, but I am sure they got him.

I turned the turret toward the front of the plane just as Maggie released the stuck bomb and it came wobbling out. I called, "Ball turret to pilot, the bomb is gone, bomb bay clear." "Pilot to crew, closing bomb bay, keep a close watch while we try to catch up with our squadron." "Tail gunner to crew, banditos six o'clock low." B-b-b-b-b-b-BAM, the tail guns were firing. I swiveled to see what Sandy was shooting at when a voice on the intercom excitedly said, "I got him. I got him." Bam-bam-bam-bam-BAM, left waist gunner firing. All I could see was the tail end of an Fw109 going up over our tail and off to our left. As calm as you please, Harvey said, "I got a piece of him." In the meanwhile, Steve and Jeff had their hands full with the Me109s coming head-on. Steve got one confirmed and hits on at least two others, while Jeff was spraying the whole sky in front of us. I am certain he had bullet holes in half those Me109s. We had several more passes, and I did get to fire Maggie's guns. The nearest I can come to describing the sound in that turret was like being in a huge washtub with someone beating on the outside with a sledgehammer.

I tried looking out the little side windows and found I could not move my head. My heart stopped…I must have been hit. I looked everywhere for blood. I called Harvey in the waist and told him to get Maggie to crank me up and change places with me. I am sure Maggie did not want to get back in that ball turret, but Ray persuaded him to change positions with me and to find out if I had been hit. "Do it quick because there are still fighters everywhere." As soon as they opened the hatch to get me out, the problem became evident. When I had gotten into the turret, my leather flying helmet got caught in the hinged door. Everyone had a good laugh, including me, and I was mighty glad to get out of that death trap. Anyone who would sign up to fly this position has got to be either crazy or the bravest human on this planet. Maggie, God bless him, I think is the latter.

By now, Ray was racing to get back into our squadron formation as we headed north to the North Sea and home. The flak got worse again as we skirted Hamburg and Bremen, but the P51s had driven off the fighters, and we could look ahead to the open water and a chance to exhale.

Sandy, in the tail, came on the intercom, "Tail gunner to pilot, there is a solid black B17 following us just out of range." "Pilot to tail gunner, thanks, Sandy, just keep him in sight. These Germans have been using B17s that have been forced down to call in altitude for flak. Some have followed our formations back to England and attempted to shoot us down."

Out over the North Sea, the black B17 peeled off and headed back toward Germany. Ray told Sandy to remember any markings and report it at debriefing.

Framlingham never looked so good. Ray had become so proficient in flying that big bird that when we landed all I felt or heard was a soft "chirp" when the wheels touched down. I reached up and made another hash mark on my radio room wall and gave Eleta's picture a kiss.

After a long debriefing, as this mission was particularly active, they were especially attentive about the bomb-release malfunction and the approach of the German fighters. As we walked back to our squadron area, I asked Maggie what he had done to release that dad-burned bomb. He grinned at me in a way that all who ever knew and loved him would recognize as a gift, a look of innocence in a mischievous child. He said, "Chuck, I took one look at that bomb, and I knew there was nothing I could do to free it. It would have to be lifted up and held, while someone used a hacksaw on the clip. The clip that held that bomb to the rack was twisted into a knot. You were already in the ball turret, and I was wondering what to do. I almost fell off that catwalk like you did. Man, that is one scary place with the plane twisting and jumping all over the place, and that is exactly how it came loose. The back-and-forth movement of the plane broke the clip and the bomb fell free." "My hero!" "Yeah."

I wrote in my diary:

> Mission #11, Hanover, Germany
> Target: Oil refinery and storage tanks
> Munitions: 3158 tons of bombs
> Results: Good to excellent
> Losses: 11 bombers, with 337 damaged and 109 men MIA

Monday, June 19, 1944

Eighth Air Force mission number 423. After being delayed for two hours due to bad weather, the 8th Air Force put up 1,167 heavy bombers and 715 fighters. Our target was 6 airfields in the Bordeaux region of France, located near the border of Spain. Because of the bad weather, we kept climbing and climbing, to more than 30,000 feet, and were still in the clouds. Four hundred fifty-three planes aborted and returned to England. The 390th Bomb Group kept going and bombed a huge airfield at Corme-Ecluse. We dropped by radar so we could not see the results, but I felt, because of the intense flak, we were pretty close. We lost 7 planes and must have torn up something with 1,675 tons of bombs.

Later, we saw the strike photos, taken by low-flying Mosquito photo recon planes, and we did a lot of damage to the airfield and the surrounding countryside. I could just see those French farmers, shaking their fists at us for bombing their farms. C'est la guerre.

> Mission #12
> Target: Corme-Ecluse airfield
> Munitions: 1675 tons of general purpose bombs
> Results: Poor to good
> Losses: 8 bombers, 16 fighters

Tuesday, June 20, 1944

When they woke us really early, I felt the chill all the way to my toes. Early missions meant long flights.

There was ground fog so thick, we could not see one hundred feet as we made our way to breakfast and briefing. Maggie said, "Anything but Big B [Berlin]." Steve said, "Maggie, there are worse things than Berlin." Maggie replied, "There ain't nothing in the world worse than Big B." It was true; the Germans shot everything they had when we got near there. If only everyone could see the sky over Berlin when our bombers were coming, they would not believe it. There would not be a square foot of space above Berlin, for thirty miles, where there was not a shell exploding. The Luftwaffe said, "If it will fly, send it up." They were fanatical about protecting their capital.

B17 DIRECT HIT BY GERMAN FLAK OVER GERMANY.

DEATH AT TWELVE THOUSAND FEET OVER PLOESTI OIL FIELDS (B24S OF THE 15TH AIR FORCE).

The Germans used every conceivable type of weapon at their disposal. Of course, their remarkable 88-millimeter antiaircraft gun (which, I think, was truly their ultimate secret weapon) was so versatile and universal. It was extremely effective when mounted on most of their tanks. They had much larger antiaircraft guns, but they could not be fired as rapidly as the 88s. There was the ever-present workhorse of the Luftwaffe, the Messerschmitt Me109 fighter and her sister, the twin engine Me110 fighter bomber, both deadly fighters. There was also the most feared Focke-Wulf Fw190, spewing 30-caliber 20-millimeter cannon shells, and some were equipped with rocket launchers.

The Germans flew large bombers, like the Junkers Ju88, Dornier 217, and the Heinkel He111, above our formations, dropping bombs timed to explode in our midst. They even used the Stuka dive bomber against our formations, but not very effectively. There was also the dreaded and fastest plane on either side, the Messerschmitt Me262 jet, fitted with 24 rockets. These rockets could be launched outside the range of our 50-caliber machine guns. They fitted some planes with bombs attached to long cables and attempted to drag them through our formations.

Their Me210s, using rockets slung under their wings, were very effective against us, but once our P51s were able to fly all the way to our targets with us, none of these ingenious methods were effective.

When the black curtain was drawn, we all gasped. It was not Big B, but Magdeburg, a little more than one hundred miles deeper into Germany. The oil and industrial sites were drawing our attention, and we had to fly right by Berlin to get to them. Woe is me!

Other groups were to bomb Hamburg, Hanover, and Fallersleben and in all, 20 different sites, one in Politz, near the border of Poland. The formation consisted of 1,965 bombers and 1,111 fighters. We encountered flak and enemy fighters, sporadically, from the time we entered Germany from the North Sea, near Denmark, until we left.

Our 390th Group, and particularly our 571st Squadron, was bounced around the sky, like falling leaves in a hailstorm, by the concussion of the German flak. My teeth were chattering, my knees were shaking, and my heart was pounding. Luckily, the fighters did not pick on our group today. All around us and in front of us particularly, B17s and B24s were smoking and afire, spiraling lazily down, while others exploded and disappeared. We counted many chutes opening; it looked like a paratrooper drop zone. Our intercom crackled constantly with reports of fighter planes on fire, planes out of control, and of parachute sightings. There were 6 B17s shot down from our formation alone and 50 overall.

When we reached Magdeburg and turned on the bomb run, I leaned over to push the bundle of chaff out through the small opening near the floor of the radio compartment, and a flak burst knocked me against the wall of the plane. When I was able to get up and back in the radio operator's seat, I found a large hole entering from the right-hand side of the radio compartment near the roof, and another hole, an exit hole, where my head normally was. We somehow stayed on the bomb run and "Bombs away," right on time. Huge oil tanks were very quickly left burning, with smoke reaching ten thousand feet.

"The first big raid by the 8th Air force was on a Focke Wulf plant at Marienburg. Coming back, the Germans were up in full force and we lost at least 80 ships—800 men, many of them pals." 1943. 208-YE-7. National Archives Identifier: 535972.

I didn't wait for Ray to ask; I jerked the bomb bay door open and yelled, "Bomb bay is clear." As the bomb bay doors were closing, I looked down through that big opening and remember thinking, *This is such foolishness. Today there would be thousands of people killed or horribly wounded and for what?* Just because one idiot, Adolph Hitler, wanted more power.

As we hightailed it for home at Framlingham, we could see our fighters really mixing it up with the Germans, and it was one of our better days. Our fighters got 59 kills, with only 8 losses.

I kept thinking, as we got closer and closer to England and our adopted home, that after such a rough mission (938 planes damaged) we would get a few days to lick our wounds. Boy, oh, boy, that was just wishful thinking. The red alert flag shot up just as we were leaving the mess hall.

We were a weary bunch. I took a long shower and thought, *Don't feel sorry for yourself. Think of those foot soldiers in the cold and rain, with no warm place to sleep, just the cold, hard ground. No way to take a hot bath and no heated mess hall."* Having talked to a number of those guys in London, they would never, no, never, trade places with us. They always said, "You flyboys can have your airplanes. We just want our feet on solid ground."

I wrote Mom and Butch long letters, and I am afraid, my trying to put up a brave front just didn't sound sincere tonight. The truthful reality of where I was and what I was doing was hard to disguise. I told them I had just completed my thirteenth mission, and number 13 had always been my lucky number and everything was fine. Then I went on to say, "Look, if anything happens to me, I want you to know I truly love you, and remember, that I am doing what I truly love to do…flying." In my heart, I could see the writing on the wall. The average life of a B17 crew is six missions. Today, we saw them falling everywhere. This was our thirteenth mission, and there was just no way humanly possible we could fly twenty-two more missions without being shot out of the sky. I have always been an optimist, and from the very beginning, I always felt sure I would be going home, but tonight, our morale was mighty low. "Good night, Mom. Good night, Butch. May God watch over us all."

Mission: #13, Magdeburg, Germany
Target: Oil refinery and storage depot
8th Air Force Mission, #425

> Munitions: 3973.4 tons of bombs, using 1965 heavy bombers and 1111 fighters.
> Losses: 50 bombers, with 938 damaged and 499 men MIA
> Enemy losses: 12 by bomber gunners and 59 by our fighters.
> Results: Excellent

Our missions were getting rougher and rougher and seemed to be coming with ever-increasing speed. I just wanted to slow things down. Dawn would come on Wednesday and give me the answer.

I looked at my watch; it said 0300 hours. I said, "Why are you waking us in the middle of the night?" There was no playing around this morning. The sergeant replied, "Let's go, men. Lieutenant Strate crew, chow in thirty minutes, briefing at four. I don't know where you boys are going today, but I can tell you it is top secret. Good luck."

I had to shake Maggie two times. He was really tired, but he gave me that grin that endeared him to all his crewmates. "Just don't get excited," he said. "We will be back in the sack by noon." In chimed Jeff, "From the sound of it, you will be lucky to be back in the sack by day after tomorrow." He didn't know how right he was. The sergeant, charge of quarters, reappeared and said, "Sergeant Fuller, you are to stand down. Don't ask. I don't know."

We assumed that this mission would require a bombardier, and this made it more of a mystery. We told Jeff goodbye and could tell he was disappointed. I didn't feel like eating very much, but forced down a couple of eggs and toast. My stomach was in a knot.

Everyone who was anyone was at that briefing. Chicken colonels were everywhere, and when the black curtain was pulled back revealing the tape showing the path of our mission, it just kept going and going. An additional map was added, and I thought for a minute, we were going right on to China.

"Settle down, men," said Colonel Von Arb, "You have heard me say before that a particular mission was very important. That was true, but today, not only is this mission important, it is the first of what will become routine. It is a shuttle mission to Russia. We will leave England, drop our bombs on Germany, and fly on to Russia. There, we will refuel, reload our bombs, and fly back to England by way of Italy. It will become an around-the-clock, relentless bombing of Der Fuhrer's Fatherland."

The shuttle mission code name, Frantic II, was to be a means of getting the Russians to cooperate and coordinate our attacks against Germany.

Frantic I was flown by the Fifteenth Air Force in Italy and was very successful. President Roosevelt, Prime Minister Winston Churchill, and Field Marshal Joseph Stalin of Russia discussed the benefits of this type of mission, while at the Teheran Conference, and decided to put it to work.

Focke-Wulf Fw190

The Focke-Wulf Fw190 Wurger is a German single-seat, single-engine fighter aircraft designed by Kurt Tank in the late 1930s and widely used during World War II. Along with its well-known counterpart, the Messerschmitt Bf 109, the Fw190 became the backbone of the Luftwaffe's Jadgwaffe. The twin-row BMV 801 radial engine that powered most operational versions enabled the Fw190 to lift larger loads than the Bf109, allowing its use as a day fighter, fighter bomber, ground-attack aircraft, and, to a lesser degree, night fighter.

Messerschmitt Me262

The Messerschmitt Me262, nicknamed Schwalbe in fighter version, or Sturmvogel in fighter-bomber version, was the world's first operational jet-powered fighter aircraft. Design work started before World War II began, but engine problems, metallurgical problems, and top-level interference kept the aircraft from operation status with the Luftwaffe until mid-1944. The Me262 was faster, and more heavily armed than any Allied fighter, including the British jet-powered Gloster Meteor. One of the most advanced aviation designs in operational use during World War II, the Me262 was used in a variety of roles, including light bomber, reconnaissance, and even experimental night fighter versions.

CHAPTER 12

Adventures In Russia And Beyond

Such was the beginning of one of the most exciting adventures of GOOD-O-YANK's crew number 86, 390th Bomb Group, mission number 134. This one took on the importance of missions such as D-DAY, and everyone was excited and chattering away.

When we finally quieted down enough, the briefing officers very methodically went through our preflight instructions. For the 8th Air Force, this was a major effort, involving 1,309 heavy bombers and 1,269 fighters.

The 1st Bomb Division, consisting of 496 B17s, were to hit Berlin, and oh, how I felt for those men. (They were to keep the fighters busy, so that we could sneak by on our way to Russia.) The 2nd Bomb Division, consisting of 368 B24s, were to hit Genshagen, Potsdam, Marienfelde, and Berlin. Many did not reach their primary targets and ended up bombing 12 different targets of opportunity, all in the Berlin area. I knew they were in for an extremely rough mission.

Consisting of 207 B17s, part of the 3rd Division was sent to Baseldorf and Berlin. The part of the 3rd Division going to Russia (which included me) consisted of 163 B17s, and our target would be Ruhland, Germany, which is south of Berlin.

The 2nd Division also sent 73 B24s to bomb the Pas de Calais, France, area in support of the invasion troops. This made a total of

2,578 aircraft over Europe at one time, with most over or near Berlin. What must the German people be thinking…the parade of planes as far as the eye could see coming to bomb. Just as the Americans were landing back at their bases, the British were taking off, in equal numbers, to bomb at night.

The mood had now turned somber as we headed for our planes. We all had different ways of relaying our thoughts to our loved ones in case anything were to happen to us. Some simply told others that were not flying that day to tell their families they loved them, some wrote letters the night before, and some just prayed silently. It was my custom to write the night before we were flying, but I was careful not to alarm them. Not every mission, but on those when I had a certain feeling of impending danger, I would write a letter to Eleta, and one to Mom, about how I was feeling. I wanted them to know how much I loved them and how much I wanted this war to be over so I could come home and be with them. The letter was to be mailed only if I did not come back. Once the mission was over, I would destroy the letter.

On the way to our plane, Harvey confided in me that he was very afraid of this mission and said that he didn't want his body to be buried in Germany or Russia. I said, "Harvey, I have those feelings myself, but if you promise to look after me, I'll do the same for you." He smiled and said, "It's a deal."

When we got to our hardstand there was some unusual activity. First, we had a new bombardier, Second Lieutenant A. P. Nielson, and a new right waist gunner, Tech Sergeant Robert F. Nichols, a squadron photographer from the 570th Squadron.

Plus, there were all sorts of additional people going along on this mission. Colonel A. J. Olds, group commander for the 45th Combat Wing (made up of the 388th, 452nd, and the 96th Bomb Groups) was our overall leader. Our 390th Bomb Group's Colonel Fred Von Arb led the 13th Wing, which was composed of the 390th, 95th, and 100th Bomb Groups.

In each plane, we carried spare plane parts and ground crew personnel (such as engine mechanics, body mechanics, or electricians), in case we sustained damage. There were also personnel from the fighter groups that escorted us. As a matter of fact, one of the men flying with us was Staff Sergeant Robert Gilbert, a crew chief on a P51 flown by Major James Goodson, commanding officer of the 336th Fighter Squadron and a combat ace.

Sergeant Gilbert, serving as waist gunner, was flown to the 452nd Bomb Group where he was placed aboard a B17 bound for Russia. Near Warsaw, Poland, his plane was attacked by Me109s, and with his plane on fire, he parachuted into Poland.

The Polish people hid him from the Germans and he was routed through Russia to Africa and, finally, back to his P51 Base in Debden, England, in August 1944. The plane that he serviced and Major Goodson were shot down the next day. Major Goodson was captured by the Germans and spent the rest of the war in a German prison camp.

Not only were there airmen and ground crews along for this trip, but also all sorts of support personnel, such as weathermen. We were surprised to see cases of K and C rations stowed aboard, as well as extra ammunition. There was stuff stashed everywhere. I could hardly walk through my radio compartment. We were so excited with all this going on, it was hard to get into our regular routine of getting ready for a mission.

We formed in the dark, over England, in the early morning of June 21, and set out on a route that had become familiar to us. Our course was charted up through the North Sea, past the Netherlands, and, keeping well to the left of the Frisian Islands and their sharp-shooting flak guns, to the mouth of the Elbe River.

Just north of Bremerhaven, we made a sharp turn into Germany, and the flak started popping like popcorn, only ten thousand times louder. As we slipped past Hamburg, to the north, we could see black clouds over the city. Doubtless, the Germans thought we were going there but, thank goodness, not this time.

North of the Elbe River, which flows by Berlin, we were shot at by flak guns mounted on flat barges that followed us as we went. The Germanic people have always been known as a fighting people, and you can believe me, they figure every way possible to kill you. Someday, I'm going to sit down and research to determine what has made the Germans so mad at the world that they wish to fight everyone.

The powers that be had done a first-class job of routing us between the heavy flak areas at Hamburg and Bremen, and Hanover and Magdeburg. It was here we saw other groups of the Eighth Air Force turning off our safe path into the terrifying areas in and around BIG B.

What a dreadful sight as we saw those planes vanish into the blackness of the German flak. I prayed unashamedly for their safety, and at the same time, I prayed that the innocent German people were safely in the bomb shelters, as the thousands of pounds of bombs rained down on them.

Shortly after passing Berlin, we changed directions and turned south on a heading about halfway between Leipzig and Dresden to our target, the synthetic oil refineries at Ruhland.

We lined up on our target and, with almost perfect bombing, lived up to our motto, "Sur le Nez," translated to "On the Nose." Results were excellent, and we could see smoke rising rapidly to 10,000 feet. We then headed northeastward and exited Germany near Hoyerswerda, on the Polish border.

The German Air Force was staying away from us, and I could see our P51 escorts crisscrossing high above us. The main reason, however, was because they were protecting their capital city of Berlin. I will never be able to describe the picture of solid black-smoke flak explosions, fifty miles across over that city, with our friends and buddies flying into that ball of hell.

I can only tell you that it could have been me except that the good Lord must have other plans for me. Seeing all that death and destruction made me wonder about all the really nice American boys. I particularly thought of Jimmy Basinger, from Charlotte, and Rex Stanley, from Dodge City, Kansas, and prayed they were not on that mission.

Everything was quiet now, no fighters or flak. All I could hear was the steady drone of our four engines. Out of nowhere the intercom cracked, "Okay, men, we have made it through the worst part but still have a long way to go. Let's do a thorough check of our plane and see if we have any damage."

"Tail gunner to pilot," reported Sandy. "I don't see any major damage, a few small holes in the rudder." "Thanks, Sandy, don't let up. Those guys are going to be mad as hell for bombing Berlin."

BOYS WILL BE BOYS

"Ball turret to pilot. I have checked everything underneath the plane and don't see anything serious, but I do have an urgent problem." "What is it, Sam?" said Ray. "I have to go pee," said Maggie. "Okay, Sam, by all means, come on out of that ball and go pee. Hah, ha, ha."

I knew as soon as I heard it. This was going to be fun! The door to the ball turret popped open, and Harvey helped Sam out. As he came through the radio compartment with a carry-around oxygen bottle, he gave me the thumbs-up sign. I could see those Irish eyes smiling through goggles. Every other part of his face was covered with the oxygen mask. He was unzipping his heavy flying suit when he opened the door to the bomb bay. He reached for the relief tube, which was nothing more than a rubber tube with a funnel attached. It was, however, a terribly complicated procedure, getting through those clothes and gear (the heavy outer fleece-lined flying suit, the inner coverall flying suit, and the long john underwear). His intercom was, of course, disconnected.

Ray said, "Is he there yet?" Steve, who was in the top turret, just behind the pilot and right in front of the bomb bay, opened the door, peeped in, and said with a snicker, "Yep, he is in there." With that the plane started to buck and roll, up and down, side to side. Oh, man, I knew what Sam was going through as I had been there more than once, standing on an eight-inch catwalk in the dark bomb bay, holding on to the bomb rack with one hand, holding a walk-around oxygen bottle in the other, while trying to hold the relief tube with the other. (Hey, wait a minute, there was no other!) With *no* plane movement, it would still take four hands to complete this maneuver successfully. (No one ever did.) I heard the oxygen bottle hit the bottom of the bomb bay and knew Sam was eliminating his options. Next went the relief tube and funnel, and Maggie was yelling at the top of his lungs. It is a good thing we didn't have to open the bomb bay doors again because they were frozen shut. All of this, mind you, was taking place five miles up. Trying to perform that delicate procedure is truly a major undertaking. Anyone who successfully performs this feat is awarded the "Order of the Relief Tube Medal." I never got one.

Can you imagine ten grown men, in the direst of circumstances, in a combat zone, taking part in such frivolity? Only if you were one of them.

When Sam was safely back in his ball turret, the damage check continued as if nothing had happened. The plane checked out fine as we passed over the Ore Mountain Range that separates Germany from Poland, and we were on a beeline for Warsaw.

Watching the country of Poland unfold below us, satisfied that we were now out of danger, we settled down to enjoy the scenery below us.

We were cruising along quietly, except for the purring of our 4 1,250-horsepower engines. I had just received a coded message from England stating the mission was going well and many targets had been destroyed, when I was interrupted by machine-gun fire. Almost immediately, our pilot, Ray Strate, came on the intercom. "All right, men, what's going on back there?"

No one answered because they didn't know. I could tell Ray was aggravated because each position must always report to the pilot as soon as there is danger to the plane.

Finally, Ray said, "Chuck, see if you can find out who is firing and report back to me." I jumped out of my radio operator's seat and opened the door to the waist part of the plane where the left and right waist gunners were stationed. They looked at me like, *We don't know*. And now, the guns were firing again, and the sound was coming from the ball turret which hangs down beneath the plane. The firing went *burrp, burrp, burrp* and shook the entire plane

I answered Ray right away, knowing that he was ready to wring someone's neck. "Radio to pilot, the noise is coming from the ball turret and when he is firing, he can't hear you on the intercom."

All at once the ball turret operator let out a yell, "Hot dang! Hot dang! I got him. I got him. He is on fire!"

"Pilot to ball turret. Why did you not tell me what was going on?"

"Didn't have time, boss man. I got me a Me109, and the pilot bailed out. He was sneaking straight up under our formation, but I saw him." Then there was a long silence…"Okay, Maggie, good work! Okay, men, settle down. Keep your eyes open and sing out if you see anything."

Sam McGee was the ball turret operator on our plane. He was very much Irish, and the Irish believe in leprechauns, usually depicted as fairylike little men with funny green hats and coats, small in stature, and very mischievous. If ever there was a true leprechaun, it surely was our Sam "Maggie" McGee.

All of a sudden, we heard over the intercom from Steve, top turret, "Bandits at three o'clock high!" Almost before we swung our guns around to meet the 7 Me109s, coming almost head-on, they shot through our formation and, turning on their backs, were gone. (In about the time it took you to read this paragraph was how quickly it was over.) I looked out my left window overlooking our left wing, and possibly 100 yards, to the 452nd Bomb Group with a square L on their tail. One B17, slowly at first, started sliding out of formation. There was smoke coming from both engines on the right side. I saw 2 crewmen pop out, and just seconds later, 2 chutes opened. Others on our plane saw several more as the B17 started spiraling down. (One of these chutes was undoubtedly Sergeant Robert Gilbert's, whom I described earlier. It would be 60 years before I discovered he landed and was rescued. Way to go, Sarge.) Our P51 escort went by us like a shot in the direction of the Me109s, who were hightailing it for home base somewhere near Warsaw. We never heard if they made it, but my guess is they were scattered all over a large area of Poland. You could almost read those German pilots' minds as they were preparing to hit our formation. "We will come in from above and in front to have the greatest amount of speed and surprise, hit the planes on the corner of their formation, flip on our backs, dive straight for the ground, land quickly, and run and jump in a hole before those Devil P51s can get to us." I would bet a month's salary they did not make it.

We had now passed between Warsaw and Krakow, the two largest cities in Poland. A few miles to our south, about thirty miles from

Krakow, we flew close to a large German concentration camp, one that claimed millions of lives, mostly Jews. What if we had been shot down and parachuted near here. **Auschwitz** will go down in history as one of "man's most inhumanity to man" places. It had its companion, Birkenau camp, just minutes away, where trainloads of unsuspecting people were marched to their deaths in German crematoriums.

We were wide awake now; the Germans had a way of getting our attention, and we began to scan the sky for more fighters.

Flying eastward toward Russia, along the fifty-eighth parallel, we crossed a huge marshland with standing water. We turned southeastward on a line to Kiev, in the Russian Ukraine, and as we descended to get off oxygen, we could see clearly for hundreds of miles. The one thing we all noticed, almost immediately, were hundreds of trenches running north and south, from one horizon to the other. We thought it must have taken millions of soldiers, digging night and day, to stop the German advance across the endless Steppes, on the road to Moscow.

We flew for hours across the most desolate country, seeing mile after mile of trenches and rocky land, with burned-out tanks dotting the countryside. A mighty battle must have occurred here as there were no trees or even bushes, just endless miles of grasslands, rocks, and water. It is little wonder the Germans were so bogged down when winter finally arrived here.

We were almost on top of Kiev, when the powers that be turned northward to fly around this Russian town. We saw a few fighters off in the distance, which we immediately recognized as P39 Bell Airacobra. Sold or given to the Russians, it was their first-line fighter. Turning southeast, we flew toward the big city of Kharkov, population over one million.

Approximately eighty miles west of Kharkov, one wing, the Fifteenth, peeled off and headed for a landing strip at Mirgorod. A town of about twenty-five thousand, the Germans had almost destroyed all the buildings.

The Germans had been defeated at Stalingrad after laying siege to it for over two years. The Russian winters were just too much for the Germans. They were fleeing westward as fast as they could, taking everything that was not nailed down and some that were, including train rails that were pulled up and sent to Germany.

We finally caught sight of our landing site, no buildings, just steel mesh laid on the ground which had not been prepared or leveled. I know Ray must have said, "What are we getting into?" With very little gasoline and no bombload, we came in very light, and it was not a bad landing at all. Being off oxygen was great, but we found without the oxygen, we tired very quickly.

The 45th Wing flew on southeast to a town called Poltava, a city of about 140,000 people. Again, there was not much left standing, and all the crews were housed in burned-out buildings, with no roofs and part of only two walls standing.

Our fighter escorts were sent on to a base at Piryatin, having about 25,000 residents, so we were all at bases less than 100 miles apart.

I remember landing at Mirgorod. There were no control tower, no trees, no trucks, and nobody in sight. We taxied to the end of the long runway, and each plane lined up, wingtip to wingtip, down both sides. It was so weird that there was no one to meet us or tell us where to go. We were tired and hungry and didn't see any place nearby where we could rest, take a shower, or eat.

We were there about an hour, and all of a sudden, there they were. They seemed to appear from nowhere. The soldier that was assigned to guard our plane was so different looking from what we expected, we were totally shocked. He was short, and his rifle, with a bayonet attached, was taller than he was. His uniform was gray, like the color of a rat, and his shirt was blousy and looked several sizes too large. His pants were also blousy and looked like English riding breeches. He wore black leather boots that came to his knees. Everything, except his boots, were the same shade of gray. The most surprising thing was his skin; it was also gray, very close to the same shade as his uniform. Looking very closely, his hair, very short and kinky, was a very similar shade of gray as his uniform. Never in my life had I ever seen anyone who looked like him. I am sure I will be accused of hallucination, but the earth, the very dirt there was this same gray. The Ukraine is one of the richest soils of the world, and

I had always heard it was black. Au contraire, mon ami, not so at Mirgorod. No wonder we saw no one; they blended into the earth.

After being there a few hours, standing around our planes, a field kitchen was erected some distance away. We were told to get our mess kits and assemble near the field kitchen, which consisted of several long tables and four or five fifty-five-gallon drums with the tops cut out. These drums were filled with something, we didn't know what, with fires built under them.

We were introduced to Russian cooking with a mess kit full of borscht, which is nothing more than boiled beets, and a chunk of black bread. It was certainly not first-class fare, but we ate it because we were hungry, and it was baaad! The bread was very coarse and hard, but acceptable. Would someone please tell me, why black? You have to do something terrible to wheat flour or any other grain to make it black.

Several of the fifty-five-gallon drums contained boiling water, and when we finished, we walked by the drums and dipped our mess kits in the boiling water, which made the metal so hot, you could not hold on to it. I used a wooden stick and still had to wait a few minutes before I was able to touch it.

The bathrooms were slit trenches about one hundred yards away. As we were leaving, one of the enlisted men from another plane threw his mess kit to the ground, making a racket, and started running across the field. Our commander, Colonel Ott, saw him running away and called out to him, "Hey, you there, soldier." He kept going, and this time he yelled, "Halt, Sergeant!" The sergeant stopped, turned slowly around, and yelled back, "To the latrine," but it was too late. The Russian GI's had gotten him, and he continued to walk slowly, spraddle legged, toward the slit trenches. I was told later that Colonel Ott apologized for stopping him, but I don't think he would have made it anyway.

We stayed close to our planes, and now we could see several P39 Russian fighters off to one side of the airfield. They were off-limits, and we were told that all the pilots were women.

HEINKEL He177

Russian P39 Airacobra

Our crew was very fortunate to have Steve Przepiorka, who was of Polish descent and could speak Polish. Although the dialects were not the same, our Russian guard could also speak Polish so we could converse. The Russian guard told us how he came to be guarding our planes.

It turns out he was a front-line soldier, and somehow, he was hit in battle, blowing off all his genitals. He spent a long time recuperating in a hospital where the army doctors grafted replacement organs that were functional, but he, of course, could no longer serve as a front-line soldier. He told us that the doctors used rolls of skin from his inner thigh as grafts. In the Russian Army, there is no such thing as retirement, so he was assigned to guard duty.

It was getting on toward dark, and we all were wondering where we were going to sleep. One of our officers came by with a Russian woman interpreter and said, "Get your heavy flying suits and follow me." Off we went, but we could see no buildings anywhere. After a short walk, we came to a hole in the ground about thirty feet across and about one hundred feet long. The Russians had dug a long hole in the ground and covered all but the entrance, which was dug at an angle, so that you could walk down into the opening. The covering was made of wooden poles laid across the opening with straw on top.

Once inside, there were two rows of racks, much like shelves, triple decked and filled with straw. They said, through the interpreter, "This is your home." You could hear that famous Air Corp moan for a half mile. OOOH, noooooo!

Things got very quiet when someone yelled, "German plane approaching!" We all rushed to the entrance of our dugout barracks and could plainly see the plane as it made a pass, right over us. We could tell it was German even before we saw it because all German multi-engine planes did not synchronize their engines as the English and Americans did. Instead of an even hum, the sound went up and down, as if the plane were having trouble.

As it passed over, it was recognized as a Heinkel He177, just like the Germans flew over our base most every night at Framlingham, England. It was an observation and photographing mission. There were a pitiful few rounds of antiaircraft fired from across the airfield by the Russians, who had no more than two guns. Then, three P39 fighters took off after the German plane, and we were told later that they never caught up with the He177.

I was tired as blue blazes, and I crawled into the straw bunk, shutting out all thoughts of war. Around 0300 or 0400 hours, we were awakened by antiaircraft fire but were told to stay in our underground bunker. Part of the noise we heard was a severe rainstorm, and I wondered if we were going to be drowned like rats down in our hole. Needless to say, we got very little rest, and at daybreak, Colonel Ott informed our officers that the German Air Force had attacked our B17s at Poltava. The entire 45th Wing was destroyed, but fortunately, all our personnel were safe.

Bright and shiny, all the B17s were the latest. The German He177 Heinkel and Junkers Ju88s, a force of about 150 planes, totally destroyed more than 50 B17Gs. Twenty-nine more were damaged so badly, they could only be used for spare parts. Wings, propellers, engines, and tail sections were salvaged to complete 9 planes that could fly. The entire 45th Wing, 3 bomb groups of over 90 planes, was devastated with only 9 planes left that would fly. The Germans dropped over 10 tons of bombs, thousands of phosphorous incendiary and antipersonnel bombs, some striking gasoline fuel trucks, conveniently left near the planes. The fires from the burning B17s and from the exploding fuel trucks lit the area like daylight, like an NFL football night game. The Germans had no trouble finding targets. They dropped thousands of Butterfly antipersonnel bombs, each fitted with a small propeller that opened outward and started the bomb spinning. The bombs settled to the ground as softly as a snowflake and were immediately armed. Although these bombs were only as large as a can of peas, they were filled with powder and razor-sharp metal pieces. They would not explode on contact with the ground, only when something or someone walked near it. Devilish, these Nazis; what kind of mind would dream up so many ways to kill or maim? One of the ground rules between the United States and Russia to permit these shuttle missions was that the Russians would have complete control over our protection while on Russian soil. Colonel Ott of the 13th Wing, and Colonel Olds with the 45th Wing, pleaded with their Russian counterparts to let our P51s defend us, but a Russian general said with absolute finality, "NYET. No. No, we will take care of it," and that was it. Our US P51s would have had a turkey shoot with the very slow German bombers, but to defy the Russians would have caused serious problems all the way up to Stalin.

When the problem was made known to higher US authorities, our lowly colonels were told to "COOL IT, NYET."

How were they going to protect us? With three P39s and a handful of antiaircraft guns? I never saw an antiaircraft gun, and neither did anyone else in our group. I did, however, hear some. One of the "passengers" that we brought along with us was a photographer with the 45th Wing at Poltava, and he had the presence of mind to set up a time-lapse photo of the airfield while the raid was in progress. I am including a copy of that photo, and although it is not a clear picture, I am sure he would not mind my using it to illustrate just how pitiful the Russian defenses were.

IMAGES FROM POLTAVA BOMBING, JUNE 22, 1944.

MORE IMAGES FROM POLTAVA BOMBING, JUNE 22, 1944.

IMAGES FROM POLTAVA BOMBING, JUNE 22, 1944.

BOMBER GRAVEYARD AT POLTAVA. Scene day after German bombers destroyed ninety-three planes, June 1944.

Probably, a lot more B17s could have been saved had there been a fire department. I hate to say it, but it appeared as though the Russians almost wanted our planes destroyed. As you can tell I was hot about it, but not nearly so mad as our commanding officers.

One of the truly great officers of the 8th Air Force was Colonel Joseph A. Moller, who came along as commander of the 100th Bomb Group in our 13th Wing. Shortly after the shuttle mission, he moved from the 100th BG to become commander of our 390th BG at Framlingham.

He was extremely bitter about how the Russians allowed our planes to be destroyed and refused to let it go. In an interview after the War, he talked with General Jimmy Doolittle and General Dwight Eisenhower about it, and although they never came right out and said so, they both left him with the understanding that it was General Eisenhower who gave the order to "SHUT UP" and carry on. Ike was a mighty warrior and a good general, and I would have followed him anywhere. (And I did, but I sure would have liked to "tweak" his little turned-up nose on this one.)

On the afternoon of June 22, I was sitting in my radio compartment, listening for news from the fighting in France. Turning a few knobs, I stopped on a fairly strong signal and heard a very familiar voice. I almost dropped my teeth when I realized it was the voice of Grady Cole, from Charlotte, North Carolina. Grady had a very popular early morning radio show that began about 0500 hours. Residents of Charlotte and Mecklenburg County, in the 1930s and 1940s, were mostly farm people, and the farmers believed every word that came out of Grady's mouth. If he endorsed a product, they bought it. He talked their language. My Pop believed! One day I said to Pop, "How do you know that tonic you are taking is any good?" He answered, astonished that I should question it, "Because Grady Cole said so, that's why!"

In radio school, we were taught that low frequency AM radio waves could sometimes be bounced off the ionosphere and skip a great distance, before coming back to earth. I was now living proof that this was true. Grady Cole's voice was as clear as it was back home.

Grady's voice was not just known around Charlotte. The radio station WBT 1110 on the dial could be heard from Maine to Florida. Grady was talking about the War, and he said, "Folks, we have turned the corner and, take it from me, your boys will soon be coming home." Man, that was good news to me, and I took off my headset to go tell the rest of the crew. I never got to tell them because our pilot was just back from a briefing, and he said, "Okay, boys, pack it up, we are moving." It seemed the same recon plane had just made another pass over us and headed back toward the German lines, with the same P39s trailing after them. He also told us that it had been determined that the base we were on would most certainly have been bombed had there not been a thunderstorm right over our base. (Here, again, I was convinced there was divine intervention.)

The plan was we were to fly up to Poltava, refuel, load bombs, and pick up all or most of the crews whose planes had been destroyed. Every plane would be carrying extra crews, and then we were to get the heck out of Dodge before the Germans came that night.

When we got to Poltava and looked down on the devastation the Germans had wrought, it almost made us sick to our stomachs. To men who loved the planes as we did our B17s, we wanted to cry. There were B17s torn and twisted, demolished, and burned everywhere.

We quickly landed and began packing up the crews, as we were on a tight schedule. Steve saw them first. The Russians, each with a long stick waving back and forth on the ground, were attempting to clear the airfield by lining up prisoners of war, shoulder to shoulder. Walking slowly across the airfield, when they came to a Butterfly Bomb, many would go off, killing the prisoners. When this happened, the bodies were loaded on a truck and hauled away. (What Geneva Convention? The Russians were ruthless.) The Russians then brought up more prisoners and followed closely along behind them with guns ready. When the line of prisoners reached the other side of the field, they were wheeled around, much like marching soldiers, and marched back across the field. The bombs popped like popcorn, and even though it was inhumane, it was very effective. I saw several Russian soldiers go down as well.

Ray said, "Boys, do not move from the plane. We don't know where these devilish things are." We said, "Yes, sir, you don't have to worry about us moving around. When are we leaving?" "As soon as we are loaded and gassed up."

With extra gasoline, bombs, and crews we had a tough time getting airborne, and I, for one, was glad to leave Poltava and all that destruction.

We headed southeast toward the Black Sea. Neal, our navigator, told us we were headed to a place called Zaporozhye, which is near the mouth of the Dniepr River, about eighty miles north of the Black Sea. We passed low over the cities of Dneprodzerzhinsk and Dnepropetrovsk and saw they were devastated, nothing standing but walls…no roofs, no electricity, nothing. The retreating Germans were burning everything before leaving.

The airfield near Zaporozhye had a long concrete runway that had been bombed and repaired with gravel, and not knowing what to expect, our lead planes eased down as softly as they could. The first two squadrons had no trouble, and thank goodness, we were just taxiing into a parking area when someone yelled, "Good Lord, look at that."

A plane had just landed and started to turn off the runway when the concrete under his left landing gear gave way and the left side of the plane dropped into a large hole. The plane was blocking the only runway, and the other planes were circling and could not land.

Man, oh, man! For the next thirty minutes, it was a Chinese fire drill, everyone running and shouting. They tried pulling it with trucks, and fifty crewmen tried to lift it with no luck at all. The props on the left side were just inches off the runway.

Time was running out. Things had gotten desperate, when a master sergeant crew chief yelled, "Get everybody away from the plane." He swung up through the nose entrance, and we saw his head pop out the pilot's seat window. "Get everyone back." He revved those four engines to the max, dropped the wing flaps as far as they would go, released the brakes, and that airplane jumped out of that hole, while everyone cheered. The other planes landed without incident, avoiding the hole.

Had I been our group commander, I would have given that master sergeant the Medal of Honor. But, you know what? I have read dozens of accounts of the shuttle mission, and not one mentions this story. Could it be that this master sergeant got the job done when all the big brass who wrote these accounts could not solve the problem?

It was getting very late in the evening of June 22, 1944, and I was having strong feelings about home. Today was my Uncle Hal and Aunt Janet Hamby's wedding anniversary, and I suppose it was that, but it seemed to be something else. Maybe it was ESP, but I had shivers up my spine; something was wrong. I wrote a few letters while we waited to go to chow, but there was no place to mail them, so I just put them away to mail later.

Ray came by to bring us up-to-date on what was going on. He told us we would be going to a Russian field kitchen to eat, and it looked as if we were going to be here for several days, until the weather cleared over our next target. We would be transporting over six hundred crewmen who were without planes due to the German bombing of Poltava.

He also told us arrangements had been made for us to go by truck the next day over to the Dnieper River, which was about two miles away, to relax, take a bath, and do some sightseeing.

The Russian Ukraine is an area of rich and fertile soil, changing from black to dark brown along the valleys and rivers that lead to the Black Sea. It is a semitropical area as you move southward from where we are. There are large tree forests, and it is a truly beautiful country. For hundreds of years, many wealthy Russians from the north, particularly from Moscow, have come to the Black Sea to vacation on the sunny sand beaches.

After viewing what the Russians prepared for our breakfast, raw fish heads with the eyes looking up at you (a delicacy in Russia), we retreated to our plane and gladly ate "K" rations.

Soon, we heard the Russian trucks coming to take us on our holiday, and we went out to greet them. There were two Russian soldiers and a couple of civilians and one small boy, carrying a rifle with fixed bayonet. The small boy looked really odd because the rifle was fully two feet taller than he. They had brand-new American Dodge weapons-carrier trucks painted olive green.

We stood looking at them, and they stood looking at us without saying anything. We eyed each other cautiously. Leave it to Maggie to break the ice. He reached in his pocket and handed each one of them a stick of Beech-Nut chewing gum. Then reaching inside his mouth, he pulled out his own gum, showed it to them, and put it back into his own mouth and started chewing. They began to smile and laugh, and finally, the young boy put his stick of gum into his mouth, paper, foil, and all, and began to chew. He said, "Da, da," which Steve translated as "Yes, yes." This really tickled our crew, and we all had gum and candy bars that we shared with them.

As they were enjoying our gifts, they were looking us up and down. Never having seen Americans before and realizing that they did not know what we were saying, someone on our crew ventured to say, "Boy, if they are not a motley-looking bunch of soldiers."

"Does any one of you speak any English?" After a long silence, one of the men in civilian clothes said, in perfect English, "Yes, I do." We were shocked, especially since we had called them stupid looking. Steve asked, "Where did you learn to speak English so well?" The man replied, "I lived in New York City for fourteen years and worked at the Brooklyn Navy yard for eleven years."

Needless to say, we cleaned up our act promptly. After talking with him about the area we were going to visit, the English-speaking man left. We felt he was placed here to learn or spy on us. Before he left, he spoke to the truck driver in Russian and, turning to us, said, "I told him to take you to a place where there are cherry trees." The man told us to enjoy our stay in Russia, then left.

We all jumped into the back of the truck like a bunch of kids on a hayride. We soon discovered our driver had received instructions on how to drive from someone in the United States, and apparently, the first thing the instructor did was blow the horn. No matter where we went, before that driver would crank the engine, he would blow the horn. It was going to be a fun day, and we laughed all the way down to the river.

The road to the river was not paved but was well traveled and smooth, except for the last quarter mile. It was more like a path, and our driver did not slow down. It was all we could do to hang on, and our brains were rattled as we came to a sliding stop. In the United States, this driver would have been killed in the first ten minutes of driving in American traffic.

When I looked up and out over the beautiful Dnieper River, it took my breath. It was not at all what I had expected, not wide or deep. It was about one hundred yards wide and very shallow, up to a man's shoulders at the deepest, but fast-moving and very rocky. We were surprised to see local women washing on almost every rock. Undoubtedly, today was washday, for there were a great number. Most were in water a little over their knees and, somehow having tucked their dress tails so their clothes would not get wet, were dipping their washcloths in the water and banging them against their rock. They would dip, bang, and squeeze, over and over. All these women were short and stout, and Maggie said, "I would not want to tangle with one of those ladies."

Now we were having second thoughts about taking our clothes off and going swimming. However, many of the others were buck naked in a New York minute, and the ladies pointed and giggled. Our crew decided to go a little further up the river where it was a little more private.

Back on the little dirt road, we approached a bend in the road which sort of followed the river. I was looking ahead, over the cab of the truck, and had a very strange feeling that I had been on this road before. I told Harvey, "I have been on this road before. I don't know how, but I can tell you that around that bend ahead and off to the right, in a grove of trees, there is a small house. It is red and has a tin roof. There is a well in front of it, and instead of having a windlass with a rope, it has a long pole with a bucket hanging on one end, and there is a small building behind it." Harvey said, "How did you know that? You are pulling my leg." I said, "I really and truly do not know." A real encounter with déjà vu.

Our driver stopped at the well and raised a bucket of water. We cupped our hands, and the water was cool and delicious. It reminded me of the well water on our farm back home in North Carolina.

We determined that the red building was a schoolhouse, and since it was summertime, there was no one around. We walked toward the river across a grassy field that looked a lot like Ireland, so very green, and through an orchard. There they were, the largest and most beautiful cherries I had ever seen. We raced over to them, and truly, five or six were a handful. They were bright red and ripe and tasted wonderful.

After eating our fill, we went down to the river, ripped off our clothes, and waded into the water, so cold, it took your breath. After a while, we got used to it and splashed around like schoolkids. We had no soap, but neither did the ladies washing clothes, and we felt clean anyway. All of us had big red whelps where the Russian lice had bitten us, and the cold water felt good on the bites.

As we lay on the white sandbar at the river's edge, warming and drying off in the sun, the horrible thoughts of the war seemed ten thousand miles away. We talked of home and what the weather was like there. Steve said, "It is still cool in and around Detroit, but my family would be shaking off the snow and ice of a hard winter. Spring in Michigan is a wondrous time with millions of bulbs breaking out." "Yeah," said Maggie, "we get a lot of snow in Connecticut, too, and the nights are a little chilly into June." Sandy chimed in, "By this time, down in Texas, it is getting hot." I said, "Down south in North Carolina, spring has already busted out all over. My mom always let us kids go barefoot the second week in May, and everyone who is going to have a garden has already got it in the ground." "Well, in Ohio, we are sort of betwixt and between you guys, but I sure would love to see home again," said Harvey. Something kept bugging me about home; something was wrong. "Beep, beep!" Our truck driver was beeping us that it was time to get started back and begin thinking about killing again.

We all agreed that this had been a wonderful day and this part of Russia was really pretty. After the war, we might like to visit to see how it was in peacetime.

"Beep, beep." That horn reminded me of the noise the roadrunners used in the movies. We went back the way we came, and the Russian women were still washing clothes and waved as we went by. These poor people had nothing. Their cities and farms had been destroyed by the Germans. It had only been a few weeks ago that the Russians had cut the German supply lines to Stalingrad, and now, the Russians were in hot pursuit all through this area.

Back at the air base, we found that enlisted men from other crews had similar experiences and were glad for a day of rest. The officers, on the other hand, were having experiences of a different nature. They were treated to food and entertainment. The Russian military drinks a lot, mostly vodka, a very high-powered alcohol drink, made from fermented potatoes. They wanted to toast everything and everyone. To get our officers involved, they would start by toasting President Franklin Roosevelt, Sir Winston Churchill, and General Dwight Eisenhower, downing shot after shot.

By the time they got to Stalin and a whole string of Russian notables, everyone was totally inebriated. To not raise a toast to Stalin and the rest of the Russian brass, however, would have been an insult. Thank goodness, we were not flying.

They wanted us to go eat the Russian food again, but we declined, saying we felt sick from drinking the water. We went, instead, to our planes and opened up a few more cans of C and K rations. Some were good, but most were just nourishment to keep you fighting. In the famous C rations were things like dehydrated eggs, mixed with water and turned an inedible green color, spaghetti, potatoes, vegetables, potted meat like Spam, and stews like a thick soup. They sound like they might be good, but had no taste...BLAH! YUCK! Then there was the infamous K ration, with mixtures and concoctions that a chemist could not identify. There was one I really liked; it contained real cheese. Take a hunk and jam it down into a chunk of Russian black bread, YUM, GOOD; I ate it three times a day. Then there was what was called a D ration, affectionately known as the D bar. It was hard as a rock and took forever to chew. It reminded me of my ole hound dog at home, with a big soup bone that Mom gave to him. He would chew it on one side of his mouth, then switch to the other side.

Tuesday, June 23, 1944

Tuesday, June 23, 1944, dawned sunny and warm. After breakfast, the enlisted men of our crew huddled around our plane, waiting for news...news from Normandy, news from England, news about when we would be leaving on the next leg of our shuttle mission. I believe it was Lieutenant George Curnes, our copilot from Charleston, West Virginia, who filled us in. He told us that our mission commander, Colonel Archie Olds, and a few other top officers had flown up to Kharkov to meet with a Russian general to determine what our target would be on our way to Italy. Kharkov is a major Russian city with over a million people and is located about 350 miles west of Stalingrad.

A RUSSIAN TRAP

Now, we knew we would not be flying today, so we looked for another Russian adventure, like yesterday. Armed with chewing gum and candy bars, we tried to converse with a small crowd who had come to see the huge Americansky B17.

With Steve's help, we became friendly with a local Russian civilian who seemed very intelligent. With Steve's Polish and a lot of hand signals and drawing in the earth, we determined that he was a leader in a small community nearby, much like a mayor in one of our American towns. He was very appreciative of the candy and K rations we gave him and invited us to his home about a half mile away. As we walked, he told us that we were very near the route the Germans had taken in retreating from Stalingrad and said that, after we visited his home, he had something very interesting to show us. Things were looking up; maybe we would have another fun day.

As we came closer to his home, we could see a large building, seven stories high. There were lots of windows and doors, but no glass or wood covering them. As we entered the main entrance, we could see it was like a large apartment building. A huge hole from the ground floor to the roof was visible and was actually an elevator shaft, but with no elevator. We climbed the stairs to the fifth floor and entered his apartment by pushing aside a cloth covering, in place of a door. There were similar cloths for curtains at the windows. We were shown into a room with makeshift furniture and a big box for a table. We met Alexanderov's wife, a short, stout woman with a weathered-like face that was deeply wrinkled and looked as if it would crack if she smiled. She did smile and showed two front teeth missing. There were several kids in the other room, but not the kind of kids we were accustomed to. There were several goats, and we learned that goats were a family treasure, furnishing milk and cheese for everyday living.

Alex, as we shortened his name, spoke a few Russian words to his wife, and she hastened off. "Ya, ya." She soon was back with a large earthen jug that appeared as though it might hold three gallons of liquid. I said to myself, "Oh, no, not vodka." She set the jug on the big box and went out for something else. We were delighted when she brought in three large round loaves of black bread from the oven. Alex walked over to the big earthen jug, which had a thick black cap on it, took his fist, and banged it down on top of the jug. Bits and pieces flew about the room, and I thought he had gone mad, but he was simply opening the jug. The thick black top was formed by goat's milk fermenting and drying to a hard crust. He raised the jug to his lips and gulped the liquid contents, much like I had seen farmers in America drink buttermilk. He then handed the jug to Maggie, who immediately became wild-eyed with a facial expression I had never seen before or since. By now the odor was permeating the room, the smell of which was so vile, one would immediately gag. There are no words in the English language to describe such a horrible odor. I reached for one of the black bread loaves, and with all my might, I could not break it open. The Russian woman took the loaf, found a narrow crack and, with very strong fingers, pried it open. The bread was hard as steel on the outside but soft and warm inside. She handed it back to me, and I freed a handful and popped it in my mouth. This sort of settled my stomach while Maggie lifted the jug to his lips and, holding his breath, pretended to drink. Quick as a wink, he turned and handed the jug to me. Now it was my time to panic and pretend I was drinking. Like Maggie, no matter how I tried to squinch my nose, that vile concoction's smell paralyzed my brain, and I could neither drink nor breathe.

Alex, seeing my predicament, promptly slapped me on the back, thereby opening my passageways and, in a mighty gulp, down went a large swallow. My eyes teared and my nose ran but it stayed down, thanks to the black bread. Sandy and Steve started for the door, but I cut them off and handed the jug to Steve. He had a terrified look which told me, "Just wait, ole boy, payback can be *bad*." By this time, Maggie was laughing like a scalded hyena until he saw Steve position himself, blocking the entrance to the room. Steve took a handful of bread, filling his mouth, then raised that fermented goat's milk and drank. Sandy, seeing how easily performed, did likewise, and then it was Maggie's turn again. This time it was either drink or jump from five stories up, and you know, for a long second, I believe he thought seriously of leaping. With the bread, he got down a swallow and now there were cheers all around. Alex and his wife drank and ate like it was Pepsi Cola and a Moon Pie, and we were all now the best of friends.

We said our thank-yous, and I honestly could not wait to get out of that building. I took the stairs in mighty leaps and the thundering herd was just behind, on my heels. Once outside in the fresh air, my nose and throat were burning, and I found I could not get rid of that horrible stink. I had apparently spilled some on my clothes and so had the others. It clung like glue and could best be described as saying, "It smelled like we had been sprayed by an aggravated skunk."

Alex was patting us on the back and hollering, "Ya, ya, goot, ya." I felt like smacking him in the snoot but knew it would lead to an international confrontation that could only be settled by Stalin and Eisenhower.

Alex walked us toward the river to show us something very interesting, as he had promised earlier. After walking about an hour, we came to the river, about a mile downstream from where the women had been washing clothes the previous day. We stopped in our tracks at an unbelievable sight. The entire width of the Dnieper River was covered with German ammunition, dumped there by the Germans so the Russian soldiers, close on their heels could not use it. Every conceivable size of rounds was there, millions and millions of 30-caliber machine gun bullets, 20-millimeter cannon shells, and truckloads of 88-millimeter artillery shells. The ammunition covered an area about a city block wide and 100 yards across. The river was slowed by all this obstruction, but flowed freely up, over, and around it. We wanted a camera to document our amazement, but no one had one. We were told later that there was no need for anyone to doubt what we saw because this was repeated many times by the Germans.

Alex took us upstream a ways, where we waded into the cool water, clothes and all, to sanitize ourselves. Until this present day, when someone asks me, "To what do you give credit for living a long, healthy life?" I will always reply without hesitation, "Goat's milk." They always laugh, and sometimes, if they really act interested, I tell them the whole story, which cracks them up. It's hilarious now, but at the time, it was deadly serious. We all had thoughts of going out that fifth-story window, near Zaporozhye in the southern Ukraine.

Before our day with Alex was over, he said, "I have one more interesting place to show you, follow me." Off we went toward the devastated city of Zaporozhye. We followed a railroad track that split off into many rail headings, and even before we got near what he was going to show us, we could see huge stacks of American war materials awaiting shipment to the Russian Army several hundred miles to the west, toward Germany.

Finally, we arrived at a huge stack of material about the size of a football field, stacked high with Prestone Antifreeze (the very same stuff I had been delivering just a few months ago in my civilian job). It is no wonder there was a shortage in the USA; it was being shipped all over the world, and there was not a soul guarding it.

We had seen how Russian soldiers handled civilians that got too close to the military. Right at the airfield where we were staying, soldiers shot and killed a civilian who got too close. We heard the soldier yell, "Stoi" (halt in Russian), and when he did not stop, the Russian soldier raised his gun and fired. The man crumpled in a heap about one hundred yards away.

We had enjoyed another day adventure, and we rewarded Alex with cigarettes, candy, and K rations. He was one happy guy, and he tried to kiss us right on the lips (which is their custom). Yuck!

Back at the airfield, we ate potatoes, cabbage, and black bread, and settled into our hole in the ground, lit with hand lanterns. We were just lying around talking to other crews about our adventures, when there was a commotion at the entrance. We looked up to see a Russian playing an accordion and another playing an instrument that looked like a mandolin. They were followed by three young women. They began playing and dancing, and the longer it went, the louder and faster it got.

It stopped abruptly when our US commander explained to the Russians that Americans were not allowed to fraternize with civilian women. The Russians left but did not go very far. Standing just outside, they played their music on into the night. The music was very soft and soothing, and I went to sleep listening to it.

We were awakened early with a message that we were on alert to fly. We were to get our gear together and be prepared to leave Zaporozhye at any time, briefing at 0900. We ate C rations and a powdered drink like Kool Aid and waited. At 0900, we were told to stand down, but were still on alert. Before you could say Zaporozhye, there were army blankets spread beneath half of the aircraft, and a poker game started. For those who wanted to lose their money faster, there was a game of craps, a dice game. It went through lunchtime and into the late afternoon.

When word came down, "Mission scrubbed," we were told it was because of bad weather, but scuttlebutt had it that our big brass was still in Kharkov with the Russians, partying. I am sure, if that were correct, it definitely was not because our officers wanted it that way. The truth is, the Russians just loved to drink that national drink, vodka, and our officers were forced to stay and drink with them.

Anyway, I was glad for another peaceful night. I wrote some letters to Mom and Eleta, thinking I could mail them at our next destination, which still had not been revealed. There was still this gnawing in my head that Eleta needed me, and here I was halfway around the world, with no way to get in touch with her. I finally pushed it to the back of my brain, thinking it must be because I was homesick. Yeah, you got that right, I was really homesick!

After dark, I went outside our bunker to the latrine. There were several men standing around talking. It was a dark night, and it was very difficult to move around. The sky was beautiful, and all the stars I had learned by name were very bright, and I felt as though I were looking at the sky from home. The same stars that pass overhead at home pass overhead here every night. I learned to trust them, and I learned to love them. I was hooked on astronomy since I was a small boy. The darkness of the Russian sky allowed me to see stars, planets, and galaxies I had not seen with the naked eye since I was twelve years old. Light pollution in the United States has made it almost impossible to seriously study the night sky. What a shame that generations of young people will never see the splendor of the night sky. I went to sleep thinking about the very clear sky and hoping that someday, I could own my very own telescope.

Saturday, June 24, 1944

We were up early with the same alert as yesterday, but this time the rumor was that we were really going. I wrote down in my logbook some of the things that we had seen while in Russia, knowing that trying to remember them later would be difficult. By far, the worst memory was the sight of all those B17s, smashed, crumpled, and still smoking at Poltava. It far outweighs all of the good things we saw, and I, for one, was ready to get gone. It was not to be, however, and once more we spent the night.

Sunday, June 25, 1944

We were called to a briefing in a burned-out building with only two walls standing and no roof. A large map of Europe hung on one of the walls. The briefing officers told us we would fly to Poltava to refuel, reload with 12 250-pound bombs, and fly to our mission target at Drohobycz, Poland. We would fly along the 50th parallel, bomb a large oil refinery, fly southwestward across the Carpathian Mountains, through the eastern tip of Czechoslovakia, along the eastern part of Hungary, across Yugoslavia and the Adriatic Sea, to our next stop at Foggia, Italy. Wow! We were going to cover a lot of ground.

I must pause here, for a short time, in the writing of this book concerning the events surrounding our 390th Bomb Group. It would be a terrible injustice not to tell you at least what I saw and know of the third group of planes on our famous shuttle mission.

That third group of planes were 68 P51s of the 8th Air Force, 4th Fighter Group, and the 486th Squadron of the 352nd Fighter Group that were our escorts. The nucleus of the 4th Fighter Group came from the famous Eagle Squadron of the RAF (Royal Air Force), composed of American pilots who volunteered to fight with England before America had joined the fight in the war against Germany.

The Americans in the RAF ES were well trained, cocky, fearless, and spoiled. They could not go anywhere without being recognized as heroes. In pubs and eating places, they could not buy a drink or meal. People on the street would put things like theater tickets in their hands before they could be thanked, and the English girls adored them.

When America joined the war, they were transferred to the Fourth and Fifty-sixth Fighter Groups, and there began a long and fierce rivalry between these two groups to see who would have the best record of German planes destroyed. The Fourth was led by Lieutenant Colonel Donald J. M. Blakeslee (the Eagles), and the 56th by Colonel Hubert "Hub" Zemke (the Wolfpack).

Early in the war when there were few aces (five kills) and the number of Germans shot down was less than one hundred, Colonel

Blakeslee set a goal for the Fourth Fighter Group at an unbelievable number of one thousand. In April 1943, with exceptional pilots like Colonel Don Blakeslee, Major James Goodson, First Lieutenant Ralph "Kid" Hoffer, Major Duane Beeson, Lieutenant Chelsey Peterson, Captain Howard "Deacon" Hively, and many more, they became the Red-Nosed Mustangs the German Luftwaffe feared most.

Exploits of these legendary pilots would fill many books, and have. One of the bravest of these men had to be First Lieutenant Ralph "the Kid" Hoffer, a true rebel who knew no fear. At the dismay of his commanders, he would go off on his own, taking it to the Germans. He was known to attack twenty-five to thirty Germans alone and lived to record it with his plane's cameras. He had twenty-seven confirmed kills. He was last seen flying into formations of from one hundred to two hundred Me109s over Budapest. His body and dog tags were found, and he was buried in Hungary. I would be willing to bet he took some of those Me109s with him. This all happened while the shuttle run was in Italy. The Eighth Air Force pilots were on a bombing mission to Budapest, Hungary. The Fifteenth Air Force was flying the mission and asked the hotshot pilots of the Eighth to go along and show the Fifteenth how it was done. The Eighth pilots replied, "Let's go." We found out that missions with the Fifteenth were every bit as rough as those of the Eighth.

The shuttle mission to Russia was a true test for fighter pilots. Colonel Blakeslee told them in briefing, "Do not engage the Germans and do not drop your wing tanks until we have crossed the Polish border. If you do, just turn around and head for England. The escorts for the bombers bombing Berlin will do the fighting. Our task is to protect the bombers on the shuttle."

For the shuttle run, it was necessary for everyone to get immunization shots and boosters. One of the Fourth Fighter Group's hottest aces with twenty-seven kills was First Lieutenant Ralph Hoffer, nicknamed Kid. A real hotshot pilot, flying a P51 he named Missouri Kid, refused to get his shots, and finally, Colonel Blakeslee ordered him to take the shots or miss the shuttle mission. He refused, but on the day we were to leave, he changed his mind, got his shots, and begged Blakeslee to go. His record was so good and the group really needed his leadership, but it had been settled. The best Blakeslee could offer was an alternate position in case someone aborted. Lieutenant Hoffer followed the group, hoping someone would drop out. On over into Germany, he finally got his chance. One of the planes had trouble, and you would think Hoffer would behave, but no, off he went on his own and, running short on fuel, landed in Kiev, Russia. No one would have ever known, except the Russians thought he might have been a German and telegraphed England to verify that he was who he said he was.

After flying 7 1/2 hours and 1,600 miles, the fighters found their landing site and were within one minute of their scheduled arrival time, a truly remarkable feat. Imagine yourself, sitting in the same position, in cramped quarters, your shoulders pressing each side of the cockpit for over seven hours. The Russians had no radio beacons for them to home in on, and believe me, Russia is one huge country. Speaking of a needle in a Russian haystack, this was it. How they found that base was amazing.

Volumes could be written of their experiences, but suffice it to say they were the greatest bunch of guys to ever put on a uniform, and I would not be writing this account had it not been for them. Thanks again, "little friends."

When we arrived at Poltava, Ray was on the intercom. "Okay, boys, listen up. We are going to land, fill up with fuel and bombs, and move out. I don't want anyone to leave the plane."

We landed smoothly, and once again, we saw the terrible destruction wrought by the Germans, even though ground crews were already salvaging useable parts. After we were gone, these parts would be used to save as many planes as possible.

Our load was so heavy, I could tell Ray and George were very worried about getting airborne, but GOOD-O-YANK performed perfectly. We headed due west, dead on the fiftieth parallel to near the Polish city of Lvov, five hundred miles away. Turning sharply southwestward, we quickly came to our target at Drohobycz, Poland. It is strange that this place has so many different spellings. The official spelling in US records books says Drohobyz; the maps we carried, Drohobycz; and the encyclopedia says Drogabych. It is a wonder we found the target, but find it we did and plastered it, with just a few bursts of flak. As we turned off the bomb run, we headed almost due south and could look back and see great domes of black smoke rising to twenty thousand feet.

We very soon crossed into Czechoslovakia, and our mission, as planned and clearly outlined on our maps, determined that we would fly an almost straight line to Foggia, Italy. However, our mission commander, Colonel Olds, began to change our route. You will remember that our high brass was partying with the Russians in Kharkov. They finally broke away, just in time to get poured into the lead plane, piloted by Captain Moylan Smith. Colonel Olds had to be helped into the plane and into the copilot's seat, according to an account by Lieutenant Colonel Marshall B. Shore, who was the task force lead navigator. Colonel Shore stated that shortly thereafter, Colonel Olds was in complete command of all his faculties and took command.

Neal Payden, our navigator, told our pilot, Ray Strate, that it looked like we were not following the flight plan, and I was able to determine by radio navigation that we were, indeed, off course. Neal and Ray decided that there was nothing to do but follow our leader. We were substantially off course and heading west toward Budapest, Hungary. According to Lieutenant Colonel Shore, he attempted to contact Colonel Olds to tell him they were off course, but was told his earphones were disconnected. Before reaching Budapest, we turned sharply south, and before long, it was determined we were way off course to the left of our flight plan and headed for Belgrade, Yugoslavia. It seems that Colonel Olds was just wanting to get a look at these two world-famous cities. After a near flyby of Belgrade, we were put on a beeline course for Foggia, flying almost directly over Sarajevo, Bosnia. It seemed as if we were shot at by a lone antiaircraft gun on every mountain we crossed. They were not accurate, but we were uncomfortable because we were flying much lower than normal and off oxygen. From the tops of these mountains, they could have hit us with a slingshot.

The sun was shining brightly, and someone up in the nose of the plane came on the intercom, "My, gosh, look at that." I scrambled to my window and looked as far forward as I could. Then, looking down, I saw it. As we roared out over the Adriatic Sea, the water was a color I had never seen before, a clear, transparent dark blue. It was breathtaking, and I said, "Someday I am coming back here with Butch for the honeymoon we never got."

There were a number of fairly large islands not far off the coast of Croatia or Dalmatia or whatever they call it now. They were beautifully green, with sandy beaches. It looked like a picture postcard and reminded me of my old haunting grounds at Myrtle Beach, South Carolina.

HOTEL BAIA DELLE ZAGARE, PROBOSCIS BEACH, FOGGIA, ITALY.

PROBOSCIS BEACH, FOGGIA, ITALY.

AMAZING...PROBOSCIS BEACH, FOGGIA, ITALY.

We were now down to about two thousand feet, and we felt like we could dip our feet in the water. As a matter of fact, that is just what a number of officers were thinking, just before we softly touched down on a very nice airfield called Foggia Main, in Italy. I thought, *Now what new adventures can we expect here?*

To give you an idea of where Foggia, Italy, is located, looking at a map of Italy, the whole country is shaped like a giant boot…a boot with a cowboy heel. Just above the heel of the boot, at about where the ankle is located, there is a large spur protruding into the Adriatic Sea. It is called the Gargano Promontory, or great protrusion. Foggia is located just below this spur, about twenty-five miles from the Adriatic Sea. It is a large flat valley, perfectly suited for growing oranges, grapes, and olives. It is an ideal location for an airfield.

Foggia is a base for the Fifteenth Air force, with B17s, B24s, and P38 fighters, and their headquarters at Bari, just one hundred miles south on the Adriatic. In the summer months, it is hot as blazes. Arriving here the last week in June was unbelievable. We stepped off our plane in sheepskin-lined leather flying suits, with heated suits and long johns, and the temperature was ninety-six degrees in the shade. It did not take us long to peel off most of our clothes and to look for something cooler. Thankfully, the Fifteenth AF loaned us enough summer wear for our short stay.

The commissioned officers were taken to officers' quarters in a local hotel, while the rest of us were trucked away to tent city. There was, of course, no air-conditioning, but very fortunately, there was a large latrine with wonderfully hot showers.

The tents were of the semipermanent variety, wooden up to waist high and canvas over the rest. We were assigned to a tent with strict instructions that it must be cleaned daily, before we left to go anywhere.

We all thought the food was excellent but weren't sure as we had not had a decent meal since we left England.

After dinner that first night in Italy, we were advised that security for our plane would be furnished for that night, but someone from our crew would have to stay with our plane twenty-four hours a day for as long as we were there. It seemed, the local Italians, particularly young boys, would make off with anything that was not nailed down.

First things first. We were sent to the dispensary. Maggie said, "What are we here for, another shot?" The medic said, "No! You are here to be deloused." "How are you going to do that?" said Steve. "First, you must take a hot shower," he said, giving us a towel and a bar of soap. As we came out of the shower, the medic met us carrying a five-gallon bucket and, as soon as we were dry enough, doused us with a white powder from head to toe.

There we were, naked as the day we were born, with white powder, like flour, that stuck to every nook, cranny, and crease. I looked at Maggie and Sandy, and they looked like two white ghosts. Pretty soon, we were all dancing around and laughing like idiots. I had that stuff in my nose, my mouth, and my ears, but, I think the corporal medic had the most fun just watching us. If there had been anyone with a camera close by, I am sure we would have killed him. The medic laughed as he went out of sight, saying, "It will wear off in a few days." Maggie said, "What the heck, I am glad to get rid of those Russian lice."

Ray and Neal came by early to check on us and to tell us that we would not be flying for at least a few days. We were free to go into Foggia if we liked, but one of us would have to stay and guard the plane. Sandy volunteered, so now, the rest were on our own until midnight Sunday.

We all dressed and headed for the shuttle bus to town. First, we stopped by headquarters to pick up our passes that Ray had arranged for us. Those who were not so fortunate were left to fend for themselves.

Stepping off the bus in Foggia, we were in no way prepared for what we saw. Here was a city desperately impoverished by years of war. Mussolini had taken all of her young men and drained the country of all industry. There were no horses or cows; these people were living on the barest of food. The city was dirty, no, filthy. With no shame, old men used the streets to urinate.

We walked the dirty streets up and down. There were very few shops, and most business was conducted in open markets, where the only meat we saw was fish. We found no restaurants, nor cafés, nor drugstores. The only thing we found to eat was loaf bread, sold along the streets, from small hand-drawn two-wheel carts. The bread was stacked like cordwood with no wrapping, and we found when we bought a loaf, the outside crust was as hard as a rock. You could swing it like a baseball bat and knock someone unconscious. But surprise, surprise, it was very good. We bought more, and that was our lunch. Now, we were thirsty and had been warned, under no circumstances were we to drink the water. In Italy, there is no age limit on consumption of wine and spirits. To the contrary, children are introduced to drinking wine mixed with water, as the water is unsanitary. Since I didn't drink wine, several others and I were between a rock and a hard place. We finally stopped at a hotel that sold bottled water which, according to them, had been purified. We took a chance, and although it did not taste good, it served the purpose and we did not get sick.

By early afternoon, we had seen all the statues and fountains we could stand. (The Italians are big on statues and fountains, very big.) We caught the bus back to the base in plenty of time before the mess hall closed. The chow that evening was *very good* for some reason.

Tuesday, June 27, 1944

We slept late, except for Steve. He had guard duty for our plane. The mess hall had closed, but we had crackers, cheese, and peanut butter that we had stashed for such emergencies. Fortunately for us, this base had a PX, and we loaded up.

Word came down that there would be no flying, at least through Wednesday, July 1. The scuttlebutt was that our mission commander and a few others had flown down to Africa to formulate our next move. We decided to forget about going in to Foggia and, instead, go over to the beautiful Adriatic Sea to swim and lie in the sun. We arranged passes and this time got some good advice from the base permanent party about where to go. They suggested a small village called Mattinata, on the Gargano Promontory. It was only thirty-two miles from Foggia, and we were there in an hour. Following the suggestion of the Foggia permanent party, we checked into a small, but very clean, hotel. Built on a high cliff overlooking the beautiful Adriatic Sea, it had an elevator, used to get down to the white sand beach. It was wartime, however, and it was not working. Even so, it was not too bad to climb the stairs, and the hotel furnished beach chairs and umbrellas. The umbrellas turned out to be a godsend because by 10:00 a.m., it was hot as blazes. For a small fee, the hotel also furnished bottled water and Chianti wine. Man, we had found heaven in Italy. The beach water was bathtub warm, with almost no waves, and you could wade out one hundred yards before the water got over your head. There were very few people, and time stood still. War? What war?

At lunch, we climbed the stairs and had lunch in the hotel restaurant. We ate spaghetti (what else) and watched the boats, large and small, way offshore.

The hotel had never heard of sunscreen and suggested we use virgin olive oil, which worked quite well. It did not, however, keep us from getting burned.

That evening, after a wonderful day on the beach, we again ate at the hotel restaurant. This time we chose the local fish, which looked like snapper. The fish was cooked whole, with the eyes looking up at you, much like the Russians served it. I could not eat the head, but I sure ate everything else.

That evening, we walked all over the village. With its whitewashed homes and red tile roofs, it looked more like a painting than a reality. It was a truly beautiful place, and the people were extremely nice.

Friday, June 30, 1944

After another morning on the beach, we headed back to Foggia and the war. I failed to write down the name of the little hotel in my diary, thinking that I surely would never forget it. As best I can recall, it was the Hotel Baia Delle Zagare[2]. If you are ever in this part of the world, look it up; you will be glad you did.

The weather was clear and hot, around one hundred degrees. So hot that the daily softball game was postponed until nearly sundown. All motion seemed to grind to a halt. The only activity still going on was the eternal poker game. The serious players seemed to never quit, and some players were broke but still playing with loans greater than their next six months' salary. I could watch for a little while, but it broke my heart to see some of those young boys, forever losing but still going. *It is a disease.*

I once knew a man whom I liked very much, who sold Bear Mfg. Company auto-frame-straightening equipment, and was the best poker player I ever heard of. His name was R. M. "Miller" Mitchell, and he was a member of every club in Charlotte, North Carolina, the Kiwanis, the Moose, the Elks, the JCs, the Eagles, and some I have forgotten. He would play every day and into the night for huge stakes and, most often, won. He once played a man for all the money he had, then his automobile, and, finally, his home and won. He didn't have the heart to take the man's home, but he took everything else.

Mitch had a son, named Jack, who joined the Air Force, and guess what, he was flying P51s out of England with the Eighth Air Force. I keep feeling as though I will somehow run into him.

---

[2] Image from booking.com website

Saturday, July 1, 1944

Still hot as blazes, we just kept looking for a cool spot to pass the day. Harvey Burr had guard duty today and tonight. They said it is awful lonely out on the airfield by yourself at night, in that big bird, that made all kinds of weird noises as it cooled down. I guess I would find out soon as my time was coming up. At least I had a big advantage. I knew how to turn on the switches and listen to my radios, get the news, and hear the music. I liked to listen to the German propaganda stations. They always played the latest American pop music and some of their own. I think I have mentioned that I really liked their "Lilly of the Lamplight, By the Garden Gate." It was so sad and mournful and made me think of home.

I FLEW IN A P38 AND LIVED TO TELL THE STORY: A WILD, WILD RIDE

We heard through the grapevine of a really great way to beat the heat on these hot days. The word was that every day a modified P38 went out on a weather patrol. Most of the radio equipment had been removed, and in its space, just behind the pilot, a second seat had been installed. Every day, for a price, the pilot would take someone along. Man, oh, man, this was right down my alley. As I have mentioned before, my greatest ambition in life was to fly a fighter plane.

I began to inquire how I might get in line for this once-in-a-lifetime ride. I had no idea that I might be chosen. The truth is that there were very few wanting to take advantage of this great offer. "What is wrong with you bunch of sissies?" But they all thought I had lost my mind.

Sunday, July 2, 1944

The officer of the day put me in touch with the pilot, who informed me that I was very lucky. He had just gotten a cancellation from a man who was in the infirmary. I was to bring forty dollars American at 0900 hours on Monday, July 3, and meet him at the weather shack. Holy mackerel, how lucky could a man get? I was so excited, I could not believe it. Here, I had made all these arrangements and had forgotten we might be flying a mission. Another important fact was that I only had five dollars to my name. I went straight to Ray and told him this was the chance of a lifetime, and could I please go? He laughed and said, "Boy, you sure are happed up on this, aren't you?" I said, "I sure am, and I will pull double guard duty if you will get it okayed." He said, "I will let you know, Chuck." I was on cloud nine until late that afternoon when the mission alert flag went up. Our squadron was scheduled to fly. Of all the rotten luck, tears came in my eyes when they told me, and I was so disappointed, I didn't even go to chow.

While the others had gone to the mess hall, I was lying on my bunk, feeling sorry for myself, when someone called out, "Chuck, are you in there?" I jumped up, opened the flap to our tent, and there was Ray. I said, "Yes, sir?" He said, "I have some bad news and some good news. The bad news is we are scheduled to fly a mission tomorrow." He hesitated and then, with a broad grin, said, "But, I have begged off, and our crew is not flying." I could have kissed that big ugly guy. He said, "Do you need any money?" I replied, "I sure do. I need thirty-five dollars," and he loaned it to me, saying, "You go and have a good time, but if you go and get yourself killed, I'll have you court-martialed." I said, "Thank you, sir, I will never forget you for this."

Harvey Burr and I decided to go to church, which was nondenominational Protestant. They had a tiny little organ; we sang some familiar hymns, and I really got homesick. I still had it in my mind that something was wrong at home, and it really bothered me. After the service, I talked with a lieutenant from Johnson City, Tennessee. He told me that he felt that everything at home was fine and to stop worrying about it, but he agreed to see if there was any way to check about my family through the Red Cross. I really did appreciate his doing that for me and felt a lot better. I spent the afternoon writing letters. I misplaced that chaplain's name, but I will never forget his kindness.

Monday, July 3, 1944

I was at the appointed place, thirty minutes early, on a bright morning, with not a cloud in the sky. I was so excited, my feet were barely touching the ground.

First Lieutenant Jeffrey Dugan[3] introduced himself and said, "Follow me." As we walked to the silver P38J sitting on the tarmac, he asked me if I had ever flown in a fighter before, and I said, "No, sir, but I have always wanted to. I applied for fighter pilot training, but was told that because of astigmatism in my eyes, my request was denied." "Do you think you will be afraid?" he asked. I said, "No, sir, I am ready!" "Have you ever been airsick?" "No, sir, flying seems to agree with me." I'll swear, I saw him grin, and he had a twinkle in his eye.

When we got to the plane, he walked completely around it, looking closely at different places to be sure everything was okay. Then, he stopped and said, "Two things, I have a plastic bag by your seat, and if you feel the least bit nauseous, use the bag. I don't want you throwing up all over me. Second, there is a seat chute in your seat. Put it on as soon as you get in the plane, and should we, for any reason, have to bail out, I will put the plane on its back. Just release your seat belt and remember to pull the rip cord." "Why do you turn on your back?" He replied, "The way the P38 is made, the horizontal stabilizer goes all the way across." The P38 is a twin-engine plane with a fuselage behind each engine, while the cockpit and pilot are housed in a compartment between the two fuselages. The lieutenant explained that if you were to exit the plane flying upright, the tail of the plane would surely catch and, probably, cut the jumper in half.

Hey, wait a minute! Why is this guy telling me all this stuff? I was not afraid, but I was beginning to get a little concerned. A flight sergeant hauled out a stepladder and told me to climb in. He then climbed up to help me get strapped in, and just as he was climbing

---

[3] Fictitious name used to protect the pilot from possible violation charges by the Army.

down, he asked, "Is your life insurance paid up?" and smiled. Were these guys trying to psych me out or what?

Lieutenant Dugan climbed aboard, and as he adjusted his flying helmet, I caught a glimpse of red hair. I thought, *Uh-oh, a redheaded Irishman hotshot.* I said to myself, "Self, it is too late to change your mind now. Just go and have a great flight."

He wasted no time after the engines were cranked. He called, advising he was ready for takeoff. They came right back, "Roger, Humpback Camel, Runway 26, winds southwest at 15, clear to go." With that, I was immediately pinned to the seat as those 2 1,225-horsepower Allison engines blasted off. Very soon we were moving faster than I had ever moved in my life. Lieutenant Dugan kept the plane on the runway until almost the last moment. Then, he pulled back on the controls, and the plane literally leaped off the ground; he pointed the nose upward at about a 45-degree angle. At 5,000 feet, the plane began a slow roll. After about 10 turns, I became disoriented and could not tell if we were upright or not. The wind rushing by the plane was whistling a mournful sound, and my stomach was doing flip-flops. I reached for my mike to tell Lieutenant Dugan to please slow things down a little, but found he could not hear me. As we raced through the sky, twisting and turning, I screamed out, "Slow it down," but to no avail. From spiraling upward, we leveled off, only to go into deep turning and twisting dives at what seemed like tremendous speeds. I was shouting, "What are you, some kind of devilish idiot? I can't stand this." My face would be flushed, then all of a sudden as we came out of a dive, the blood would drain out of my head. I was praying, "Dear God, just get me out of this contraption. Sweet Jesus, stop this maniac while I still have my mind and body." There is no roller coaster ever made or ever will be made that can approach the wild maneuvering of this satanic invention. If I could only reach this devil, I would twist his head off. He was trying to wring me out and doing a very good job of it.

My eyes were spinning, my nose was running, my mouth was dry, and my ears were humming. I was nauseous to the point of throwing up, and my fanny was chewing up my parachute. I did not know whether I was upside down or sideways. I was weightless for long periods and felt as though I weighed a thousand pounds at others. There were times when it was impossible to lift one finger, never mind my hand or arm.

As quickly as it began, I felt a snap, and it all stopped. He had snapped the plane from an upside-down position to upright. I gathered enough courage to look up and everything was beautiful again. Lieutenant Dugan turned his head to one side, held up his headphone cord, and motioned for me to plug mine in. His voice came through, loud and clear. "You doing okay?" I said, "Sir, I thought you were trying to separate my body parts." He laughed. "I thought you wanted to be a fighter pilot!" All I could do was shake my head.

"That's the Mediterranean down there, and all those ships are ours." From twenty thousand feet, they looked like play toys, but there were literally thousands of them.

Lieutenant Dugan remarked, "We have to stay at altitude to get the weather readings they need, but on the way home, we will drop down so you can get a good look. That is Sicily on your right, and you can see Mount Vesuvius in the distance. You will see it better on your way home." My faculties were finally coming back, and I was really beginning to enjoy it. Lieutenant Dugan flipped me a candy bar. "That's your lunch." With a wicked little grin, he said, "You went through that pretty well. Did you say you had never had any pilot training?" "No, sir!"

"We will be flying over Sardinia dead ahead, with Corsica on your right." The water was a brilliant turquoise. Flying low and level, we headed straight for Spain, then turned southwest toward Africa. Flying was now the joy of my life again. We crossed into Africa near Algiers, over the Atlas Mountains, and even at this height, I knew I didn't want to go there. Everything was brown and dry.

Back out over the Mediterranean on a beeline for Turkey, clouds up to thirty thousand feet were closing in. We turned north and east to fly back toward Italy, over Greece, and were dropping down as we went. We crossed Greece, near Athens, and this area was so bright and beautiful. I made a mental note to someday come back and see this place from ground level. The snow-white houses with red tile roofs, set on the hills along the coast, were like a painting.

As we neared Italy, flying low over the Adriatic, Lieutenant Dugan said, "We will be back in Foggia in a few minutes, and I wanted to show you the Adriatic up close." And with that, he flipped the plane over on its back and flew low level for a view I will never forget.

"Foggia Main, this is Humpback Camel, request landing instructions." "Roger, Humpback Camel, Runway 26, winds at 16, clear to land." And, it was over. I hopped down from that wonderful airplane, happy as a child who had gotten everything he wanted for Christmas. Lieutenant Dugan asked, "Well, Chuck, how was it?" I didn't know at first whether to kill him or kiss him, but my joy overruled, and I thanked him over and over.

Back in our tent area, I talked with my crew. They wanted to know how I liked it and what it was like. I told them it was wonderful, and to best describe the aerobatics, I borrowed a description of another sergeant who had gotten the same treatment. He said, "It was like someone had inserted an eggbeater in his heinie and a madman was turning the crank." I could not describe it better than that.

I wanted to know about the mission our group had flown today, along with several groups from the Fifteenth Air Force. They told me that fifty-seven B17s, escorted by forty-two P51s flew a mission to Arad, Romania, bombing railroad marshalling yards, with excellent results. We lost one B17 to flak, and it was a crew we knew well. I thought to myself, how lucky for me, flying around, having a ball, while our friends were being shot down. It was a sad night. I hate writing letters home when I am sad and down because I can't hide my feelings, and I do not want to worry my wife, Eleta or Mom. I was still concerned about something being wrong at home.

I thought to myself and I mentioned it to Harvey, "How can it be that I had a mountaintop experience today, absolutely thrilled flying in that P38 Lightning, and then tonight, be utterly in the dumps over losing our friends?" Harvey said, "Try not to worry, get some sleep. Things always look better tomorrow." I tried to unravel that advice in my head until I fell asleep.

Tuesday, July 4, 1944

"Good morning, Chuck, it is 0500, and guess what?" I rolled over and said, "What?" The duty sergeant said, "Your day and night in the barrel to babysit the Good-O-Yank." "Thanks a lot, Sarge. I'll try to do something nice for you sometime." He said, "Don't forget to go by the mess hall and get something to eat and drink to last you through the night." "Okay, Sarge, now go harass somebody else." He laughed. Sometimes he really enjoyed his job.

While I was out joyriding in a P38, the rest of our crew had planned a trip to Naples today, and I truly would have liked to go. Naples is one of Italy's famous cities, with nearby Pompeii and, still smoking, Mount Vesuvius. It was not to be, and I had really had enough excitement yesterday to last me a long while. But, fate can rise up and kick you in the tail, as I am about to reveal. What could possibly go awry guarding an airplane?

I had planned tuning in to local and long-distance radio stations and writing to Eleta; Mom and Dad; my little brother, Preston; my older brother, Eddie, in the Navy in (God bless him) Honolulu, Hawaii; my Aunt Louise Booker; and my Aunt Janet Hamby; plus a few others. So, my day would go quickly. Oh, yeah!

"Have fun in Naples, boys, and don't let Vesuvius get you." "Yeah, sport, and don't you let anyone steal our plane."

Everything was quiet on the flight line as I climbed aboard Good-O-Yank. Our plane number was 2102673, and she was gorgeous, bright silver, and still smelled new, like a new car. She had completed fifteen missions and now felt like home. When our crew climbed aboard, it was like she came to life; we were all like one, with each part dependent upon the others.

I snapped on the light above my radio compartment desk, looked up, and there was Butch (Eleta), looking down at me, and a chill ran up my spine. "Hi, honey, I'm worried about you. Please be okay."

I went through the bomb bay, dark as pitch and kind of spooky, and into the cockpit to turn on the main switch so I could listen to the radio. I looked out the pilot's window, and as far as I could see, there were long rows of B17s. It was just beginning to get light, and nothing was stirring.

Sitting in the pilot's seat, I pretended I was taking off on a mission, going through the preflight check off, revving the engines, taxiing to the runway, turning on to the runway, full throttle forward, releasing brake pedal, watching the air speed indicator, racing down the runway, near the end of the runway, easing back on the controls, feeling the easy liftoff. I had watched Ray so many times, I believed I could fly this big bird.

Back to reality, I watched the sun come up from over the Adriatic and dreamed of home. I went back to the radio compartment, picked up my tablet, turned on my radio, and listened to the BBC (British Broadcasting System) and the news. Allied forces were making progress, but very slowly. Will this war never end? Back to the pilot's seat, where I wrote letters to everyone I could think of.

Near 1200 hours, I decided to take my lunch outside and sat on the ground, under the wing. A jeep came by with two British soldiers. They stopped and invited me to come over to their position, about fifty yards away. It was an antiaircraft unit, dug in with camouflage nets over their bunker. I gave them C and K rations, and they gave me tea and biscuits (a hard cookie). We talked of war and home. One of the soldiers was from Cambridge, very near our base at Framlingham. He told me he used to go fishing in the English Channel, not far from our base.

I really enjoyed my short visit with them and told them I would be in jolly old England in a few days. They were teary-eyed at the thought, but being British, they bravely showed a stiff upper lip. I can tell you that they were one group of very homesick boys.

I hurried back to the plane because the sky was getting black toward the west, and it looked like a summer storm was coming. I had just gotten into the plane when the thunder and lightning began, and again I settled down in the pilot's seat. I watched as the storm got closer and the wind began to shake the plane. Then, the full fury of the storm unfolded right over the top of the airfield. It was a horrible storm, and the wind shook the plane and seemed to pick it up right off the ground. Did I feel the plane moving? Just my imagination. The lightning was everywhere, and the thunder boomed, amplified by being inside the metal plane, like being inside a bass drum. I was afraid to touch anything. Yes! I did feel the plane move! What is going on here? I put both feet on the brake pedal, but nothing seemed to stop the plane from rolling. Oh, no! I was heading right for a group of B17s, which did not seem to be moving. I could see it now, plowing into three or four planes and wrecking them all. The plane was actually lifting and bouncing. Everything that was not nailed down came blowing down. It was like a tornado, and what seemed like hours was no more than thirty minutes. It died down, and in thirty minutes it was gone. There I was, almost touching another B17, and turned ninety degrees and two hundred feet from where I was originally parked.

Apparently, the control tower saw what was happening and sent a maintenance truck to drag the Good-O-Yank back to its assigned position. I don't mind admitting and am not ashamed to say that experience "scared my mule," an old Southern expression meaning, I was scared to death.

I never told Ray that we almost lost Good-O-Yank, not in combat, but just sitting on the Foggia airfield, minding her own business.

A jeep raced up to the rear hatch, and someone was banging. "Hey, Sarge, wake up, open up." I was hurrying back through the bomb bay, the radio room, and the waist windows to the hatchway. "What the heck could they want?" What started out as a peaceful day had turned into anything but. I flung open the hatch, and there, all excited, was a corporal who said, "Get your stuff and come with me. The 390th is alerted to fly in the morning." I said, "Who is going to stay with our plane?" He replied, "Don't worry about it. They are on the way." He took me and others back to the tent area and went back for more. I didn't tell anyone, but I was glad my guard duty was cut short.

Our crew came straggling in from their trip to Naples, all talking at the same time about what they had seen. They were excited to find we were alerted to fly. They asked, "How were things here?" I answered, matter-of-factly, "Oh, fine, nothing much happens around here."

Wednesday, July 5, 1944

We were awakened very early, told to have chow in thirty minutes and report back to our tent area to tear down our beds, turn in our bedding, clean our tent, and be ready for briefing in one hour.

Well, that was final; we were leaving, and it would be bittersweet because we had become accustomed to the warm weather and sunshine. But, it was good to know we were going back to Framlingham to get on with our missions and go home.

Indeed, the briefing officer drew back the curtain, and we all squealed when it showed the last leg of our shuttle mission ending back in England. The mission would be a long one, flying from Foggia, Italy, across Italy, out over the Tyrrhenian Sea, over the island of Corsica, the Ligurian Sea, along the south coast of France, over the Gulf of Lion, making landfall very near the border of Spain, to our target at Beziers, France. Then, on a beeline across France to the English Channel, to the south coast of England, and straight up the coast to Framlingham.

Everyone was in good spirits. Sandy was humming and whistling, "Rose of San Antone," and for a quiet guy, he set the mood for the rest of us. We were going home.

It was well after sunup when we climbed aboard the Good-O-Yank, and I checked the list of our previous missions. This would be our mission number 16. Wow, only nineteen left, but wait, we haven't gotten to England yet.

After takeoff, we circled the airfield to get into formation and gain enough altitude to get over the Apennine Mountains. Once over the mountains, we flew straight to Rome. Looking down on that ancient city that was truly beautiful from the air, I thought of the once mighty Roman Empire and their dictator, Julius Caesar, thinking also of how Christians were slaughtered by humans and wild animals. Caesar thought he could rule the world, only to be killed by his supposed best friend. You would think the Italian people would learn, but not so. Along comes Benito Mussolini, only to be crushed again. We saw Rome in bright sunlight, and it glistened with its Vatican City.

Leaving Rome, we flew across the top of Corsica, not far from the isle of Elbe, where again I was reminded of another infamous dictator, Napoleon Bonaparte. Bonaparte set out to conquer the world and did a pretty good job of it until he, too, was squashed. He spent several years in exile on the isle of Elbe, only to escape back to France. He proceeded to collect eighty thousand men to take over France, only to be defeated at the Battle of Waterloo.

Now only Hitler was left, and we could feel the tide of battle quickly turning, but there was still a lot to be done.

BRITISH SUPERMARINE SPITFIRE.

As we neared the coast of France, with the city of Nice to our north, we turned to fly along the beautiful south coast of France… ah, the French Riviera in brilliant sunlight under French blue skies.

We flew by beautiful beaches with palm trees, the playground of millionaires with their million-dollar yachts. We flew by Saint Tropez, Cannes, and Monte Carlo, home of Prince Rainier of Monaco, the country of no taxes. Now heading westward, past Toulon, past thousands of ships and boats, very close to Marseille. We could actually see the invasion of France from the south about to begin. That was the purpose of our target at Beziers, which is about 50 miles north of Spain. We lined up on the train marshaling yards with little antiaircraft fire and no fighters. Bombing results were excellent, and the target was destroyed. We dropped 183 tons of bombs and had no losses.

Beziers, France, has a little-known distinction. It is the home of Pierre-Paul Riquet, who spent his entire life and fortune on the wildest idea of his time. He proposed connecting the Atlantic Ocean and the Mediterranean Sea by digging a canal. Everyone thought he was crazy, but one year after he died, the canal was completed, and literally, thousands of small boats and cruise ships still use this wonderful waterway, the Canal du Midi.

We turned directly north, past Toulouse, through the center of France, past Tours, LeMans, and Paris off to our right, over the battlefields, and exited France at Dieppe. Flying across the English Channel, high above the hundreds of barrage balloons protecting the English coast, we made landfall over Brighton on the southeast coast. With London off to our left, we were escorted by British Spitfires, diving, twisting, and turning as if to say, "Welcome home." We continued up the east coast to (at last) Framlingham. I think our mission commanders had planned to buzz the field, but by the time we got there, everyone was so tired, we just flew low over the tower and peeled off for a much-awaited landing.

I think the entire base personnel was out to greet us. The Red Cross welcome wagon was there with coffee and doughnuts. There was a lot of commotion, but we were whisked away to debriefing. We skipped chow and went directly to bed. We were so glad to be in our own beds after flying over seven thousand miles.

Thursday, July 6, 1944

We slept 'til noon, went to chow, and went back to bed. The 390th went on a mission to the Pas de Calais area, along with 1,342 bombers and 1,138 fighters. They dropped 3,101 tons of bombs, with the loss of 3 B24s over Kiel, Germany. Our fighters had 15 kills and lost 5 planes.

Friday, July 7, 1944

This day will long be remembered in the history of the 8th Air Force.

My squadron, the 571st, stood down. I suppose it was because we were so very tired from the Russian shuttle mission, but I believe it was the providence of God, at least in my case. By all reason, we should have been flying today. It turned out to be a very deadly mission.

We heard the 390th taking off. In a tin building that magnifies sound, how could we help but hear it, hundreds of B17s, throttles wide open, 4 huge engines on each plane. After they were airborne and struggling to gain altitude, the distant roar of 1,129 heavy bombers and 756 fighters gradually lessened during the next hour. Then the sound was gone, and it got graveyard quiet.

We didn't learn of their mission until late that evening when the roar began again from far off. The ground crews had assembled in the grassy areas near the runway, and the sound began to build as the planes got closer. We then saw the red flares (wounded aboard), and the ambulances and fire trucks came up. The sound grew so great, you could not think, and the ground trembled as they made a pass over the field. The planes with the wounded aboard peeled off, landed, and were quickly unloaded, and the planes taxied or were pulled to their parking areas.

We learned that the 2nd Division, with 373 B24s, went to Lutzkendorf, Halle, Aschersleben, and Bernberg. The 2nd dropped 850 tons of bombs on oil storage and aviation plants. We lost 28 B24s, 3 P51s, and 1 P38. There were 126 planes damaged and 274 crewmen missing in action. We shot down 39 enemy aircraft.

The Third Division (my division), we learned, flew to targets in central Germany with 303 B17s and 197 fighters, dropping 516 tons of bombs on oil storage tanks at Bohlin and Merseberg, airfields at Lutzkendorf and Kolleda, and train marshaling yards at Gottingen. We lost 2 B17s, both from our 390th Group, and 20 men MIA, with 112 planes damaged.

The 1st Division, with some airplanes from the 3rd Division, consisting of 453 B17s and 294 fighters, hit oil storage plants, airfields, and train yards in Leipzig, Kolleda, and Nordhousen. Dropping 856 tons of bombs, they lost 7 B17s and 1 P51, with 65 men missing in action and 152 planes damaged.

All told, we lost 43 planes. Bomber crews destroyed 39 German planes, and our fighters shot down 75. In addition, a P51 collided with 3 B17s over Leipzig. A P51 also collided with a Messerschmitt Me210. Two B24s collided with 2 B17s from the 384th Bomb Group over Withersfield, and all were killed.

This was a major mission, deep into the heartland of Der Fuhrer's Germany. The Germans lost 118 fighters, and the brunt of their attack was against the 15th Bomber Wing, of which our 390th Bomb Group was a part. Here again, it was God's will that I not be on that terrible mission, where planes were falling like autumn leaves in a windstorm. I was surely glad I wasn't, as two planes of our group were not so lucky.

Saturday, July 8, 1944

Our 390th Group was alerted to fly, and our crew was chosen to lead the 571st Squadron. The entire 8th Air Force was asked to soften up the German defenses just ahead of our Allied advances.

One thousand twenty-nine heavy bombers and 714 fighters were to bomb bridges, airfields, road junctions, and buzz bomb launch sights, from the Netherlands to Nantes, located close to Spain.

There were 29 different targets. The 1,029 bombers and our group of 24 were assigned to hit an airfield at Conches, France. Well below the Brittany Peninsula, near the large city of Nantes, our target was right on the Atlantic Ocean and more distant than all the other targets.

The 8th Air Force lost 9 bombers and 1 fighter and claimed 20 aircraft destroyed. The total bombload delivered on target was 1,176 tons.

It was a long way back to Framlingham, but uneventful. We wanted to relax and enjoy the ride, but being over enemy territory, we needed to be on constant alert. We found this more tiring than when being attacked.

The tremendous buildup, all along the coast, of American and British forces and equipment was evident everywhere. There was a steady stream of ships of every description. You could just feel that very soon now, there was going to be a horrendous push to break through the German defense, and we, of the 8th Air Force, had most certainly done our part today.

Sunday, July 9, 1944

Due to bad weather over the continent, the 390th did not fly. Only 331 bombers and 441 fighters actually flew missions, all of which were in close support of ground forces. Losses were one B17, one B24, and 3 fighters. Enemy losses were 6 planes destroyed.

Monday, July 10, 1944

The bad weather over the continent forced cancellation of all flights by the 8th Air Force, and that was good news for us. The good news lasted until mail call. All the mail that had been accumulating since our mission to Russia was delivered at once, with large rubber bands around the bundle. I put them in order by date and lay on my bunk for a lazy afternoon of reading. The second letter I opened from Eleta made me sit straight up and shout, "Oh, no." Harvey knew something must be horribly wrong and came to see if there was any way he could help. Everyone in our crew grew very quiet as I read her letter aloud. "Dear Chuck, I know you are busy fighting, but I can no longer keep it from you. Please forgive me for worrying you but, as you know, I have been working in Belk's Dept. Store and, as I was walking between two departments, I tripped and fell, landing on a granite step on my tailbone, and shattering it. I am going to be operated on tomorrow morning at 6 AM and they will remove the last two joints of my spine. As you can imagine, I have been in a lot of pain and the doctor says there is no alternative. I am sorry to tell you this, but I could not wait any longer. I don't know how long I will be in the Charlotte Memorial Hospital, but please write me there until I tell you to stop. Please try not to worry, I am sure everything will be all right." I could not read any more; the tears were streaming down my cheeks, and I could not stop them. Everyone tried to reassure me that everything would be okay, but it didn't seem to help. I gathered up my letters and my writing tablet and went off to be alone.

I stopped by squadron headquarters to see if it were possible to call home. The officer of the day explained that it was just not possible, with literally tens of thousands with problems worse than mine. It would seriously affect important military communication. I told him I understood, but felt I should try something. I even considered going AWOL, but common sense finally ruled. I sat down and wrote letters like crazy. When I gave them to Lieutenant Neal Payden, he said, "Chuck, for gosh sakes." I then explained, and he was so kind and understanding that after talking to him, I felt better. Thanks again, Neal.

Tuesday, July 11, 1944

I woke up as our group took off. We could tell it was a maximum effort by the sounds of hundreds of planes assembling. It was not 'til later that we found they went to bomb Munich, an awful and deadly place. A force of 1,176 B17s and B24s with an escort of 795 fighters took part.

It was not until the planes returned that we found out just how lucky we were, as we lost 20 bombers and 6 fighters. Munich was a tough target, and it was reported that they had some of Germany's best antiaircraft batteries.

Wednesday, July 12, 1944

Eighth Air Force mission number 468. For some reason, known only to God and a very few high people, our 390th was chosen to fly today, but my squadron, the 571st, was ordered to stand down. We were certainly not unhappy to learn we were spared, but couldn't understand why. Particularly, when we found they were going back to Munich. **Great gobs of goat meat!** Not back to that terrible place. We went around all day thanking everyone we could think of for sparing us, still again.

Of 1,402 bombers dispatched by the 8th Air Force, 1,150 were to bomb Munich, again. Another maximum effort, with 2,766 tons of bombs dropped, how could there be anything left? Could it be that we were missing our target? With 803 escort fighters, we could only imagine what it was like…few fighters getting through to our bombers, but unreal and horrendous *flak*. Just as we figured, when the planes came limping back and our wounds were counted, we lost 24 bombers (240 men) and one fighter.

Bad weather caused the bombing to be made by radar, but photos made by Mosquito recon planes, flying under the overcast were good, though still not satisfactory. Munich was so big (over one million) that no matter where bombs were dropped, they were sure to hit something. Our 390th was lucky; we only lost one plane. It was sad to hear that one group had two bombers collide over the target and all were lost.

CHAPTER 13

Mission To Munich

It was Thursday, July 12, 1944. The 390th heavy bomber base at Framlingham, England, was socked in. No way was there going to be a mission tomorrow. Burr (Harvey Burr, right waist gunner), Maggie (Sam McGee, ball turret gunner/armorer), and I, Chuck Richardson (radio operator/gunner), on the B17G GOOD-O-YANK, were sloshing back to our barracks from the mess hall. It had been an unusually good meal, and Burr was teasing Maggie about eating so much, he would not be able to get into the ball turret. It was hard enough for a skinny guy. Believe me, that ball turret, hanging just 34 inches beneath the belly of a B17, was also not the place for anyone with claustrophobia.

As we passed the 571st Squadron headquarters Nissen hut, Maggie stopped walking and said, "Well, I'll be d… Will you look at that?" Burr said, "Maggie, what is wrong with you?" And then I saw it; the red flag was blowing in the half light of late evening. They have scheduled a mission in this soup. It would never clear out of here before morning. Our jolly mood was broken, and we went into our Nissen hut home and broke the news to the rest of our crew.

Steve (Steven Przepiorka, top turret and engineer) said, "Don't worry about it, boys. Even if we do go, it will be an easy milk run, and we will have another one behind us." Good ole Steve, he was just trying to keep our spirits up, or was he just "peeing in the wind" (an

Eighth Air Force expression for saying one thing and knowing all along it was not true).

I tried to get my mind off that red flag, but it clung like dirty socks. I grabbed my towel and soap and headed for the shower, which was two huts over. Maybe I could wash that uneasy feeling right out of my head.

When I got back, I settled down in my bunk and reread the two letters I had gotten today from Butch (Eleta, my wife and new bride) and the letter I had from Mom. Mom had brought me up-to-date on my older brother Eddie, an ensign in the Navy, who had just been assigned to permanent party in, where else, Honolulu, Hawaii. Can you beat that? Mom wrote that my younger brother, Preston, was just itching to get into service, in spite of the advice I had been writing him to stay out as long as he could.

I was writing a letter to Butch when suddenly I realized what day it was, and I yelled, "Hey, you guys, do you know what day tomorrow is?" Jeff Fuller (waist gunner/togglier) said, "Yeah, it's Christmas." He was always full of fun and pranks. "No," I said, "it's Friday the thirteenth, a sure sign of bad luck." But I quickly added, "Not to worry, the number thirteen has always been my lucky number." Months later when I got back home, my hometown newspaper wrote a long article about the lucky thirteens in my life.

After finishing my letter to Mom and Eleta, I took them over to our officer's quarters as they were responsible for censoring them for security leaks and removing anything that might be helpful to the enemy. As always, Lieutenant Neal Payden, our navigator, took them and said, "Good night, Chuck, get a good night's sleep. Looks like we are going to need it."

As I hurried back to my barracks I was wondering, "Why did he say that? Does he know something?" I worried, but it was now dark, and I could see searchlights coming on in every direction. The Germans were coming to bomb as they did almost every night.

Our base at Framlingham was near the English Channel, on the east coast, and the area between our base and London was known as BUZZ BOMB ALLEY. You could watch those devilish pilotless German V1 flying bombs, launched from across the channel in Holland, putt, putt, putt their way toward London. The V1 was Vergeltungswaffe 1 or Vengeance Weapon 1. It was the first of Hitler's promised secret weapons. Equipped with an Argus pulse jet engine, its effective range was about 150 miles. It carried a warhead of 1,870 pounds and, once it was launched, would reach an altitude up to 3,000 feet. Traveling at 400 miles per hour for about thirty minutes or until its fuel ran out, it would fall to the ground and explode. WHAM! Look out below.

The V1 assault began on June 13, 1944, and the Germans were firing 190 per day. The last launch was on March 30, 1945. By then, over 10,500 had been used, and of that number, 2,419 fell on the city of London, killing 6,184, and injuring 18,000.

From nearby towns and airfields, we could hear the air raid sirens wailing and hear the British antiaircraft guns, *thump, thump, thump*. London was about 90 miles away, but the sky glowed a reddish orange in that direction. My heart and prayers went out to those very brave people.

I finally got to bed around 9:30 p.m. Even though lights out was at 9:00 p.m., we learned to maneuver in the blackout. I thought of home and Eleta, my brother Eddie, way over in Hawaii, my brother Preston, my sister Jeannie, and my mom and dad. As I said my prayers that night, I distinctly remember how much easier it was to talk to God than when I first got to England. We had come through many hard missions, and I found the more we flew, the more I prayed.

Thursday, July 13, 1944

Eighth Air Force mission number **471. Target: Munich.** Finally, a fitful sleep was shattered by the squadron CQ (charge of quarters) shouting and turning on the lights, "All right, Ray Strate crew, up and at 'em, let's go. Breakfast in thirty minutes, briefing at 0430." Someone yelled, "Hey, Sarge, where are we going?" "YOU'LL FIND OUT, AND YOU'LL BE SORRY!"

I don't know how he did it, but Sandy (Rogelio Sanchez), our tail gunner, was always the first one dressed and waiting for the rest of us. I laughed as I thought of a Bible phrase about the first shall be last and the last shall be first. Sandy was a Texas boy from San Antonio who was an inspiration to us all. He kept those Germans off our tail.

We made our way to the mess hall and were met by a bleary-eyed mess crew, who had been awakened about an hour before us. Needless to say, they were not very social at that hour of the morning.

Even so, they had a good breakfast of canned orange or grapefruit juice, oatmeal or cornflakes, and either fresh eggs or pancakes, with toast and coffee. Only flying crews received fresh eggs, and we went right into the kitchen to get them prepared any way we liked them, hot off the griddle. Everyone else ate powdered, dehydrated eggs which, when mixed with water, turned a gosh-awful green color. Everyone hated them, but when we were not flying, we all ate them. Flying with gas on your stomach, at altitude, could be a terrible thing, much like deep-sea divers with cramps. I always visited the latrine after breakfast. Once we got into all those flying clothes, including our heated suits, it would be almost impossible to go to the bathroom, and it would be many hours before we were back on the ground.

We were transported to the briefing rooms, which were large Nissen huts with a platform on one end and folding chairs for all the crews. There was a podium and a large map of Europe, covered with a black cloth. The operation's officer had marked out our mission route using pins and red ribbon before covering it with the cloth. It was all very dramatic, and as we were all seated, the group briefing officer and our group commander, Colonel Frederick W. Ott, and 571st Squadron commander, Colonel George Von Arb, entered the rear of the room. The briefing noncommissioned officer yelled, "Attention!" Everyone jumped up as the string of briefing officers walked quickly down the center aisle.

My heart was in my throat as the briefing officer said, "Be seated, gentlemen." As he pulled the string that opened the curtain, Colonel Ott said, "Men, this is a mission of utmost importance." There was a loud gasp, and many "Oh nos," as the red ribbon stretched way across the map into deepest Germany.

"Our target today is Munich, known to the Germans as Munchen. To be more exact, we will be bombing the Bayerische-Motoren-Werke. The Bayerische-Motoren-Werke manufactures jet aircraft engines, and if these engines start being turned out in large numbers, woe be unto you and all other Allied planes. You have already seen one or two of them, and, gentlemen, we do not have any aircraft that can come close to flying as fast as the Messerschmitt 262 jet planes. They have been reported as flying at 540 miles per hour. It is imperative that we shut down production as soon as possible." Using a projector, the group weather officer gave us a rundown on what the weather would be like on the way to the target and on the way home. Almost every mission site was flown over the night before by weather-gathering planes. They were usually British Mosquitos that could fly very high and very fast. Built with very lightweight wood and metal, they had the most powerful engines available.

Next came the intelligence officer who showed pictures of our target and our checkpoints. He also pointed out the German defenses, and this drew a few more "Oh nos." Antiaircraft guns completely surrounded Munich, and there were a number of fighter airfields nearby, including a squadron of thirty Me262 jet fighters.

The weather over Munich was completely overcast, and we would almost assuredly have to drop our bombs by Pathfinder, which was a B17 fitted with high-tech radar that could see right through the clouds. There was usually one Pathfinder plane with each formation, and when the target could not be sighted visually, the Pathfinder would drop smoke bombs over the target, and all the planes following would drop at the same point.

Before leaving the briefing, we were given a time "hack," which was a way of setting all watches on the exact same time. Counting down each second and calling out "hack" at the correct moment, technically, it was called watch synchronizing.

After the main briefing, which took about forty-five minutes, all the pilots, bombardiers, and navigators went to another briefing for additional information concerning their specific duties. They were given flimsies, which were maps and other information that we did not want to fall into enemy hands. The flimsies were made of very thin rice paper so they could easily be destroyed. By wadding them up and stuffing them in your mouth, your saliva would dissolve them.

Even though the group lead plane would do all the navigating, each navigator was briefed just as if he were doing all the navigating, in case he had to take over or if his plane became separated from the rest. This was also true for bombardiers.

All radio operators, too, were given a separate briefing. We were given a sheet of rice paper, sandwiched between two pieces of plastic, which was to protect it. It included our mission call signs and codes, as well as frequency procedures. The plastic also gave the paper some weight so it would not be blown about or possibly blown out of the airplane.

We then went to another hut which contained lockers with our special flight equipment. We each had a large carrying bag, and we picked up our electrically heated suits, parachutes, Mae Wests (inflatable life jackets), heavy lamb's wool flying suits and boots, and our all-important oxygen masks.

We then were loaded into jeeps or trucks and transported to our individual planes. Each plane was assigned two mechanics, and they were already helping prepare the GOOD-O-YANK for flight. There were also a couple of armorers on the ground crew.

Preparing the plane began by priming each engine and what we called "pulling through the props." Each propeller blade was manually turned, and usually, all crew members except Pilot Ray Strate and

Copilot George Curnes assisted. This turning over the engines was to get oil to all cylinders so when the engines started, there would be no metal-to-metal wear. It also served to flush out any fuel remaining in the cylinders.

Ray climbed into the cockpit for the priming procedure. A gasoline-driven auxiliary starter was cranked up and plugged into a receptacle under the wing. While the engine cranked, a ground crewman stood near the first engine with a large fire extinguisher, just in case of a backfire and explosion. This was just one of the many small things that was very dangerous and could occur before we even got off the ground.

The engines were started one at a time. The first (number one on the left wing farthest from the pilot) actuated the plane's internal generators so the many electrical circuits on the plane were operational. As the engines were run up to maximum revolution, Ray and George checked on oil pressures, prop feathering, turbo chargers, all electrical and hydraulic circuits, and magnetos.

Everything checked okay, the engines were shut down, and we waited for the petrol wagon (English for gasoline truck) to top off the fuel tanks. Every drop we could squeeze in now might just save our lives later. Keep that thought in mind as we get further along in this mission.

In the meanwhile, the ground crew armorers were finishing up loading twelve five-hundred-pound general-purpose bombs into the bomb bay. (Even though we were many miles from the Germans, this was another of those routine, but very dangerous times.) A five-hundred-pound bomb sometimes can have a mind of its own, and we learned quickly, if it decided to roll a certain direction, just jump back and let her roll. Not this morning, but once while loading, a bomb rolled off the loading hoist, right out of the bomb bay, and rolled all the way to the end of our right wing. Luckily, it was not armed. Each bomb has two doughnut-shaped lugs on its side, and as they were hoisted up into position in the bomb bay, they were attached to the vertical bomb rack with two shackles. When securely fastened, the lifting device was lowered to pick up the rest of the bombs. The fuses were then fitted into the nose of the bomb, secured with a pin and wire which kept the vane (small propeller) on the fuse from turning and arming the bomb. When the bomb fell, it pulled the pin from the fuse, and when the vane turned five hundred turns, the bomb was armed, and whatever it came into contact with would explode.

While this was going on, other ordinance personnel were delivering heavy boxes of 50-caliber machine-gun rounds that had been belted together with steel spring clips. We could clearly tell what kind of mission we were going to have by how much armor they gave us. Usually, it was five thousand rounds; today (the 13th of July), it was eight thousand rounds. OOOH! NOOO!

As they were always removed after each mission to be checked and repaired, the 50-caliber guns were also delivered to us. If the previous mission had enemy fighters, almost all the guns would get new barrels because, after a lot of firing, the heat would ruin them. They would bend in the middle, and you would not know where the bullets were going.

After the guns were installed and rounds chambered, Maggie made his rounds to each gun position to assure all guns were ready for firing. Occasionally, as a gunner was chambering his first round, there would be what we called a "runaway gun." A gun would malfunction, and every round in the ammo box would be fired. You could hear the unmistakable sound, rat-a-tat-tat, and someone screaming, "Get down, get down." Imagine that gun firing, spewing 50-caliber bullets in every direction like a nozzle on a water hose, in the midst of hundreds of five-hundred-pound bombs, airplanes filled to overflowing with 100-octane fuel, hundreds of boxes of ammo and incendiary flares, and flying and ground crews everywhere. Just another of those times when it was so dangerous, even though not in combat. This never happened to our crew, but it happened on the hardstand next to ours, and there were fatalities.

As I entered the radio compartment, which was a small room located behind the bomb bay and just halfway between the nose and tail of the plane, protected by wings on both sides, I took consolation that it was one of the safest parts of the plane. I began the routine check of my radios and intercom, turned on my IFF (Identification Friend or Foe), set and fed in the mission code.

I glanced up from my seat position, and above my radio command set which was attached to the bulkhead, a partition between the radio room and the bomb bay, where I kept a running account of the missions I had completed, I saw the hack marks (|||||-|||||-|||||-|||) indicating that we had completed eighteen missions. Next to it was a small picture of Eleta. I thought to myself, *Will this be my last one?* This would be my nineteenth, and I could not wait to mark it completed. Only seventeen more, and I would be going home. It seemed impossible and forever.

I was jarred back to reality at the sound of Lieutenant Strate calling for a position check over the intercom, "Look sharp, boys, are we ready? Report in!" Bombardier, check. Navigator, check. Top turret, check. Radio, check. Left waist, check. Right waist, check. Ball turret—"Hold a sec while I connect my oxygen." (The lower ball turret operator could not enter the ball turret until we were airborne). Maggie finally got hooked up and reported in, "Tail gunner, check." Sandy reported, speaking from the waist gunner position. He, too, could not take off in the tail of the plane. This was only the first of several reports that Lieutenant Strate or Lieutenant Curnes would call for before we crossed into Germany.

The weather was still socked in. We could barely see the control tower, and most of us were convinced we would stand down and not have to fly this time. Conditions, however, were not any worse than a lot of missions we had already flown.

We could hear the mighty roar as plane after plane cranked their engines. It sounded like the whole English Isle was vibrating. Just as we were ready to move out, out raced a jeep and an operations officer, motioning to Lieutenant Strate to cut the engines and yelling, "Stand down," but quickly added, "Temporarily."

I failed to mention that this mission was a *MAXIMUM EFFORT*, meaning every plane that could fly, would fly...1,043 bombers and 609 fighters, a total of 1,652 aircraft. Imagine 1,652 airplanes, all loaded with high explosives, flying around in the thickest fog you have ever seen. Sheer lunacy! Surely those big shot generals would not send us off in this mess. Thirty minutes later, the same jeep was back with new instructions. The message was "GO," and the engines roared again like angry lions. The flares went up, and the giant B17s moved out of their revetments from every corner of Framlingham Airfield.

We slowly moved out and waited for our takeoff position. Since this was to be a very long flight, the fuel trucks were at the end of the runway to top off each plane before takeoff. I could hear and feel, even now, the engines rev up, moving us a short distance, then the horrible screech of our brakes being applied.

Finally, we reached our position, and I could hear our copilot, Lieutenant George Curnes, calling out the instrument readings as Pilot Lieutenant Ray Strate got ready to get the show on the road. The GOOD-O-YANK groaned and jerked and shook all over as Ray locked the throttle controls for all four engines together, moving them forward, while both pilots held the brakes on with all their might. Curnes locked the tail wheel, and when the control tower fired off a flare, we leaped forward, slowly gaining speed until, nearing the very end of the runway, Ray pulled back on the wheel, and we gradually lifted off. This was another of those terrifying moments when you hold your breath. If we didn't get airborne now, they wouldn't find enough of us to send home. No turning back now, but 135 did turn back. They aborted because of engine trouble or electrical or oxygen problems. However, our 390th Bomb Group sent 37 planes to the target.

Now came a time of intense excitement, a very serious maneuver of assembling all those airplanes into a fighting formation…in total blindness. This was another of those deadly times, even though we were nowhere near the enemy. The 8th Air Force had developed a procedure for using radio transmissions, along with colored flares shot from a Very pistol, located above the pilot's head. The radio transmitters were known as bunchers, and were located near all bomber airfields. These bunchers had a range of twenty-five miles. They transmitted once per minute, using a predetermined call sign in Morse code, followed by a signal created by holding the transmitting key down. This allowed the pilot to use a radio compass to determine from which direction the signal was being sent. This radio compass was an instrument with the face of a compass and a large needle that pointed to the degree of the radio transmission on the ground.

Each squadron and group assembled around their buncher, and ours was number eleven, located near the town of Ipswich, on the East Anglia coast. After takeoff, the lead bomber climbed straight out from the base for two minutes, flying at 150 miles per hour, at a climb rate of 400 feet per minute. This meant the lead bomber was at 800 feet before beginning a left turn. The other bombers followed at 30-second intervals. They would fly a course of 5 miles, turn left, fly for 15 miles, turn left, fly 5 miles, turn left, fly 15 miles, completing an oblong course that put them back over their home airfield.

"Pilot to crew…this weather is pretty bad, keep a sharp watch from your positions for other planes. We are right on schedule, but we don't know about all those other guys. Sing out if you see anything."

At 9,000 feet, we broke through the cloud cover, and all heck broke loose. Steve Przepiorka (top turret) yelled, "Take it down. There is a plane right on top of us." We dropped like a rock, back into the overcast. Gradually, Ray pulled us back on top of the clouds, telling everyone to yell if we saw anything close. All was clear this time, and we could see hundreds of planes forming up into groups of threes. The lead plane in our squadron (571st) fired off predetermined colored flares as we maneuvered into position. Our takeoff time was 0542 as logged in my radio logbook, and our squadron formation was completed in 32 minutes. Once the squadron was assembled, we started to look for our sister squadrons, the 568th, 569th, and the 570th. We were flying the right wing in the lead squadron and soon hooked up with our other squadrons forming the 390th Bomb Group.

Now, we started looking to hook up with other bomb groups in our wing. We always flew with the 95th and the 100th Bomb Groups. The 95th distinguished itself by being the first bomb group to bomb Berlin (Big B as we knew it). The 100th had the dubious distinction of being the group the German fighters went for first. We really felt for those guys. On every mission, they would lose more planes than any other group, but they kept coming. I think the Germans knew they were a lot of new, inexperienced crews, and would pick on them. I am sure this fact saved my life and our group many times. I salute the 100th.

Ever climbing, the sky was full of planes and flares to assemble. It looked like the *Fourth of July.*

We headed out over the English Channel, and all those planes that were not in their correct position were fast catching up. The sun was out because we were now flying above the overcast, and what a beautiful sight. How could we be going out to kill or be killed? OH, GOD, how can this be?

"Test your guns," came Ray's voice over the intercom, and I was once again brought back to reality as the whole plane vibrated. There were no dampeners or noise suppressors, just metal-to-metal clatter. I looked out to see hundreds of planes firing their 50-caliber machine guns, with every fifth bullet a tracer, so we could follow where our shots were going. It is an absolute wonder we didn't shoot down our own planes. Then all was quiet, and I was monitoring my radios. This was an especially important time. If reconnaissance planes over the target area reported cloud cover up to and over our bombing altitude, they would notify headquarters in England, and predetermined signals would be sent to us to either abort the mission or bomb another target. Rarely did we return to base with our bomb-loads. The last resort was a target of opportunity, usually picked by the command pilot and lead-plane bombardier.

While I was monitoring these messages, I was not connected to intercom and I missed Ray's instructions to go on oxygen at fourteen thousand feet. At eighteen thousand feet, I started to get lightheaded and giddy. Lack of oxygen can make you silly. Harvey Burr (waist gunner) banged on the radio room door and motioned for me to hook up. We had a buddy system to check on each other.

We were now at twenty thousand feet when I heard that terrifying sound, *whump...whump,* of the German 88s as we crossed the Belgium coastline, heading for deep Germany. Our route to the target, Munchen (Munich), was almost a straight line, generally following the border between France and Belgium, to a point just south of Strasbourg, France, right on the border of Germany. We could not see the ground because of the thick overcast, but the ever-loving weathermen assured us the target would be clear or, at worst, broken clouds. Wrong again, Oh mighty and wise guessers, but I give them credit; they were right a lot of the time, and being right probably saved a lot of lives.

I forgot to mention that as we were leaving the coast of England, I looked out of the Plexiglas hatch in the top of the radio room, and I could see a line of British planes just returning from their night-bombing missions into Germany. There were giant Lancasters and Wellingtons, huge four-engine planes that were certainly not built for beauty, but they could carry much larger bombloads than we could…three and one-half tons of bombs for Lancasters and even more for the Wellingtons. To accommodate the very large "blockbuster" bombs, they had extra-long landing gear which, when sitting on the ground, made them look for the world like giant grasshoppers. Regardless of good looks, they got the job done. My hat was off to a courageous group. They flew in darkness, so not only could they see the terrifying flak smoke they were flying into, as there was a bright flash each time an antiaircraft shell exploded, but also worse still, they flew at half the altitude we did.

As I was saying, we were passing them, and as each plane came by us, they would dip their wing to salute us. It was an inspiring sight.

Whump…whump…whump. I could hear them getting closer and closer, and I could hear a sound much like that of sitting in a car during a hailstorm. As the shrapnel hit our plane, "*Good Golly, Miss Molly,* them crazy guys are trying to kill us. Let's get the heck out of here." My teeth were chattering, and it felt like a million ants were racing up and down my spine. *Scared* was not the word for it, more like *terrified.* Then, just as quickly as it had started, it quit. "Whew!"

"Bandits…three o'clock high," sang out Harvey Burr (right waist gunner). "Hold your fire, boys," called out Ray. "Be sure they are not ours." "I can see their yellow noses. They are Focke-Wulf 190s," said Steve (top turret). "Okay, when they get into range," Ray said calmly, "let them have it." They never got to us as, all of a sudden, from out of nowhere, the sky to our right was full of fighters, going at it. Our escorts, P38s and P47s came out of the sun.

Our Third Division had ninety-eight P38 Lockheed Lightnings, fifty-one P47 Republic Thunderbolts, and forty-six P51 North American Mustangs escorting us today. The P38s were the first to escort us, and we could clearly see them because of their double fuselage. It dawned on me why we were getting enemy fighters so early in our mission. Our route to the target at Munich took us within fifty miles of Abbeville, France, home base for the notorious Yellow-Nose Abbeville Kids, the most elite and most feared of all German fighter groups. They were Goering's handpicked and most fearless pilots, with more combat kills, by far, than any other fighter group.

Why did those big shots back at headquarters send us so close to Abbeville? Are they nuts? On second thought, why not engage them while we still had the most escorts, with still plenty of fuel. There were some pretty smart guys back there at headquarters.

As we watched from our front-row-seat vantage point, we could see hundreds of fighters going in all directions, looking very much like a hive of angry bees. Some were hit and smoking, and we saw a number of parachutes. Our fighter escorts had saved us one more time.

As they faded to our rear, I thought, *Man, oh, man, we have got to come back this way. Oh, Lord, will I ever see Eleta and Mom and my family or home again?* This war business was for the birds. "Let it soon be over, Lord, like today," I prayed.

Whump…whump…whump…bang! That was too close. I looked through the Plexiglas roof of the radio compartment to see that the flak bursts were brown looking. I made a mental note to report when we got back, as all the other flak bursts we had seen were either black or white. We had been briefed on another mission that some flak batteries would fire shells that burst green, as a signal to the German fighters that they were interrupting fire, so their fighters could safely fly into our formations and not be hit by their own antiaircraft fire.

We flew peacefully for the next hour or so with our P47 escorts crisscrossing high above us. Thank you, Jabbos, which is what the Germans called them (meaning "devil plane"). The Germans were terrified of this plane and for good reason. The P47, with a huge eighteen-cylinder radial engine, equipped with wing tanks, could fly up to seven hundred miles, and when they reached their range limit and turned for home, they hit the deck and look out below. They shot up airfields, convoys, trains, and anything else they could find worth shooting at. With eight 50-caliber machine guns, they were a holy terror.

As we approached Germany, just south of Strasbourg, France, we came into an area known as the Kammhuber Line, a defense system named for Josef Kammhuber, its organizer. It was a concentration of fighter airfields, radar tower installations, flak batteries, searchlight batteries, and ground observers that stretched 650 miles, from Switzerland to the south of Germany, to Denmark to the north.

You could tell when you got near it because the flak increased dramatically, as did fighter sightings. Fortunately for us, this was where our P51 Mustang (bless them) escorts took over, all the way to our target and back. Unfortunately, the flak just got worse and worse. We could always tell which targets were most important to the Germans because of the number of antiaircraft guns we encountered. I told Harvey Burr that it started out like popcorn in a pot. First, a single puff and as the fire got hotter…puff…puff…puff, then into a steady bursting like popcorn as it almost finished popping. The only difference being that it was a thousand times louder and it was spewing deadly shrapnel in every direction.

During my stay in England, between missions, sometimes radio operators from several crews would talk about problems we each had. One of the problems most of us had in common was monitoring messages from home base in England and listening to our intercom at the same time. Many operators were known not to hear the order, "Abandon ship or bail out," even though there was an emergency bell the pilot always rang. The problem with the bell was it did not function when the plane was shot up or on fire.

Another problem, as I have mentioned earlier, is that we did not get the message to go on oxygen when we reached altitude. We also monitored German transmissions, when possible. Several of us modified our headsets so we could hear two different transmissions at the same time. On this mission, I was listening to our plane intercom and the German Air Force Luftwaffe alerting their squadrons that we were coming. "Achtung! Achtung, Luftwaffe!" ("Attention! Attention, Luftwaffe"), and then a lot of German I didn't understand. But I knew they were coming, and in a very short time, the Me109s and Me110s appeared way off to one side, not close enough to shoot at. They were calling in our altitude and direction to the antiaircraft batteries below.

The reason for doing this was because of a very simple procedure the English had devised to render the German radar practically useless. It was called code word "Windows," and consisted of slivers of aluminum foil about twelve inches long and one-half inch wide. They were packed in bundles and were first dropped by the British on the night raids. The procedure was so successful, it was adopted by our American bombers. One bundle of two thousand slivers would send a radar echo back to the German operators, indicating that there were, literally, tens of thousands of planes coming from every conceivable altitude. The Germans were going mad with confusion and were saying to themselves, "This is impossible."

As we approached Munich, it was one of my duties to throw out the chaff, as the Americans called it. I had about one hundred bundles, and I opened a small hatch, which was just large enough for one bundle to go through, and started chunking.

Someone up front, Neil Payden (navigator), I believe, said over the intercom, "Wow, look at that flak. The whole sky is black." I heard Steve (top turret) say, "We do not have to go through that, do we?" Needless to say, I could have done without those words of warning. I was already wound up as tight as adrenaline could get me.

Just as we turned on the bomb run, we were over the little town of Oberammergau. Little did I suspect that this little town, later on, would play an important part in my life, but that is another chapter. Our IP (initial point) or beginning of our bomb run was the northern end of a large lake, Lake Starnberg, southwest of Munich and easily discernible by radar in our lead Pathfinder plane.

As we neared our target, I could hear the bomb bay doors groaning and a clunk, which signaled they were open. "Chuck, check the bomb bay doors," said Ray. His voice, usually very calm and reassuring, was a little higher. I opened the door to the bomb bay and said, in a much-higher-than-usual voice, "Bomb bay doors open." Through the bomb bay, all I could see below were clouds and flak bursts. I closed the door, which was not easy because the freezing air was rushing through.

I no sooner sat down at my radio table, when I heard it coming. *Whump...whump...whump, wham.* The plane felt like it stopped abruptly, tilting over on our left side. The noise was deafening, and holes appeared everywhere. I knew we were hit and hit hard. I snapped on my chest chute and listened as Ray began getting damage reports from all positions.

Meanwhile, Neal (navigator) had his hands full as Malinsky (bombardier) was hit in the chest by shrapnel. Neal, a real cool dude, got Malinsky laid out on the floor, moved into the bombardier's chair, and dropped our bombs, just as the Pathfinder plane dropped his smoke bombs. Neil yelled, "Bombs away," and I opened the door to the bomb bay again and confirmed to Ray that the bombs were gone. He immediately closed the bomb bay doors, but not before I got a radio room full of smoke. Man, oh, man, my heart was jumping and my knees were weak and my teeth were chattering. I was ready to jump if Ray gave the word. As we flew over Munich, we flew directly over Dachau, the concentration camp where thousands of prisoners were put to death. I thought, *Lord, please do not let me be killed here in this awful place.* (I had not the slightest idea that fifty years later, I would be standing on the ground, here in the middle of Munich where our bombs had fallen, looking up into the sky where I had passed.)

We were still being rocked by exploding flak as Ray and George tried to gain control of the airplane.

"Top turret to pilot, number three engine is smoking," called in Steve.

"Okay, Steve, keep an eye on it."

"Ball turret to pilot, number three is getting worse and there's a hole the size of a bathtub."

"Okay, Maggie, keep me posted. Anyone else?"

"Right waist to pilot, I can see flames in number three and fuel is pouring out."

"Copilot to pilot, number three manifold pressure is dropping and that prop is going to run away and fly all to pieces. I'm moving the fuel mixture control to the 'off' position, cutting the booster, pressing the feathering button, and closing the cowl flap." The prop windmilled and finally stopped.

"Good work, George," said Ray and, over the intercom, said, "Hang on, boys, we have lost number three, and we have fire in the engine well."

The extinguisher did not put the fire out, and Ray continued, "Steve, start transferring fuel out of that right-wing fuel cell."

Steve slipped out of his top turret and went aft into the bomb bay, where the fuel transfer valves were located. He operated the valve while Curnes watched the gauges.

"Okay, boys, it looks like the fire is not going out. Buckle up, we are going to dive to try and blow it out."

"Radio to pilot, the flames are getting worse and extend beyond the rudder."

"Roger that, Chuck, check to see if Steve is back in his turret."

I opened the door to the bomb bay and saw Steve just climbing back into his turret.

"Radio to pilot, okay, Steve is back."

The plane tipped forward into a deep dive, and I was lifted out of my seat. Everything that was not fastened down began to float around. My steel helmet, the extra flak vest I had confiscated, and an oxygen bottle were pinned to the ceiling.

"Waist to pilot, number four is smoking," said Harvey.

"Check it out, George, and what is that vibration? Pilot to crew, check out your positions and see if you can locate what is shaking."

"Ray, this is George, manifold pressure on number four is low but holding."

"Waist to pilot, fire in number three is going out."

"Roger that, Harvey."

"Radio to pilot, cowl on number three was flapping, but has broken off and is gone."

"Roger, Chuck, the vibration has stopped."

At fifteen thousand feet, Ray and George began pulling us out of our dive, straining with all their strength to pull the steering yoke back. Expecting at any moment to hear Ray say, "Bail out," I looked out and could tell it was already too late. As we leveled out at five hundred feet, we were under the cloud cover, and I could see the ground.

Ray, assessing our situation, talked to all stations on the intercom. "We have two engines out on the same side, our bombardier is critically wounded in the chest, we are out of formation and flying alone, over five hundred miles from England, and have a large, undetermined loss of fuel. We are in sad condition, indeed." Ray determined that we had too many strikes against us. He broke radio silence and called the group command pilot, asking permission to land in Switzerland, which we could almost see. If we landed there, Switzerland being a neutral country, we would be interned and held there until the war was over.

The command pilot did not waste any words. *"Do not land in Switzerland. Bring that plane home, repeat, do not land in Switzerland!"* I am sure this decision was influenced by the fact that a great many planes had been taking the easy way out, flying to neutral countries, and later finding the planes to be in good working order. Some pilots just did not call their superiors in the lead planes and just flew on to those neutral countries.

In the meanwhile, our old bombardier, Lieutenant Vic Estes, flying in our group lead plane as group bombardier observed that our group was taking a beating with planes, one of which was ours, leaving formation. He saw something that perhaps was never repeated. A B17 whose nose was sliced off, the plane completely turned around, was flying back into the following formations. Wow! I can just imagine what those pilots in the following planes thought. Thank goodness, Vic and crew made it home safely.

With the very strict orders from the command pilot, Ray began to size up our next move and lay plans to bring the GOOD-O-YANK home.

Several things were in our favor. There were still the clouds that we could pull up into to keep the German fighters off our tail. We were now also flying at treetop level which would keep us off the German radar screens. We had one of the best navigators in the Eighth Air Force, Lieutenant Neal Payden. Ray told Neal to plot a course to England and to avoid as many antiaircraft guns, airfields, and large towns as possible.

As Neal began plotting our course, I thought to myself, *Neal, ole buddy, you are a great navigator, and I have complete confidence in you. But please do not take us near Magdeburg or Stuttgart on the way home.* Those two places, not far away, were extremely fortified and had fighters based nearby. He was well ahead of me and took us well to the south. When we finally got our bearings, we were near Strasbourg, France, which is almost on the German, French, and Belgium borders.

"Pilot to crew, well, boys, we have gotten ourselves into one heck of a mess, but we have a good chance of making it. We need to lighten our plane as much as possible, so start ripping everything you can get loose and toss it out. We are fighting to keep this bird in the air, so the quicker the better. Your chutes will not help you at this altitude, so they can go, too."

With that, all stations got busy throwing out everything they could. I threw out just about all my radio equipment, except my command set and my IFF, both of which we would need as we got closer to home, the command set to send SOS or Mayday, and the IFF (identification friend or foe).

Out went the parachutes, the flak suits, the oxygen bottles, extra ammunition, our heavy clothing and electric suits, and the ball turret. It was installed with a few special bolts, so could easily be jettisoned in just such an emergency as this.

We popped the rear hatch door off and watched as our stuff hit the ground. The first small town we came to was Saverne, France, which was on a small river, and there was a German guard in a little house at one end of a bridge over the river. He saw us coming and jumped into his house and picked up a machine gun, just as we roared over. He emptied his clip at us at point-blank range. The walkway in a B17 is about eighteen inches wide and is made of plywood. That soldier shot holes in our walkway from the bomb bay to the tail. Splinters were flying everywhere, and I sat down in my steel helmet. I was glad I had not thrown it out. It was all over in a moment, but I can tell you our crew learned a new dance step.

I do not know what those French people thought when they saw all that stuff come falling down as we passed over the French countryside, so low we could read signs. Ray, with two engines out on the same side, was having a terrible time flying the plane. He had to keep the right side higher than the left; if not, we would have fallen right out of the air. We were so low that when we came to high hills, high trees, or water towers, we had to fly around them. So low, that when standing in the rear escape hatch door and flying over a French farmhouse, we could see a woman running for her house with her dress pulled up over her head, and chickens were flying as high as we were to get out of our way.

At every little crossroads, there seemed to be a German outpost that wanted to get some shots at the GOOD-O-YANK, and the plane was getting so many holes, we could see daylight in any direction. Now, sitting right in our path was the city of Metz, a hotbed for flak guns. It is a city of over one hundred thousand people on the Moselle River. I never found out what the Germans had there that was so all-fired important, but they sure did protect it. Neal plotted our course around it as best he could, but we still got shot at.

The Germans were masters at antiaircraft installations. There were flak towers everywhere, platforms built high above the ground, with dreaded 88-millimeter guns. From a distance, they looked like water towers, but boy, were they deadly.

"Pilot to crew, thanks, boys. Getting rid of all that weight has helped a lot, but we still have a long way to go. Steve, can you give me any idea how we stand on fuel, our gauges are out?" Steve replied, "We moved all that was left in the right-wing tanks over to the left side. I could tell when it quit flowing because the pumps got hot. I can tell you we do not have much left, and if we make it, I will be surprised." When I heard this, along with all the other woes we had, including a bombardier with a terrible shrapnel wound in his chest, lying bleeding on the floor of the bombardier/navigator compartment in the nose of the plane, it was just too much.

I walked out of the radio compartment, past the hole in the floor where the ball turret used to be, to where Harvey and Bill Holter (waist gunner) were looking out the escape hatch door. The ground seemed to be going by so fast, my eyes could not focus. We were so close to the ground, and our air speed was around ninety to one hundred miles per hour.

With everybody and his brother shooting at us along the way, we had not even gotten to the area where the greatest concentration of antiaircraft guns was located, which was near the coast. I remembered also that we had to pass the Abbeville area where Herman Goering and all his yellow-nosed Focke-Wulf 190s were based. I looked down at the peaceful French farmland and, to my great surprise, became very calm whereas only a short time ago, I was shaking all over. I thought of home. Yes, I prayed, and trembled. I remember praying the Lord's Prayer and saying the Twenty-third Psalm, over and over. "Yea, though I walk through the valley of the shadow of death, I will fear no evil, for Thou art with me." Then this calm came, and it was not that I was sure that God was protecting me (though he most certainly was), but I finally decided there was absolutely no way I was going to live through this. I accepted God's promise that whosoever believed in His son, Jesus, though he may die, will have eternal life. I believed that, and I was perfectly calm and no longer afraid.

As we flew around Metz, we flew near Homecourt and Verdun. I thought, this is where one of the bloodiest battles of World War I was fought. The French and Germans have been fighting here since the year 450 AD and in the day of Charlemagne's rule. Now, men are still fighting here. Why?

We were now about seventy-five miles from Germany, and looking ahead, we could see the trees of the Argonne Forest, where thousands of soldiers died. Would we be next? Of course, we did not know it, but just a few miles north in the trees and forests of Ardennes, Belgium, a bloody battle was yet to be fought, the Battle of the Bulge.

We crossed the Neuse River, near Charleville, and even the soldiers on small boats shot at us and, again, the splinters flew on the catwalk. They could not miss us; they could have done real damage with a slingshot. How all those bullets going through our plane missed us, I will never understand. We flew south of Lille, a city of more than seven hundred thousand people and another hotbed of flak guns, with our course set to exit France just south of Dunkirk, where thousands of British soldiers were trapped in their retreat from the fast-moving (blitzkrieg) German Panzer troops. They made a miraculous withdrawal using hundreds of very small boats. The Germans had concentrated literally thousands of big guns along the coast between Dunkirk and Calais (closest point to England) and, almost daily, lobbed huge shells across the channel. We were going to fly right through the middle of them. "Oh, God, is this where it is going to happen, here in the cold water of the English Channel?"

As we neared the coast, all heck broke loose, and Ray and George were trying to maneuver left and right as best they could, knowing that if they dropped our right wing, we were gone for sure. Ray called to Neal, "Neal, head us to the nearest English airfield." Neal came right back, "That will be Manston. Only trouble is, we have to get over the Cliffs of Dover." I thought about the song "White Cliffs of Dover," but not for long. Ray yelled, "Chuck, get on your radio, get me a heading, and send a Mayday, just in case we have to ditch." I tapped out, ...***..., dit-dit-dit-da-da-da-dit-dit-dit, three times then screwed my Morse code sending key down, so it sent a continual signal, and reported back to Ray that it was done. About that time, we were just off the coast and the big German naval guns began to zero in on us. If we thought those 88-millimeter flak guns made a noise, these were fourteen- and sixteen-inch naval guns that could follow us all the way to England, and then some. The shells exploded closer and closer, and when they exploded ahead of us, the plane sounded like someone had thrown a handful of gravel on us. Then we flew through black smoke. The German gunners were excellent shots due to practicing every day. But God was on our side, and I heard Ray yell, "Landing gear down," and then he told George to give our two engines all the power we had to get up and over the

White Cliffs of Dover. Our troubles, however, were not over as a red light told Ray that our landing gear was not down. Neal confirmed this by looking out his window in the nose. More shells, more bouncing, will it never end?

Steve was already out of his top turret when Ray said, "Steve, get down there and see if you can get our wheels down." I opened the door to the bomb bay, and Steve already had the manual hand crank to crank down the wheels. He turned and he cranked, but it was binding, and the sweat was pouring off him. I cranked awhile and then Maggie. It looked like we would have to belly-land because we were coming up on the English coastline.

Steve took another turn and just as we crossed the beach, I felt the plane lurch upward as we cleared the Cliffs by inches. We heard the landing gear snap into lock position, and the red light went out. Hallelujah!

When I got back to the radio room, Bill Holter was pointing behind us, and I could see the Spitfire dipping his wing as if to say, "Everything is okay now." Back in the Channel, we could see the air-sea rescue ship that had met us at mid-channel, peeling off to go help some other poor, unfortunate souls. As I looked out my radio window, I noticed our number one engine was smoking. Fortunately, we were right on top of the emergency landing field at Manston. Neal had brought us in *sur le nez* (on the nose), which, by the way, was the official slogan for the 390th Bomb Group.

When we first saw Manston tower, I heard a loud thud and said to myself, "Oh, no, surely nothing else can happen to us. We are so close," but then I saw the two red flares high above us. Ray had fired the Very pistol flares, alerting the emergency crews that we had wounded aboard, and they would be waiting as soon as we stopped rolling to take Lieutenant William Malinsky to the base hospital.

Ray dropped the GOOD-O-YANK right on the beginning of the nine-thousand-foot runway, and we coasted to a stop. I sat in the radio room for some time, unable to move. Finally, realizing we had made it, I said, "Thank you, Lord," and grabbed my radio logbook and hopped down on Mother Earth. There was whooping and shouting and kissing the ground. "Whew!"

I told Ray I had to get over to the control tower to report concerning my SOS (Mayday) transmission. All radio operators were required to report as quickly as possible that they had landed safely, so that the air-sea rescue could be notified and the search called off. The English control tower operator thanked me and said, "GOOD-O-YANK, good show." That was one of their favorite expressions, and how our plane happened to be named GOOD-O-YANK.

When I got back from the debriefing, it was normal procedure that each crew member got a shot of whiskey. Harvey Burr and I were the only two on the crew that did not drink, and our portion was quickly divided among the others. Afterward, I thanked Ray for a fantastic job flying and for saving my life, especially since I had been so sure I was going to die. But God had other plans for me.

The next day we all slept late and, after lunch, went back to the airfield to take what was to be our last look at GOOD-O-YANK, a truly remarkable airplane. Some said there were over 360 holes of various sizes in her, but I, personally, counted over 600, the largest behind the number three engine, as big as a bathtub. It is true, some of the holes were where shrapnel had entered, and others where it had exited. There were several holes in the wings that were perfectly round where shells had passed completely through without exploding. As I looked at all those holes, I was reminded of the old magician's trick of putting a woman into a long box and then sticking swords through the box from all directions. How all those holes got in there and only one person was hit, I will never comprehend. I retrieved two pieces of shrapnel that had ricocheted around in the radio compartment and landed at my feet on the floor. One piece has four numbers on it that match four numbers of my Army serial number. Coincidence? I don't think so. I still have those two pieces.

We all said our goodbyes to the GOOD-O-YANK and thanked her. We were told that a ground crew tried to crank the two remaining engines so they could taxi off the runway, but there was not enough gas to start them. My thought was that she had just given her all and died. They had to tow her away with a truck.

We were told some weeks later that an engineer from Boeing looked at her and reported that it was impossible for a plane in that condition to fly, but she had.

They sent another B17 to pick us up to fly back to our base at Framlingham, and much to our surprise, it was Lieutenant Colonel George Von Arb, our squadron commander. We had to straighten up and behave like professionals because he was very strict.

The flight back to Framlingham was smooth and uneventful, and we were taken directly to our Nissen hut. Much to our surprise, our personal belongings were in a box about the size of a cigar box, lying on our beds, which had been stripped down to the three small pillow-like mattresses stuffed with straw.

After successfully returning from a very hard and stressful mission, I was humbled to see that all that would be sent home to remember me by could be placed in a very small box, but I was alive and very thankful.

The third successive mission to Munich was highly successful. It was carried out by 1,043 heavy bombers, 617 B17s and 366 B24s, dropping 2,356 tons of bombs. We were escorted by 609 fighters, consisting of 185 P38s, 149 P47s, and 275 P51s. Losses were 10 bombers and 5 fighters, and many sleepless nights.

These three Munich missions in succession were so terrible and costly, that later they were to be called "The Three Days In July."

Friday, July 14, 1944

The crew of Lieutenant Ray Strate was grounded. The mission to Munich had taken everything we had. We were dead tired, mentally and physically exhausted. We were given a three-day pass and told to relax.

Our plane, the Good-O-Yank, was inspected by a team of Boeing experts who reported that a B17 in its condition was impossible to fly. They dragged it to the B17 graveyard.

Note: It was not to be denied. They looked it over and pronounced it to be salvageable. It got four new engines, a new right wing, and a number of other new parts, and was returned to duty to fly again. Not under the name of Good-O-Yank, but by the name Preferred Risk. Aircraft number 2102673 flew a total of 43 missions. It was shot down by enemy fighters on January 14, 1945, on a terrible mission to Durban, Germany. Our 390th Bomb Group lost 9 planes, and the 8th AF lost 31. Our plane crashed near Goerne. Four men parachuted safely and were interned for the war. The rest were killed.

If my records are correct, Lieutenant William Malinsky (bombardier), who was wounded on our Munich mission, flying on this same plane in place of our togglier, Jeff Fuller, was wounded again on January 6, 1945, on a mission to Kusel.

CHAPTER 14

Time-Out From The War

THOSE "BLAWSTED" GERMANS

Saturday, July 15, 1944

After a good night of rest, all the enlisted men on our crew said, "Let's get away for a couple of days and try to forget about Munich and the Germans and the war." So off we went to London, already planning what we were going to do, none the least of which was to sleep in a real bed with clean, white sheets, to eat fish, and to laze in the sunshine.

As we pulled into Liverpool Station, the weather had truly turned bright and sunny, and we hailed a cab to five of us singing, "Look out, London, here we come." We turned onto Bishopsgate Street, passing the Bank of England, and on to Victoria Embankment, which would take us downtown to Charing Cross, where the hotels catered to American soldiers. We were in a jolly old mood, and our worries were light-years away. Sailing along at about thirty miles per hour, we noticed our cabdriver cocked his head to one side as if he were listening for something. Suddenly, he whipped the steering wheel to the left (they drive on the left side), screeched the brakes to a jarring halt, and ducked under the dashboard. We were all thrown to the floor in a heap. Someone yelled, "What the—" and that is all I heard before the loudest noise I have ever heard in my life. "Whooooom." The cab jumped four or five feet off the pavement and bounced onto the sidewalk. Still upright, it then began to rain brick, mortar, dust, fire, and smoke down on top of the cab until we could no longer see out the windows, which were all shattered. I thought, *This is it! Fighting a war in the air with every conceivable way to get killed is one thing, but coming to London and having a building collapse on me is another!*

I faintly remember an air raid siren and an ambulance or fire truck going, EEEEE-AUGH-EEEEE-AUGH. It got deathly silent…I am sure I was fading away and they would not find my body until long after the war. I then heard Steve say, "Will one of you guys get off my back. I'm suffocating down here." He was on the bottom of the cab, in the floorboard. There was smoke and dust and dirt in our eyes, noses, and mouths.

Next, I heard someone sobbing, and strangely, it sounded like a woman. She was saying, half-talking and half-crying, "Hang on, boys, I'll have you out of there quick enough. Those blawsted Germans and their blawsted Buzz Bombs." *Sniff, sniff.* "Those dirty bawstards! Stinking cowards is what they are."

Piece by piece that lady dug us out from under that cab roof which had collapsed over us, with nothing but her bare hands, surely saving our lives. Our driver was not so lucky; he was crushed by the building wall.

It turned out that the lady was Fire Marshal and Air Raid Warden for the neighborhood. Still sobbing and swearing, she led us across the street to her apartment and washed our faces and hands. She brushed off our uniforms and gave us a cup of Earl Grey hot tea. The English people truly believe that a cup o' tea has magical healing powers, and I, for one, am beginning to believe it. She said, "Stay as long as you like, boys, but I am off to see if anyone else needs me." Man! What a country, and what a lady, and what a courageous people!

Later, as we left, we could see across the street where the V1 or V2 bomb had exploded and had taken out an entire city block.

Maggie said, "Okay, boys, what's it going to be? Do we head back to base, or do we go on for more of the same?" I said, "Man, I am not afraid to die, but chances are we are going to if we tempt fate too much. I'm heading back to Framlingham." Harvey said, "Me, too." Jeff called out, "Tallyho and toodle-oo," as they hopped into another cab and waved goodbye. Harvey and I, two ole married men, walked back to Liverpool Station and caught the next train north, to Framlingham.

After all, what could be worse than being in London when it is raining?

I can tell you what is worse; it is being in London when it is raining Buzz Bombs.

It was so good to get back to base and, surprise, get a handful of mail from home, two letters from Eleta and one each from my Aunt Louise Booker, my Aunt Janet Hamby (Mom's two sisters), Eddie, my big brother in the Navy in balmy Honolulu, Hawaii, and one from Mom.

I sat on my bunk and cried when I read the first letter from Eleta. After removing the last two vertebrae from her spine, she spent three weeks in the hospital, lying facedown on her stomach, unable to even turn over. When they got her up to sit in a chair with pillows, she fainted from the pain, but it was a start. I can only imagine the pain and suffering she went through, alone.

The second letter was written three days later while sitting on the sunporch, high on top of the hospital, looking out over the city of Charlotte, North Carolina, with the sun shining brightly. My heart was lifted; my whole world was right again, and I felt like singing. I didn't finish my other letters. I got my bike and rode out to the flight line to be alone with my thoughts, and I prayed, "Lord, just let me get through this, and I promise I'll never let Butch go through anything like this alone again."

Before long, the 390th Group was returning from today's mission, with 131 bombers and 712 fighters hitting targets along the French coast and dropping food and arms to the French Freedom Fighters. Over 4,000 containers were parachuted to the Guerrillas, and we did not lose a single plane. The Germans lost 6 fighters, and I was happy for the crews. It was a successful mission and a safe one. I went back to read the rest of my mail.

Sunday, July 16, 1944

The mission today consisted of 1,087 bombers, back to Munich, Augsburg, Stuttgart, and heaven forbid, Saarbrucken, through the most heavily fortified region of Germany. We lost 11 bombers and 3 fighters.

Harvey and I went down the little path to Parham, to the village church. I remember they sang, "A Mighty Fortress Is Our God," and I thought, *A mighty fortress is our B17*. God was, indeed, leading us. The church was so cold (no heat), even in the summer, but the warmth of the people made it a wonderful place to worship.

Monday, July 17, 1944

The 8th Air Force flew two missions today, the 478th and 479th, with 854 bombers hitting targets along the front lines, from Belgium all the way to southern France. There was little opposition, and losses were 1 bomber and 1 fighter.

Tuesday, July 18, 1944

Missions today were in direct support of ground troops trying to break through the tough German defenses, mostly in the area near the D-Day beachheads. One thousand three hundred ninety-four bombers and 476 fighter escorts dropped 3,074 tons of bombs. B17s of the 1st Division bombed Peenemunde, Germany, a highly sophisticated German base. This is where the Germans developed the first jets and rockets, home of the V1 Buzz Bomb and the V2 high-altitude rocket bomb. Although we did not know it at the time, it was where work was being done on the atom bomb. This base was located on the very north coast of Germany, on the Baltic Sea.

The red alert mission flag was flying when we went to bed tonight. We would be flying our twentieth mission, and we wondered where we would be going. The missions just don't seem to be getting any easier.

Wednesday, July 19, 1944

It was very early when they woke us, which we took to be a bad omen, suggesting we had a long way to go. But Sandy was in good spirits, meaning perhaps it would be a good day. Maggie had an earache, and he was cranky, a sure sign of something. Harvey Burr was still sound asleep in his top bunk. No one liked that to happen because you were sure to be awakened in some ungodly fashion, such as with a freezing-cold 50-caliber machine bullet slipped down your back, or worse, down your front. He woke just in time to avoid this and beat everyone getting dressed.

Steve was nowhere to be found, and Jeff, always kidding, suggested he was AWOL. He was in the latrine and very hacked because he had gotten up to go to the latrine, expecting to hop right back in the warm sack for a few more hours of sleep. We were all laughing and kidding around at breakfast and that was a *good* sign.

When they pulled back the curtain, I almost died...Schweinfurt, one of the very worst targets in all of Germany, smack in the *middle* of Germany. The 8th Air Force in a maximum effort with 1,242 bombers and 761 fighters were scheduled to bomb 21 targets. Some of the worst were Augsburg, Strasbourg, Saarbrucken, Koblentz, and Schweinfurt. Our morale hit rock bottom.

Messerschmitt Bf 109

The Messerschmitt Bf 109, commonly called the Me 109, is a German World War II fighter aircraft designed by Willy Messerschmitt and Robert Lusser during the early to mid-1930s. The "Bf 109" designation was issued by the German ministry of aviation and represents the developing company Bayerische Flugzeugwerke and a rather arbitrary figure. It was one of the most advanced fighters of the era, including such features as all-metal monocoque construction, a closed canopy, and retractable landing gear. It was powered by a liquid-cooled, inverted-V12 aero engine

REPUBLIC P47 THUNDERBOLT

As we were forming, the weather was clear, but we saw 2 B17s collide and go down. Some chutes were seen, and we never learned what group they were in, but it was not the 390th.

Schweinfurt is the home of a large ball bearing factory and a number of other important industrial factories. It is remembered as being one of the most fiercely protected areas in Germany and a place where many planes were lost. We were exceptionally alert.

Nearing our target at Schweinfurt, the flak got thicker and thicker. It looked like a thunderstorm over the target, as we turned on the IP (initial point) and started our bomb run. We opened our bomb bay doors, and I was feeding bundles of chaff (aluminum strips) through an opening just behind my seat in the radio compartment. I was looking out my side window, and in the next few minutes, I saw fighters coming from ten o'clock high. I heard the thump, thump, thump of their 20-millimeter cannons as they blazed through our formation and the sound of our own 50-caliber guns firing in staccato bursts. The sound was like that of many air hammers you have seen and heard, as work crews dig up pavement. Our plane stuttered, jerked, and bounced but held its course. To my amazement, I saw P47s on the tail of the Me109s, twisting and turning through the formations below us. Smoke and fire streamed from B17s and fighters, both ours and theirs. Then, the fighters went into the kind of air battle that I had always dreamed of being a part of. Me109s and Fw190s were everywhere, off to our right and left, but bless those "little friends," they kept them away from us. The red-nosed P47s seemed to be all over the sky, and the intercom was alive with chatter. Ray came on and said, "Okay, men, hold down your chatter. Just call in when you see them coming in."

This was by far the largest air battle I had witnessed, even though we had faced many more fighters on other missions. The sky was full of smoke, fire, airplane parts, exploding shells, planes in every conceivable attitude, sideways, upside down, falling headfirst and tailfirst, severed engines and tail sections. It was weird to see a B17 flying upside down, a copilot falling from his position window, and their tail gunner jumping from his rear hatch at the same instant. Our plane was bouncing in all directions. I could hardly keep my feet on the floor, and even with earphones on, the noise rattled my brain. Are we hit? Should we jump? No, we had not heard the bailout bell, but maybe Ray was hit and couldn't sound the alarm. I couldn't think; it was panic time. Put on your chute; destroy the radio equipment. This is where all that training comes flooding back. You do things automatically, and your brain slows things down. "Radio to pilot, any instructions?" "Pilot to crew, just hang on. We will be out of this shortly, and if there are any wounded, let me know." No one spoke. All were shell-shocked, but still functioning as a team.

After "Bombs away," I checked the bomb bay to be sure the bombs were gone, and looking down at Schweinfurt from twenty-seven thousand feet, with bombs exploding endlessly, was truly awesome. How could anything survive that? I called out, "Bomb bay clear." The doors ground and closed, and the bombardier called out, "Back to you, Ray." Immediately, we turned sharply to the left and dropped five hundred feet. We knew the flak guns were tracking us on our long bomb run, and it took our breaths away as the plane dropped. It is absolutely amazing how these pilots can maneuver like that in tandem. These guys never get enough credit for their unbelievable flying skills.

Sure enough, after the bomb run, here came the German fighters again, only this time they didn't get to us. The P47s had a field day. Evidence of the ferociousness of the fighting were the results. We lost 17 bombers, with 350 heavily damaged. We lost 7 fighters, but the Germans lost 72 and many more damaged. Our squadron lost 1 B17, and the 8th Air Force dropped 2,780 tons of bombs.

After a number of evasive action maneuvers, the flak let up, and we set sail for England, truly thankful to have survived our 20th mission. I thought to myself, *I never want to go there again.*

After finishing a lengthy debriefing and returning to our squadron area, it was hard to believe the red alert flag was flying in the breeze. Could they not just let us get over one mission before we started worrying about another? Someone yelled, "Say la gare," meaning, "C'est la guerre."

Thursday, July 20, 1944

Lieutenant Ray Strate crew mission number 21, 390th Bomb Group mission number 154. "Surely!" we said. "It will be a short mission after what we went through yesterday." Our ground forces were stuck and unable to move. The big brass must certainly know that we needed to saturate the front lines, didn't they? We were up early again, a bad sign, but the weather was beautiful. I don't think I have mentioned it, but the sun coming up over England is a glorious sight. The grass and the trees are a color of green that is unlike any other place I have ever seen, probably because it rains so much. When the sun does shine, it makes it exceptionally beautiful, which I think is a good sign.

The mission curtain was drawn back, and once again, my heart sank. Why had I said, "I don't want to go back there ever again?" Another maximum effort. Our ground crews most certainly worked all night long, repairing the 350 heavily damaged airplanes. I pray they did not overlook anything. We joked among ourselves—maximum effort, every plane that can fly will fly. We knew that meant some very old planes, held together with baling wire, would be called on for one more battle.

The ribbon stretched deep into central Germany, meaning three-fourths of all the guns and fighter planes in Der Fuhrer's Deutschland would have a crack at us, both from the ground and in the air. Jeff said, "Maybe they shot up all their ammo yesterday and have not gotten it replaced yet." Oh, yeah!

That sinking feeling I got when the odds of our returning safely were weighted against us was back. The more missions we flew, the more I thought about what they had told us when we arrived at Framlingham. As of the day we arrived, the chance for surviving was one in six. Every sixth plane would be shot down. If you lived through six missions, you were average. Twelve missions doubled your chances of going down. Now it was our twenty-first mission, and we were on borrowed time.

Steve said, "Hey, Chuck, snap out of it. We have a job to do, and this is going to be a ditto of yesterday." We would be on a similar route into and out of Germany. Would they be waiting for us again or, perhaps, be fooled into thinking we would not possibly try it again?

In addition to our (MY) other worries, we would be flying a different plane. Since the Munich mission destroyed (or so we thought) our wonderful Good-O-Yank, we were assigned to fly a B17G, serial number 337564, with the name Little Moron painted on the nose. Now don't you think a name like *that* gives you a good feeling? It was one of the oldest planes on the base, with seventy-eight missions. Six into seventy-eight equals thirteen average lifetimes. It had patches on top of patches. Every surface and every major part on it had been replaced at least once. The one thing that stuck in my mind was the pilot and copilot controls were worn smooth like the steering wheel on a very old automobile.

On the other side of the coin, this old plane had proven its mettle and brought back its crew safely, time after time. Two crews had completed their tours with her, and we felt good about flying such a lucky lady.

The 8th Air Force sent 1,172 bombers and 542 fighters back to the Leipzig area, which is about 120 miles south of Berlin, to hit oil and manufacturing plants. There were 30 different targets, the largest of which were Dessau, Leipzig, Kothen, Lutzkendorf, Merseberg, Wetzlar, Erfurt, Gotha, and Schmalkalden.

The 390th target is Lutzkendorf, which is very near Leipzig. Our escort consisted of 50 P38s on the first leg in and last leg out, 60 P47s on the second leg in and second leg out, and 100 P51s near and over the target. They did a remarkable job of keeping the German fighters away from our formations (bless them), but they could only look down on us as we took blistering flak from the time we hit the coast of France until we crossed the English Channel on the way home.

We were mercifully spared fighter attacks on our group, but there were B17s and B24s falling in every direction we looked. One of the things our debriefing officers had told us to look for were parachutes from stricken bombers, and today, it looked like a parachute drop zone.

Bomber crews shot down 11 German fighters and damaged 9, claiming 7 probables. Sadly, we reported 19 bombers lost and 372 damaged, with 159 crewmen MIA. Our fighter losses were 8, but they shot down 15 Germans. Unfortunately, we also lost one of our greatest fighter aces, Lieutenant Colonel Francis "Gabby" Gabreski, who was shot down while strafing.

I can't say enough about our fighter escort pilots. It took courage and guts to fly 500 miles into enemy territory, knowing you were far from home and outnumbered many times over, to jump right into the midst of it. To see literally hundreds of Me109s and Fw190s rising up in waves headed for the front of our bomber formations must have been a terrifying experience. I was privileged to be able to listen in on our fighter radio frequencies and hear the absolute calmness in their voices. It would sound something like, "This is FIREBALL LEADER, Jim, follow me and watch my tail. The rest of you pick out a target and stay on it." "Go after the bandits attacking the lead formation." "Okay, here we go." "Bill, you have two on your tail, break." "Well done, Fireball, assemble on me at 31,000 'til the next wave." "Watch those Me210s and He111s off to the left, firing rockets into our bombers."

And so it would go, until we were well on the way home. The fighters were gone, but the flak never seemed to let up. It is a terrible feeling to be shot at and to hear it coming closer and closer. You just draw up in a knot and shiver. Talk to any bomber crewman and he will tell you, the flak is the thing that got to you most. Many men cracked up and couldn't take it any longer. Others held on by their nails, until they got what was called FLAK leave, which was a week to ten days, usually at the "Miami beaches" of England. Most were on the southernmost coast of England at the peacetime resort areas. I don't think the water temperature ever got above sixty degrees, but that is another story. We yet had to get home from this hellish mission.

Finally, we crossed the English channel near Dunkirk, France. We saw a B17 smoking and in trouble ahead of us, and watched as they hit the water about halfway to the English coast. There was a flight of P38s circling, and we could see the English rescue boats heading toward it. I felt badly about that crew but encouraged to see how well the rescue unfolded. We later learned the B17 was from the 306th Bomb Group and all but one crew member was saved.

I can't remember when our crew was so completely drained. After back-to-back missions deep into Germany, we couldn't get the sound of flak to stop. At debriefing, I gave my shot of Scotch to Ray. He was wringing wet. How he and all the other pilots handled all the pressure they were under was amazing. Just flying that big four-engine bird and keeping in close formation, with sometimes feet or inches between planes was hard enough, much less having flak, fighters, and a thousand other things to think of. We were fortunate to have been chosen to serve on Ray's crew.

As we stumbled back to our squadron area, just holding it together 'til we got to our bunks, we heaved a sigh of relief. Even though the weather was clear, there was no alert flag flying over squadron headquarters.

As I drifted off to sleep, I hoped the 2,667 tons of bombs we dropped on Der Fuhrer today had taken its toll so we would not have to repeat that trip.

Friday, July 21, 1944

We were awakened early by the sound of our 390th Group taking off, long before daylight. Thankfully, our 571st Squadron was not flying as those last two missions had left us, literally, shaking in our boots.

When we found out where they were going, we were even more thankful. The 8th Air Force, in still another maximum effort with 1,110 bombers participating, dropped 2,415 tons of bombs on 26 targets. The largest were Saarbrucken, Munich, Regensburg, Schweinfurt, and Ludwigshafen. Again, they flew deep into southwest Germany, and again to targets that were heavily defended, both with flak and fighters. This was an area protected by several squadrons of the new Messerschmitt Me262 jet fighters, the fastest fighters of World War II.

The 2nd Division, with 433 B24s, attacking targets at Oberpfaffenhofen, Saarbrucken, and Munich, got the worst of it, losing 22 B24s, damaging 181, and losing 205 crewmen. In turn, they shot down 10 German planes.

The 1st and 3rd Divisions lost an additional 9 bombers, for a total loss of 31, 362 damaged, and 288 men lost. They were escorted by 795 fighters who destroyed 9 enemy planes and lost 8. It was a very rough mission and a very costly one.

Saturday, July 22, 1944

Bad weather over the continent kept everyone grounded except 7 B17s that dropped leaflets on Kiel, Hamburg, and Bremen. Escorts were 34 P51s with no losses; however, our fighters took out 2 Me109s.

Sunday, July 23, 1944

The 390th did not fly, and only 280 bombers flew ground-support missions along the front lines in France. One bomber was lost, with 193 fighters flying escort.

Monday, July 24, 1944

The 390th Bomb Group mission number 156. As we went into the briefing hut, there was the same kind of excitement in the air that we felt on D-Day, June 6. There was a crispness in the walk of the briefing crew as they walked down the aisle from the rear of the room to the podium. Harvey leaned over and whispered, "Uh-oh, something is up."

"Tens-hut. As you were."

"Men, let's get right to it. Our ground forces are building up along the beaches by the tens of thousands. The Germans, give them credit, are using the centuries-old hedgerows, having stopped our troops in their tracks just a few miles inland from the beaches." He pulled back the curtain, and the entire gathering gasped. The ribbon showing our mission route to the target was so short, it didn't look like we were leaving England. It crossed the Channel, right over the invasion beaches. Our target is a strip of land 7 miles long and 1/2 mile wide, on a line from Saint Lo to Periers, France. Imagine, if you can, 1,586 bombers and 671 fighters converging on that little strip of land and dropping their bombs on the German defenders.

Problems arose as we neared the target area. Clouds at ground level kept most of our formations from releasing their bombs, and they were ordered back to England. Those that did dropped 944 tons of bombs, but were having difficulty identifying their exact targets. The thing we feared most happened as someone dropped short, killing 20 and wounding many more of our own soldiers. We lost 3 bombers and 5 fighters to ground fire, and I would not be at all surprised if it were not from our own troops being tired of being bombed. Our fighters shot down 5 German planes and destroyed 13 on the ground.

Tuesday, July 25, 1944

Eighth Air Force mission number 494, 390th Bomb Group mission number 157. It was a cloudy day, and we all thought our mission would be scrubbed, but no such luck. Briefing was short and sweet, the identical mission as yesterday. The only thing different was a warning, repeated over and over. *"Do not drop short. We killed some of our own men yesterday, and we absolutely do not want a repeat."*

The target, again, was a 7-mile-long, 1/2-wide strip between Periers and Saint Lo, near the Cherbourg Peninsula, just in front of our ground forces. One thousand six hundred eighty-seven bombers and 720 fighters were to saturate this small area again, and General George Patton was going nuts to get his 6th Armored Division moving.

Over 3,000 Allied bombers dropped more than 4,000 tons of bombs in just over 2 hours. How anything could survive this onslaught is truly unbelievable, but later reports said a very few German soldiers, although incoherent, did survive. The bombing caused the German front line to fall back toward Cherbourg, leaving a huge gap in the German lines. American troops of the US 1st Army and Patton's Armored raced through. This was the beginning of the end for Hitler.

We lost 5 bombers and 2 fighters to ground fire and were saddened to learn when we landed at Framlingham, in spite of all the precautions, someone had dropped short again. One hundred two US soldiers were killed and 380 wounded. We never saw the ground from the moment we left England until we returned. It is a true miracle that many more ground troops were not lost.

I marked down my 23rd mission, leaving only 12 more. If only the rest could be as easy as the last two, I would be really happy.

Wednesday, July 26, 1944

Eighth Air Force mission number 496. No heavy bombers flew today, but 192 P47 fighter bombers attacked fuel dumps in France.

Thursday, July 27, 1944

Eighth Air Force missions numbers 498 and 499. Escorted by 164 fighters, 146 bombers bombed coastal batteries at Brussels and Ghent, dropping 192 tons of bombs without any losses. An additional 204 fighter bombers bombed and strafed trains and railroads near Rouen, France.

Along about this time, combat crews' morale was being sorely tested. Up until late May 1944, crews were required to fly 25 missions. Just as our crew started our missions, because so many crews were being killed, captured, or wounded, replacements could not keep up. As a result, the number of missions was raised to 30, and even that didn't solve the problem. We were just losing too many men, so subsequently, it was raised to 35 missions. It looked for the world like they were determined to kill us all. Then, an order came down from US Army Air Force that there would be no minimum number of missions. **We would be required to fly as long as we were needed.** However, they also directed that flying time could be determined by the 8th Air Force flight surgeons, who immediately wrote a directive that under no circumstances would flight crews be required to fly more than 35 missions. Thank heaven for our flight surgeons. I am certain they saved my life and many others.

Friday, July 28, 1944

Eighth Air Force mission number 501, 390th Bomb Group mission number 158. Any ideas we had that we might possibly get another easy milk run were dashed when the curtain was drawn, and the ribbon showing our mission path, starting in Framlingham, stretched on and on into east central Germany. The target for our 390th Group is Merseberg, not far from Leipzig. The purpose for our mission is to destroy the German oil reserves.

The 8th Air Force dispatched 1,057 bombers and 753 fighters. Reports were coming in to intelligence that the German war effort was experiencing serious shortages of oil, and we were being sent to help finish it off.

Just getting to the target area in central Germany was hard enough in itself. Hitting the target and getting back home safely was getting harder and harder to do. However, since I did not control our destiny, *off we went into the wild blue yonder.*

Since our plane, the Good-O-Yank, had been battered and sent off to the B17 graveyard, we now had to fly whatever was available. This time we were assigned a B17G named Gentleman Jim, veteran of 83 missions with enough patched holes to prove it. There again, she had survived; maybe she had a few more lucky missions left. She had helped three crews finish their tours and go home.

The 2nd Bomb Division, with 180 B24s and 111 B24s from the 3rd Division, was sent just across the Channel to bomb fuel supplies and V-weapon (Buzz Bombs and high-altitude rocket bombs) sites in northwest France and around Brussels, Belgium. Bad weather prevented them from dropping their bombs. They lost no aircraft, but still got credit for a mission. Now, that is what I call a milk run.

Our part of today's missions, consisted of 766 B17s to hit targets at Merseberg, Leipzig, and Wiesbaden. The way the Germans defended this area, you would think Hitler himself was there. We had to fight our way all across Germany.

The Germans are an intelligent and cunning adversary, and they had many terribly destructive weapons. It seems as though every couple of months, they introduced a new secret weapon. Among them were the blitzkrieg; the Tiger tank; the V1 Buzz Bomb; the V2 Rocket Bomb; the Fw190 Focke-Wulf fighter plane; the Me110 Messerschmitt, with bombs dangling on a cable and lowered into our formations; the Me210 Messerschmitt, fitted with rocket launchers; and the Me262 Messerschmitt jet engine fighter. Today, for the first time, we saw a new secret weapon, the Messerschmitt Me163 rocket fighter. It is demoralizing to see a plane with that kind of speed, streaking across the sky at over seven hundred miles per hour, capable of breaking the sound barrier. What we didn't know was that it was only capable of maintaining that speed for a very short time, and then it became a glider and easy prey for our P51s. The Me163 never became a threat to our bomber formations, but we didn't know that at the time.

In my opinion, the greatest secret weapon of the Germans was the 88-millimeter antiaircraft gun. The Germans virtually used it on everything—tanks, rail cars, boats, artillery, and, of course, aircraft. I have never seen any statistics on this gun, but I do know, they shot literally hundreds of Allied aircraft down. Today was no exception; we lost 7 bombers and 2 fighters. While our fighters shot down 5 German airplanes, our 1,754 tons of bombs started large fires that could be seen up to 10,000 feet.

On the way home, we regretted having gone there, but were content in that we had done enough damage that we would not be going back for a while.

Also, on the way home, we saw two B17s from the One-hundredth Bomb Group crash into each other for no apparent reason. We watched but did not see any chutes, a constant reminder that just flying in formation is a very difficult and dangerous task. I felt for the One-hundredth, who carried the square D on their tail. This square D also acted as a magnet for the German fighters.

The crew of Lieutenant Ray Strate had now completed twenty-four missions, and we were beginning to feel it. Surely, we will get a few short missions now.

After debriefing, most of us skipped chow and went straight to bed. The stress that comes from being alert and in combat for hours on end can completely drain you.

Saturday, July 29, 1944

I wrote in my diary the night of July 28 that I hoped we would get a few days' rest. The next thing I remember was "Tens-Hut. Lieutenant Ray Strate crew number 86, up and at 'em." I could not believe it. We were flying again?

I took a quick shower. After sweating in my flight suit on that long mission to Merseberg yesterday, I really needed it. It also got my eyes open. A good breakfast of orange juice, pancakes, and fresh eggs made me feel like a new man. I was ready to go. "Let's get number 25 behind us."

At briefing, the operations officer said, "Men, you did a wonderful job yesterday at Merseberg." He hesitated. "However," he said, as he pulled back the curtain, "you only did half the job, so today we are going back to finish them off."

The ribbon showing our mission route was almost identical to the one we flew only yesterday. The moan was loud and long. "Weather on the target will be clear, and we are expecting excellent results. Now, go get the job done. And, oh, yes, good luck."

In spite of the outlook of another rough mission, our crew seemed in good spirits.

This time there were 1,228 bombers and 775 fighters, circling around in the clouds, in the dark, trying to get into formation in an area 200 miles long and 100 miles wide, 13,055 men, off to battle (boys, I should say, since the average age was around twenty-one years old)...a piece of cake! Speaking of cake, on all these long missions, we had been missing our noon meal, and would come home so dog-tired, we would go straight to bed, without the evening meal. Maybe that's Hitler's supreme weapon. He would starve us to death.

As we crossed the coast of France, we fired all our weapons to be sure they were ready. It was a coincidence, I am sure, but we almost immediately began getting flak bursts. Ray came on the intercom and said, "We must have made them mad."

We did it a little differently this time. We split into two major groups with 657 B17s going back to Merseberg, and 571 going to Bremen. Both groups' targets were oil refineries. This also served to split up the German defenders, and as a result, our 390th BG got hit by only half as many fighters as yesterday. Even so, it didn't seem any easier. A flight of Me210s flew over us, dropping bombs into our formations. This was not very effective, however, and they only got one chance before our fighters got on them, and they hightailed it out of our sight.

The most effective tactic used against our formations was to line up 20 to 30 Me109s or Fw190s abreast and come straight at us from 12 o'clock level. Every time they did this, bombers fell from the sky. Our best defense was for our fighters to get to them before they got to us. With 10 guns on each bomber, and 12,280 50-caliber machine guns firing at one time, we always got some of them. On this day, we made them pay. Our bombers shot down 15, damaged 8, and had 3 probables. Our fighters downed 24 Germans. Along with their flak, however, the Germans accounted for 17 bombers and 7 fighters.

It was a wild and woolly time, with airplanes of every kind and description, in every conceivable attitude, right side up, upside down, climbing, diving, corkscrewing, spinning, and exploding. We saw an American fighter on the tail of a German, who was on the tail of an American.

The Fw190s flew right through our formation, between B17s, where there was just enough room for them to get through. We thought, *What kind of idiot would dare do that?* only to see an American P51 on *his* tail. It took courage and a little insanity.

I didn't *see* it happen, but I *know* it did. Bomber guns following a German fighter did not always release their trigger soon enough to keep from hitting our own planes. We were constantly reminded by Ray, "For God's sake, don't shoot our own 'little friends.'"

Although we were not singled out for a pressed attack, our close friends in the 100th Bomb Group were. Our 390th Group lost 2 planes, but the 100th lost 8. The bloody 100th bore the brunt, yet again. All told, we lost 17 bombers, with damage to 445. Thankfully, the sky was full of parachutes, so hopefully, many survived. We were all tired and shaken, but thankful to be alive as we made our way back to England.

I know it will be hard for my readers to believe, but as we landed red flares filled the air, denoting there were many wounded aboard. Those planes got immediate clearance to land, and there was a steady stream of ambulances taking the wounded to the hospital.

Once on the ground, we were taken to an assembly area where there was a Red Cross truck, with a side that let down, exposing several Red Cross girls passing out doughnuts and coffee.

When we finished the doughnuts, we were moved to another line where we received a booster shot in each arm. These shots made your arms go limp like they were filled with lead. Some passed out cold, on the ground.

Once through that line, we were lined up one more time, as it was the end of the month and payday. We would stand in front of the payroll officer and a sergeant helper who would read our name, rank, serial number, and state the amount we were to get, then have us sign the payroll ledger and hand us our few dollars.

Afterward, we went to debriefing and to stow our flying gear. I heard Jeff Fuller say as he went out of sight, "Let's hit the sack, boys, no chow again tonight."

I am convinced that had we been called to fly again tomorrow, we just could not have physically been able to go. Thankfully, they did not call us, and we slept 'til noon.

Sunday, July 30, 194

Eighth Air Force mission number 505. The only planes flying today were 255 fighters, sweeping up and down the front lines in support of our ground troops.

Monday, July 31, 1944

Eighth Air Force mission number 507, 390th Bomb Group Mission number 160. We were glad when we found out we were not flying today because the mission was to Munich and Ludwigshafen, where they were to bomb chemical and industrial plants. What was it with bombing Munich? It seemed every other mission was back to Munich. You could always count on heavy losses when bombing in this area, and today was no exception. The Germans accounted for 16 bomber and 3 fighter losses. We delivered 3,096 tons of bombs, and our fighters were credited with 18 German planes destroyed.

Tuesday, August 1, 1944

Eighth Air Force mission number 508, 390th Bomb Group mission number 161. Tactical support for the ground forces began in earnest. The entire 8th Air Force struck at targets along the battle lines, from the southeast coast of France, across the Riviera, and up the west coast to Belgium.

Our 571st Squadron did not fly again. They must have known how badly we needed rest, after two back-to-back missions to Merseberg. All the other squadrons in our group (the 568th, 569th, and 570th) did go and took part in a unique mission, code-named Buick. This was a mission to drop supplies to the French Resistance fighters in the Chalon-sur-Saone and Savoie area. Over 2,000 containers were successfully dropped to those brave men behind the German lines. This mission, and others like it, contributed greatly to shortening the war. With the equipment they received in these drops, many railroad lines were blown up, and numerous bridges were destroyed.

The rest of the 8th AF bombed more than 30 different targets, mostly airfield and bridges. Of the 1,291 bombers and 432 fighters that completed these missions, we lost 5 bombers and 4 fighters. More than 2,100 tons of bombs were used. This was a milk run mission, short and fairly safe. Maybe we will get a few more like it.

Wednesday, August 2, 1944

Eighth Air Force mission number 510, 390th Bomb Group mission number 162. My squadron, the 571st, did not fly again, and we were told it was because our planes were so badly damaged on our two Merseberg missions. The 8th Air Force put up 836 bombers and 690 fighters to attack supply lines and bridges in and around Paris. There were more than 30 separate targets.

The pace of the Allied offense had now been speeded up sharply. With General Patton and his tanks outrunning their supply lines and preventing the Germans from rushing reinforcements to where they were needed, the Air Force was called upon to bomb railroad marshaling yards, oil dumps, bridges, and airfields.

B24s of the 2nd Division were sent to bomb an important bridge on the River Loire at Neuvy, which is south of Paris. Although they did extensive damage, the bridge was not closed, and Germans were pouring northward to plug a hole in their defense line. I point this out as it is customary when a target is missed that it is reassigned for another strike.

The 8th AF losses today were 5 bombers and 1 fighter. Our bombers dropped 1,992 tons of bombs, and our fighters destroyed 9 German planes.

Thursday, August 3, 1944

Eighth Air Force mission number 512, 390th Bomb Group mission number 164. You guessed it, our target for today was the bridge at Neuvy-sur-Loire, the same one the 36 B24s missed. They were determined to knock out that bridge or else. Today, 38 B17s would try again.

In addition to our mission, 54 B17s were to bomb a railroad yard at Mulhouse, France; 62 B17s were to bomb a railroad yard at Saarbrucken; 106 B17s, an oil refinery at Merville; 68 B17s, the railroad yards at Strasbourg; 15 B17s were assigned a railroad bridge near Saarbrucken; 36 B17s, a bridge at Joigny / La Roche-Guyon; 27 B17s, targeting an airfield at Conches; 11 B24s, an airfield at Etampes-Mondesir; and 12 B24s were to bomb a railroad yard at Melun.

In the afternoon, another Eighth AF mission number 513 had 126 B17s and 121 B24s bombing V-weapon sites at Pas de Calais; 76 B24s, bridges and V-weapon sites at Brussels, Vivoorde, and Ghent in Belgium; 22 B24s to bomb V-weapon sites in Pas de Calais; 10 B24s bombing road bridges at Lille/Marquette; 10 B24s, bridges at Lille-Sequedin; 24 B24s to bomb road and rail bridges at Courchelettes; 49 B24s to bomb road bridges at Harnes; and 8 B24s to bomb rail marshaling yards at Ghent.

I list all this to show what a fantastic job the Eighth Air Force did in coordinating just one day's missions.

In addition, the fighter bombers were out in force, dropping 18 tons of bombs on oil supply dumps and bridges near Paris and Strasbourg. In all, there were 1,154 bombers and 726 fighters flying every which way, at all kinds of altitudes, and from east, west, north, and south. It is an absolute miracle that we didn't run all over each other.

A low cloud cover kept some groups from hitting their targets, but most got good to excellent results. Over 2,500 tons of explosives were unleashed on the German war machine which was, for the first time, beginning to get the feeling that their momentum was changing and that they were backing up instead of moving forward.

We lost 8 bombers and had 273 damaged, mostly from flak. The Luftwaffe was nowhere to be found, although the final totals show that bomber crews shot down 4 enemy planes, and escort fighters accounted for 13.

Friday, August 4, 1944

Eighth Air Force mission number 514, 390th Bomb Group mission number 165. In the briefing room today, the mood was somber. Everyone was hoping for another short mission to support the frontline troops, but when the curtain was drawn, there was a mighty groan and a lot of "Oh, nos."

The mission route tape for the 390th Group ran up the English Channel, past the Frisian Islands, home of 5,000 flak guns, but we were staying out of their range. A funny thing about the enemy there, no matter how far out of range we flew, they always threw up a barrage, as if to say, "Stay away."

We flew on up toward Denmark, then took a quick right down the Elbe River to Hamburg. Hamburg was heavily defended as it was the largest port in Germany, the hub of German manufacturing, and had miles of huge oil storage tanks. We had flown past it many times, and you could always tell how many flak guns they had by the amount of heavy black smoke left from their exploding flak above the city. It appeared like a giant thunder cloud, just hanging in place. One other thing about Hamburg, different from most other German cities, was once our planes got within a certain distance, it triggered an elaborate smoke screen that completely obliterated the ground. Only Berlin and very few other places had this defense. You would be amazed at how well it hid the city and how quickly it was deployed. The Germans had completely encircled the city with smudge pots so that no matter which way the wind was blowing, they covered the city with black smoke, thereby blocking our targets from view.

I knew by the amount of sweat pouring off Ray's head that he was worried about this mission. Fortunately, the 8th AF chose to bomb four major areas of Germany, and that would assist in splitting up their fighter defenses.

All the B17s in the 3rd Division, 358 total, were assigned to bomb targets, mostly oil refineries, in the Hamburg and Bremen regions.

The 1st Division, with 425 B17s, were being sent to Peenemunde, the large facility on the Baltic Sea used to develop secret weapons.

We did not know it yet, but this mission was an attempt to destroy Germany's secret plant for making heavy water (altered water) used in the making of atomic bombs. We had never heard of heavy water or atomic bombs, but had Germany not been stopped, they would have had the ultimate bomb before we did, and the outcome of World War II might have been vastly different.

With 426 B24s, the 2nd Division was being sent to bomb aircraft industry plants along the north coast of Germany, from the torpedo plants at Kiel to Rostock. Seventy-eight B24s were sent to bomb an oil refinery at Heide, southwest of Kiel, and an airfield at Husum.

Utilizing 1,307 bombers and 883 fighters, most of our targets were in a concentrated area, which allowed the Germans to deploy their fighters in one direction, but they were still separated enough to divide them.

As usual, when we turned out of the North Sea at the mouth of the Elbe River, the German fast-moving flak boats were firing at us all the way to Hamburg. We were being blasted all over the sky, and then we saw the fighters coming at us. It looked like the entire German Luftwaffe, mostly Me109s and Focke-Wulf Fw190s, twenty abreast, head-on. The ugly sound of their 20-millimeter cannon, thump, thump, thump, and the smell of their black-smoke gunpowder was like rotten eggs. I saw a Me109, turned on his back, come within 10 feet right over the top of us. Someone yelled, "Great God, did you see that? He was trying to ram us." Our plane was so noisy, with all our guns blazing away, the flak booming like thunder all around us, plus the German fighters with their 20-millimeter cannon and 30-caliber machine guns wide open. We could hear the metal tearing through our plane, and see spots of daylight opening up the aluminum shell like a can opener. Off to our right, four Me210s were flying parallel with our formation, and we could see flashes of light, followed by a trail of smoke, headed straight for us. They were lobbing rockets into our close formation. Where were our escorts? As we looked around, we saw they were engaged with a large force of German planes. The fighters left us as we started our bomb run, moving out of range of their own flak guns, but we knew once we moved away from the heavy flak, they would be coming back.

Being right on the Elbe River, Hamburg was an easy target to spot from the air as it has two large tributaries within the city. Our target was the large oil refinery northwest of the center of the city, not far from the Elbe River. We were being knocked all over the sky but, finally, got "Bombs away" and turned on a heading for home.

I yelled, "Bomb bay all clear," and watched the doors close. I noticed ten or more large holes in the doors, and one door was twisted so that it would not completely close. I could see Hamburg twenty-nine thousand feet below. Smoke was everywhere, so I figured we must have clobbered our primary target. We didn't learn until a few days later that due to the terrific beating we were taking and the smoke screen, we had missed our target miserably. The good news was we had dropped our bombs in an open field, and the whole area lit up like fireworks. Apparently, we had hit a camouflaged munitions storage dump.

Immediately after the bomb run, we made a steep left turn and went into a deep dive, both to gain speed and to take evasive action. That dad-burned flak didn't seem to care where we went; it went right with us. I was still throwing out the bundles of foil, but nothing seemed to work except getting the heck out of there. Later, in debriefing, we were informed that the Germans were trying a new tactic in which they did not try to follow our formation, but simply shot at a certain spot and altitude over and over. We were doing saturation bombing, which meant when the lead ship dropped its bombs, everyone dropped simultaneously. The flak gunners, firing at one point in the sky, hoped we would run into it, and we did.

It was not far to the relative safety of the North Sea, and you can be sure, we were hightailing it to get away from the booming, twisting and turning, smoking, stinking hell in the sky. I found myself and others on the crew screaming, "Go! Go! Go! Get out of here!" Ray and all the other pilots were using our descent from around twenty-nine thousand feet to obtain maximum speed. I could not remember another mission where our whole group was redlining all of its engines, scrambling to get away from that awful place.

I looked back, and the German fighters were back, but thankfully, our escorts were keeping them at bay. Never had we experienced such savage attacks, without regard to life or limb. The entire sky was full of fighters, from high above us down to treetop level, below us, turning, twisting, firing, smoking, and exploding. They kept coming, and our "little friends" made them pay. Even our usually quiet tail gunner came on intercom and said, "Won't this thing go any faster?" Looking back at the carnage, with planes and parachutes falling, Maggie, from his ball turret vantage point underneath our plane, kept repeating, "Holy cow! Holy cow! Holy cow!"

We lost 15 bombers, mostly from our 15th Bomber Wing, consisting of the 95th, the 100th, and the 390th Bomb Groups. We also lost 16 fighters, but the Germans paid dearly, losing 81 with 20 probables.

We later learned that for the first time, as one of the diversionary flights, a number of war-weary B17s were filled with bombs and were crewless, guided by radio control from other planes for strikes against V1 missile sites. They were mostly unsuccessful, and I believe that type of bombing was discontinued.

I wrote down mission number 27 in my logbook as we passed over the English Channel and the coast of East Anglia. We had dropped 3,321 tons of bombs, and I can speak for our entire crew, our nerves were shot. We were shaking, trembling, and wild-eyed from this wild ride. Exhausted almost to the point of nausea, it was difficult for our interrogators to get a clear picture of what had happened. Ray took three straight shots of Scotch and seemed the most coherent. I suppose that is why he was the captain of our team, but you could tell, at this pace, we were all headed for a collapse. One cannot stay in extreme pressure for hours without a wheel coming off.

I took the time to write Eleta before falling asleep with my flight clothes on. Just before falling asleep, someone said, "What if the alert flag is flying and we are flying tomorrow?" Everyone groaned. Maggie said, "Just tell them we can't go. We are shot." Harvey said, "I'm not going," and Steve said, "Me neither." Jeff chimed in, "But we have to go, we are soldiers." Sandy tiredly said, "Hey, you guys, shut up and go to sleep." And we did.

OFF TO THE FLAK-HAPPY FARM

Saturday, August 5, 1944

Eighth Air Force mission number 519. I woke up with a start. Something was definitely wrong; there was deathly silence. I hopped out of the sack and saw no one was moving. I looked outside. The sun was bright and high in the sky. Still, no sound. I didn't see a soul where usually, there were people going in all directions. I walked up to squadron headquarters; no flag was flying. I thought to myself, *I must be dead or dreaming*. I went inside the headquarters Nissen hut, and the desk sergeant looked at me and I looked at him. I must have looked perplexed because he said, "The 390th is standing down today, aren't you lucky?" Then, he added, "They have gone back to Magdeburg." I replied, "Thanks, Sarge," and rushed back to our hut to tell the crew the good news. Some were still asleep, but they didn't mind at all being awakened to tell them we were not flying today. We were all laughing and rejoicing when a corporal runner came in and said, "Lieutenant Strate's crew?" We all said in unison, "Oh, no, what is it?" "Lieutenant Strate wants to see one of you guys, PDQ." "Okay, we are on the way." Steve volunteered to go for what could only be bad news.

Steve was back in ten minutes and said, holding back a big grin, "Guess what?" Harvey said, "They have changed the rules and we are going to fly fifty missions!" "No, no," said Steve, "Ray said that beginning Monday, we will be on a one-week flak leave." **WOW!** The crew went nuts, hollering, banging on the walls, jumping up and down like a bunch of kids. You would have thought we were going home. "It's about time," we all shouted. "Where are we going, Steve?" Maggie asked. Steve replied, "We are going to a summer resort in Bournemouth." "Where the heck is that?" yelled Sandy. "I don't know, and I don't care, just as long as we won't be flying for a week," said Steve. We were truly ready for this, and I am sure, our flight surgeon thought we were too. What a relief!

We rode our bikes around the base and, after lunch, washed our clothes, sewed our stripes on our dress uniforms, and stopped by headquarters to get the latest scoop on how the 8th Air Force mission went. We already knew they went to Magdeberg and the surrounding area, but we learned they also bombed 25 other targets. Large strikes were at Brunswick and Hanover.

We lost 13 bombers and had 492 damaged out of 1,212. There were 658 fighters who lost 6, but destroyed 33 German planes. The mission hit, primarily, oil refineries and aircraft manufacturing plants in central and northern Germany. Dropped bombs totaled 3,220 tons.

Sunday, August 6, 1944

Eighth Air Force mission number 524. I was up early, and Harvey and I went to church down in Parham. Knowing that we would not be flying for a while gave us a whole new outlook. After lunch, we went for a long bike ride in the English countryside. We were two old married men with a lot in common. Harvey was a really good friend and a genuinely fine boy.

The 390th flew today, along with 1,186 others. The 95th and 390th were part of the 3rd Division that flew on to Russia on the second shuttle mission. Again, this group was given a fairly easy target at Gdynia, Poland, while the rest of the 8th hit targets in Berlin and Hamburg and, as expected, paid a precious price, losing 24 bombers. Our fighters destroyed 33 German planes, while losing 6. Major George Preddy shot down 6.

We were up early, having breakfast with our friends on other crews who knew we were going on flak leave. They were all having fun kidding us about being "flak happy" and having to be sent to the "funny farm." We didn't care; we were glad to be getting away from this gosh-awful war and all the killing and maiming going on, even if it were for only seven precious days.

Our crew officers were being sent to another resort area since officers and enlisted personnel were not allowed to fraternize. It was always a mystery to me why we could fly into battle, in the closest companionship, to die together, but were not allowed to have a cup of coffee together. We were best and closest of friends, but back on the base, it was a crisp salute and a "Good morning, Lieutenant, sir."

We were a happy bunch as we were taken by truck to the train station to catch the train that ran from Scotland to Liverpool Station in London. It was only ninety miles to London, but we stopped at every small town on the way.

We had to transfer by taxi from Liverpool Station to the Cannon Street Station since no trains ran through London. It is like Chicago. Cannon Station is very near the London Bridge, which crosses the Thames River on the south bank at the London Bridge Station. We were delayed for about an hour, as there was a V-bomb (Buzz Bomb) air raid attack. Most of the bombs fell on the north side, with a couple near Liverpool Station and the Bank of England, the area we left just before coming here. It reminded us of our last visit to London.

We were thinking it would just be our luck to be killed here in London after surviving all those terrible missions. Soon, we were moving again, and we kept looking for Stonehenge and the town of Romsey on the Test River, and Broadlands, the home of Lord Mountbatten, a beautiful home where Prince Charles and Lady Diana stayed during their honeymoon in 1981.

Just down the road, we came to the great port city of Southampton, whose history of shipping goes back to the year 1100 and beyond. This is one of the great ports of the world and still is, even today. It was home port for such mighty ships as the *Mayflower*, the *Queen Mary*, and the *Titanic*.

From Southampton, we could see the Isle of Wight, the Miami of England, where the English rich and powerful have their summer homes or castles. For instance, Queen Victoria lived here much of her life and she died here.

Everywhere you turn in this part of England abounds with rich history. Whereas, in America, we think two to three hundred years is history, in England, they consider history by centuries, back to 800 or 900 AD.

We made a right turn at Southampton, and in about 10 miles, we came to Lyndhurst where, in the year 1079, William the Conqueror set aside 150 square miles of forest and meadowland as his private hunting reserve. There is still much wild game with deer and ponies.

Slowly, we covered 20 more miles to arrive at our destination of Bournemouth, on the southernmost coast of England.

FLAK LEAVE AT BOURNEMOUTH, ENGLAND

Bournemouth was founded in 1810 by an Army officer who liked the way it was situated on a high cliff, overlooking the ocean, and its seven miles of beautiful white-sand beaches. It has become one of the most popular resorts in all of England.

It was evening when we arrived, and we were trucked to the Langtry Manor Hotel, where they received us as if we were royalty. We had just enough time to get checked in and shown our rooms before the evening meal. We had huge individual rooms, with a high ceiling and highly polished wood floors. The thing that caught my attention was the large four-poster bed, high enough that you needed a footstool to get in. And clean white sheets, WOW! This is heaven. There was a writing table, with fruit in a bowl, and a couch with two chairs, with a connecting water closet (bath) and hot-water showers. I just wanted to jump right into the middle of that big bed and sleep 'til December, but a soft bell rang, telling us it was dinnertime.

We entered the very large dining room with tables spaced around windows that stretched from floor to ceiling, overlooking a beautiful English garden, with little paths leading to benches, and flowers everywhere. The tables were set with white tablecloths and real silver. There were three glasses at each setting and three of every kind of silverware, spoons, forks, and knives. I was amazed! What in the world do you need all these dishes and silverware for? We had gotten so used to eating off an army metal tray, with little compartments, I felt I would be embarrassed, not knowing what each piece was for. Four forks, five spoons, and three knives…soldiers had fought battles with less than that. The waiters made us feel right at home. There were seven courses, and each time something was brought to the table, they told us what to use. Man, what a meal, roast beef and ham, four fresh vegetables, wine or beer if we wanted it. Then came a big dish of plum pudding with real ice cream. Man, oh, man, the Good-O-Yank crew pigged out. This room, with its long drapes by the windows, was so pleasant, we didn't want to leave.

After dinner, an Army officer explained the dos and don'ts for our stay and told us of the points of interest, and when he was through he said, "Boys, you are on your own. Have a good time." We never saw him again.

After sunset, it was dark as pitch; the English really knew how to "black out." We wanted to see what was going on, so we strolled over to the promenade along the top of the high cliff, overlooking the beach and the English Channel. It was deathly quiet, with no lights visible anywhere. There was a nice breeze, and the odor of fir trees filled the air. One reason the Britons loved to come here was because of the trees. They are supposed to have a medicinal healing effect for those with breathing problems, sort of like the eucalyptus trees of California.

As we turned to go back to our hotel, Harvey said, "Look over to your left." We looked and saw very bright searchlights snapping on, one at a time, until there seemed to be hundreds of shafts of light stabbing high into the dark sky. Someone said, "That's London, getting ready for an air raid." It was not long before the bombs began to drop on those poor souls in London. Soon, the sky was a rosy red, as the bombs exploded and the fires began. We could not see the barrage balloons, but we knew they were there. We had seen literally hundreds, hanging over the east side of London, with their long cables tethered to the ground to keep the low-flying planes and Buzz Bombs from getting through.

We watched the sky get brighter and brighter on into the night, then the searchlights started snapping off, and the fires diminished. Maggie shared all our feelings as we made our way to the hotel, "I am proud that we are helping the English people. They have suffered so much."

A warm bath in a luxurious tub, and I jumped into that beautiful bed. I can't remember saying a prayer that night. I was asleep before I even thought of it.

Tuesday, August 8, 1944

Oh, what a beautiful morning! Last breakfast was at 10:00 a.m. We were all awake on this bright sunshiny morning, served at our tables with fresh eggs, pancakes, bacon, and potatoes, with coffee and real orange juice. We also had melon if we liked. What war? There's no war here.

If the Air Force's aim was to boost our morale and our spirits, they certainly did it that first morning in Bournemouth. The dining room was on the corner of our building, and windows, floor to ceiling on two sides, with sunshine pouring in over flowers in the garden, was a sight you don't soon forget. I couldn't wait to write home to Eleta about this place.

After a leisurely breakfast, we walked out to the promenade along the edge of the cliff overlooking the English Channel. The panoramic view of the beach, far below, was absolutely breathtaking. As far as we could see was the blue water and the white sand, with people sunbathing. The beach formed a crescent and reminded me of home and Myrtle Beach, South Carolina. The big difference being that at Myrtle Beach, there are no high cliffs.

Some of our guys wanted to go swimming, but Harvey and I opted to wait until the afternoon. We wanted to look around the town to see where things were situated, so we went back to the Manor House to pick up bicycles. There were bike stands with bikes for us to use, and off we went.

Bournemouth is situated on a series of hills, and we found it easy to drift off down a long hill, forgetting that we would, eventually, have to pedal back up that same hill. Near the bottom of the hill seemed to be the center of town, and we stopped at one of the shops to buy a bathing suit. We were surprised that the only suits the stores had were made of wool. We shopped everywhere, but that was all there was. We said, "We know things are very bad in England, but this is ridiculous." We were told that cloth was in very short supply, and many people were having to use old, used clothes. The bathing suits were three pounds, six pence, which was just over fifteen dollars American. Off we went, back up the hill, to the Langrty Manor

House. We dressed with our bathing suits under our uniforms and headed down to the beach. It was seventy-two degrees and cool, but everyone was enjoying the sunshine. We walked down a ravine, a cutout place the English called a cline. It zigzagged down hundreds of steps to the sandy beach.

We noticed there were not many people in the water. Most were just sitting around, sunbathing. Harvey and I stripped off our uniforms and headed for the water. Not too far from the beach there were barricades, with rolls of barbed wire sticking out of the water, a defense against German invasions. Still further out in the water were steel frames, which were anti-tank barriers. We stopped at the water's edge to test the water temperature, and in up to our ankles, we quickly retreated. We looked up the beach and noticed that many stopped, watching us. When they saw us step back out of the water, they smiled and went back to what they were doing.

It's no wonder they looked at us and smiled. The water temperature today was fifty-two degrees which, we found out later, is the mean temperature for the Channel. With the water at fifty-two degrees Fahrenheit and the wind blowing, it would take your breath away. There was a thermometer near the stairs that led down to the beach, and it showed both air and water temperature. However, the British use the Celsius scale, and never having been exposed to it, we didn't know how that translated to Fahrenheit. We do now.

We said to one another, "We are not going to pay fifteen dollars for a swimsuit and not even get it wet." So, out we went up to our waist in the coldest water I had seen without ice in it. We were shivering and shaking, and Harvey said, "I don't know about you, Chuck, but I am getting the heck out of here." Now we understood why the downed airmen in the Channel had a life expectancy of fifteen minutes. That was enough swimming for us, and to further irritate us, the wool suits began to itch like crazy. We learned quickly to do as the British do. Wrap a blanket around yourself, take off that dratted bathing suit, and slip on your uniform.

The sun was warm, and further back on the beach out of the wind, we spread our blankets and lay down to absorb some rays. It was very pleasant here as we lay on the beach, looking up at the blue sky and talking about home.

I was beginning to get a little sunburned, so I climbed the stairs back up to the hotel. There was a table set up in the garden, with soft drinks, orange juice, hot tea (for the British help), and I must admit, I had really begun to like their afternoon tea and crumpets or crackers (we called them cookies).

I staked out a claim on a little bench over in the far corner of the garden and brought out my writing equipment. I went off into another world, writing to everyone I could think of, beginning with my beautiful wife, Eleta. I wrote Mom and Dad, my sister, Jeannie, married to an officer in the US Army Engineers whose specialty was building bridges. I wrote to my brother, Eddie, in Honolulu, Hawaii, and my younger brother, Preston, who was fast approaching draft age. He most recently had been working, after school and on Saturdays, with a brick mason company. His job was to toss bricks up to the masons building walls. After a whole year, he had built up the muscles in his arms, and all his buddies called him Rock, which came about because he would let them hit him on his shoulder as hard as they dared, only to hurt their hands. Even as a kid, he was already strong. We used to tussle, and it was all I could handle, and he was two years younger. Pres and I were very close; we were brothers, buddies, and friends. We never fought, but I cannot say that about older brother, Eddie. Pres was an exceptionally good boy, and we had many wonderful days playing together.

I wrote to my Aunt Louise, whom I dearly loved. She was a redheaded knockdown, beautiful lady. Hollywood missed her somehow, a straight-up perfectly poised, royalty type. I remember when our family on my mom's side had get-togethers at Christmas, Thanksgiving, and other special occasions, my Aunt Louise was the one chosen to play the piano, while we all gathered around to sing. My mom, my Aunt Louise, and my Aunt Janet were sisters, and all were accomplished piano players, but Aunt Louise was the best. In the words of today, she could really "get down." Her son, Harry "Sonny" Booker (too young yet for the war and I pray it will be over before he is called up) made a name for himself at Central High,

Charlotte, North Carolina's largest high school. We were all terribly proud of the very handsome Sonny Booker.

I wrote to everyone in the family and then started on some of my old high school friends who were in service at bases all over the world. Wilbur Cook, a close friend and former singing partner in our old Tin Can Quartet, was in the Navy somewhere in the Pacific. I wrote to Robert Little, recently sent to fight in Europe, and to Jack Heafner in the Army, in charge of a laundry unit. I am sure he was put there because of his training as a plumber in his dad's plumbing business. I also wrote to George Brannon. Although he had already been killed in action while flying in Africa, I did not hear about it for a couple of months.

Someone shook me and said, "Hey, Chuck, are you not going to eat dinner?" Time had completely gotten away from me. I said, "Yeah, I'm coming. I'm hungry as a bear."

After dinner, we strolled over to the top of the white cliff again, and facing toward France out over the bay, Steve said, "Boys, can you believe that just about one hundred miles straight out there, this very minute, our Army buddies are engaged in one of the greatest battles in history?" Maggie said, "Yeah, and they won't have a bed with clean sheets." Wow! He is so right. It sort of put us in a serious mood, and we didn't do much talking for the rest of the night.

Wednesday, August 9, 1944

On the morning of our third day, I was awakened just after sunrise, *wide awake* for some unknown reason. It was so quiet and peaceful, so unlike being back at our base at Framlingham, with a thousand engines roaring. The sun was bright, and for the entire time I was in England, it came up in the wrong place. It was disorienting to see the sun come up from over Europe. It seemed to me it should rise from the ocean side of England.

None of the rest of the crew were stirring, so I went down the hall to the dining room, where the smell was heavenly, fresh ground coffee, orange juice, pancakes with real butter, and a choice of English jellies and jams. Sitting by the open window, with the sun streaming in, I could hear the sound of the garden and the twitter of English sparrows. I thought to myself, *God is in His heaven, and all is right with the world*. How could we be in this terrible war, just a few miles away, with all the killing and maiming? I said a prayer of thanks for the food and this wonderful moment of peace.

I didn't want to wake any of the crew, so I checked out a bicycle and decided to ride to no place in particular. I rode through the town square, with its tall pine trees whistling in the breeze, and rode to the top of the cliffs. Out in the Channel, I could see hundreds of boats and ships passing by, no doubt coming or going from Cherbourg, France, just across the Channel. It seemed to me that Cherbourg should be to my east, but from where Bournemouth is located, it was directly south. Boats are a part of England, like nowhere else in the world. They are inseparable, and all English people live and breathe a love for the water.

After riding for what seemed like hours, I headed down Exeter Road toward downtown. The hill was long and steep. The wind in my face reminded me of home, when I first got a bicycle and used to take long rides in the country alone.

I found myself sailing down the street with my thoughts, far away. Coming up on Hinton Street was Saint Peter's Church, a huge building with a two-hundred-foot steeple. Buried here is one of England's great poets, Percival Shelley. Even if you do not like poetry, you owe it to yourself to read his "To a Skylark." His second wife, Mary, is equally famous. She was the author of the book *Frankenstein*.

So many great authors are from this area of England, such as Thomas Hardy, who wrote *Far from the Madding Crowd* and *Mayor of Casterbridge*, and Jane Austen, who wrote *Sense and Sensibility*, *Emma*, *Persuasion*, and *Pride and Prejudice*. The places they wrote about in their books are, for the most part, still there, just as they were when they wrote about them. We think in America, a home that is seventy-five to one hundred years old is really old, but in England, a three-hundred-year-old home with a thatched roof is common.

Daydreaming and speeding now, I slowed my bike to a mere fifty miles per hour at an intersection on Hinton Street, when I caught sight of something coming at me from my right. The next thing I remember, I was sprawled on the cobblestone street, my bike twenty-five feet away. At first thought, I must have been hit by a Buzz Bomb, but no, I wouldn't be crawling around. Still dazed, I could make out a small crowd standing above me and someone saying, "I say, ole boy, are you all right?" I tried to answer, but could not get my breath. I then noticed another bicycle, its front wheel twisted and bent beyond repair. As I struggled to get on my feet, I saw a man in uniform looking down at me. He said, "Sergeant, what in the world were you thinking, speeding down this hill without looking left or right?" Then I noticed the person I had clobbered was a captain. I thought, *Oh, no. I'll probably spend the rest of my time in England in the guard house*. But then, the captain took me by the shoulders and yelled, "Chuck, Chuck Richardson from Derita, you ole son of a gun, I'm glad to see you." As my wits came back and the fog lifted, I could see it was Marvin Little, with whom I had gone to school. He graduated two years ahead of me, and his brother, Robert, my same age, was the one I wrote a letter to yesterday.

How is it possible to go halfway around the world and have a bicycle accident with someone you went to school with? But, here it was.

This is the day that the hard and fast Air Force rule of no fraternizing between officers and enlisted men was tossed out the window. We dusted ourselves off, picked up what was left of our bikes, and retreated to a nearby pub, where Marvin would not let me pay for anything. We had a wonderful lunch and spent the next few hours talking of home.

Needless to say, this turned out to be one of the brightest moments of my entire time in England. In high school, the Littles, Marvin and Robert, were not particularly close friends. My closest connection was their sister, Margaret. She was not the most beautiful girl in school, but she had a wonderful personality and was so easy to talk to. I learned early on that the prettiest girls were out of my league. Girls like Hilda Gibbons (a true Hollywood-type beauty) and Janice Barnhardt (with beauty and brains) were surrounded by good-looking, upper-class boys (with cars). The fact is from the time of this bicycle accident until this writing (sixty years), I never saw the Littles again. Just knowing that he was from home and we were both homesick made it a special meeting, and as Marvin put it, "God has ordained that we, for some reason, run (actually crashed) into each other so far from home." The reason must have surely been to cheer us up and get us through the rest of the war.

Later in the afternoon, we reluctantly parted, promising to keep in touch. Even though he was assigned as an executive officer (non-flying) at the 306th Bomb Group only a few miles away, I never saw him again. *Such is the color of war.*

That night, I spent a quiet evening at a writing desk, sending picture postcards to Eleta and my family back home, telling them of my unbelievable experience of today. Thinking we may never get another chance, Harvey and I made plans to visit some of the places of interest in nearby towns the following day.

CHARLES J "CHUCK" RICHARDSON

THE DAY THE EARTH TREMBLED

Thursday, August 10, 1944

The morning of the fourth day, I got up early, and Harvey and I began our excursion. After a short ride of about thirty miles, we arrived in Winchester. Dating back to the year 800, it is one of the oldest cities in England and, before being moved to London, was once the capital.

One of the first things we visited was Winchester Cathedral; yes, the same one the Beatles made famous. It was started in the year 1066. William the Conqueror was crowned here, and his son is buried here, and so is the great English author Jane Austen. From its bell tower, you can see for miles, all the way to the Isle of Wight, pronounced "white," about twenty miles away.

Winchester is a lovely city with many beautiful gardens. We visited the Great Hall, where the English Parliament had its beginning. It was here that Sir Walter Raleigh (the one directly connected to my home state of North Carolina, our capital being named after him) was tried for conspiracy against King James I. He was convicted and beheaded in 1618.

We enjoyed Queen Eleanor's beautiful gardens and stopped to have tea and cookies at the City Mill, an old watermill that is still in operation on Bridge Street. I bought some postcards which I still have. Since our time was limited, we decided to go on to Salisbury, about 25 miles west of Winchester. Long before we arrived, we could see their most famous attraction, the Salisbury Cathedral. The granddaddy of all cathedrals in England, its spire reaches 404 feet, an inspiring sight from any point within 20 miles. We were told that the tower, which was added to the church in 1320, is not exactly straight up. It is about 4 feet off-center from being vertically straight. Inside is a clock said to be the oldest working mechanism in the world. The cathedral houses one of the four original copies of the Magna Carta.

This city is built where three different rivers come together. Its many gardens and early architecture provide wonderful places for those who enjoy history. We could have spent weeks here and not been able to visit all the interesting sights, but we wanted to visit Stonehenge, just 8 miles north.

STONEHENGE

When we got to Stonehenge, the mysterious arrangement of stone monuments, we walked up the stone pathway to the crown of a hill. It is the most visited attraction in England, and was first begun around 3000 BC. Except for the puzzling nature and the "How in the world did they do it?" with none of the modern tools we have today, it was somewhat of a disappointment. As we heard some Englishmen say, "It's nothing more than a pile of stones." Looking at it gives you the idea that the people who built it were no ordinary people. The thing is huge, about 1,500 feet across and more than 3/4 of a mile around. It originally had 98 stones spaced in a circle, with each stone denoting an astronomical event, such as where the sun came up at vernal equinox. There are other places in England where these stone circles are found, but none nearly as large as Stonehenge. When you consider that many of these huge stones were quarried from the mountains of Wales and transported either by land or sea over 200 miles, you can get some idea of the enormous undertaking for building this "whatever" it is. Some say that because of its circle within a circle, it was the forerunner of our current-day computer.

Stonehenge is set in a vast open field, and Harvey and I started back to the parking area and bus stop. We had not gone very far when we felt the ground tremor. We thought at first it must be an earthquake, but the further we walked, the more we shook. Someone passing by said, "Look to the south in the sky." We could barely see them coming into view, the MIGHTY 8TH AIR FORCE, on their way home from a bombing mission somewhere in France. As they drew nearer, the noise of those planes grew louder and louder, to a deafening roar. They were letting down from altitude.

We realized that we were experiencing what many English people heard almost every day. Many of the planes flew directly overhead, and a sergeant, with a pair of binoculars, was calling out the bomb group letter designation. He never called out the square J, our 390th Bomb Group letter, but we knew they were up there somewhere. To see these hundreds of planes flying over, still in very tight formation, made us feel good and proud. We waved and shouted, knowing how glad they must be to be coming home safely after a mission.

I called it the day the earth trembled, for that is exactly what happened. I thought about all those people near the targets we bombed, of the very magnitude of thousands of bombers flying over with their never-ending, deafening, droning engines, knowing that the worst was yet to come, of the thousands of high explosive bombs raining down, day after day, and night after night. How the German people kept their sanity, I cannot understand. Thank God, our American families back home didn't have to endure this.

There are so many interesting and historical places near Bournemouth, it would take months to visit, but our time was getting short, and we felt we needed to relax before going back to the hell of war. It was getting on toward evening, and we caught a bus back to Bournemouth. It had been a busy day, and we had enjoyed our little excursion, but we were tired and hungry. It worked out well as we got back to our manor house just in time for dinner.

Friday, August 11, 1944

I spent the day, with a cup of tea and orange juice, enjoying the sunshine in the beautiful gardens that surrounded the Manor House, writing letters, reading, and listening to music from home. We never got the urge to go swimming again… That water is strictly for polar bears!

Saturday, August 12, 1944

The next two days literally flew by, and it was time again to think about going back to fighting a war. "Just think," I told Steve, "nine more missions and we will be going home." That seemed to perk everyone up, and Maggie said, "Let's go get them over with." Sandy said, "Yeah, the rest will probably be short, helping out our ground troops."

Sunday, August 13, 1944

Harvey woke me about nine o'clock and said, "Hey, Chuck, would you like to go to church downtown at Saint Peter's?" I replied, "Yeah, I would like that." We rode our bikes down the long hill, and much to our surprise, there were a lot of American uniforms in the congregation. It was a good way to start our day and a very good way to end a wonderful and much-needed week.

CHAPTER 15

Back To The War

Monday, August 14, 1944

The morning of the seventh day, we boarded our little English train and with a toot, toot, Bournemouth was a memory, a very pleasant memory. Thank You, God, for this time of relaxation, and thank you, Eighth Air Force, for making it possible. We felt totally refreshed.

We arrived late in the evening, after a three-hour layover in London, where you could look down almost any street, and as far as you could see, there was rubble lying in the streets with just a narrow passageway cleared down the middle. It was surprising that we got through at all, but the people of London seemed to somehow get it done.

The first thing we noticed when we got to our squadron area was the red alert flag was flying, and Steve said, "I hope that don't mean us." The next thing we noticed was all the crews around us that we knew were gone, either lost in combat or finished their tours. That was a shock! Some new crews crowded around us, wanting to know what it was like and what to expect. We told them to just take it one day at a time and learn as much as they could as fast as they could.

Our crew officers were already back and came to check if we were all back and okay. Then, "Good night, see you in the morning. We are flying." Well, that settled that. We were back, and it was time to get on with it. Right away we got that sinking feeling in our stomachs, realizing that our seven days at the "funny farm" flak camp were over.

We were anxious to find out all that had happened since we left and get the POOP from our friends on an older crew.

The day we left on flak leave was Monday, August 7. The 8th Air Force mission number 527 was to bomb bridges, highways, train yards, and fuel dumps in central France. Many on this mission had to return home due to bad weather. We learned our 390th Group had again been sent to Russia on the second shuttle mission and would return by way of Italy, as we had in July. We probably would have been with them, and fortunately for them, they did not lose a single plane.

On Tuesday, August 8, the 8th AF mission number 530 put up 1,095 bombers and 632 fighters, not including the 78 B17s and 55 P51s on the Russian shuttle run. The bombers suffered 8 losses, while the fighters lost 13. There were many targets, mostly in support of ground troops. Bomb tonnage used was 2,548.

On Wednesday, August 9, mission number 533 was one of those rough ones with targets at Ulm, Saarbrucken, Karlsruhe, Sindelfingen, and others in southeast Germany. Targets included armament works, aircraft factories, airfields, and fuel depots. We suffered 18 bomber and 3 fighter losses, but the Germans paid dearly as well. Our fighters shot down 39 in the air and destroyed 24 on the ground.

The 2nd and 3rd Divisions encountered bad weather and had to drop their bombs on secondary targets. One thousand, three hundred ten tons of bombs fell on Germany. "Heil Hitler."

On August 10, mission number 537 was limited because of bad weather. Only 175 bombers and 573 fighters bombed bridges and rail targets, dropping 522 tons of bombs. One bomber was lost.

Mission number 538, 338 medium bombers bombed troop concentrations. It was a very good day, for our fighters destroyed 27 planes with 14 losses. The 20th Fighter Group destroyed 37 locomotives, bringing their total to 264.

Friday, August 11, the 8th Air Force flew 3 different missions. Number 541 hit fuel, rail, and troop concentrations in and around Saarbrucken and Strasbourg. Mission numbers 542 and 543 concentrated on targets on the French Brest peninsula, dropping a total of 2,371 tons of bombs and losing 5 bombers and one fighter.

Mission number 545 on Saturday, August 12, sent 650 bombers and 1,330 fighters along the front lines. Targets were airfields and transportation hubs. In dropping 1,713 tons of bombs, we lost 3 bombers and 13 fighters. As our fighters turned more and more to strafing, our heavy fighter losses were due to ground fire. The Germans lost 19 planes.

On Sunday, August 13, the 8th Air Force mission number 548 sent 1,269 bombers and 1,065 fighters to drop 3,712 tons of bombs in direct support of our ground troops. Losses were 12 bombers and 13 fighters. Worth noting on this day, the 388th Bomb Group used TV controlled 2,000-pound guided missiles. They had poor results, and this kind of bombing was not perfected until the Gulf War, 50-plus years later.

Monday, August 14, sent mission number 552 with 1,183 bombers and 584 fighters to bomb targets in Mannheim, Ludwigshafen, Sindelfingen, and Stuttgart. Dropping 2,914 tons of bombs with excellent results, they hit oil and aircraft engine plants. We lost 2 bombers and 4 fighters, while destroying 13 German planes. Due to many accidental mistakes, all strafing of ground troops in France was discontinued.

That brings us up-to-date on what went on while our crew was on flak leave. We thought things would be getting better with short trips and support of ground troops. Time would tell.

Tuesday, August 15, 1944

Eighth Air Force mission number 554, 390th Bomb Group mission number 174. At 0445 our Nissen hut door (I am going to demolish that thing before I leave this place) slammed open, and a familiar voice penetrated my brain, "Lieutenant Ray Strate crew number 86, arise, arise. Your day to shine. Chow in thirty minutes, briefing at 0545. No bitching now, you are all rested up." With that the sergeant made a hasty retreat.

It was difficult for us to get moving. It was as if we were walking in molasses. I think a great part of it was that we didn't want to go back to war, but with only eight left, we wanted to get them over with, so we pushed one another.

When that black curtain was opened, we saw at once this was going to be an exciting day. The 1st Division was going to Frankfurt and Cologne to bomb airfields. The 2nd was going to bomb airfields in western Germany, and the 3rd Division (our division) to bomb airfields and Buzz Bomb launching sites in Belgium and the Netherlands.

The target for our 390th Group was a large airfield at Venlo, Netherlands. Venlo is located on the River Haas, right at the German border, about 50 miles from Cologne, Germany. Cologne is in the middle of the rich industrial Saar Valley of Germany, and one of the most heavily protected areas in the world.

This was not one of those days when the Luftwaffe would run and hide, especially for the 1st and 2nd Divisions. They were met head-on by swarms of Me109s and Fw190s in groups of 20 abreast, as well as very heavy flak.

In the meanwhile, we were making our bomb run with very few German fighters and only moderate flak. The Germans were far too busy defending their own country to bother with us. Our bombing results were excellent, and later photographs would show, the Germans were just too busy to reopen this airfield. It was totally demolished.

In all, there were 18 different targets today, and our 571st Squadron had one of the easier ones. Sometimes, it is like that when the Germans decide to concentrate their defenses on several groups and leave the others be. Thankfully, today was not our day in the barrel.

Over 2,200 tons of bombs were dropped, and we lost 16 bombers, with 156 badly damaged. We also lost 6 fighters. The 1st and 2nd Divisions' bombers shot down 13 German fighters, and their escorts took out 14 in the air and 7 on the ground. We all felt badly for the 303rd Bomb Group, who lost 9 bombers.

The 390th was one of the first groups to get back to England, and as we cleaned up our plane, removing our guns and ammo boxes, our parachutes, and flak suits, we could hear the other groups coming back. Many were firing off flares, alerting ground crews of dead and wounded aboard. We felt very fortunate.

I wrote Eleta a long letter tonight, telling her that we now had Hitler on the run and it would all be over soon. With her just recovering from a major back operation, there was no need to worry her.

As we went to bed, the red alert flag was flying, and good ole Steve said, "Don't worry, boys. It will probably be a short milk run." Maggie retorted, "Yeah, Steve, that's what you told us the night before our Munich mission."

THE ZEITZ FIREWORKS

Wednesday, August 16, 1944

Seems like we had just gotten to sleep when our Nissen hut popped like a firecracker. "All right, all right, Lieutenant Strate crew number 86, hit the deck. Do you expect to sleep 'til noon?" Sandy said, "Good gosh, Sarge, it is just 0330," and sure enough, we knew immediately it would be a long mission and a hard day.

We knew it was coming, but we didn't want to face it. The black curtain was pulled back, and after the "Oh, nos" and groans, many of the pilots just shook their heads.

The 8th Air Force mission number 556 and the 390th Bomb Group mission number 175 was being sent to bomb 20 different targets, all within a 100-mile radius in eastern Germany, just 50 miles from the Czechoslovakian border. The targets were airfields, synthetic oil refineries, and aircraft manufacturing plants.

The 8th Air Force hierarchy could sense victory and were striking death blows on Germany's most vital parts, aircraft and oil. The odds that we would lose a great number of planes and crews by going deeper into Germany had been weighed, and the decision had been made.

The Germans had a remarkable defense system in place. From the moment the 8th Air Force started assembling high over England, information began to flow in to German defense headquarters. As the first groups of bombers headed toward the continent, Luftwaffe airfields from the Baltic Sea to the Mediterranean were alerted. As American planes neared France or Germany, hundreds of planes were moved to meet them, sometimes moving from one base to another waiting to see where the strikes would be. Sometimes, hitting the bombers near the Channel, then falling back to air bases along the determined track of the bombers, refueling and adding ammunition. Concentrating their forces and, finally, after determining the route and the target areas, they had the maximum number of fighters where they were needed.

The 8th countered these maneuvers by sending strikes to several widely separated target areas, thereby diluting the number of fighters.

Today, there was no attempt to fool the Luftwaffe. We headed out, 1,090 bombers and 692 fighters strong…a maximum effort, in-your-face assault, right through the center of their highest concentration of flak and fighters, as if to say, "Okay, Hitler and Herr Goering, we are coming at you. Give us your best shot because we are going for the kill."

Listening to the German radio frequency, I can truthfully state that I have never heard more activity in preparation for a strike. "Achtung, Luftwaffe" ("Attention, Luftwaffe") was repeated over and over with coded instructions. They were getting set for an all-out engagement. The battle lines were drawn. An air war was set on a stage so vast that observers could only see bits and pieces. Only God could see it unfold, and only He knew the outcome.

As we headed northeast over the English Channel, we could look ahead and behind and see our armada, hundreds of bombers and fighters, slowly getting into their formations. Pilots alerted their crews to prepare for battle. "Test your oxygen systems, your intercom, and your guns." When all those guns began firing, the plane shook like a huge vibrating machine and made your hands and feet numb when they stopped.

Further and further, up to the North Sea, heading for the Denmark peninsula, we made our turn into Germany. Entry was to be, as so many times before, near the point where two great rivers, the Weser and the Elbe, empty into the North Sea.

Ray came on the intercom with a voice as calm as if we were going to the corner drugstore for ice cream, "Okay, men [he no longer called us boys], give me one hundred percent from here until we come back this way and I will bring you home. Keep your eyes open and your mouths shut unless you have something important to tell the rest of us. Good luck."

The Germans were already firing at us from boats and barges as we entered Germany very near Bremerhaven, and about an equal distance from Hamburg and Bremen.

The commander of our 390th Group, Colonel Fred W. Ott, was leading the 15th Wing as command pilot, and we felt we were in good hands. He was a fearless soldier and a great pilot and was not averse to making a second run over the target if he felt we were not properly aligned or if clouds obscured our target. Hopefully, that would not be the case today. One time over the target is quite enough for one day, if you please.

As we threaded our way from the northwest toward the southeast, past Hamburg on our left and Bremen on our right, just out of range of most of their big guns, the sky was black on both sides. On toward Hanover and Magdeburg we flew, cities whose mere mention of their names would bring shudders and goose pimples to many crews that had been on missions to their fiercely defended skies. Now we could see fighters attacking in swarms the groups up ahead of us, and the dogfights as our escorts began to tangle with them. Soon, from a distance, you couldn't tell to whom which fighters belonged; they just resembled a bunch of mad bees.

The flak was getting our range as we approached our target, an oil refinery, at Zeitz. We were on that part of our mission resembling a giant roller coaster, buffeted from side to side, up and down by enormous flak bursts. Imagine you are in a giant popcorn popper where the sound of one explosion after another, seemingly, becomes one big boom. Your teeth are chattering, and your knees are trembling. There is a part inside your body that you never use except in circumstances like this, but you can take it from me, it is there and it is real. It is just above your stomach and just below your heart, like a strong magnet that pulls and draws on every part of you, squeezing tighter and tighter until it feels as though you are drawn into a rock-hard knot that will never again relax.

Someone shouted, "Bandits, twelve high," and, now, there was the target. "Pilot to bombardier, it is all yours." As we started the bomb run, I was busy tossing out aluminum strips to baffle their radar and looking out my side port window. It seemed the whole sky was ablaze with bombers, burning and falling. Almost nothing can be worse than seeing those majestic B17s torn apart and reduced to rubbish in a split second, right before your eyes. There were engines still running and props turning, with entire tail sections broken off, twisting and falling, and down below a pitiful few chutes sail by.

Shaken by blast after blast, "Bombs away. Controls back to you." Ray took control of the airplane and shouted, "Check the bomb bay, Chuck." I was already standing with the door open to the bomb bay and yelled, "All clear." I stood looking straight down at the earth, 28,500 feet below, watching the bombs from the groups ahead of us as they hit the ground, exploding just milliseconds apart. I thought, *How could anything survive that?* I was relieved as the bomb bay doors ground closed, shutting off the chaos below. What could possibly be so all-fired important about a little town of 20,000 people named Zeitz? We lost 23 bombers and 3 fighters. I made it a point to check out why we were sent there.

Zeitz was a manufacturing plant and storage depot for synthetic oil, a very high priority for the German war machine. I found it was first bombed on May 12, 1944, and on that mission, the 8th Air Force lost 46 bombers. Pictures and intelligence reported that the target was destroyed, but give the Germans their due. It was back to full capacity in two weeks, at which time it was scheduled to be bombed again on May 28, with heavy losses of 23 bombers.

Pictures again showed destruction so great that it was thought not possible for it to be rebuilt. Again, there it was in almost full operation. As with many other targets, it turned into a contest of who would eventually win out. Our bombers would destroy a plant, and within a week, it would be back in operation. This time, however, was a barn burner, and not only Zeitz was laid waste, but neighboring supply dumps and transportation lines as well.

The importance of this area to the Germans was made clear when we were told that large batteries of 88-millemeter, 105-millimeter, and 128-millimeter guns, called Grosse batteries, were laid all around this area. These batteries did not follow single aircraft across the sky but simply shot at one point continuously. When they did move, hundreds moved in tandem, synchronized so that no area of the sky was left uncovered. This was a devilish operation, conceived to knock down the maximum number of enemy planes. This type of system made my job of tossing out chaff useless, as the Germans were no longer dependent on radar to find the altitude of their prey. The new ways they found to kill us were unending.

Another thing seemed different about the sound of the flak. The 88-millimeter, with their *thump, thump, thump*, was shattered by the new sound of the 105-millimeter and 128-millimeter. Their sound was more like a crack of lightning, ricocheting through the sky, like when you were caught outside in a summer storm. We were bounced about like pins in a bowling alley.

As we passed Leipzig, which was only 20 miles from Zeitz, the flak and fighters renewed. Every station on our plane was reporting something, fighters from head-on and from six o'clock low, simultaneously, bombers smoking and afire on both sides of us, chutes streaming down, many trailing a crewman with the canopy foiled. They didn't seem to be getting any air under the chute to make it snap open. Why were they not opening? George Curnes (copilot) had the answer…too much turbulence in the air, from the prop wash of hundreds of planes, plus the turbulence caused by thousands of shell explosions.

Hopefully, as the chutes dropped closer to the ground, they would all open. We lost 23 bombers; that's 207 crewmen, if they all got out. There were six enemy planes shot down by our bomber crews and 32 downed by our fighters. If all bailed out, that would be a total of 268 possible. It seemed like a whole lot more to me; they were in every direction.

It was not over yet. As we passed Magdeburg, over to our left, the sky was black with AA gunfire, and we began to see a steady stream of crippled bombers dropping out of the protection of their groups, unable to maintain their airspeed. Mercifully, a squadron of our P51 escorts was designated to stay with them as they became easy prey. Slowly, we made our way past Frankfurt and Bremen and into the relative safety of the North Sea.

After over eight hours in flight, we touched down in Framlingham, dog-tired, mentally and physically. When you have been on oxygen for a long time and take off that mask, just normal breathing becomes labored; you get instantly tired. When on oxygen, breathing becomes easier. I have always thought doctors should use it more to treat people. It will stop a terrible headache in a New York minute.

Off we went to debriefing, and it was long, as we had a lot to talk about. We got word to report to squadron headquarters, in dress uniform, to receive an advance in grade. I was elevated from staff sergeant to tech sergeant. Then came the presentation of medals. It had now become routine and seemed to mean a great deal more to the visiting dignitaries than to any of us. We would gladly have traded it all for a good night's sleep and a day off. Maggie summed it up when he said, "Man, oh, man, I am glad this day is over. Thank you, Lord."

Thursday, August 17, 1944

The weather over England and all of Europe had deteriorated so badly that all heavy bomber operations were suspended, with the exception of mission numbers 558 and 559 on which 10 bombers were dispatched, but did not drop their bombs. Five hundred four fighter bombers hit targets in and around Paris, dispensing 172 tons of bombs and losing 7 aircraft.

Friday, August 18, 1944

B24s of the 3rd Bomb Division, with 52 planes, dropped 102 tons of bombs on the large Roye-Amy airfield, while 670 bombers hit airfields, bridges, fuel dumps, and an aircraft manufacturing plant in France and Belgium. There were only 2 bombers lost, but our fighters lost 17. The Germans lost 56 planes and 20 probables. Our 571st Squadron did not fly, most likely because they knew we were not able.

Saturday, August 19, 1944

The weather was completely socked in, and there were no missions scheduled for August 19, 20, 21, 22, and 23. We were thankful for the rest.

Thursday, August 24, 1944

The weather finally cleared, and it was a beautiful day. The 8th Air Force was sending a mammoth strike, mission number 568, with 1,310 bombers and 739 fighters, deep into the heart of Germany, hitting such terrible targets as Brunswick, Hanover, Meersberg, Weimer, Merseberg, Leipzig, Brux, Ruhland, and Kiel. Oil and armament plants were the targets, and 2,982 tons of bombs were dropped. We lost 26 bombers and 4 fighters.

THE 390TH BOMB GROUP 100TH MISSION PARTY

The good Lord was certainly watching over me and our 390th Bomb Group. The only reason we were not on that awful mission was because the 390th Bomb Group was celebrating its 100th mission flown, though we had already flown 175. Scheduling these celebration parties had to be done well in advance, and since we were fortunate enough to get the most famous band and orchestra of our time, we had to wait our turn.

Everyone was truly excited. Ground crews spent all day cleaning out the big hangar and building a bandstand. Truckloads of beer in kegs were hauled in and placed, side by side on sawhorses, all around the inside of the hangar. Red, white, and blue paper streamers were strung everywhere, even from the rafters. All was ready.

Major Glenn Miller, with his entire band, would play for our 100th mission party to be held in a huge aircraft maintenance hangar. I am including the information from the invitation, which I still have. The cover of the program was hawking our servicemen to buy war bonds, with words like, "ATTACK, ATTACK, ATTACK, with our Victory Squadron 8th Air Force," "BUY YOUR SHARE," "See your unit personnel officer" (who encouraged us to have war bonds deducted from our monthly pay). It pictured war planes bombing a Nazi swastika.

Inside the program was printed, "Presenting—Captain Glenn Miller [he had been promoted to major since the programs were printed], the Moonlight Serenader and the 50-piece American Supreme Allied Command Band, featuring:"

Sgt. Ray McKinley	*Drummer*	*Who led his own band*
Sgt. Carmen Masters	*Guitar*	*Who played with Tommy Dorsey*
Sgt. Johnny Desmond	*Vocalist*	*Who sang with Gene Krupa Orchestra*
Sgt. Bobby Nichols	*Trumpet*	*Who played with Vaughn Monroe Orchestra*

And supported by a special 20-piece string section who were former soloists and members of the Philadelphia, Boston, and Cleveland Symphonies. With a quintet from Glenn Miller's last civilian band, including:

Lt. Don Haynes	*Glen Miller's Personal Representative*
S/Sgt. Trigger Alpert	*Bass Fiddle*
M/Sgt. Zeke Zarchy	*First Trumpet*
S/Sgt. Jimmy Priddy	*First Trombone*
T/Sgt. Jerry Bray	*One of America's foremost Composers*

On the back of the program is a thumbnail sketch of the "Serenader," Glenn Miller, The Top-Billed Band Leader in America for Three Consecutive Years.

Starred in two Motion Pictures, *SUN VALLEY SERENADE* **and** *ORCHESTRA LEADERS WIVES.*

He has been featured on NBC Radio and *The Chesterfield Hour.*

Our crew got there early, dressed in our best uniforms, ready for the show. We were hoping to talk with anyone in the band and get news from home before the music started. Just before the program was scheduled to start, up drove our base commander, Colonel Fred Ott's car, and out stepped Colonel Ott and Glenn Miller. Everybody went nuts, shouting and whistling. He was definitely an American idol.

Right behind him came a big green bus, and the band popped out. The crowd got louder and louder as each band member, with their instruments, unloaded.

As the band set up on the platform, the crowd was still yelling. Ray McKinley walked over to the microphone and said, "But we ain't done nothin' yet." With a big grin on his face, he went back to his drums and br-r-r-r-r, bip, bam, bam, and I heard him holler over the crowd, "Now, we done somethin'." *And the partying began.*

Within a few minutes, several military trucks arrived, filled with giggling English girls from nearby communities, who had volunteered to dance with members of the 390th. It turned out they were for the commissioned officers only. The doors closed, guarded by MPs (military police), and no one was allowed out of the hangar with any of the girls. The big brass, however, underestimated the ingenuity of the American flyboys. There were girls and boys going in and out of the latrine (bathroom) temporarily designated for ladies, like a revolving door.

Glenn Miller was introduced by Colonel Fred Ott and by "Moonlight Serenade." He and the band hopped right into one of the greatest, entertaining shows of all time. At that time, Glenn Miller was at the peak of his popularity and was tops in the entertainment business, bigger than Elvis and the Beatles combined.

I hope my readers will forgive me for listing the music the band played that night, but Glenn Miller's music means a great deal to my wife, Eleta, and me. You can just skip the next paragraph, as I would understand.

They made the place go wild with "Bugle Call Rag," "American Patrol," and "Chattanooga Choo Choo." Then Tex Beneke sang, "I Gotta Gal in Kalamazoo"; then, there was "People, Like You and Me," made famous by Marian Hutton and Tex Beneke.

There was slow dancing with "Moonlight Sonata," "In the Mood," and "Serenade in Blue." We watched as the officers moved gracefully in the warm, low lights that set the mood, like high school dances at home.

As the night went on, there was an awful lot of drinking going on. The beer kegs were flowing, and the place smelled like a saloon.

During the three break periods, I was intent on getting to meet members of the band and to get their autographs. I was talking with Ray McKinley (drummer), when Glenn Miller walked up to talk to Ray about the next set. Ray surprised me by saying, "Glenn, this is Sergeant Chuck Richardson, from Charlotte, North Carolina," and Glenn shook my hand and said, "Nice to meet you, Chuck. You boys are doing a hell of a job here. Thanks from everyone back home, and by the way, the band played Charlotte for a war bond drive just before we came over here." He was so easy to talk with, not a big shot at all. Meeting him and others, like Johnny Desmond, was a thrill I will never forget.

After playing for two and a half hours, he closed with "Moonlight Serenade," and tears rolled down my face as I thought of home and Eleta. What a night!

They told us goodbye, and no one there expected that, within a very few days, Glenn Miller would be lost over the treacherous English Channel, on his way to play concerts for the troops in France.

We went back to our huts, pleased and honored to have been one of the last to hear that great band. I am not ashamed to tell you that the tears rolled well into the night. Talking about being homesick…I was not the only one. "Good night, Honey, I love you."

It was not until years later that I learned that our Colonel Ott invited Glenn Miller to spend the night at our base and observe the early morning preparations and briefing. He was in the room the next morning as we prepared to fly a mission.

Friday, August 25, 1944

Eighth Air Force mission number 570. There is an unwritten law or rule in the Air Force that states, "If you find something good, you better make the most of it because it will not last very long."

At 0400, the door to our hut snapped like a gunshot. I always wanted to take a look at that door to see what could possibly make it crack like that, but the excitement and irritation of the moment made me forget it until the next time it happened.

"All right, Lieutenant Strate crew number 86, did you think the party was going to get you another day off? Up and at 'em, chow in thirty minutes, briefing at 0500. Oh, by the way, have a good day." And he was gone. "One of these days, I'm going to choke that guy," said Maggie.

How in the name of heaven were all those guys who had drunk so much beer last night going to get out of bed, much less fly a mission, especially the pilots? Maybe they will have mercy on us and give us a short trip just across the Channel.

It was a motley-looking bunch that sat quietly at briefing, waiting for our top brass to come down the aisle and draw back the black curtain. In they came, snappier than usual. "Tens-hut! At ease, men." With not one word about the knockdown, drag-out party last night, they went from one to the other, spelling out the important points of today's mission. When the curtain was drawn showing our routes to and from the target, it seemed to stretch to China. The ribbon went up through the North Sea, across the Denmark Peninsula, on to the Baltic Sea to a province of Germany called Mecklenburg, to the region around Rostock. Once before, I had mentioned going into the Mecklenburg Province, which rang a bell for me as my hometown of Charlotte, North Carolina is in the county of Mecklenburg. Mecklenburg had its roots right here, and Queen Charlotte of Germany is where the name of Charlotte originated and has, from its beginning, been known as the Queen City of the South. How terrible it would be to be shot down or, worse still, be killed here. We passed through Rostock and Peenemunde to get to our target in Politz. Politz is located, like so many other of Germany's oil refineries and storage depots, on Germany's eastern border. I am sure the Germans thought it would never be attacked by planes from England, but they fortified it well because the Russians were coming.

It meant that we had to fly all the way across Germany and pass all those flak guns and fighters. I believe the strategy behind this entire day's mission was not the oil refinery at Politz, nor the aircraft plant at Rostock, nor the liquid oxygen and ammonia plants in Belgium, but the main focus was the highly secret experimental station in Peenemunde. Again, this is where all of Hitler's secret weapons were developed and tested.

The most secret and feared had never been heard of outside of HIGH intelligence circles. We came to know of it as heavy water. Fifty years from now, the mere mention of heavy water, or water enriched with uranium, would instantly be recognized as a basic ingredient for the development of an atomic bomb. All we knew was it was Hitler's most secret weapon and this target at Peenemunde *must* be destroyed, no matter what the cost.

Our opposition at Politz was fierce, but only from flak. Our escorts did a wonderful job of keeping the fighters away from us. You will remember our plane the GOOD-O-YANK was so badly damaged on our mission to Munich on July 13, it could no longer be flown. Since then, we had been assigned to fly a veteran plane of many missions, plane number 237868, better known as Gentleman Jim, named by a previous crew who had completed their tour.

Today, we got so many holes shot into us that I had my doubts about getting Gentleman Jim back to England, much less flying any more missions. But we did, and as a matter of fact, only 14 planes in the 390th Bomb Group flew more missions than Gentleman Jim. It is truly a good airplane.

When all the bombing and shooting was done, we had lost 18 bombers and 7 fighters, while the Germans lost 41 planes. On the first leg of our return to England, what was left of the 1,308 bombers and 916 fighters that began the mission turned north toward the Baltic Sea. A number of planes that had been badly damaged, realizing they were not going to make it home, decided to land in Sweden, just a short distance away.

We were still a long way from England, and although we flew over the Denmark Peninsula and out into the North Sea, we only saw a few bursts of flak. It was as though the Germans were saying, "We have had enough of you today."

Several airplanes did not make it back. A few ditched in the North Sea, and some were rescued by the ever-faithful British Air Sea Rescue. I have never seen any figures on this, but I am certain their rescues were in the thousands. They were another one of those branches of service that were unsung heroes, almost as precious to us as our little fighter escort friends.

It had been a long and tiresome mission, and we barely made it through debriefing before heading back to the sack. I felt as though I wouldn't be able to go on another mission tomorrow, and mercifully, we were not scheduled to fly on Saturday, August 26.

Saturday, August 26, 1944

Eighth Air Force mission numbers 575 and 576. One group was sent to bomb enemy forces on the Brest Peninsula, while another was sent into central Germany to bomb fuel depots, oil refineries, and a chemical plant. Losses were 10 bombers and 12 fighters. Bombing was visual and produced good results.

Sunday, August 27, 1944

Mission numbers 583 and 584. I don't know why our crew was not scheduled for these missions, and I have mixed emotions about it. I am very glad, on the one hand, we were not chosen, for the target was Berlin and was led by our 571st Squadron commander, Major Bill Pennebaker. As they neared the target, high cloud cover forced them to turn back. The other groups on mission number 584 went on to bomb Emden and Wilhelmshaven in northwest Germany. Also, to my personal delight, they bombed the tiny islands of Sylt and Fano.

The reason I would like to have been on this mission is because these small islands in the Fresian chain, which run along the coast of Germany, are much like the Outer Banks of North Carolina.

Many of our missions into the heart of Germany took us on a route into the North Sea, and I was usually busy with my radios, monitoring the channels that, for any of many reasons, may send us a message to abort our mission. Everything would be quiet except the drone of our engines. Our formations would make a ninety-degree turn southward, toward the German coast. Out of nowhere, there would come a blam, blam, blam, blam, BLAM. It was the flak gunners on these small islands, just off the coast, getting in their first licks. They always scared the daylights out of me, and now, for the first time, we were going to get a chance to fight back.

Our bombers did a lot of damage, but those islands had concrete bunkers and were back in business in a few days. I'll just bet they were plenty surprised at being bombed. I understand that the 8th Air Force finally got enough of their foolishness and about a year later, in 1945, sent enough bombers to destroy the Islands. The next day all who survived (about 1,500) were evacuated to the German mainland. It serves them right.

In all, 1,203 bombers and 871 fighters took part in these two missions, and we lost 3 bombers and 11 fighters, while destroying 16 enemy planes.

Monday, August 28, 1944

The weather over Europe deteriorated to the point that no heavy bombers were dispatched. There were 835 fighter and fighter bombers sent to bomb and strafe rail transportation in Germany, Holland, Belgium, and France, with 195 tons of bombs. Twenty German planes were destroyed.

Tuesday, August 29, 1944

Eighth Air Force mission number 589. Today's mission was almost a duplicate of yesterday's mission. Due to bad weather, 200 fighters and fighter bombers bombed and strafed, at low level, anything that was moving.

Wednesday, August 30, 1944

The weather finally cleared enough to send 941 bombers on 2 separate missions. Three hundred forty bombers dropped 560 tons of bombs on launching sites for V1 Buzz Bombs in the Pas de Calais area, just across the Channel from London.

The other 637 bombers followed our favorite mission route, up through the English Channel, into the North Sea to attack port cities of Kiel and Bremen. We were not with them, but I would bet a month's salary, those gunners on the Heligoland Islands got in their licks. Of the 941 bombers and 310 fighters, we unloaded 2,008 tons of bombs without a single plane being lost.

Thursday, August 31, 1944

Due again to bad weather, no bombers or fighters were dispatched.

Friday, September 1, 1944

Eighth Air Force mission number 590. Today, 973 bombers were sent to Haslach, Germany, but were recalled because they ran into very high clouds over Germany. Fifteen other bombers, using guided bombs, destroyed a bridge in the Netherlands, and 856 fighters and fighter bombers bombed and strafed targets behind enemy lines in support of Allied ground troops. The 8th lost 6 fighters, while destroying 10 German planes. But, back to Framlingham, where this day will long be remembered.

CHAPTER 16

The Prehistoric Monster

The Day a Prehistoric Monster Devoured Framlingham Air Force Base, Chewed It Up, and Spewed It Out

For those of us who were there that Friday morning, September 1, 1944, it seemed like a terrible nightmare, but I can assure you, it was real and will always be remembered as the day a prehistoric monster rose out of the foggy mist...a mist that almost always lingered until well after sunrise in this part of England near the coast and, particularly, near the deep, marshy area known as The Wash. It reminded me of a book I once read in school called *The Hound of the Baskervilles*. It must have been written about this; it is a sorry place, and you can imagine all sorts of demons, ready to pounce upon you. It happened this way.

Harvey Burr, Maggie McGee, and I were up early this morning, happy that we had not been chosen to fly because it was so foggy. We had just finished breakfast and were walking back to our hut, discussing the fact that we only had five missions left to complete our tour of duty of thirty-five missions.

Harvey, who had exceptionally keen vision and hearing, said, "Hey! Wait a minute! Do you hear that?" I said, "Hear what?" Maggie said, "I don't hear nothing." Then we heard it. It was a low moaning, mournful sound and the pitch raised and lowered, like the sound of a huge animal mortally wounded. It groaned louder and raised the hackles on the back of my neck.

We changed directions and began walking toward the sound coming from the direction of the flight line. As we neared the runway where our plane was parked, we looked toward the east and we saw it. Maggie said, "What the heck is it?" There, coming toward the end of our longest runway, was the monster, an incredibly large prehistoric GRASSHOPPER, five stories high with long skinny legs, legs much too skinny to support such a large body. Out of the fog it came, writhing, twisting, spouting flame and smoke and roaring like a mad bull.

Returning from a mission over Germany, it was firing red and green flares. A British Lancaster, it was not more than head high as it raced down our runway, barely missing our control tower, then pulling up, making a wide turn, only to line up again on our long east-west runway and gently touch down, roll to a stop, and not move.

A jeep raced out to the plane, which looked for the world like a giant green grasshopper, in its brown and green camouflage colors. A British Lancaster heavy bomber, it was the very first one we had ever seen up close and on the ground. Built by Avro and later modified, it was continued in production by the Armstrong Vickers Company. It had a wingspan of 102 feet, was 67 feet, 4 inches long, and stood 19 feet, 7 inches tall. The bulbous plastic turret in the nose gave the appearance of huge insect eyes. We were fascinated by this strange-looking machine and waited until it was pulled off the runway onto a hardstand and secured, not far from the control tower.

AVRO LANCASTER B 1

The Avro Lancaster is a British four-engine Second World War heavy bomber designed and built by Avro for the Royal Air Force. It first saw active service with RAF Bomber Command in 1942, and as the strategic bombing offensive over Europe gathered momentum, it was the central implement for the nighttime bombing campaigns that followed. It became the main heavy bomber used by the RAF, the RCAF, and squadrons from other Commonwealth and European countries serving within the RAF, overshadowing its close contemporaries the Handley Page Halifax and Short Stirling. The Lanc, as it was affectionately known, thus became one of the more famous and most successful of the Second World War night bombers, "delivering 608,612 long tons of bombs in 156,000 sorties." The Lancaster, an evolution of the troublesome Avro Manchester, was designed by Roy Chadwick and was powered by four Rolls-Royce Merlins, or, in one version, Bristol Hercules engines.

The seven-member crew was taken to the interrogation (briefing) hut and, I suppose, allowed to contact their home base. In the meantime, the plane was loaded with petrol.

We discovered that this particular Lancaster belonged to a Canadian Group and had run out of fuel. In about forty-five minutes, the crew was trucked back to their plane, and we noticed that the pilot was a very short Canadian. Everyone thought American pilots were brash and cocky and a little whacko, but you only had to observe for a few minutes to discover, by their manner, they were the ones who invented "brash." They made American fighter pilots look like choirboys. Their strut was akin to a John Phillip Sousa marching band.

We learned there were English airfields nearby where they could have landed, but chose American because we did not make them pay for the fuel. When Americans landed on English fields, they were made to pay for any fuel received. The Canadians were treated more like someone from home on the American bases.

As this huge plane readied for takeoff, we could see, with 4 1,460-horsepower Merlin engines that seemed to purr rather than roar, how they could carry enormous bombloads. It could carry a 10,000-pound bomb, which was used to destroy dams and fortified submarine pens. Under normal conditions, the front and top turrets carried 2 each 0.0303-inch Browning machine guns, and the tail turret carried 4 0.0303-inch Browning machine guns. The normal bombload is 22,000 pounds.

The only thing puzzling to us was there was no armament for the underside, and I am sure the Germans took full advantage of this fact.

As the Lancaster taxied away, we waved goodbye. We had a great respect for these fellows, flying at night and at altitudes that were within the range of a good slingshot. They took extremely heavy losses but inflicted terrible damage and suffering on the Germans.

We watched as they made the turn at the end of our longest runway and, with power that we could feel in our feet, came racing by us. The officer in charge of our tower saluted as they jerked up their landing gear and settled toward the runway, almost touching.

We oohed and aahed at the devil-may-care attitude. Then, pulling up in a very steep climb, we watched as the monster out of the east disappeared to the northwest.

As we started back toward our squadron area, Harvey said, "Listen," and we stopped. Sure enough, the sound of the Lancaster had not gone away, and in fact, it was getting stronger. Maggie said, "Something is wrong. They are coming back."

We turned to see it, coming low from the east. The closer it came, the lower it got. Maggie said, "Look, he doesn't have his landing gear down. Heeeee...he is going to belly-land." We started backing up, expecting a big ball of fire. Now, he was within feet of the runway, but the engines were close to redline. "He's not going to land. He is going to buzz the field," said Harvey. Almost before you could think, that huge Lancaster disappeared behind our control tower and we could see the hot rod pilot salute as he came tearing by us. I screamed, "WOW! Did you see that? He buzzed us, he buzzed us good." We were laughing and dancing around. "What a pilot!" And before we could gather our wits, Harvey yelled, "Oh, no, no, here they come again!" They, indeed, came again, this time from the north and down on the deck with engines moaning. This guy was flying that Lancaster like a fighter pilot as they flew by the control tower and off over the haystacks in the nearby field. Next thing we saw was the base commander's jeep skidding to a stop by the control tower. Whoever it was, they were taking three steps at a time up the stairs to the top of the observation roof.

By the time he got to the roof, the Lancaster was gone, and we, as well as everyone else in sight, were yelling and whistling and jumping around. Then all was quiet; it had really gone. We moved away slowly, thinking about the guts of this brash kid of about twenty years. What a show!

And lo, we heard it again as he turned steep on his left wing and, diving for the east-west runway one more time, came in low and stayed inches off the runway all the way to the end, pulled up in a steep climb and disappeared, this time for good. I will never forget our base commander (if it was him) shaking his fist at that big Lancaster as it came screaming by. I'd bet our base commander was smiling at something all flyers would like to do, but just didn't have the nerve to try.

It was a memorable day, the day the great grasshopper monster buzzed our field. Not only did he buzz us, but also he chewed us up and spewed us out. WOW!

We never heard another word about the greatest BUZZ JOB of World War II.

Saturday, September 2, 1944

The weather was so bad today, the only thing flying was a group of 36 P47s, 8th Air Force mission number 596 assigned to strafe targets on the ground in Belgium.

At mail call today, I received 9 letters and 2 packages. Five of the letters were from Eleta, who is home from the hospital now and recuperating very well. She had gone through so much, and I was stuck 5,000 miles away and couldn't help her. I promised her in my letters that I would, someday, make up for it.

I received a box of cookies from Mom. They were dried out and hard as a rock, but the rest of the crew and I thought they were wonderful.

The alert flag was flying tonight, and tomorrow we would be also, even though the weather reports said that all of Europe was covered with thick clouds.

Sunday, September 3, 1944

We got a wake-up call, which usually meant we would have a short mission. It was raining, and most of our buddies were betting that we would not fly, but we had flown under worse conditions.

Mission number 601 put up 404 B17s from the Third Division to bomb gun emplacement and coastal defenses in Brest. When we got to our target, the sky was clearing, and we bombed visually, with many direct hits. The Germans took refuge into concrete bunkers, 20 feet thick, so I am not at all sure that we did much damage.

Mission number 602 sent 345 B17s from the 1st Division to Ludwigshafen, Germany, a much tougher mission than ours. They bombed by radar, and all told, we lost 3 bombers and 2 fighters. Our fighters accounted for 7 German planes, and we dropped 2,009 tons of bombs.

LOVE LIFTED MCGEE

Monday, September 4, 1944

There were no missions flown today because of bad weather, but there was one other mission of a different nature that needed to be attended to.

Because our ball turret operator, Sam "Maggie" McGee was so well-liked by his crewmates and because he was suspected of being the instigator and perpetrator of a process known as lifting, it was decided that he should not go unrewarded. Since we only had four more missions to fly to complete our tour of duty, we should honor him on this day.

While he was taking a bath in the latrine, all preparations were made in and around his bunk. One of the great joys of doing this just right was to set the stage, with everyone in their bunks except the igniter, writing letters or pretending to be deeply engrossed in another matter, to make everything look normal.

The bomb, a large empty juice can, was filled with a predetermined level (depending on how high the honoree was to be lifted) and placed inconspicuously under the honoree's bunk. I might add that, in some cases, a little more 50-caliber machine-gun bullet powder was added and a flak jacket was installed under the straw-tick bed covering, so no one would be killed. Everyone agreed that this was to be a major effort as sort of a payback.

A cigarette was stuffed into the small hole in the juice can (bomb), and doused with lighter fluid. The lighter fluid was then drizzled down the side of the can, across to the Nissen hut wall, then up the wall as far as one could reach, back again under several bunks, up and down the wall to the door and around the corner, out of sight of the honoree, to the lighter's position. The plan was to wait until Maggie was in his bunk, with nothing on but his shorts, lying back with his hands behind his head, as was his usual custom. Then, someone would tap on the wall for the fireworks to begin.

I don't know why Maggie was so slow this evening. We were afraid the lighter fluid would dry up, so while Maggie was sitting on the side of his bunk, I believe it was Jeff who tapped on the wall, and here came the flame. Maggie saw it coming but didn't know who the victim was, so he jumped in his bunk and pulled the bath towel he was holding over his head. There was a terrible moment of silence as the flame completed its journey. **BLAM!** Maggie was gloriously lifted to a standing position, a perfect blast. He would have been proud if he had done it.

After the smoke had cleared, the duty sergeant from the 571st Squadron surveyed the situation and, turning to leave, said nonchalantly, "Happy Birthday, McGee."

Well, it wasn't his birthday, but it was a great celebration.

Tuesday, September 5, 1944

Things had been going too well, and we were getting kind of nervous because we knew, from past experience, that it could not last…like holding your breath.

At our early morning briefing, we were both excited and worried. With so few missions left, our chances of completing our tour depended a great deal on where we were sent. A short trip to France would be ideal, but we knew that was not to be because we were up too early. We just prayed that it was not the Big B, Berlin, or one of the other tough targets.

The operations officer slid back the black curtain, and my heart sank. The mission route ribbon stretched all the way across France and into southwest Germany. Our target for today was the industrial city of Stuttgart, the home of Mercedes Benz and Porsche automobiles. (Little did I realize that many years from now, my life would be inextricably connected with these two names.) Only now, the famous plants were turning out aircraft engines by the thousands. We were also to hit an oil refinery and a rail yard.

There were two 8th Air Force missions today. Number 605, which was ours, was split into three targets, Stuttgart, Ludwigshafen, and Karlsruhe. Mission number 606 was sent to Brest, France, to support ground troops. We would much rather have been on this one, but it was not to be.

Stuttgart has long been known as one of Germany's brightest gems in industry and technology. It sits on the Neckar River and is surrounded on three sides by mountains. Needless to say, it is well protected with antiaircraft guns atop these mountains. Since it is such an important war-machine-making city, you can double the number of flak guns and nearby fighter bases.

The route we were on to Stuttgart was almost identical to the one we took to bomb Munich on July 13, and it brought back some pretty bad memories.

As we neared our target, Ray came on the intercom, "Okay, men, look sharp. These guys are not going to look kindly on us, trying to knock out one of their prize aircraft engine plants. We only have a few more to go, then we can all go home together." *Yea, Ray*, I thought, *let's get this one over with and head for home.*

When we crossed into Germany, their fighters were waiting for us. Out of the sun they came, from twelve o'clock high, their cannon and 30-caliber guns winking like fireflies. The lead groups always took the worst of their first pass, and almost always, one of our lead planes would go down. The Germans were intelligent and cunning. (It's their politics where they are stupid.) Their pilots would fly at our giant formations, usually from head-on, but you could see them veer to a particular angle before they commenced firing. What they were doing was lining up several bombers in a row, so when they began firing, if their shells missed the first bomber, it would hit a second or even a third or fourth. More likely than not, they would be hitting a plane somewhere in the formation, if not the lead plane. Today, there were about three passes before our fighters got to them, and from then on, they were too busy staying alive to bother with us. Our main concern now was that wicked flak.

There were dogfights in every direction; some fighters were smoking and falling. We saw today, for the first time, a Messerschmitt Me109 on fire, with parts separating, falling straight through our formation. The P51 that got him pulled up just before going through behind him. I suspect half the gunners in our formation took credit for the kill, but I saw the pilot who "done him in" through the Plexiglas window in the roof of my radio compartment.

We turned on our IP (initial point), starting our bomb run, and we could see up ahead the black sky over our target. They were firing for altitude, and it looked like they had found us. I began throwing out chaff, but the German gunners no longer depended on their radar to find our altitude. They just sent up an observer plane to fly alongside our formation and radio their altitude back to the flak gunners on the ground.

We looked at the flak explosions ahead and wondered if it were possible to fly through it, but with nerves of steel, Ray turned into the hell of that barrage and started our bomb run. The plane bucked like a rodeo bull. It twisted, shook, and rocked, but we were on the run and must keep straight and level for the bombsight to do its job.

I could see holes appear in the skin of our plane, as if by magic. I prayed that no one was hit.

Jeff Fuller, our togglier, yelled, "Bombs away." I jumped to the bomb bay door. "All clear," I shouted, and I could see the doors closing as I looked down at Stuttgart, 28,500 feet below. As soon as the doors clunked closed, Ray took evasive action that left me hanging in midair and floating around the radio room, weightless, until we pulled out of our dive.

"All stations, report damage." "Bombardier, okay." "Navigator, okay." "Top turret, okay." "Radio, okay." "Everything looks okay underneath," said Maggie from the ball turret. "Waist, okay." "Tail gunner, okay," said Sandy. "Pilot to crew, everything checks okay, now hold on to your seats 'til I can get us out of this flak." So the roller-coaster ride began. We would dive to the right to gain speed, then pull up to the left, all the while looking out for our own planes doing the same thing. Once out of the flak, we began to regain our tight formation, which was so important in case of fighter attacks. Thank goodness, our fighters had kept them busy.

As I sat at my desk writing these accounts, almost 60 years to the day after this mission, how absolutely ironic that I was bombing the manufacturing plants of Mercedes and Porsche, from which later I would derive my living, as I was parts manager for both Mercedes Benz and Porsche dealers after the war.

But on this day, we destroyed their plants and a great part of the city. We dropped 2,117 tons of bombs, lost 8 bombers and 11 fighters. Our fighters were credited with 21 planes in the air and 192 on the ground. We were told the Germans did not want to risk losing more planes in the air; but I am sure the truth is, as the Germans told us later, they just did not have the pilots and, more importantly, they did not have the fuel to get them off the ground. So our "little friends," said, "If you won't come up, we will come down." WOW! One hundred ninety-two destroyed on the ground; that surely is some kind of record.

When we landed back at Framlingham, Ray, after shutting down the engines, swung down from the front hatch, uncharacteristically gathered us around the front of the plane, and said with a smile, "Well done, men, only three more to go. Keep up the good work." As we put our equipment away, Harvey looked puzzled and said, "What was that all about?" Steve said, "Ray has been carrying a heavy load of responsibility for a long time. He knows our time together is getting short, and that is his way of thanking us."

Wednesday, September 6, 1944

The weather over England and all of Europe was terrible. Two hundred fourteen fighters braved the cloud cover with visibility 3/4 of a mile, strafing transportation targets in the Netherlands and western Germany. We lost 4 fighters and 1 of our best pilots, Captain Quince Brown. He was shot down by ground fire and bailed out. Captain Brown was captured, shot in the back of the head and killed by a German civilian.

Thursday, September 7, 1944

The weather completely shut down the Eighth Air Force today, and there were no missions flown.

Friday, September 8, 1944

Eighth Air Force mission number 611, 390th Bomb Group mission number 185. The weather cleared, and on a cool, clear morning, we were awakened early, signifying a long mission so we were prepared when we got to briefing. They did not disappoint us. This mission had 3 prongs. The 1st Bomb Division, with 364 B17s bombing Ludwigshafen, dropped 1,008 tons of bombs on industrial targets and an oil depot.

The 2nd Division, with 300 B24s, bombed Karlsruhe, dropping 667 tons of bombs on rail marshaling yards.

Our 3rd Division, with 386 B17s, targeted aviation plants at Mainz and Gustavsburg, and an oil depot at Kassel, dropping 1,001 tons of bombs. We used a very direct route to our target at Mainz, an important industrial city, located at the juncture of the Main and the Rhine, making it easy to locate from the air.

I have almost run out of words to describe how terrible the flak is, but this time it is multiplied many times over, because we are bombing aircraft plants less than 2 miles from Frankfurt, one of Germany's principal cities. As I look out my window on the left side of our plane, I can clearly see the city and the black cloud that is hanging over it. The sky is blacker than black as we turn toward our target. The explosions quicken and intensify, rocking and shaking our plane like a baby's toy. There is a series of shells bursting, blam, blam, blam, ka-boom, and I hear fragments ripping through the plane. The sky now is so dark that it blots out the sun; it is like flying at night. There is another loud explosion, and I look out to see a B17 split in two and parts going in all directions. The front section of the plane, from the wing forward, is now pointing straight up, all four engines still running, and I can clearly see the copilot's face looking to his right. In his mind, he must be saying, "What is going on, the whole formation is diving straight for the ground or else we are flying straight up." They must have figured it out quickly, for soon we saw chutes dropping away, and the whole tail section was falling like a giant leaf. There were no chutes from this falling part, and I can only imagine the horror of the ball turret gunner, trapped in his spherical coffin. Our plane seemed to be sideways, and up on one wing, when I heard Jeff call out, "Bombs away." I scrambled to get my footing, but fell facedown on the floor. My legs were churning, but the plane was rotating, and I could not get my legs under me, so I crawled toward the bomb bay door. Ray was on the intercom, "Chuck, how about it, are we clear?" Holding on to the bomb bay door as we rocked from side to side, I screamed, "All clear." George Curnes (copilot) said very calmly, "Bomb bay doors closed." Then, someone yelled, "Get the h—out of here!" Within minutes, the flak subsided, and I exhaled. The acrid smell from all the flak smoke filled our plane, and even with oxygen masks on, we could still smell it.

It seemed to me that, after the bomb run, Ray turned up the air speed more than usual. We were hightailing it out of Germany. We lost 10 bombers and 2 fighters, and our escorts shot down 10 fighters.

I didn't know it at the time, but our own 571st Squadron commander, Major Bill Pennebaker, was our command pilot, and he brought us home safely. Someday I hope I will have a chance to thank him. He is a great pilot and has nerves of steel, or no nerves at all.

A footnote here seems to be in order. Almost 50 years later and nearly the same day, my wife, Eleta, and my son, Ron, and I came back to Frankfurt. Flying over the same scenery, this time we were to come as tourists on vacation, to wander through the enchanted scenery of Austria, Northern Italy, and Switzerland. I had mixed feelings as I walked where I had once bombed. I dared not mention, especially to the older people, that I once flew with the feared and hated 8th Air Force.

Saturday, September 9, 1944

Eighth Air Force mission numbers 613 and 614, 390th Bomb Group mission number 186 and mission number 34 for Lieutenant Ray Strate's Crew number 86. We were moving slowly, and we were in a good mood, for two reasons. First, it was our 34th mission with only one more after today to complete our tour. Second, we had been awakened later than usual, giving hope that it would be a short mission, just across the Channel to support ground troops.

In reality, mission number 613 was a very easy mission, with 72 B17s dropping 200 large containers of food and munitions to the French Underground in southern France. It was called Operation Grassy, and there were no fighters, no flak, and no losses.

When the curtain was pulled for our mission number 614, the target was Dusseldorf, Germany, which sits in the juncture of the Rhine and Dussel Rivers, smack in the center of the highly industrialized area of the Rhur Valley and the area called the Rhineland, with thousands of antiaircraft guns concentrated along the Rhine River for 150 miles.

No missions to Dusseldorf and the cities of this Ruhr had fared well, and to the crews of the 8th Air Force bombers, many would rather bomb Big B, Berlin.

Now, that old scared feeling was back, the one that sent chills up and down my back. It seemed that the powers that be, seeing that we were about to finish our tour, were determined to do us in.

At briefing, we saw that 419 B17s of the 1st Division were being sent to Mannheim, Germany, to bomb the train marshaling yards there. Two hundred thirty-four B24s of the 2nd Division were to bomb the rail yards at Mainz, Worms, and Koblenz, near where we went yesterday. We, of the 3rd Division, with 384 B17s, were to bomb munitions plants at Dusseldorf.

It was a comparatively short mission, with 714 fighter escorts, just across the Channel, through Belgium and 20 miles into Germany. Ray was very nervous and told us we probably should not see any fighters, but the flak would be as bad or, perhaps, worse than any we had yet encountered. He said, "Remember, we have been through everything they have, so don't let up. Give me your best and I will do the rest."

From the time we tested our guns over the Channel and hit the coast of Belgium, I do not remember a moment we were not being shot at. The sound of exploding flak started gradually, and the further we went, the louder it got, like the music of a great concerto building to a momentous crescendo, until we neared our target at Dusseldorf. We were being rocked, bumped, blasted, banged, and shook and still had miles to go to the bomb run. After an eternity, I heard, "Bomb bay doors open." I snatched the door to the bomb bay open, and I shouted, "Doors open." The time on the bomb run seemed forever, and the intercom was filled with voices. Maggie's was loudest, shouting, "Pull up, pull up, the plane under us is on fire." Steve echoed, "Pull right, plane on our left is hit and going down and is headed for us." Through the Plexiglas above my head, I could see parts and pieces being blown and scattered in all directions. Some, hitting our plane, made a terrible noise. "Bombs away." "Bomb bay clear." "Move to the left, quick, quick." "My God, every plane in our group is smoking." "All stations, report damage." "Two holes about the size of a football in the nose." Steve said, "Ray, we have a bunch of holes in both wings, but look okay." "Ray, this is Chuck, don't expect to use our dinghy. There is just a hole where it used to be, above the bomb bay." "A little smoke or fuel coming out of number 3 engine, otherwise okay," said Maggie. "Waist is okay, but won't hold water." Sandy in the tail was last to report, and he said, "Looking back over the target, we smashed it, but I don't see how we got through that." We continued to take flak and bump and jump back over the Channel. And just so we wouldn't forget, the big German naval guns opened up on us, just like the day at Dunkirk. You could feel the concussion of those big naval guns for half a mile.

Out of 1,212 planes, we had major damage on 449. We lost 14 bombers and 5 crews of our friends in the 390th Group that we had flown with many times. Our escorts lost 9, but destroyed 14 German planes.

Man, oh, man, oh, man. I was so glad that this mission was over. It was terrifying, it was rough, it was mean, it was very sad, it was nerve-racking, it was mind-boggling, it was hell, it is war, and I hate it with a passion. Except by the grace of God, I would not be telling this story.

Sunday, September 10, 1944

The red alert flag was flying, but Ray had sent word that our crew would not be flying. I was very thankful and planned to attend church service down in Parham. I wanted some quiet moments with my God, to thank Him for watching over our crew. The last few missions had been devastating to our 390th Bomb Group, and why we had been spared is, to me, a true miracle.

We heard the 390th leave early this morning, but we went back to sleep. Harvey and I woke up about the same time; we showered, dressed, and had a leisurely breakfast before walking down the pathway to Parham. We were talking about what had happened since our flak leave on August 7. It had been like a whirlwind.

After a pleasant and restful worship service, we stopped by the 571st headquarters to inquire where our group had been sent. We found that the 8th Air Force Mission number 619 had been sent to three different target areas. The 1st Division, with 372 B17s, hit a tank factory in Gaggenau, an aircraft engine plant in Sindelfingen, and a jet airplane plant at Zuffenhausen, all in southwest Germany.

The 2nd Division, with 358 B24s, was sent to Ulm and Heilbrunn. Both are rail marshaling yards, deep in Germany, near the Swiss border.

The 3rd Division, with 385 B17s, was sent to an aircraft factory at Furth, a tank factory at Nürnberg, and an airfield at Giebelstadt, in south central Germany.

All these targets would be difficult, and I prayed for their safety. It was a slow and easy day, and in the late evening, our planes began to come in. We rode our bikes to the flight line to learn just how bad it had been. First of all, our 390th lost 2 more planes. That made 9 lost from our group in just one week. We lost 7 bombers and 13 fighters, while destroying 78 German planes, and dropping 2,803 tons of bombs.

Monday, September 11, 1944

I do not know why our crew was not chosen to fly this mission, but I do know, it was by Divine Providence. Eighth Air Force mission number 623 and 390th Group mission number 188 began at 0230, and as you know by now, that meant a very long mission, usually deep into Germany.

Since our crew was not flying, most of us slept in, missing breakfast. We had heard our planes leaving long before sunrise, but quickly dropped back off to sleep.

After lunch, we stopped by headquarters to find out about the mission. The sergeant in charge said, "You guys have got to be the luckiest crew on this base." We looked at the mission map, and our 3rd Division was sent to Ruhland, Germany, the same synthetic oil plant we had bombed on June 21 on our shuttle mission to Russia.

Others in our 3rd Division hit oil refineries in Bohlen, Brux, and Chemnitz. All these targets were all the way across Germany and only 30 miles from the Polish border. There were 384 B17s dropping 759 tons of bombs.

The 1st Division, with 351 B17s, was to hit oil refineries at Merseberg, Lutzendorf, and Eisenach, which are located even further inside Germany, within seeing distance of Czechoslovakia. They dropped 733 tons of bombs.

The 2nd Division, with 241 B24s and 588 tons of bombs, was to hit oil storage depots and refineries at Misburg and Magdeburg, which are near Leipzig.

We recognized immediately that this was a really tough mission and went to the flight line, late in the evening, along with all the ground crews. We were hoping for the best, but expecting the worst. As our 390th began to arrive, we could see the red flares blossoming from one plane after another, indicating wounded on board. The formation was ragged, telling us that a number of them were shot up pretty badly.

After debriefing, we had a chance to talk with some of our friends on other crews, who told us that, without a doubt, this had been their worst mission ever. Even though we had 440 fighter escorts, our losses were the largest in over a year. We lost 40 bombers (360 crewmen), with 370 damaged, and 17 fighters.

Our 390th BG had been extremely lucky because the German fighters singled out the 100th Bomb Group, just as they had in the past. Since the 100th BG was flying on the 390th left wing, the Germans bypassed the 390th to get at the 100th. No wonder they called it the BLOODY HUNDRETH. They lost 11 planes.

Whoever said we had almost destroyed Germany's fighters had their eyes opened today. We encountered over 500 German fighters in an all-out defense of their precious fuel supply. *Defend* at all cost.

Tuesday, September 12, 1944

The red alert flag was flying, and our group and our squadron were being sent on mission number 626, but again, our crew was told to stand down. I have asked many times why we did not fly, and I have never gotten an answer. One possibility was the plane we had been flying had taken an awful beating on the September 9 mission, but it rarely took that long to repair them. And I ask you now, why were we not asked to fly that day?

We waited 'til after lunch to inquire about the mission and, knowing our planes left very early, confirmed that this was another difficult mission. We were told that the 1st Division, with 299 B17s, was sent to Ruhland, Brux, Pluen, and Lauth to bomb the synthetic oil refineries again. An extremely long and dangerous mission, these targets are near the Polish border.

The German fighters were awaiting our planes again, and even though there were 662 fighter escorts, our fighters were kept busy with dogfights, while other German planes pounced on the 1st Division bombers. We lost 19 bombers and got credit for shooting down 14, with 7 probables.

The 3rd Division, with 348 B17s, went back to Magdeburg, Bohlen, and Fulda, about 90 miles from Berlin, for strikes at the enemy's dwindling fuel supply. They had it no easier than the 1st Division, losing 12 bombers and taking damage on 161 others. This time, the 493rd Bomb Group bore the fury of the German fighters, losing 9 B17s.

The 2nd Division, with 241 B24s, was dispatched to a number of targets, from Kiel in the very north, to Hemminstedt, Misburg, Lehrte, Northeim, and Hanover in north central Germany. These targets were primarily oil and gasoline storage depots. The 2nd did not receive the attention the other division got and lost 4 bombers.

In all, our bombers shot down 27 enemy planes and got credit for 12 probables. They dropped 1,990 tons of bombs, while our fighters destroyed 80 German planes and lost 12.

It was another hellacious day over Germany, and I can only say, "Thank God that we did not have to go." My heart hurts for the crewmen and families of the 35 bombers and 12 fighters lost over Germany today.

Wednesday, September 13, 1944
A Day to Remember!

The red alert flag was flying, and so was Lieutenant Ray Strate's crew number 86. This is the day we had been looking forward to since we left the USA. It was our thirty-fifth and final mission on our tour of duty with the 8th Air Force.

I did not hear the usual moaning and groaning as the duty sergeant called us for our last mission, and he did not joke as usual. "The time is 0400, chow in thirty minutes, briefing at 0500. Good luck, men." And he was gone.

As I got dressed, I thought about what the sergeant said. He called us men, and I realized he was absolutely right. When we came to Framlingham, Base number 153, we were mostly kids, fresh out of high school. As we worked and flew together, through the horror and killing of war, it was like growing up overnight. Now, we were war veterans and battle-tested men.

When the curtain was drawn, revealing the target for our last mission, I watched the face and expression of our pilot, Ray Strate, and he lowered and shook his head. I could almost read his thoughts as the route ribbon stretched across France and into south central Germany.

The responsibility of flying that long distance, through fighters and flak, hitting our target, and getting his crew home safely weighed heavily on his mind; he was weary and exhausted to the bone. "Could he do it just one more time?"

They told us the weather would be good and the bombing would be visual. "You will encounter flak here, here, and here, somewhat heavy and accurate over the target area." The target area was Sindelfingen, about five miles west of Stuttgart. It was an oil refinery we have hit before, but they kept building it back. With good bombing and the incendiary bombs, plus the added five-hundred-pound bombs with delayed fuses that would continue to explode for weeks after being dropped, it should delay the rebuilding.

The trucks dropped us off at our plane hardstand, and our ground crew was unusually busy getting the plane ready. We talked to the crew chief, Tech Sergeant Bill Masters. Maggie said, "Hey, Bill, what is going on with you guys, you have checked everything twice already?" Bill said, "Yeah, a little extra precaution, we know this is your last mission." "Thanks, Bill," said Steve, and we all said, "Amen."

Sindelfingen and Stuttgart are in almost a straight line, running from our base at Framlingham, across the Channel, along the border between Belgium and France, all the way to Germany. We had used this pathway many times, as I described on our mission to Munich on July 13. We could tell when we neared a point where we would receive flak, and we could feel our bodies tighten for the action that was sure to come.

This was the 8th Air Force Mission number 628 and 390th Bomb Group mission number 190, and as usual, it was split into 3 different target areas, for each of the 3 air divisions.

The 1st Division, with 297 B17s, was assigned to bomb oil refinery targets at Lutzkendorf and Merseberg.

The 2nd Division, with 342 B24s, was to bomb airfields and munitions dumps at Schwabisch, Ulm, and Weissenhorn.

The 3rd Division, with 378 B17s, was to hit oil refineries at Sindelfingen and Ludwigshafen, and also military equipment manufacturers at Darmstadt, Wiesbaden, and Mainz.

Our 390th target was the oil refinery at Sindelfingen. There was another group of 74 B17s scheduled to bomb near the German-Russian front at Diosgyor, Poland, then fly on to Russia on another "Frantic" shuttle mission.

Fighter groups were sending 603 fighters to escort us. Of these, 63 were to fly on to Russia, and eventually, return by way of Italy.

Had our intelligence gotten it all wrong? For weeks, since June and July, we had met fewer and fewer Luftwaffe, and now, they were coming out of the woodwork. As we approached our target, we saw them coming, climbing up to meet us in fours, eights, and twelves. There was the ever-present Me110, all alone, sitting off to our right just out of range of our 50-caliber guns, supposedly calling down our altitude for the flak gunners.

Our P51 escorts were already engaged, and we could see their contrails, twisting and turning in the sky around us.

"Bandits at two o'clock high and at twelve o'clock level. They are turning in to us right now, get ready," said Steve from the top turret. They tailed off to our left to hit the low groups in our wing. They seemed to be after the 490th Bomb Group, who were new. How did the Germans know that? *Burrrrrr-rap-rap-rap.* Someone was firing. But who, and at what? *Burrrrrr-rap-rap, burrrrrrr-rap-rap.* "Pilot to crew, who is firing?" "It's me, tail gunner," said Sandy. "There is a Me210 behind us, shooting rockets. Oh, wow. A P51 just blasted him to pieces." "Thanks, Sandy, good work. Remember to sing out when something is going on, I need to know." "Roger, will do." But, nothing, no, nothing, could keep us away from the devilish flak.

We turned on our bomb run at the Initial Point and headed straight into the midnight black cloud, hanging over the target. By now I could see planes falling ahead of us, and I am not sure if it was from fighters or flak. Above us and to our right, I just saw a Me109 plow into a B17, both going down. The B17 was spiraling, and the Me109 was falling in a clump, like a rock. Smoke and flame made it easy to watch as we left it behind. I don't think the Me109 meant to ram the B17, but it was almost impossible to fly through our formations without hitting something. I counted 4 crewmen bailing out, but soon, it was too far behind to see what happened to them.

Our plane was now right in the middle of our bomb run, and we were being rocked and tossed like weeds in a windstorm. If you are not buckled down, you are sure to get knots on your head. I knew that shortly I would have to unbuckle my seat belt and check for "Bombs away." Almost immediately Jeff shouted, "Bombs away," and I grabbed the door to the bomb bay, trying to stay upright, scolding myself for not snapping on my chest chute as a sudden lurch would have me flying right into the bomb bay and 27,000 feet, straight down. I yelled, "Bomb bay clear," and scrambled back to my seat. I heard the grinding of the doors closing and the clunk that told me they were closed tight.

Ray took back the control of the plane and did some wonderful maneuvering, getting us out of that flak, and turning for jolly ole

England. As soon as we were out of flak range over the target, someone yelled, "YIP-PEE!" and Ray was quick to tell us, "We are not home yet, so save your celebrating for later." I was already thanking God, not only for watching over us on this mission, but all the others as well.

For the next hour, as we got closer and closer to England, I could feel the terrible tension that had built up since our first missions, now was beginning to release. It was like a balloon slowly releasing the air. By the time we crossed the Channel, I was singing and even Sandy, who was always quiet, began to bubble with joy.

We touched down so gently; the wheels kissed the runway with a "nuuurrp" so soft, we could barely feel it. It was, by far, Ray's gentlest landing. It was as though his muscles were completely relaxed.

CHAPTER 17

Against All Odds

We made it! WE MADE IT! **WE MADE IT! HALLELUJAH, WE MADE IT!** You could hear shouts from every corner of the plane. Sandy, Harvey, and Maggie all came into the radio compartment, and we all gave each other hugs and high fives.

Mission number 628 had taken its toll. We lost 15 bombers and 135 brave comrades and 10 fighters. We dropped 2,063 tons of bombs, and our fighter escorts destroyed 58 planes. We had taken everything the Germans could throw at us, and we had survived.

After our engines were shut down for our last time and our gear stowed, we gathered underneath our plane to thank one another and, especially, our pilot. Our ground crew joined in, for it was as much a celebration for them as for us. We reveled in this precious moment. Against all odds, we had made it. Thank you, Lord.

We continued to celebrate through debriefing, and when we were through, I gave my shot of Scotch to Ray and thanked him again. We were told to take a couple of days off, relax, and report to headquarters on Friday the 15th at 1400 hours for further instructions.

After writing Eleta, Mom, and Dad my good news, I slept like a baby, knowing that I would not be flying tomorrow or tomorrow, nor the day after.

THE HAYSTACK CAPER

That night, while we lay sleeping, our pilot, Ray Strate, was celebrating over at the officer's club until they closed the place. Still wanting to celebrate, he went to the flight line, "borrowed" the base fire truck and, with engine roaring and siren wailing, proceeded to speed about the entire airfield, with the base MPs in hot pursuit. Finally, after dodging around and between the huge haystacks that bordered our base, he plowed into one headfirst and came to a halt. He was promptly and judiciously escorted to wherever bad boys were put to sober up and sleep it off. What a way to finish his tour!

Within days, the remarkable crew of Lieutenant Ray Strate, the GOOD-O-YANK team, was unceremoniously separated, one and two at a time, and shipped out to parts unknown. We hardly had time to say thank-you and goodbye. I suppose it was both good and bad, for we had grown closer than blood kin. We had been bonded by blood and fire, and could truly never be separated.

It was good we didn't have time to dwell or mourn on the sadness of our separation and bad that we hardly had time to shake hands when we could have been making plans to reassemble someday in the future to, once again, hear our leader say, "Okay, boys, look sharp." I was the last to leave our hut, and I was sad but excited about going home. That last day on the Framlingham Base, I rode my bicycle out to the flight line and parked on our hardstand. I said a prayer for those who were flying today, and thanked God for seeing me and my crew through some really tough days. I felt like a new person, and from now on I would be free, free to spend the rest of my life as I had planned.

A corporal caught up to me just as I got back to our hut. "Sergeant Richardson, Base Commander Colonel Fred Ott wants to see you at base headquarters right away." I said, "What in the world for?" Did they miscount my missions? Will I have to fly more? My brain was in a whirl as I rode my bike over to base HQ.

The sergeant in charge said, "Sergeant Richardson, you are to go right in." I saluted Colonel Ott, who told me to be at ease. (How could I? I was shaking in my boots.)

He said, "Sergeant Richardson, you have completed your tour of duty, and I want to personally thank you, and present you with a certificate outlining your accomplishments and welcome you to a very exclusive group, the Lucky Bastard's Club." He handed me a certificate that reads as follows: "Diploma, 390th Bomb Group. This is to certify that T/Sgt. C. J. Richardson, a member of Ott's Wallopers Bombing College, has successfully completed his tour of Operations against Hitler's Hot Shots and is now eligible to return to God's country (THE LUCKY BASTARD)." It listed my thirty-five missions flown and was signed Colonel Fred W. Ott, Professor of Bombing, and Major Lewis W. Dolon, Dean of Formation. I was so relieved and happy, I hardly remember thanking him, giving him a snappy salute, and backing out of his office. Once on my bicycle I yelled, "Whoopee!" Colonel Ott had made me proud of what we had accomplished.

I took one last look around Framlingham Air Force Base number 153, trying to burn into my memory what it was like. I was gone before today's mission got back and didn't get a chance to say goodbye to friends on other crews. Perhaps, it is just as well.

Diploma

390th BOMB GROUP

This is to Certify that **C. J. RICHARDSON** a member of OTT'S WALLOPERS' BOMBING COLLEGE HAS SUCCESSFULLY COMPLETED HIS TOUR OF OPERATIONS AGAINST HITLER'S HOT SHOTS AND IS NOW ELIGIBLE TO RETURN TO GOD'S COUNTRY (THE LUCKY BASTARD)

Missions Completed

#	Location	#	Location	#	Location
1.	STRASBOURG FRANCE	13.	HALLESLEBEN GERMANY	25.	NEUVY FRANCE
2.	TROYES FRANCE	14.	RUHLAND GERMANY	26.	HARBOURG GERMANY
3.	OSNABRUCK GERMANY	15.	DROHOBYCZ POLAND	27.	VENLO NETHERLANDS
4.	PARIS FRANCE	16.	BEZIERS FRANCE	28.	ZIETZ GERMANY
5.	BOLOGNE FRANCE	17.	CONCHES FRANCE	29.	POLITZ GERMANY
6.	ABBEVILLE FRANCE	18.	MUNICH GERMANY	30.	BREMEN GERMANY
7.	CAEN FRANCE	19.	SWIENFURT GERMANY	31.	BREST FRANCE
8.	NANTES FRANCE	20.	LUTZKENDORF GR.	32.	STUTTGART GERMANY
9.	DINARD FRANCE	21.	ST. LO FRANCE	33.	MAINZ GERMANY
10.	MONS BELGIUM	22.	ST. LO FRANCE	34.	DUSSELDORF GERMANY
11.	HANOVER GERMANY	23.	MERSEBURG GERMANY	35.	SINDELFINGEN GR.
12.	CORME-ECLUSE FR.	24.	MERSEBURG GERMANY		

F. W. Ott
PROFESSOR OF BOMBING

Louis W. Slaw
DEAN OF FORMATION

CHAPTER 18

The Home Stretch

I retraced the path that had brought me to Framlingham, back through Liverpool Station in London, and over to Euston Station. All seemed to blur, like in a dream as I rode along, wondering how in the world so much could have happened in so short a time, and how I could have possibly survived. Now, thinking ahead of home and Butch and about Poogin (my pet name for Mom), would they be surprised to see me? Had I changed? Oh, yes, my whole outlook on life was different. Knowing what could have happened, I was spiritually changed. I now knew for a fact that God had spared me. How could I ever thank Him for answering my prayers?

Everything seemed to move in slow motion as my train headed back through Manchester and on toward Glasgow, Scotland. Looking out my window at the beautiful countryside, I remembered I had written a poem about how truly beautiful and peaceful this place really is. I quickly wrote a few more lines to be added to those I wrote just five months (and a lifetime) ago:

> Ah Scotland, how fair thee still
> 'Ere I passed this way afore
> 'Tis wonder to see from Clyde
> To heathered rill
> As being at paradise door.

> Yea, your bonnie lasses weep
> For their brave lads lost
> On land, sky and seas deep
> The terrible tempests tossed
> Your people bear their burdens
> And cry, "carry on"
> For yours will be the victory
> 'Ere the few come home
> Ah, Scotland, how fair thee still.

My destination is Gourock, Scotland, a debarkation station for tens of thousands of troops leaving England for America. Gourock is on the River Clyde, just north of Glasgow. There was this huge base surrounded by wire fences, with single-story barracks built around the perimeter, one connecting to another, with doorways facing inward to an open court. At one end was a very large building converted to an enormous chow hall. Facing it on the other side of the compound was the headquarters building. The open area was larger than several football fields. The first thing I noticed about this place were long lines (or queues) of servicemen waiting to get in the chow hall. These lines circled the entire compound several times. In the open area, there were many softball games, as well as other games being played simultaneously.

I was directed to one of the barracks, and assigned a bunk. I knew no one. I looked around, hoping to find someone from my crew, but I never saw them again. All these soldiers had finished their tours and were heading home, so all in all, it was a happy place. There was no duty except to keep your quarters clean and stand in the chow lines. From early morning, you got in line for breakfast, and as soon as you finished breakfast, you got back in line for lunch, and the same for dinner. This had to be the longest chow line in the world.

Knowing how inventive American boys can be, they soon devised a system whereby someone would hold your place in line while you played softball. By keeping your eye on the line, you would know when it was time to swap places with someone just coming out of chow, and resume your place in line.

We soon learned that this was a holding station, and when a ship arrived from the USA, it was loaded and sent on its way. I am not sure if it was a blessing or not, because the next ship leaving was the gigantic *Queen Elizabeth*. The good part was it is extremely fast and needs no escorts to avoid submarines; it just outruns them. The bad part was it holds over fifteen thousand men, and we would be here until we get a shipload. How long would that be? No one seemed to know, so one day I decided to get an estimate of how many were there. I counted up to six hundred, and they were moving around too much. I gave up.

Need I tell you what the other games played were? The ever and eternal poker and craps. There was a game for every five hundred people, at least. Money changed hands like the Federal Reserve.

After I had been here for one week, I began to think we were never going to leave. I played so much softball, I didn't want to see another softball. One afternoon, I was almost to the chow hall, and heard a faint "Chuck." I looked at that mass of humanity, but could not tell where it had come from. "Chuck," it came again. I thought I recognized this voice, but it was useless. By this time, there were a hundred guys being funny, saying "Over here," and pointing. The voice came again, and this time it said, "Over by the latrine." Then, I saw him waving like a madman. Now, the rule was you can always go backward in the line, but to cut in front was strictly a no-no. So, I forfeited my place in line, which meant at least an hour and a half, and went back to be reunited with an old buddy from radio school, Rex Stanley, from Dodge City, Kansas. We hugged and danced around like two kids. I was so glad to see Rex, especially since I knew no one else. We ate together and brought each other up-to-date on all that had happened since we got separated in Salt Lake City, Utah. It turned out that we were stationed about fifty miles apart and flew on many of the same missions. We vowed to stay close, at least as long as we could.

CHAPTER 19

At Last, I Finally Meet The Queen

I was in Gounock for twelve long days. Finally, they posted our orders to board ship the next day. We were driven to the dock, and I looked at that ship with my mouth open. It was enormous; it was the *Queen Elizabeth*, more than 3 football fields long, 1,031 feet to be exact, and 118 feet wide. It just had to be the largest moving thing in the world.

It took all day to load 15,000 troops, and sometime during the night, we slipped out of the River Clyde and said goodbye to jolly old England. When I woke, we were well out to sea, and after breakfast, the officer in charge of our deck put me in charge of our stateroom because, being a tech sergeant, I was the ranking noncom. My duty was to see that everyone got to chow on a very strict schedule, and to see that our room was kept clean. We slept in what they called tiered Standee bunks. They were stretcher-like contraptions, made of canvas and slung between poles. A stateroom that usually housed two people would now sleep 20 soldiers. It took a minimum amount of space, and the bunks were 6 high.

Very early, I discovered that there was no way to control 20 happy-go-lucky guys who had seen it all and were going home. I just put up a notice showing chow times and said underneath, "Miss it and you don't eat." We had very few who missed any meals. The ship's company was English Navy, and the meals were what the British

Navy ate. We ate beans and potatoes at every meal. It was not what we were accustomed to, particularly at breakfast, but we were going home, and we would have put up with just about anything for a little while. We were fed in the main dining salon and the grand ballroom, which were fitted with long tables to feed thousands at a sitting. I could only picture in my mind bygone years when millionaires in their fur and finery, orchestras playing, walked down those wide stairways to the most sumptuous food money could buy. And *we* were being fed beans and potatoes.

The normal ocean crossing time was 3 to 4 days, but wouldn't you know it, there was a horrendous hurricane speeding toward the USA. If we stayed on schedule, we would hit New York about the same time. The storm followed the Atlantic Seaboard from Florida to New England, and we had to detour into the southern hemisphere, down by South America. We followed the hurricane up the east coast at 31.5 knots, zigzagging to avoid submarines.

HONK! HONK! HONK! "Attention, all passengers, this is a lifeboat drill. You will report immediately to *A* deck with your life preserver." Man, you talk about a Chinese fire drill, this has definitely got it beat. There were soldiers going every which way, some hollering, "Where the h—is *A* deck," some going upstairs, some going downstairs. When most finally found their emergency station, an officer came around inspecting to see if the life jackets were put on correctly and explain what we had done wrong and what to do next time. Next time? Are we going to have more of this madness? We had them every day and at night.

Quite by accident, I found Rex Stanley again. I was walking down a passageway going to the stairs that led to the main deck. I heard his voice coming from one of the staterooms, and I should have known, he was shooting craps. He had a fistful of dollar bills. I watched for about thirty minutes, and he was still winning. "What's your room number, Chuck? I'll check you later. I'm on a roll right now." We ate together twice after that, and he told me he had won seven thousand dollars. He was the luckiest man I ever met. I never saw him after that, but I have talked to him on the phone, and he has done very well in the cattle business, buying and selling hundreds of thousands of cattle in Dodge City, Kansas.

HONK! HONK! HONK! Oh, no, not another lifeboat drill! "Attention, all passengers, you will report to *A* deck with all your bags and equipment. It is against Army regulations to transport war souvenirs of any kind, pistols, knives, helmets, etc. You will remain on *A* deck until all staterooms have been searched. Be prepared to have your bags inspected." Well, now, it seemed that half the guys on the ship had contraband, and the FAN had been hit. When I got to *A* deck, there were guys throwing things overboard like crazy. It was not that they had not been told. We were told many times, if we had it, get rid of it, and that we would be inspected. We never were. Many thought that this was a bluff also, but we saw several officers coming down the deck inspecting, and now, there was another wave of stuff going overboard. The inspecting officers were not asking us to open our bags. They had this two-foot-long thin metal rod they would shove through our bags from several angles. If the needlelike rod hit anything metal, then you were asked to lay out everything. Sure enough, they caught some. Some had German Lugers, helmets, and even pearl-handled pistols. The stuff was confiscated, and the soldier's name, rank, and serial number were taken. What happened after that, we never found out.

As we followed the storm up the east coast of the United States, I was out on deck and looking behind the ship. I could see the turbulence created by the four giant screws, coupled to the mammoth steam engines. We left a track in the water that you could see for miles. The great ship had slowed considerably because we didn't want to overrun the hurricane. The ocean became so rough that hundreds of guys became ill. The huge waves caused the *Queen*, as she was called, to roll in one direction, then fifteen minutes later, roll in the other direction. I remember walking down the long passageways, and as the ship rolled way in one direction, my feet would be on one side, while my head would be in the opposite corner near the ceiling.

THE GOOD OLD USA

Seven days after we left England, we steamed into New York Harbor and were met by tugboats. We sailed right by the Statue of Liberty, and all were on deck to see this glorious sight. Some were crying, some were saluting, and others were just screaming their heads off. The fireboats were shooting water over one hundred feet high to celebrate our arrival.

Again, it took all day to disembark, and as we were leaving, they were inspecting our cloth barrack bags and our canvas B4 flight bags with the long metal needlelike rods. We were too happy to be upset now. Many new items were found.

As we went down the gangplank, we could see hundreds of busses waiting to take us to a receiving station. We were bussed to Camp Kilmer, New Jersey. When my feet touched American soil again, I said, "Thank you, again, Lord." Others kissed the dirty wharf.

Camp Kilmer was another one of those holding areas where tens of thousands waited for their records to be processed, before we were checked off and sent to the nearest Army camp for separation. I spent one night there and was put on a train—destination, Fort Bragg, North Carolina, with a fourteen-day furlough en route. I was put in charge of forty-eight guys who were insane with joy, and whom I had no more control over than a fly. As usual, they jumped off and on the train every time it stopped. I solved my problem by giving each one their records and meal vouchers, and told them they were on their own. Good luck.

CHAPTER 20

Home At Last

I arrived in Charlotte, North Carolina, at 7:00 p.m., and immediately caught a cab to 700 Mount Vernon Avenue, where Eleta had a room in a private home. She had no idea that I was even in the USA. I had not told her when I would arrive.

When the lady of the house saw me she almost fainted. She had me come in and explained that Eleta was having dinner with a girlfriend, but not to worry, she would call and have her come straight home. She told Eleta on the phone that something had come up, and she must come home at once. Within ten minutes, a cab brought her home. Mrs. R. B. McCord met Eleta at the front door and ushered her into the living room. She was so beautiful. All I could say was, "Hi, Honey," and we both wept tears of joy. I can remember she was wearing a pink angora sweater. She was so soft, I thought I would crush her. We embraced for what seemed like hours.

Home at last, thank you, God, I was home at last!

Addendum, 2012

Several months ago, I received a very surprising letter written on official letterhead of the 390th Bomb Group of the 8th Air Force. It was a letter inviting me to attend a reunion of the 390th Bomb Group to be held in New Orleans, Louisiana.

I wanted to attend very much, but because of my wife, Eleta's, illness, I wrote back that I would not be able to attend. That, however, was not what got me really excited. It was the fact that the invitation letter was from Lieutenant Colonel William "Bill" Pennebaker. I almost dropped the letter because Lieutenant Colonel Pennebaker was my commanding officer in the 8th Air Force in England, commanding my squadron, the 571st, during my combat duty as a radio operator on a B17 bomber. I had not spoken to him since September 1944, when I had finished my 35 missions and was heading home. What a surprise! I looked at his return address and was amazed. It read number 1 Battery, Charleston, South Carolina.

For a very long time, I have been searching for someone who was there in England while our crew was flying. Sad to say that I am the last living member of the GOOD-O-YANK crew and could not call on them to verify that what I had written in my book was really the truth.

I wanted to talk to them about the night our crew finished our missions and our pilot, Ray Strate, had a few too many, celebrating at the officer's club. He subsequently "borrowed" the base fire truck and went on a joyride around the entire base and into the neighboring farm. The crew was only told that he crashed into a farmer's haystack and was hauled away by base MPs for disciplinary action.

I had mentioned this report in my book, *The World War II Years, The Life and Adventures of Tech Sergeant, Charles J "Chuck" Richardson, U.S. Army Air Force, 1940 through 1945*, but noncom members of the crew were never told of Ray's midnight ride.

I somehow felt my book was not complete until I learned more about this wonderful escapade. I have written several officers, but they did not know or would not tell, so now was my chance to find out, officially, from the horse's mouth, our squadron commander, "Bill" Pennebaker.

I called him on the phone. My heart was racing as I fully expected to hear the gruff military voice of a strict old Army disciplinarian. What I got was the voice of an elderly lady, asking if she could take a message. I told her my name and that I had served under Bill in England, during World War II. She was very gracious, saying he was out but would be back in an hour and a half, and she would have him call me.

In exactly one and a half hours, the phone rang, and my heart raced again. "This is Bill Pennebaker. I am sorry I missed your call earlier. I understand that you were in the 390th Bomb Group in England. What Squadron?" I answered, "The 571st," and started to say "sir," but caught myself. We were civilians now. "Yes, Bill, I was a tech sergeant, radio operator on Ray Strate's crew." "Oh, yes," he said, "I remember Ray very well, good pilot. I am always glad to talk with anyone from the 390th, and especially my 571st Squadron."

"Bill, I called you for several reasons, and I hope I am not taking a lot of your time." "No, not at all, Charles, what did you have in mind?"

"First, I have written a book about my experiences during the World War II years, and quite naturally, I think it is very accurate. I was wondering if I sent you a copy you would check it for accuracy and authenticity."

"Yes, Charles, I would be happy to do that. Just send me your book and when I have finished it, I will return it."

I mailed the book the next day, and four days later, while I was at the grocery store, Bill called. Eleta told him I would be back in about an hour. I had hardly gotten in the house when the phone rang and it was Bill. "I have finished your book, and I am delighted to tell you that it is absolutely factual and entertaining. I was taken back in time to those frightening times when none of us knew we would be alive the next day. I still do not see how we got through those horrendous missions."

He talked for an hour, and I could have listened all night. Bill is ninety-three years old and told me he is in perfect health, never takes a pill, and every afternoon, weather permitting, runs across the Cooper River Bridge and back. Yes, runs, every day. His voice is strong, and his memory is keen.

He told me he flew 42 missions, 16 of which he was the command pilot, leading the 13th Wing, consisting of the 95th, 100th, and 390th Bomb Groups. He said he was curious and checked his records to find that he had flown as group commander on six of the missions that our crew flew.

Now, the revelation that has kept me exhilarated for more than a week now. If you have read my book, you will remember that it told of our crew's worst mission. It was on July 12, 1944. The weather over Framlingham, England, Air Base was socked in, foggy and rainy and miserable. We waited for the sky to clear, but it never did, so we went anyway.

Our target for today was Munich, more exactly Bayerische-Motoren-Werke, where hundreds of jet engines were being built for use in the new German secret weapon, the Messerschmitt Me262 jet engine fighter, the fastest plane in the world at the time.

This secret weapon of Hitler's was so precious to him that he ordered it be protected by thousands of antiaircraft guns and encircled the city of Munich with airfields for his best fighter planes. With mountains circling the city and flak guns high up in those mountains, Munich was one of the formidable targets the Eighth Air Force had to attack.

Major Pennebaker, one of the most skillful B17 pilots in the Eighth Air Force, carefully approached Munich, avoiding the huge batteries of 88-millimeter guns. We flew right over the center of Munich and began our bomb run. We could tell by the loud crack of the flak exploding that the Germans had our exact altitude. They were zeroed in on our formation. Just before "Bombs away," there was a terrifying blast that rattled my teeth. We were hit and hit hard. Just back of engine number three, there appeared a hole as large as a bathtub, and smoke and fire erupted.

Ray calmly assessed our damage by having each crew position call in what they could see. Lieutenant Curnes feathered the number 3 engine and applied the fire extinguisher, but the flames would not die.

Ray advised all aboard of our damage and said he was going to dive at high speed to extinguish the flames. He then broke radio silence and called the command pilot for permission to land in Switzerland, which was just a few miles away.

The command pilot came right back, "Negative. I repeat, negative. Do not land in Switzerland. Bring that plane home."

That voice was the voice of Major Bill Pennebaker. He told me he watched as our plane, the GOOD-O-YANK slowly left formation, with fire streaming from her right wing. What a horrible sight to see one of these mighty warbirds wounded and falling from the sky.

Now, after sixty-eight years, I have found who had given us that command. I am dumbfounded it was our own squadron commander. What courage it must have taken to order one of your own, with people you live and die with every day. He had the character of a great leader.

Bill told me that his heart went out to us as our plane faded into the distance, but he knew that Ray Strate was an excellent pilot, and although it would be hard, he could save his plane and his crew. He also knew that any wounded B17 falling out of formation was easy prey for the German fighters that followed the formations. Thank the good Lord for the cloud cover we found at low altitude. We made it by the skin of our teeth, and now, Bill just chuckled and said, "I knew you could make it."

Bill asked me for permission to send his copy of my book to the 390th Memorial Museum in Tucson, Arizona, to be placed with other memorabilia of the 390th Bomb Group. Of course, I said yes. I felt honored that he thought well enough of the book. He seemed pleased that one of his men would be contributing to this very excellent museum.

Anyone wanting to learn more about the 390th can e-mail *390th@aol.com*. There are thousands of items on display, including a completely rebuilt B17G. Now, at least, for as long as Bill Pennebaker is with us, anyone can verify what I have written, can e-mail or call Lieutenant Colonel William Pennebaker[4].

I still have not contacted anyone who was there the night our pilot was celebrating completing our thirty-five missions, but I am still looking. I am sure it will make a fine ending for my book. Until then, this story is not complete.

---

[4] Lieutenant Colonel William Pennebaker passed away October 14, 2016

AIR MEDAL AWARDED TO
T/SGT. CHARLES J "CHUCK" RICHARDSON

Criteria

The Air Medal was established by Executive Order 9158, signed by Franklin D. Roosevelt, on 11 May 1942. The Air Medal was awarded retroactive to 8 September 1939. The medal is awarded to anyone who, while serving in any capacity in or with the Armed Forces of the United States, distinguishes himself or herself by meritorious achievement while participating in aerial flight.

The original award criteria set by an Army Policy Letter (dated 25 September 1942) was for one award of the Air Medal...

- per each naval vessel or three enemy aircraft in flight confirmed destroyed. (An entire aircrew would be credited for the destruction of a ship but only the pilot or gunner responsible would be credited for destroying an enemy aircraft).
- per twenty-five (25) operational flights during which exposure to enemy fire is probable and expected.
- per one-hundred (100) operational flights during which exposure to enemy fire is not expected.
- **Army Air Forces (1942-1947**
- During World War II, the medal's award criteria varied widely depending on the theater of operations, the aircraft flown, and the missions accomplished.
- In Europe, the airspace was considered completely controlled by the enemy and heavy air defenses were encountered—so the criteria was altered from that of the original medal. Bomber, photographic reconnaissance, or observation crewmembers and air transport pilots received it for five sorties, fighter pilots received it for ten sorties, and individual pilots or aircrewmen received one award per enemy aircraft shot down.
- Elsewhere in the Pacific and CBI the pilots and crews flew mostly over uncontrolled or contested airspace for long hours and lighter air defenses were encountered, so much higher criteria were used.

CHARLES J "CHUCK" RICHARDSON

HEADQUARTERSC-A-6
AAF STATION 153
APO 559

23 October 1944.

SUBJECT: Transmittal of Awards.

To: Commanding General, III Bombardment Division, APO 559
U.S Army
Attn: Awards

Transmitted herewith General Order Extracts awarding Oak Leaf Clusters to the Air Medal for the following officers and enlisted men transferred 70th Replacement Depot per authority of listed below:

T/Sgt. Charles J "Chuck" Richardson 34602539 so #258, Hq 3RD, 14 Sep 44

For the Commanding Officer:

/s/ John A. Williams,
/t/ John A. Williams,
Captain, Air Corps,
Adjutant.

1 Incl.
GO #671, Hq 3rd Bomb Div, 20 Sep 44.

AGPD-R LZ/AMM/mjc

1st Ind.

WD, AGO, Washington 25, D. C., 27 February 1945.

To: The Commanding Officer of:
3501st. Army Air Forces Base Unit,
Eaton Air Field, Forida.

1. Forwarded for notation of award of <u>an Oak-leaf Cluster to the Air Medal</u> in service record of enlisted man, or qualification card of officer concerned.

   T/Sgt. Charles J. Richardson 34602539 so #258, Hq 3BD, 14 Sep 44

2. If the individual is no longer assigned to your Command, this paper will be referred to the unit to which transferred.

3. If the <u>Decoration</u> has not been issued, requisition therefor should be made under the provisions of Section III, Circular 46, W. D., cs

BY ORDER OF THE SECRETARY OF WAR

Louis Zuckerman
Adjutant General.

1 Incl.
n/c

To Sp-A.
Entered on Emm record.

RESTRICTED

HEADQUARTERS 3RD BOMBARDMENT DIVISION (H)
Office of the Commanding General
APO 559

(GENERAL ORDERS)
(NO   559)   1 September
1944

AWARDS OF THE DISTINGUISHED FLYING CROSS

Under the prvisions of the Army Regulation 600-45, 22 September 1943 and pursuant to authority contained in letter 299.6, Headquarters Eight Air Force, dated 4 August 1944, Subject; " Awards and decorations," the DISTINGUISHED FLYING CROSS is awarded to the following named Officers and Enlisted Men, for extraordinary achievement as set forth in citation.

PAUL G JONES, 0-758573, 1st Lieutenant, Army Air Force, United States Army.
For extraordinary achievement while serving as Pilot on many high altitude heavy bombardment missions over Germany and German occupied Continental Europe. Under duress of heavy fighter attacks, anti aircraft fire, and often under adverse weather conditions, Lieutenant Jones by his superior airmanship, contributed to the success of all these operations. The untiring effort, skill and determination under stress of combat displayed by Lieutenant Jones are in keeping with the highest traditions of the Army Air Forces of the United States.

MAX K. NAUMAN, 0-7533237, 1st Lieutenant Army Air Forces, United States Army.
For extraordinary achievement while serving as pilot on many high altitude heavy bombardment missions over Germany and Derman occupied Continental Europe. Under duress of heavy fighter attacks, anti-aircraft fire, and often under adverse weather conditions, Lieutenant Nauman, by his superior airmanship contributed to the success of all these operations. The untiring effort, skill and determination under stress of combat displayed by Lieutenant Nauman are in keeping with the highest traditions of the Army Air Forces of the United States .

NEAL F. PAYDEN, 0-709061, 2nd LIEUTENANT, Army Air Forces, United States Army.
For extraordinary achievement while serving as navigator on many high altitude heavy bombardment missions against the enemy over Continental Europe. Lieutenant Payden, expertly navigating his aircraft, has contributed materially to the successful destruction of targets highly important to the enemy's war effort. The skill, energy, and resourcefulness displayed by Lieutenant Payden on all these occasions reflect the highest credit upon himself and the United States Military Forces.

CHARLES J. RICHARDSON, 34602539, Technical Sergeant, Army air Forces, United States Army
For extraordinary achievement while serving as radio operator gunner on many high altitude heavy bombardment missions against the enemy over Continental Europe. By expertly operating his radio equipment during long hours of combat and by warding off vicious fighter attacks with his gun, Sergeant Richardson made a substantial contribution to the success of these operations. The heroic determination and disregard of personal safety displayed by Sergeant Richardson on all these occasions reflect the highest credit upon himself and the Military Forces of the United States

By command of Major General PARTRIDGE:

OFFICIAL: A.W. KISSNER
                                                                                               Brigadier General, U.S.A.
                                                                                               Chief of Staff

RÉPUBLIQUE FRANÇAISE

CONSULAT GENERAL DE FRANCE A ATLANTA

Le Consul Général

Mr. Charles J. RICHARDSON
6824 Linda Lake Drive
Charlotte, NC, 28215

October 31, 2006

In recognition for your noble contribution during World War II, and in remenbrance with endless respect and affection of those who sacrificed their lives for the cause, the Consulate General of France will organize a ceremony at which time the "Thank you America" certificates will be presented.

This ceremony will take place at the :
American Legion
Post 380, 4235 W. Tyvola Rd
Charlotte, NC 28208.

On **thursday November 30th, 2006 at 2:30pm.**

Please confirm your attendance with Céline Galland at celine.galland@diplomatie.gouv.fr or (404) 495 1671.

If for any reason you cannot attend this event and would like to receive the certificate by mail, you can also let us know and we will be glad to comply.

In hopes of meeting you on November 30th, I would like to thank you again for the incredible service you rendered to my country and assure you of my deepest gratitude.

Sincerely,

Philippe ARDANAZ
Consul General of France

Prominence in Buckhead - 3475 Piedmont Road NE - Suite 1840 - Atlanta GA 30305
T. 404.495.1660 / F. 404.495.1661
Info@consulfrance-atlanta.org · www.consulfrance-atlanta.org

| ПОСОЛ РОССИЙСКОЙ ФЕДЕРАЦИИ В США | AMBASSADOR OF THE RUSSIAN FEDERATION TO THE USA |

Mr. Charles J. Richardson
6824 Linda Lake Dr.
Charlotte, NC 28215

June 10, 1996

Dear Sir,

    On behalf of President Boris Yeltsin, the Russian Government and the entire Russian people, I am pleased to inform you that you have been awarded the Commemorative Medal "The 50th Anniversary of the Victory in the Great Patriotic War" (World War II).

    This medal is awarded to you in recognition of your courage and personal contribution to the Allied support of Russia during her fight for freedom against Nazi Germany.

    Please accept my heartfelt congratulations and wishes for your good health, well-being and every success.

Sincerely,

Yuli M. VORONTSOV

Enclosures: Commemorative Medal, Medal Certificate.

„50 ЛЕТ ПОБЕДЫ
В ВЕЛИКОЙ ОТЕЧЕСТВЕННОЙ ВОЙНЕ
1941—1945 гг."

Х №17849469

Чарлз Дж. Ричардсон

НАГРАЖДЕН(А)
ЮБИЛЕЙНОЙ МЕДАЛЬЮ

„50 ЛЕТ ПОБЕДЫ
В ВЕЛИКОЙ ОТЕЧЕСТВЕННОЙ
ВОЙНЕ 1941—1945 гг."

Указ от 24 апреля 1995 года

- *THE MEDAL* -

This medal was instituted on April 24, 1995, to commemorate the coming 50th anniversary of the victory over Germany in World War II or as it is known in Russia, The Great Patriotic War. The anniversary is celebrated in the Russian Federation on May 9th.

The medal is made of bronze and is 32 mm in diameter. The obverse shows the Red square with the Spassky Tower and the Wall of the Moscow Kremlin on the right and St.Basil Cathedral on the left. Lights from fireworks are on both sides of the tower. In the lower part of the medal are the dates "1945" and "1995" with the Order of the Great Patriotic War in the center, and in the lower part behind the Order one can see two laurel branches.

The reverse has an eight line inscription in the center which reads "50 years of Victory in the Great Patriotic War 1941-1945". Below the inscription are two laurel branches tied with a ribbon.

The ribbon is 24 mm wide, is divided into two equal parts. The left part is 12 mm wide and consists of three black and four yellow strips. The right part of the ribbon is red, also 12 mm wide.

The Certificate to the medal bears the name of the recipient and the date of issuance, is stamped with the seal of the President of the Russian Federation and signed by President Boris Yeltsin.

Sources of information about the original crew of Good-O-Yank came from obituaries of the crew members and, additionally, from descendants. Oral permission from descendants was granted to use this information. Information was also added from military archives, as well as research from American Air Museum and Parham Airfield Museum in England and the 390th Bomb Group Museum in Tucson, Arizona.

RAYMOND STRATE, PILOT

- BORN MAY 21, 1917 IN HENNEPIN, MINNESOTA, SON OF GERHARD E. AND DAGMAR STRATE.
- DIED JANUARY 23, 1993 IN FRESNO, CALIFORNIA.
- ENLISTED AS PRIVATE IN ARMY AIR CORPS ON JUNE 8, 1942 IN LOS ANGELES, CALIFORNIA (ENLISTED MEN).
- SERVED AS PILOT ON GOOD-O-YANK CREW 1943-1944. FLEW 35 MISSIONS OUT OF FRAMLINGHAM, ENGLAND MAY, 1944-SEPTEMBER 1944.
- OWNED AND OPERATED LOS ANGELES WHOLESALE ELECTRIC COMPANY, WHICH OCCUPIED MOST OF HIS TIME.
- HOBBIES WERE OCEAN FISHING, WHICH HE ENJOYED WITH MILBURN STONE OF "DOC" FAME ON THE TELEVISION SHOW "GUNSMOKE", AND WAS ALSO AN AVID DUCK HUNTER AND MEMBER OF A DUCK CLUB NEAR FRESNO, CALIFORNIA.
- RAY MAINTAINED GOOD PHYSICAL CONDITION WITH VOLLEYBALL AND WORKOUTS AT THE PACIFIC COAST CLUB IN LONG BEACH, CALIFORNIA.
- PRIOR TO ENTERING THE AIR CORPS IN 1942, ATTENDED 3 YEARS OF COLLEGE AT UNIVERSITY OF MINNESOTA, WHERE HE PLAYED ON THE FOOTBALL TEAM.
- MARRIED JUNE MARGARET DWAN IN 1941. SHE PASSED AWAY MARCH 18, 1992.
- ONE DAUGHTER, JULIE M. STRATE BORN SEPTEMBER 17, 1944, WHILE RAY WAS STILL SERVING IN ENGLAND.
- JULIE MARRIED KENNARD R. SMART, JR. ON JUNE 23, 1968 AND PASSED AWAY IN MAY, 1988. THEY HAD TWO CHILDREN, KENNARD

R. SMART III, AND ELIZABETH LAURA SMART, 2 GRANDCHILDREN, AND SIX GREAT GRANDCHILDREN.
- MY THANKS TO KENNARD R. SMART, JR. FOR MUCH OF THIS INFORMATION.

GEORGE C. CURNES, COPILOT

- BORN APRIL 25, 1920 IN SAINT ALBANS, KANAWHA, WEST VIRGINIA, SON OF JOHN W. AND SALLIE CURNES.
- DIED NOVEMBER 17, 2007 IN CHERAW, SOUTH CAROLINA, HAVING RESIDED PREVIOUSLY IN WEST VIRGINIA AND GREENSBORO, NORTH CAROLINA.
- ENLISTED AS PRIVATE IN ARMY AIR CORP ON AUGUST 14, 1942 IN CHARLESTON, WEST VIRGINIA (ENLISTED MEN)
- SERVED AS CO-PILOT ON GOOD-O-YANK CREW 1943-1944. FLEW 35 MISSIONS OUT OF FRAMLINGHAM, ENGLAND MAY, 1944-SEPTEMBER 19
- WAS A PHOTOGRAPHER/LITHOGRAPHER DURING THE LATE '40S IN CHARLESTON, WV
- ATTENDED UNIVERSITY OF WEST VIRGINIA EARLY 1940'S.
- MARRIED GRACE BEATRICE TAYLOR, IN 1948 IN SAINT ALBANS, KANWAHA, WEST VIRGINIA. SHE PASSED AWAY DECEMBER 9, 1992.
- BOTH BURIED IN CHATHAM HILL MEMORIAL GARDENS, CHERAW, SOUTH CAROLINA.
- ONE SON, DR. JOHN CURNES, GREENSBORO, NORTH CAROLINA AND 5 GRANDCHILDREN

NEAL F. PAYDEN, NAVIGATOR

- BORN APRIL 3, 1920 IN MOLINE, ILLINOIS, RAISED BY HIS MOTHER AND STEPFATHER, JENNIE WAHLSTROM PAYDEN AND CHARLES SEAMS.
- DIED APRIL 27, 2011 AT HIS RESIDENCE IN MOLINE, ILLINOIS.
- ENLISTED AS PRIVATE IN ARMY AIR CORPS ON JULY 3, 1942 IN CHICAGO ILLINOIS (ENLISTED MEN).
- SERVED AS NAVIGATOR ON GOOD-O-YANK CREW 1943-1944. FLEW 35 MISSIONS OUT OF FRAMLINGHAM, ENGLAND MAY, 1944-SEPTEMBER 1944.
- A CIVIL ENGINEER AT WESTERN STRUCTURAL COMPANY IN MOLINE FOR 27 YEARS, RETIRING IN 1989, AND PREVIOUSLY WORKED AT BELING ENGINEERING.
- A LONGTIME MEMBER OF FIRST CONGREGATIONAL CHURCH, MOLINE, SERVING ON THE BOARD OF TRUSTEES
- A MEMBER OF THE 390TH BOMB GROUP VETERANS ASSOCIATION.
- AWARDED A DISTINGUISHED FLYING CROSS, THE AIR MEDAL WITH FOUR BRONZE OAK LEAF CLUSTERS, AND THE EUROPEAN THEATER RIBBON WITH FOUR BATTLE STARS.
- MARRIED ANNA BLANCHE STOELTING, BORN APRIL 11, 1923, ON NOVEMBER 12, 1944 IN MOLINE. ANNA PASSED AWAY MAY 17, 2013 IN EAST MOLINE, ILLINOIS.
- GRADUATED FROM UNIVERSITY OF ILLINOIS WITH BS IN ENGINEERING IN 1946.
- THREE SONS, (ONE SON, RICHARD DIED IN INFANCY), REV. THOMAS PAYDEN AND

CHARLES J "CHUCK" RICHARDSON

WILLIAM PAYDEN, THREE DAUGHTERS, DEBORAH PAYDEN TYLER, BETTY PAYDEN HERZFELDT, AND JENNIFER PAYDEN GESKE, 11 GRANDCHILDREN, AND THREE GREAT GRANDCHILDREN

VICTOR HENRY ESTES, BOMBARDIER

- BORN JULY 3, 1913, OUTSIDE TELEGRAPH, TEXAS, SON OF JOHN THOMAS ESTES AND MARTHA (TALBERT) ESTES.
- PASSED AWAY JULY 16, 2008 IN HOUSTON, TEXAS.
- ENLISTED AS PRIVATE IN ARMY AIR CORP ON JANUARY 13, 1941 IN HOUSTON, TEXAS (ENLISTED MEN)
- SERVED AS BOMBARDIER ON GOOD-O-YANK CREW 1943-1944. FLEW 26 MISSIONS OUT OF FRAMLINGHAM, ENGLAND WITH THIS CREW, BUT WHILE SERVING WITH ANOTHER CREW, PLANE SUFFERED SERIOUS DAMAGE AND WAS FORCED TO LAND. INTERNED BY THE SWISS GOVERNMENT DURING THE WAR, ESCAPED TO FRANCE AND HELPED TO RETURN TO ENGLAND BY THE FRENCH UNDERGROUND RESISTANCE.
- MARRIED ALDIA MAY ESTES IN 1950.
- EMPLOYED MOST OF HIS LIFE IN THE OIL INDUSTRY, MAINLY FOR DOWELL IN GAINESVILLE, TX AND FT. SMITH, AK.
- WAS A DEVOTED MEMBER OF BAPTIST CHURCH AND AN ENTHUSIASTIC FAN OF BAYLOR UNIVERSITY.
- TWO SONS, BOB BARRETT AND VIC ESTES, JR., 5 GRANDCHILDREN, AND 2 GREAT-GRANDCHILDREN.

CHARLES J "CHUCK" RICHARDSON, RADIOMAN/GUNNER

- BORN JUNE 7, 1923, IN CHARLOTTE, NORTH CAROLINA, SON OF FRANK AND MARY RICHARDSON.
- ENLISTED AS PRIVATE IN ARMY AIR CORPS ON JANUARY 20, 1943, AT CAMP CROFT, SOUTH CAROLINA
- SERVED AS RADIO OPERATOR/GUNNER ON GOOD-O-YANK CREW 1943–1944. FLEW THIRTY-FIVE MISSIONS OUT OF FRAMLINGHAM, ENGLAND, MAY 1944–SEPTEMBER 1944.
- AWARDED CERTIFICATE IN RECOGNITION OF CONTRIBUTION/SERVICE IN LIBERATION OF FRANCE AND PARTICIPATION IN THE NORMANDY INVASION, THE DISTINGUISHED FLYING CROSS, AIR MEDAL WITH FOUR OAK LEAF CLUSTERS, TWO PRESIDENTIAL UNIT CITATIONS (SCHWEINFURT-REGENSBURG), RUSSIAN MEDAL OF VICTORY IN THE GREAT PATRIOTIC WAR ON BEHALF OF BORIS YELTSIN, GOOD CONDUCT MEDAL WITH FOUR BRONZE STARS, FRENCH LEGION OF HONOR MEDAL.
- RETURNED TO USA TO RESUME CAREER AT SOUTHERN BEARING AND PARTS COMPANY, A FAMILY OWNED BUSINESS. SOUTHERN BEARING AND PARTS WAS SOLD, AND HE SUBSEQUENTLY WAS EMPLOYED IN THE AUTOMOTIVE PARTS INDUSTRY, REMAINING UNTIL RETIREMENT IN 1991.
- FREE TIME SPENT WRITING, GOLFING, ENJOYING CLOSE FRIENDSHIPS, AND SERVING AS YOUTH LEADER, SUNDAY SCHOOL TEACHER, ELDER, AND DEACON IN PRESBYTERIAN CHURCH SINCE 1946.

- ATTENDED CENTRAL PIEDMONT COMMUNITY COLLEGE FOR BUSINESS CLASSES AND VARIOUS TECHNICAL TRAINING.
- MARRIED ELETA PITMAN JANUARY 23, 1943. ELETA PASSED AWAY IN 2012.
- TWO CHILDREN, RONALD C. RICHARDSON AND CAROL RICHARDSON DUDLEY, TWO GRANDCHILDREN, AND TWO GREAT-GRANDCHILDREN.
- SON, RONALD RICHARDSON, PASSED AWAY IN JANUARY 2018.
- CONTINUES TO ENJOY TIME WITH FRIENDS, CHURCH LIFE, AND STAYING ACTIVE WITH MAINTENANCE OF HOME OWNERSHIP.

STEVE PRZEPIORKA (PRESTON), ENGINEER/TOP TURRET GUNNER

- BORN JUNE 23, 1922 IN DETROIT, MICHIGAN, SON OF JOHN AND MARY FURGAL PRZEPIORKA. HE WAS REARED IN HAMTRAMCK, MICHIGAN.
- DIED AUGUST 2, 2009 AT HIS HOME, SURROUNDED BY HIS FAMILY.
- ENTERED THE US AIR CORPS ON FEBRUARY 26, 1943 AT FT. CUSTER, MICHIGAN AND WAS DISCHARGED SEPTEMBER 13, 1945 AT FT. SHERIDAN, ILLINOIS AFTER HAVING ATTAINED THE RANK OF TECH SERGEANT.
- SERVED AS FLIGHT ENGINEER AND GUNNER ON THE GOOD-O-YANK CREW, COMPLETEING 35 MISSIONS OUT OF FRAMLINGHAM, ENGLAND MAY, 1944-SEPTEMBER 1944.
- WORKED FOR WOODY PONTIAC AND JOHNNY MOTORS SALES AS SALES MANAGER BEFORE RETIRING AFTER 30 PLUS YEARS AS ONE OF THE TOP INSURANCE AGENTS FOR AAA.
- INTO RETIREMENT FORMED PRESTON ASPHALT WITH HIS SONS.
- MARRIED ALICE JACHNA, NOVEMBER 11, 1944, 2 CHILDREN, KATHLEEN AND CRAIG.
- MARRIED ELEANOR KLEPAK IN 1957, 4 CHILDREN, STEVEN, ELAINE, DARLENE, AND DWAYNE, 14 GRANDCHILDREN, AND ONE GREAT GRANDCHILD.
- VERY CIVIC-MINDED AND DEVOTED MUCH OF HIS TIME TO OPTIMIST INTERNATIONAL, AS WELL AS HELPING TO DEVELOP LOCAL AND STATE OPTIMIST CENTERS.

HARVEY A. BURR, JR., LEFT WAIST GUNNER

- BORN 1922 IN BADEN, BEAVER, PENNSYLVANIA, SON OF HARVEY AND JENNIE BURR.
- DIED JULY 11, 1973 IN MIAMI, FLORIDA.
- ENLISTED AS PRIVATE IN ARMY DECEMBER 14, 1942 IN BUFFALO, NEW YORK, (ENLISTED MEN).
- SERVED AS LEFT WAIST GUNNER ON GOOD-O-YANK CREW 1943-1944. FLEW 35 MISSIONS OUT OF FRAMLINGHAM, ENGLAND, MAY 1944-SEPTEMBER 1944. RELEASED FROM SERVICE IN OCTOBER, 1945.
- GRADUATED FROM AMBRIDGE HIGH SCHOOL; ALSO GRADUATED FROM THE UNIVERSITY OF BUFFALO IN 1953.
- MARRIED LOUNELL BOGGS IN DALHART AIRFIELD CHAPEL, DALHART, TEXAS, MARCH 4, 1944. SHE PASSED AWAY JULY 15 2013 IN VIERA, FL. (JEANNE LOUNELL CARLSON)
- ACCOUNTANT WITH NATIONAL GYPSUM AFTER WORLD WAR II IN BUFFALO, NEW YORK.
- AN EXECUTIVE WITH NATIONAL AIRLINES IN MIAMI, FLORIDA FROM 1964 UNTIL HIS DEATH IN 1973.
- ONE DAUGHTER, MRS. JOSEPH (CAROL) RUSSO, MELBOURNE, FLORIDA AND HAMBURG, NY AND TWO GRANDSONS.

JEFFERSON C. FULLER, JR, RIGHT WAIST GUNNER

- BORN DECEMBER 30, 1921 IN HEALDTON, OKLAHOMA, SON OF JEFFERSON C. AND ELLA FRANCES OGLESBY FULLER.
- DIED SATURDAY, FEBRUARY 21, 2009,
- ENLISTED AS PRIVATE IN ARMY AIR CORPS, MARCH 26, 1942, IN OKLAHOMA CITY, OKLAHOMA. (ENLISTED MEN)
- SERVED AS WAIST GUNNER ON GOOD-O-YANK CREW 1943-1944. FLEW 35 MISSIONS OUT OF FRAMLINGHAM, ENGLAND, MAY, 1944-SEPTEMBER 1944.
- AWARDED THE AIR MEDAL AND DISTINGUISHED FLYING CROSS.
- GRADUATE OF OKLAHOMA A&M, NOW OKLAHOMA STATE UNIVERSITY.
- MARRIED BETTE WARD FULLER IN 1945, MARRIED FOR 59 YEARS, PASSED AWAY JANUARY 1, 2004.
- MARRIED MARTHA MATTHEWS KAUFMAN, JUNE 2005, WHO PASSED AWAY MAY 28, 2010.
- TWO DAUGHTERS, REBECCA RICE AND KATHERINE BELL, AND ONE SON JEFF FULLER, III, 8 GRANDCHILDREN, AND 4 GREAT GRANDCHILDREN.
- RETIRED FROM S. C DEPT. OF NATURAL RESOURCES AS DIRECTOR OF WILDLIFE AND FRESH WATER FISHERIES. HE WAS ESPECIALLY PROUD OF HIS WORK IMPROVING WHITE TAIL DEER, WILD TURKEY AND HYBRID BASS POPULATIONS SERVED AS DEACON IN HIS BELOVED PRESBYTERIAN CHURCH AND WAS ALSO A 32ND DEGREE MASON.

SAMUEL J. MCGEE, JR., BALL TURRET GUNNER

- BORN MARCH 31, 1923 IN FALL RIVER, MASSACHUSETTS, SON OF SAMUEL J. AND MARY MCGEE.
- DIED NOVEMBER 6, 2002 IN LONGMEADOW, MASSACHUSETTS, BURIED IN MT. OLIVET CEMETERY IN WATERTOWN, CT.
- ENLISTED AS PRIVATE IN ARMY MARCH 12, 1943 IN NEW YORK CITY, NEW YORK (ENLISTED MEN)
- SERVED AS BALL TURRET GUNNER ON GOOD-O-YANK CREW 1943-1944. FLEW 35 MISSIONS OUT OF FRAMLINGHAM, ENGLAND, MAY, 1944–SEPTEMBER 1944.
- ORIGINAL OWNER OF MCGEE WELDING COMPANY OF WATERBURY, CT, WHICH IS STILL IN OPERATION.
- COMMUNICANT OF ST. BERNARD'S CHURCH OF ENFIELD, MEMBER OF THE AMERICAN LEGION OF ENFIELD.
- MARRIED CELIA YVONNE "MIDGE" COTE IN 1945, WHO PASSED AWAY AUGUST 6, 2009.
- ONE SON, SAMUEL J. MCGEE, III, OF BREWSTER, MA, AND ONE DAUGHTER, MRS. DEBRA BIRTWELL OF LONGMEADOW, MA., FIVE GRANDCHILDREN AND TWO GREAT GRANDCHILDREN.

ROGELIO SANCHEZ, TAIL GUNNER

- BORN APRIL 1, 1923 IN SAN ANTONIO, TEXAS SON OF CARMEN AND JULIA SANCHEZ.
- DIED JANUARY 6, 2008
- ENLISTED AS PRIVATE IN ARMY JANUARY 19, 1943 AT FORT SAM HOUSTON, TX. (ENLISTED MEN)
- SERVED AS TAIL GUNNER ON GOOD-O-YANK CREW 1943-1944. FLEW 35 MISSIONS OUT OF FRAMLINGHAM, ENGLAND, MAY 1944-SEPTEMBER 1944.
- PURSUED CAREER IN THE UPHOLSTERING BUSINESS AFTER WORLD WAR II.
- MARRIED ESTILLE GONZALES, TWO DAUGHTERS, DIANA (SANCHEZ) CARTER AND IRENE (SANCHEZ) PARMETER, 6 GREAT GRANDCHILDREN, 13 GREAT GRANDCHILDREN, 2 GREAT, GREAT GRANDCHILDREN.
- MARRIED ANTONIA L MARTINEZ ON DECEMBER 31, 1975.
- BOTH BURIED AT FORT SAM HOUSTON NATIONAL CEMETERY IN SAN ANTONIO, TX.

About the Author

Charles J "Chuck" Richardson was born June 7, 1923. He is an avid reader/writer on various subjects. His favorite genres are history, particularly that of World War II, astronomy, and science. He has penned six additional books of fiction and non-fiction, one of poetry, two fictional novels, two nonfictional writings, and is currently working on his seventh.

Charles was employed in the automotive parts industry prior to his engagement in the European Theater of Operations in 1944, and returned to this career after his return to the United States after the war. He remained in this industry until his retirement in 1991.

He was fortunate to be able to return to many of the destinations which he bombed during World War II and to witness the numerous changes that had developed over the fifty years since his presence there.

Mr. Richardson's free time is spent reading, writing, enjoying time with close friends, listening to music, singing tenor in the church choir, and maintaining his residence in Charlotte, North Carolina. Charles is active as a speaker and is very active in the 390th Bomb Group Historical Society Chapter in Charlotte, North Carolina.

He has served as elder and deacon in the church, beginning in 1946, as well as having served as youth leader and Sunday School teacher. He is physically active with water aerobics several times weekly at the YMCA.

Prior to her death in 2012, he was married to his wife, Eleta, for almost seventy years. Two children were born of this marriage, a son, Ronald Richardson, who passed away in January 2018, and a daughter, Carol Dudley. He enjoys time with his two grandchildren, two great-grandchildren, and his miniature schnauzer, Lee.

T/Sgt. Charles J. Richardson
Radio Operator/Gunner on B17G, World War II

CPSIA information can be obtained
at www.ICGtesting.com
Printed in the USA
BVHW090452040123
655467BV00021B/805